MANAGEMENT
OF HOSPITALITY
OPERATIONS

The Bobbs-Merrill Company, Inc.

Hotel-Motel Management Series

Series Editor: DAVID HERTZSON

MANAGEMENT OF HOSPITALITY OPERATIONS

Bruce H. Axler

The Bobbs-Merrill Company, Inc.
Indianapolis

The Bobbs-Merrill Company, Inc.
4300 West 62nd Street
Indianapolis, Indiana 46268

First Edition
First Printing 1976

Cover photo by Van Bucher
Reproduced by permission of
Photo Researchers, Inc.

Library of Congress Cataloging in Publication Data

Axler, Bruce H.
   The management of hospitality operations.

   (Hotel-motel management series)
   Includes index.
   1. Hotel management.   2. Motel management.
I. Title.   II. Series.
TX911.2.A94   647'.94   76-9843
ISBN 0-672-97001-5

Contents

CHAPTER 8

CHAPTER 9

CHAPTER 10

1 | Operational Management in the Hospitality Industry

PERSPECTIVE

The total sales of the hospitality industry approach 80 billion dollars. Seventy thousand hotels and motels, and 500 thousand foodservice establishments employ approximately 5.6 million people. Every one of these establishments has someone in charge, every one of those millions of workers reports to someone: a manager.

Because of the growth of the industry, and because of the huge number of individual operational units, every year for the foreseeable future an additional 25 thousand managers will be needed. Unlike the management employees entering other major segments of the American economy, steel and autos for example, the individual joining a hospitality organization as a manager is very likely to have total responsibility for an operational unit in a short time. It is not unusual for a person 22 or 23 years old to be in charge of a property representing a 3-million-dollar capital investment, and employing 70 or 80 people.

On a smaller scale, he will have most (but not all) of the functions and responsibilities that concern only the senior executives of industrial corporations. He may not be asked to articulate the organization's business philosophy or formulate plans for obtaining additional capital, the frequent concerns of senior executives, but he will be expected to assume profit and loss operational responsibilities for his unit. If it is successful, he is successful. If it fails, he fails. Managers of comparable age and experience in other industries generally perform in much more limited roles in much larger organizations that vest this ultimate responsibility with individuals much higher in the organizational structure.

The hospitality industry, therefore, offers the operational manager much more of a personal challenge and more opportunity. His mettle is soon tested; if he proves himself, he advances rapidly. No other industry demands so much of its junior management; no other industry boasts so many young corporate presidents and executives.

The key to both the individual's and the organization's success is the quality of his operational management—his day-to-day management of a hospitality unit with a profit and loss perspective. He *makes* the unit produce a profit. He *controls* events so that consequences benefit it. He *acts* to promote its interests. It succeeds because he made it happen.

What an Operational Manager Needs to Know

Operational managers might be classified, generally, in three categories: those who are unaware of the factors influencing the success of their organizations, and this makes up the vast majority; the many who are aware of these forces and unable to control them; and the few who are aware, able to act, and do. The same categorization might well be applied to the hospitality industry.

The essential question then for anyone entering the hospitality industry, anyone employing him, and anyone presuming to guide him is: What does he need to know to function effectively?

Discussion with entry level managers, surveying of senior hospitality executives, and analysis of industry management job descriptions make it apparent that there should be certain priorities in the development of a hospitality manager. At the start of his career he cannot possibly know everything about the hospitality industry, from the interpretation of feasibility studies to financial restructuring. He cannot know everything about the scores of hospitality crafts and technologies, from plastering to data processing.

What the manager has to *know* has to be related directly to what he has to *do*.

The nature of the work of the entry level manager, the problems of young managers in managing, the emphasis of job descriptions, and the job specifications of industry executives all point to the specific techniques and areas of knowledge in which operational managers must be competent to function effectively. Hence the concept of operational management as a discipline that differs from corporate or executive hospitality management, which addresses itself to the principles of planning and owning a hotel or restaurant rather than its actual operation. What does the individual involved in the day-to-day management of a hospitality unit owned by someone else need to know to do the job right?

After some brief discussion in this chapter defining the operational manager's role in the organization's total management program and outlining the operational manager's field of activity, as well, necessarily, as that which is beyond it, succeeding chapters present these priority subjects with exactly that perspective: need to know, how to do.

The subtleties of some very interesting disciplines have been deliberately (and perhaps reluctantly) excluded, on the simple basis that the operational manager in all likelihood will not require this knowledge. Some independent study on the part of a manager should, indeed must, accompany career progression, and these disciplines he can pursue on his own. On the other hand, some subjects which are not particularly glamorous have been included because it is in precisely these areas that the operational manager has the greatest opportunity to affect organizational health and progress.

THE OPERATIONAL MANAGER

Who are the Operational Managers?

Simply defined, the operational managers in the hospitality industry are those individuals managing a hospitality unit for which they have primary responsibility but not complete authority. They are actually in charge of day-to-day operations, but they are subordinate to someone else. It follows from that definition that operational managers can have a variety of titles, some very posh, others very ordinary, without their essential roles being much affected.

The general manager of a motel or hotel that is part of a chain, the director of a restaurant in a large hotel, the manager of a restaurant under the direct control of the restaurant's owner, the steward in a large kitchen, the food production manager in a hospital, the housekeeper in a resort hotel, and the night club manager are all operational managers with a great many concerns, problems, and responsibilities in common even though their individual jobs might demand different specific knowledge. If they are good operational managers they could, by special study in a specific area, e.g., specifications for purchasing produce, or operating a reservations system, exchange jobs with other managers in the operation. Put another way, they are professional managers exercising a particular specialty at the moment. In five years, like so many hospitality "veterans," they may be practicing another specialty but they still will remain operational managers.

Their assistants, if they have them, are also operational managers with operational responsibilities and management concerns which differ in scale but not in substance.

Operational management, in contrast to administrative management and executive management, is characterized by day-in and day-out

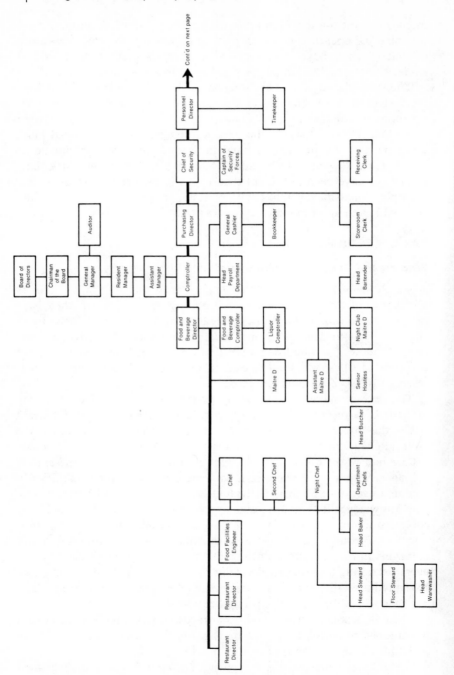

Figure 1.1. Management organization of a major resort hotel.

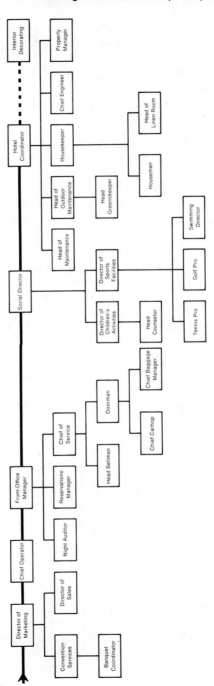

concern with the service and production workers, with the operation's product facilities, and with the individual customer. Administrators and executives have these concerns also, but their role in respect to them is to formulate guidelines called *policies* which the operational manager is expected to implement.

Operational management does not become involved in activities that are reserved for higher level management:

1. *Determination of a business philosophy.* This is the concern of the executive level of management and involves such areas as business ethics, fundamental employee relationships, competitive activities.
2. *Establishment of an organizational structure.* Another concern of executive level management: How should the authority and the power of the management as a whole be apportioned among the managerial group?
3. *Formulation of goals for the organization.* Executive management determines objectives and articulates them in terms of sales volume, profit, growth, acquisitions, and market share.
4. *Provision and allocation of financial resources.* Development of capital sources, planning capital investments in the physical property and in major equipment are executive or administrative responsibilities.
5. *Determination of policies.* Setting guidelines by which goals can be reached within the organizational structure, consistent with the business philosophy of the organization, and using the financial resources available can be described as an administrative function.

What Operational Managers Do

Workers, including skilled craftsmen, who are made operational managers usually are amazed at the extent of their new responsibilities. The operational manager's time is fully occupied by a diversity of activities the worker may never have considered. The operational manager *works,* the newly promoted worker observes, without ever slapping a steak on the broiler or lifting a guest's bag.

The 25 functions listed below represent some of the operational manager's major responsibilities (all of which are discussed in subsequent chapters).

1. *Planning:* anticipation of future events; establishment of temporal priorities.
2. *Budgeting:* immediate allocation of resources for their most effective utilization; planning in quantifiable terms.
3. *Organizing:* structuring the operational unit around definite jobs

including the delegating of some of the operational manager's work to subordinate employees.

4. *Decision making:* weighing of alternative courses of action which have long term implications for the operational unit.
5. *Problem solving:* dealing effectively with circumstances, people, and things that immediately menace the operational unit's progress.
6. *Forecasting:* assessing the impact of future events on the performance of the operational unit and adjusting to them.
7. *Communicating:* serving as a conduit for information, directives, policies, etc., from higher level management to the employees and as a conduit from the employees to higher level management; coordinating efforts with other operational managers.
8. *Leading:* providing the goal-oriented direction for the employees.
9. *Motivating:* developing among the employees a willingness to perform; stimulating them to particular goals.
10. *Keeping peace:* maintaining a productive atmosphere among employees.
11. *Disciplining:* correcting employees whose behavior menaces the operational unit's goal achievement.
12. *Supervising:* demonstrating, directing, surveying, and inspecting to insure that the operation's standards of quality and quantity are met.
13. *Training:* instructing employees in necessary skills; in proper organizational behavior; in their rights and benefits as employees.
14. *Morale building:* developing and maintaining a healthful and productive group spirit.
15. *Protecting:* insuring that the operation complies with the various laws and regulations that govern hospitality operations.
16. *Representing the organization:* positively influencing the community, the communications media, the other members of the industry, and the workers' labor organization on behalf of the organization.
17. *Developing productivity:* simplifying work and method engineering so that the amount of work produced is increased.
18. *Scheduling:* maximizing the use of labor and the efficiency of work flow.
19. *Cost cutting:* reducing the operation's expenditures for supplies, equipment, and physical facilities.
20. *Quality and quantity control:* monitoring the product of both goods and services to insure that standards are being met and that the unit operates effectively and efficiently.

21. *Reporting:* supplying upper level management with the data which will become the basis for administrative and executive decisions.
22. *Protecting profits:* securing the operation against theft, fraud, and other similar activities that menace profitability.
23. *Developing profits:* increasing sales revenues by developing profit centers, encouraging additional and more frequent patronage.
24. *Accommodating guests:* actively purveying the spirit of hospitality as well as hospitality products and services.
25. *Assuring health and safety for employees and the public:* protecting the people using the operation against physical injury and illness.

How Organizational Structure Affects the Operational Manager's Work

Managers function within organizations. What they do and what they can do depends on their position and their level in the organization and the nature of the organizational structure. Six hundred thousand lodging and foodservice organizations does not mean that there are six hundred thousand totally different organizational structures. Two basic models can be identified: (1) the departmentalized organization and (2) the single executive organization.

Perhaps two thousand establishments, and this includes most of the largest properties, are organized around a departmental structure. A definite management hierarchy is created, conveniently represented by a pyramid. At the base of the pyramid are the workers. The territory in between is occupied by people in managerial roles, with each ascending level being narrower because fewer people occupy it.

If the pyramid were further analyzed it would be seen to consist of smaller pyramids within the pyramid serving as building blocks. At the apex of each of those pyramids is a department head. In a particular organization not all of the department heads may be of the same rank, not all of the departments may be of the same size, and several departments may share a common pool of workers (which would make graphic representation of that particular organization as a pyramid rather difficult).

The basic structure is apparent, however. The executives occupying the upper reaches of the pyramid do not directly control the workers or their product. Rather there is a middle-management level, the administrative level, the department heads with definite areas of responsibility. Likewise, within each department there may be a level of managerial personnel between the department head at the top of the pyramid and the workers at the bottom.

On the other hand, in the single executive organization, which may be a very small motel or a behemoth resort, the pyramidal structure does not exist. There may be ranks, titles, salary differentials, and apparent hierarchical status symbols such as office size and secretaries, but the essential managerial *functions* are concentrated in a single individual or in several individuals of equal rank.

The single executive actually operates the establishment. Other individuals may serve as conduits for his instructions and as his means of gathering information, but he is totally in charge.

Organizations exist which share some of the characteristics of both of these models. An individual may dominate an organization completely except for one particular area in which he defers to an expert, for example, the golf pro or the chef. Several individuals may split an operation into the "front of the house and the back of the house," that is, into areas where activities are directly concerned with the customer and into others where these activities are supported.

Historically, organizations have "progressed" from the single executive model to the departmentalized model as they have either grown or aged. Whether any actual progress, as measured by profits or organizational health, was made during the process depended entirely on the quality of the persons involved. Some individual operators do a better job than would any group of individuals they could employ.

The general success of an establishment, however organized, is of less concern for the entry level manager than the implications that these differing organizational structures have for his performance on the job. He is in no position to change the organization or, indeed, to pass judgment on it. Whether an organization tilts to the departmentalized pyramidal model or the single executive model determines *which* managerial functions he will be expected to perform and *how much* overall responsibility he will have for those functions.

Figure 1.2 indicates which managerial functions of the 25 listed above are likely to be emphasized within the two organizational structures.

The manager serving in a single executive organization will be primarily concerned with keeping peace, supervising, control, reporting, and protecting profits. While the manager in the highly departmentalized organization will be more concerned with budgeting, problem solving, forecasting, leading, productivity, scheduling, accommodating guests and representing the organization. In both types of organizations important secondary concerns will include communicating, disciplining, training, and cost cutting.

In the departmentalized hospitality organization those functions which are not high level concerns for the manager still concern him, but functionally they may be assigned to higher level administrators or craft specialists, for example, the head baker. The manager in a depart-

Departmentalized Organization		Both Types of Organizations	Single Executive Organization
Primary Functions	Secondary Functions	Secondary Functions	Primary Functions
1.	Planning		
2. Budgeting			
3.	Organizing		
4.	Decision making		
5. Problem solving			
6. Forecasting			
7.		Communicating	
8. Leading			
9.	Motivating		
10.			Keeping peace
11.		Disciplining	
12.			Supervising
13.		Training	
14.	Morale building		
15.	Protecting		
16. Representing the organization			
17. Productivity			
18. Scheduling			
19.		Cost cutting	
20.			Control
21.			Reporting
22.			Protecting profits
23.	Developing profits		
24. Accommodating guests			
25.	Assuring health and safety		

Figure 1.2. Functions of operational management under different organizational structures.

mentalized organization may also be supported by individuals whose primary function, whatever their rank in the organization, is to facilitate his activities. These departments, called "staff" departments, do not have customer contact or immediate customer impact as "line" or operational departments do. For example, training and record keeping could be the functions respectively of a personnel department and an electronic-data-processing department.

In the single executive organization the operational management functions which might normally be performed by the managers are either performed by the executive himself, by anybody handy on an immediate basis, or by individuals who serve as direct assistants to the executive, functioning as instruments of his will.

Employment in either type of organization, or in any of the multi-plicity of variations in between, may be pleasant and rewarding, or un-pleasant and unrewarding. A departmentalized organization could be staffed by petty individuals jealous of their territories, while a single executive organization might be headed by a benevolent, brilliant, paternalistic autocrat. On the other hand, departmentalized operations may be based on "teams" whose collective effort far exceeds the sum of the individuals' efforts involved, while a single executive might be barely competent, tyrannical, and abusive.

SUCCEEDING IN MANAGEMENT

Business publications often write of major executives completely switching industries. A man retires from one corporation making auto-mobiles and becomes the head of a business machine conglomerate. Or the head of a law firm becomes the chief officer of an airline with seem-ing success.

Their success is attributed to the universality of executive skills. While certainly their expertise in areas which occupy all executives, for exam-ple, financial planning or operations research, is a contributing factor to their success, much of it as such is due to their ability to completely control the factors that affect their jobs. In the articles discussing their efforts there is almost always mention of their demanding and getting a "free hand" or "carte blanche" from the board of directors or financial institutions that hired them.

The operational manager never has a free hand or carte blanche. His success, no matter if it is his first job or his tenth, is going to be affected by factors over which he has little immediate control.

He functions in a situation which he did not create. Most likely he inherits second-hand procedures, hand-me-down policies and used peo-ple. He is part of a system, a functionary in an organization which may encourage his contributions and innovations or which may be structured so that all "creative" activity is submerged. He is supposed to "do the job."

It is pivotal to the manager's success that he recognize that there are factors that influence his effectiveness in his job about which he can do nothing, factors about which he can do something, and factors about which he can do a great deal. Obviously he must order his priorities ac-cordingly, at least until he rises in the organization and simultaneously gains more control over his personal success and that of the organiza-tion. The following are factors over which the operational manager has limited control but by which his performance is affected.

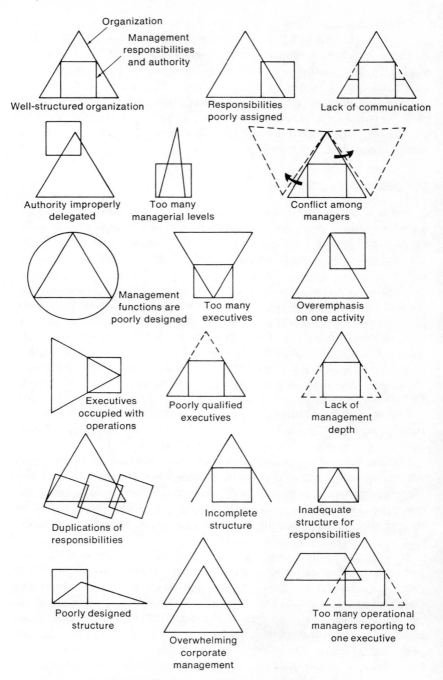

Figure 1.3. Structural defects in organizations.

1. Organizational philosophy
2. Organizational objectives
3. Organizational structure
4. Organizational health
5. Quality of higher level management
6. Peer performance
7. Major policies
8. Equipment, materials, and facilities
9. Availability and quality of human resources
10. Personal qualities

1. *Organizational philosophy.* An enterprise's organizational philosophy deals with community relations, business ethics, employee relations, social accountability, etc. It is not an operational manager's concern except as it affects his ability to function. For example, in the area of employee relations, one major company's corporate attitude is unabashedly paternalistic and indulgent. Another major company has adopted the attitude that employees are like facial tissues, they can be used up, thrown away and replaced readily. Both represent the philosophical positions held by the founders of the firm. The managers (and the upper level administrators) cannot change the philosophy. In the first company the managers are untroubled by a rapid turnover of employees, although they may have other problems that the company philosophy creates. In the second company, there is sometimes not enough time to process an employee's payroll forms before he quits. The economic wisdom of either practice is not the issue, a case could be made for or against both. To be considered is how the manager must function in these different situations, created by organizational philosophy.

2. *Organizational objectives.* Because of his position and level in the organization the operational manager has little opportunity to influence marketing strategy, reaction to competitive pressures, long range profit planning and similar upper echelon management activities. Yet, indisputably, these decisions affect him. For example, if a decision is made to seek convention business for a resort property, every operational activity is affected. If the convention business is attracted there must be an operational response. The manager must effect changes in procedures, planning, priorities even if he does not agree that they are in fact "good business."

3. *Organizational structure.* What a manager can do, and what he cannot do, is defined for him by someone else. He may be ac-

countable to an individual with whom he does not share attitudes, approaches, opinions, procedural standards, style, work philosophy, or views on other important matters such as the advisability of wearing brown shoes with a gray suit. But the structure is there. The manager's defined functions are there, although he may be chomping at the bit to enlarge his responsibilities. Unless he is a master strategist at corporate politics, there is little he will be able to do to change things for a long time.

Put another way, the manager is given a certain amount of managerial "risk capital." He is expected to make decisions himself for the good of the organization. In a healthy organization he is also expected to make some small errors while making some significant gains.

Upper level management tries to limit this risk capital to protect the organization by concentrating most critical decisions at levels where there is more managerial experience or competence. A detailed procedure manual is an example of this kind of effort. The requiring of forecasts, projections, and budgets has a similar effect.

The nature of the hospitality business makes it difficult for upper level administrators to pre-audit or directly supervise the operational manager. Rather, managers are held accountable for the results of their operations. This is not simply a semantic distinction. The manager's authority-responsibility and discretionary areas may be described as the difference between clearing an activity with a superior and accepting the consequences for its results.

4. *Organizational health.* Every year several hundred hotels and thousands of food service operations go out of business. Until the moment when they hang the "Closed" sign on the door, or the marshall tacks up his notice, they are being "managed" by someone. Managing in an operation beseiged by creditors, constantly maligned by employees and luckless guests, plagued by equipment failures is totally frustrating. The manager is completely impotent.

5. *Quality of higher level management.* It is difficult, if not impossible, to fire the boss. A fairly high position in a hospitality organization does not necessarily mean an individual is brilliant or even bright. There are other explanations for his success. Without being unnecessarily cruel to specific individuals many "executives" owe their current positions of authority to an early fortuitous association with someone who was genuinely brilliant. Just as a soldier or two in the Light Brigade must have questioned the tactical wisdom of the charge but was powerless to do anything about

it and went into the valley, the operational manager follows the orders of his superiors.

6. *Peer performance.* Business organizations are often compared to sports teams. The analogy is apt but perhaps it should be pursued. Great quarterbacks are smothered by defensive players because weak lines collapse. Super pitchers lose games 0-1 because nobody on their side can hit. Rebounding centers find themselves with nobody to pass off to.

The existence of a "team" does not mean the team's success. Superlative players lose because of their fellows' mediocrity and there is nothing they can do about it.

7. *Major policies.* Junior management does not make the rules or the major decisions. Undoubtedly there are operational managers in organizations among the thousands of hospitality operations who are seething with better ideas. Although they have been hired to think, what they are permitted to think about is rather restricted, and opportunities to make major changes in procedures, rules, and regulations are severely limited. Employee policies are an excellent example. A rather conclusive case has been made for the economic wisdom of developing career ladder opportunities in the hospitality industry, that is, of trying to develop individuals so that they can make progress within an organization. The manager may accept this, just as he may accept the idea that individuals can be motivated by other than financial incentives, or threat of dismissal. Accepting the concept is one thing, doing something about it is another. The steward in charge of the warewashing facilities of a major convention-hotel center, in all respects a manager in a fairly well paid job, does not necessarily have the right to pay a warewasher another dime an hour, or to develop a head warewasher from among the crew of itinerant laborers, or even the right to issue each man a beer unless he expects to pay for it himself, and perhaps not even then. Ultimately he may earn, by his performance within the constraints of his present job definition, permission to make changes. As an immediate concern, policy matters are beyond his purview.

8. *Equipment, materials, and facilities.* Elsewhere in this book are several forms dealing with purchasing. On each is a very significant line, a place for a superior manager to approve an operational manager's requests. Money which might be spent on equipment, better facilities, better materials can also be spent on debt retirement, advertising, promotion, executive salaries, decorating guest rooms, flowers for VIPs. The allocation of a limited resource—money—is not an operational manager's concern. He

certainly can make recommendations, he can do studies indicating how capital investment will save operating expenses, he can moan about lost productivity because of breakdowns and ancient equipment, but the final decision is not his.

9. *Availability and quality of human resources.* The hotel-motel segment of the hospitality industry produces less dollar product, with twice the number of workers, than would several single industrial corporations. The nature of the product offered is a factor. Capital investment is a factor. There are a number of acceptable explanations but it would be unrealistic not to identify the "worker" as part of the problem. Historically, hospitality organizations have been structured to function with individuals who were not otherwise employable. This is a fact, not a moral judgment. Many of the individuals a manager is likely to encounter in his crew have rather grave social, physical, and emotional problems which severely limit their work potential. The hospitality industry has used these people "successfully" and currently pays the price in its inability to attract better workers to jobs which have historically had an abysmally low social status. Eventually the bright, college-educated young engineers will be tinkering with the automatic controls on the giant chrome-plated, sparkling, bed-making-dishwashing-garbage-eating-lawn-raking machine. At the moment, and for the foreseeable future the manager will have to make do with the lost, the troubled, the scruffy, and the derelict. How he will perform will depend on how they will perform.

10. *Personal qualities.* Managers do not succeed or fail in the hospitality business because they know or do not know the weight of a lug of tomatoes or the purpose of the city ledger. "Sudden death" on the basis of specific information or a single act is infrequent. Most organizations evaluate the manager on the basis of his general competence over a period of time. But even managers who are technically competent can be ineffective or so minimally effective that they will never progress because of addressable personal characteristics.

Some deficiencies of management style are discussed in the following chapters fairly extensively. The list below is meant to prompt some self-appraisal and then, it is to be hoped, some preliminary development. Learning about oneself on the job has to be a most expensive educational process.

Immaturity. The play attitudes of the school assignment, the summer job, and the part-time hustle cannot be carried over to an individual's career.

Play it safe attitudes. There is an acceptable area of venture-someness between recklessness and passivity. The successful manager cannot hide out.

Problem solving vs. opportunity seeking. The operational manager is expected to solve problems in his operation; he is also expected to anticipate them. Problem solving at best maintains the status quo and protects the operation from deterioration; it does not represent progress. Opportunity exploitation does.

Poor tempo. The hospitality industry is fast paced. There is a need for quick, correct decisions, fast thinking, and fast action.

Lack of confidence. A know-it-all probably has a better chance of success than the competent individual who lacks personal confidence. The manager who lacks confidence is distrusted by his superiors and dominated by his subordinates.

Fear of criticism. Mistakes are expected of any individual, he is just not supposed to make too many. In a healthy organization, yes-men and toadies may be kept around to amuse the boss but they never become the boss.

Lack of emotional control. It is sometimes a good tactic to become angry or otherwise emotional, however, the manager must be capable of assessing the proper moment. "Blowing up" indiscriminately deprives the manager of a valuable tool.

Need for the familiar. Some hospitality jobs are extremely routine. The pay and the responsibility of a job are directly commensurate with the amount of change and pressure a manager can handle.

Inability to concentrate. Perseverance, follow through, the ability to focus one's attention are among the most valuable traits of a manager. He does his most important work, he makes his most important decisions in the midst of tremendous static.

Absence of a managerial attitude. The operational manager is an officer (although not necessarily a gentleman) rather than a soldier. To succeed he has to make the emotional and intellectual transition to his status. He has new obligations.

Rigidity. Flexibility in attitude, procedures, priorities is essential in a service industry.

Over-conformity. Conformity in dress and grooming is necessary, conformity in thinking is not. The manager who tries to submerge himself in the crowd, may succeed too well.

Paper-craziness. The major battles of management are not fought with a clipboard. Record keeping, written communications, forecasts, analyses are essential to successful performance, but "making it happen" is the first priority.

Showboating. Being able to do any job in a particular operation is an indisputable advantage for a manager. Actually doing the job, except in the rare crisis situation, is a mistake. One man bands never get to play Carnegie Hall.

Offhandedness. Hospitality crews are not generally self-motivated. An off-hand managerial style most of the time results in sloppy performance.

Soft-mindedness. Accepting that the hospitality industry is a "people business" does not make the manager a therapist, missionary, or mother to the workers in his employ. He absolutely cannot solve his workers' personal problems. He hopes that he can avoid aggravating them.

Overaggressiveness. Managers effect changes and progress by compromise, reconciliations, persuasion, back scratching, etc., more successfully than by frontal attack.

Cupidity, insincerity, nastiness. The qualities which are undesirable in a man are undesirable and dysfunctional in a manager.

Self-satisfaction. A continuous process of self-development is needed. Many upper echelon hotel-motel managers say they learn something new every day: a fair number actually do. In the next twenty-five years a score of technologies from electronic data processing to freeze drying will substantially alter the hospitality industry. Economic events, social changes and just plain good thinking will affect the manager's work. A growth industry grows in every way. The manager's success will depend on his ability to grow with it.

2 | Management Techniques

An analysis of the typical manager's day would show that most of his time is spent on matters that concern people—guests and fellow workers —and money. It might also be that for the most part he is functioning as the director of a situation, that is, he is attempting to control events to a consequence that favors the organization. He is hustling, juggling, charging, maneuvering, side-stepping, pushing, saving, scrimping, making-do, and manipulating until finally the clock stops, or the spring winds down, or the doors close.

His success during a particular day is not measured by his frenzy but by his results. He achieves results only if he has managed to impose some order on all the activity so that it is purposeful as well as hectic. Thus, at some time, he has had to think as well as do. He has also tried to share his thinking with his subordinates so that when the crunch comes they are part of the solution, not part of the problem.

Management technology has sufficiently evolved so that specific processes and techniques may be applied *before* the actual situation to be managed occurs. These processes include planning, budgeting, organizing, delegating, decision making, problem solving, forecasting, and communicating.

PLANNING

Planning is essentially an effort to anticipate future activities and predispose their elements so that a desired objective is achieved. Planning is goal oriented. The planner attempts to find a course of action that expeditiously achieves a goal while minimizing the expenditure of resources. He tries to determine which of the many things his unit can do is the right effort toward this goal.

Planning has definite practical advantages. In the hospitality industry many efforts are cooperative, different individuals and departments are involved. By planning, a manager can identify his coordination needs. Planning also allows the manager to marshall his resources before they are actually needed. A requisition for equipment or personnel is a plan, or at least a part of a plan.

Planning permits an examination of objectives with at least some time for a re-ordering of managerial priorities. Making a "plan" to change a filing system at the front desk makes the manager address the fundamental questions implied: Is the change necessary? Is the change a high-priority objective?

Every employee in an organization, except perhaps those completely involved in mechanical routine activities such as warewashing, makes plans. The difference among plans is in the level of importance of their objectives for the organization as a whole. A good cook plans his preparation. A good corporate executive plans the marketing strategy of the company.

The manager's plans fall somewhere in between the two: the objectives toward which he can plan are limited yet he plans more than his own immediate work. Generally, his planning emphasizes short-range objectives. His plans have a small time span, for example, a plan to reduce overtime this month, or a plan to cater a five-hour wedding celebration.

Several types of plans by management might be identified: *project plans* directed toward a single activity, for example preparing the swimming pool for the opening of the season; *phased plans,* which cover a continuing activity with the expectation that early actions based on the plan will affect the nature of later actions, for example, a plan to reduce food costs; *get started plans,* which address a situation with a great many unpredictable elements, for example, building convention business, so that only the objective of the plan and the initial steps are really determinable.

Plans may be originated by the manager alone, or the actual planning may involve other people. Often the manager is developing sub-plans to implement a master plan promulgated by upper-echelon management. Obviously, this type of planning is restrictive, for the objectives established are really intermediate objectives in some grander scheme to which the manager may have made no contributions.

Often the manager will involve other people in his planning. He may simply want to share the work with an assistant or a worker with specialized craft knowledge. Some organizations have staff specialists whose function is to assist the operational or line manager. A manager planning a more efficient garbage disposal routine might consult with a staff specialist in transportation, engineering, equipment design, etc., in developing his plan.

Sometimes the manager invites the workers who will have to implement the plan to participate in its formulation. The restaurant director trying to avoid repeating today's chaotic performance could develop a plan with the help of the maitre d', chef, kitchen steward, and head busman. They might very well have something to contribute from their collective experience, but even if they don't, talking with them about the plan and making them feel they have had a part in its formulation predisposes them to it.

A plan need not have any particular format. If it must be communicated to other people—superiors for approval, peers for cooperation, subordinates for implementation—then it should be articulated so that they can understand it. The planning process is not a piece of paper. As a managerial technique it should include the following steps:

1. *Identify the purpose, need, objective of the plan.* What is the course of action described by the plan supposed to do?
2. *Investigate the precedents.* There may already be a plan. The manager can review his own experience, he can read a book, he can ask someone.
3. *Assemble the relevant data.* If a plan is going to be accurate then the planner must have as much knowledge as possible about the situation for which he is planning. This calls for a consideration of past performance and a determination of the external elements that could affect the activity described in the plan: market mix, weather, competing activities, etc.
4. *Build in deadlines, a time element.* The essence of planning lies in achieving the objective within a definite time period. A plan can very well include a schedule (see Chapter 5).
5. *Identify the resources needed.* If the plan is going to succeed, what men and material are needed? In an organizational situation there is usually the need for a plan on how to get them.
6. *Preview the action.* What is going to happen, how is it going to happen, when is it going to happen? Examine several alternative scenarios and choose the best one to implement.
7. *Develop contingency plans.* Take into account that there may be unforeseen developments, or that at a certain point in the plan several alternatives may present themselves.
8. *Identify the needs for outside cooperation and coordination.* See if *the* plan fits in with the plans of those whose cooperation you will need.

9. *Address obstacles to the performance of the plan.* Consider upper echelon resistance, worker resistance.
10. *Translate the plan into a punch list.* What has to be done, by whom, and when?

Why Plans Fail

The plans of managers frequently fail (the objective is not achieved) because they lack fundamental information. A plan for stripping and waxing a ballroom floor has to be based on solid information about the size of the floor and the capabilities of the men and equipment.

Plans also fail because too much is attempted in a single plan. Good plans are characterized by their directness and simplicity. Many plans, not a single omnibus plan, are needed.

Other common causes of plan failure include the manager's failure to integrate his plan into the organization's general plans; his failure to consider the "people" element; everyone's failure (including the manager's) to follow the plan; administrative hindrance; and, finally, the use of the planning process to delay the necessary action so long that the opportunity to act is lost.

BUDGETING

Budgeting is essentially a part of the planning process. A budget is in fact a plan expressed quantitatively to allocate and control the use of limited resources. A budget is not a "shopping list"; it is a plan. It is not an accounting device; it is a control device.

In the hospitality industry budgets are often prepared on the operational level so that the plans, judgments, and expertise of the manager can be communicated to the corporate management. Even when budget preparation is not formally required of the manager, it is a most useful technique for improving his unit's performance. By budgeting the resources at his disposal (materials, labor units, and salaried time), that is, by expressing his anticipated requirements for a given period in numbers, he provides himself with a number of valuable tools.

The control aspects of a budget are especially significant (see Chapter 7). By budgeting for a day, or week, or month, the manager is disciplining himself.

The act of budgeting is making him address changes in the operation's occupancy and sales volume. It is easy to ignore changes in occupancies when scheduling maids, waiters, or bellmen if there is no device for quantifying the cost of their labor units as a percentage of sales volume. Making a budget for the next week's labor cost makes the manager address the problem.

SIX-MONTH BUDGET PLAN WORK SHEET AND SUMMARY

DEPARTMENT_____YEAR_____BY_____

	JANUARY				FEBRUARY				MARCH			
	This Year		Last Year		This Year		Last Year		This Year		Last Year	
	Amount	%	Amount	%	Amount	%	Amount	%	Amount	%	Amount	%
Sales												
Sales % Income												
Gross Profit												
Payroll												
Expense												
Profit												

	APRIL				MAY				JUNE			
	This Year		Last Year		This Year		Last Year		This Year		Last Year	
	Amount	%	Amount	%	Amount	%	Amount	%	Amount	%	Amount	%
Sales												
Sales % Income												
Gross Profit												
Payroll												
Expense												
Profit												

	FOR 6 MONTHS ENDING			
	This Year		Last Year	
	Amount	%	Amount	%
Sales				
Sales % Income				
Gross Profit				
Payroll				
Expense				
Profit				

Figure 2.1.   A six-month budget plan work sheet and summary form.

Budgets also allow the manager to see where trade-offs are possible. He budgets for a certain dollar cost of cooks. With the budget before him he sees that he can reduce that cost by bringing in utility workers for one additional hour overtime.

Using a budget over a period of time, the manager finds relationships between labor units expended and sales volume, between materials used and sales volume, between labor units and materials used, and he can manipulate these relationships to lower costs significantly.

A budget can also be used to test several alternate plans by comparing the budgets for each.

Budgets first establish standards of performance and then give the operation manager standards of performance to beat. He may not know how many housemen can clean the ballroom floor. His first budget is way off. His second budget reflects his experience, establishes a tentative standard, and gives him a performance goal for which to shoot.

A budget is also a measure of commitment. In organizations which use them regularly they serve as a contract between the manager and his superior. Incentives for above standard performance are sometimes incorporated into the contract. Even when the manager makes the budget for himself, having his objectives quantified makes it easier for him to keep to the plan.

When a manager is in charge of other managers, the budget he prepares for them, or with them, is also a communications device. Numbers are indisputably clearer than words in articulating an operational plan.

Guidelines to Budgeting

1. *Identify controllable items as specifically as possible:* labor units in hours and dollars by job category, for example.
2. *Establish tentative numerical relationships between cost items and revenues.* For example: 3 waitress hours for every 100 customer hours, or a labor cost of $9.30 for every $155.00 of revenue. (An expression of the same relation: If the waitresses earn $3.10 per hour, and 100 customers with a cover average of $1.55 each are processed in an hour.)
3. *Record past performance.* Generally the standard is placed in one vertical column.
4. *Indicate budgeted amount for a definite period.* In a standard budget this would appear as the second vertical column.
5. *Record actual performance.* In the third vertical column.
6. *Note significant variations.*
7. *Systemize variations which are under budget.* Find out why the greater labor productivity or economization of materials was achieved, and make it standard operating procedure.
8. *Correct variation over budget.* The budget figure may be wrong, or, the manager could not anticipate some event that required an exceptional expenditure. On the other hand, the budget figure may represent a well established standard, and the manager is obliged to insure that the cause of deviation is corrected. Very often the budget includes a statement of either the absolute cost to date or the absolute cost percentage to date (of the month or year) with a comparison of a prior period. Including this data allows the manager to identify whether the excessive cost is truly exceptional (one time only) or a systematic problem. If he were operating the bars in a convention hotel, and the group booked into the hotel was delayed by an airline strike, the cost of the bartenders that day would be an excessively high percentage of revenues. Their contract might provide that they be paid for three hours if they were called in at all. On the other hand, the monthly cost figure would be almost normal.

ORGANIZING

The manager in a hotel-motel organization may be provided with a detailed presentation of the positions, inter-relationships, and responsibilities of the individuals in his unit. His first activity on the job may be to paste his name over his predecessor's on the organization chart posted on the departmental bulletin board. In recent years, higher management in the hospitality industry has reacted to periodic organizational convulsions by attempting to establish some written organizational structure.

An organizational structure prepared by higher management does not necessarily explore the organization of each operational unit. The manager most often organizes his own unit. Even when there is a formal organizational description of the unit, the manager still must fashion an informal organization which allows for his functioning as a person within the unit.

Organization is always necessary. It is the difference between continuity of operations and creating the unit in all its dimensions every single day. Ideally it will take the form of manuals, charts, job descriptions, job specifications, and procedural designs, and it must at least be a concept in the manager's mind.

The manager's difficulties in organizing vary considerably with the particular hospitality units being organized. Likewise the nature of each organization will differ. Organizational structures might be described as traditional or quasi-military, and modern or progressive. The operational manager in charge of a crew of warewashers will be obliged to create a quasi-military structure, and he will have continuous difficulty in maintaining it. The principle of routinization described in the organizing process methodology below will have to be intensively applied. A constant turnover in this department severely limits any possibility of decentralization of authority or the creation of "rewarding" positions: desirable objectives which are absolutely beyond the capabilities of the manager to achieve.

On the other hand, the manager functioning as a chief steward may be able to create a much less formal structure for a group of men in the receiving and storage areas. The "right" crew can work together informally, dividing duties in response to a changing situation. Each man in a fairly stable crew could create the natural boundaries of his own job with the collaboration of his colleagues as long as the unit was productive.

It might also be observed that the first organization is simple and the second is complex, that is, it allows for a criss-crossing of functions and responsibilities.

The manager can create a complex organization in a unit with a stable crew because he will not constantly be faced with the cost of training new members and integrating them into the crew. In the ware-washing unit he is obliged to keep it simple so he can explain it in a few seconds: "Stand here and take the dishes from the bus box"; "Stand here, and sort and stack the dirty dishes." The organizational structure in this instance consists entirely of the warewashing procedure.

The "process of organizing" which follows does not necessarily have to be applied completely or with the same emphasis to every operational unit. Its application like most of the manager's work is situational.

Process of Organizing

1. Determination of the purpose of the unit
2. Assessment of resources
3. Task identification
4. Reduction of tasks to simple routines
5. Grouping of routines into job "slots" (titles or positions)
6. Generation of job descriptions and specifications
7. Creation of an "ideal" organizational structure
8. Establishment of the chain of command
9. Introduction of the principle of exception
10. Codification of the organization

1. *Determination of the purpose of the unit.* In the organization as a whole the particular unit has a function. The warewashing unit processes the dirty serviceware.
2. *Assessment of resources.* The organization of competent, well motivated, experienced workers is necessarily different from that of itinerant workers.
3. *Task identification.* The activity of the unit is the sum of individual tasks accomplished. In a dining room the tasks might be identified as cooking, serving, busing, cashiering, etc.
4. *Reduction of tasks to simple routines.* The principle of routinization, dividing each task into simple, routine, repetitive action, protects the organization against losing "key" personnel. Nobody is doing anything that cannot be taught to the first person off the street in two minutes. Competent people are soon offended by the personal implications of this system and quit, thereby perpetuating the vicious cycle that prompted the creation of the system. If the manager can evolve a new system (and necessarily a new organization) he must first sell it to the policy-making executives who are understandably reluctant to make changes in a system that works.
5. *Grouping of routines into job "slots" (titles or positions).* A single

routine may not be a day's work. It is necessary therefore to group several routines and give the combined activity a place or slot on the schedule and some descriptive title. "Tray Carrying and Removing Dishes from Tables" may both be simple routines necessarily combined into the "Busboy" title.

6. *Generation of job descriptions and specifications.* Essentially this is the communication of the decisions reached in step 5 to other people: superiors, personnel departments, workers.

7. *Creation of an ideal organizational structure.* At the point where the operational manager has the elements of his organization, i.e., he has established "positions," he can place the positions in relation to each other so that lines of authority are established; so that there is ideal process flow; and so that there are ideal communications. Organization charts with neat boxes and straight connecting lines are a graphic representation of this ideal structure. The presumption is that everyone follows the rules, lives up to his job description, never empire-builds, never shortcuts superiors. Although the presumption is false, the manager at least has an ideal toward which to strive.

8. *Establishment of the chain of command.* This is a real process that takes into account the people involved. The chain of command therefore can change as the composition of the crew changes. The manager tries to establish an organization of leaders and followers: each subordinate has but one superior to whom he is accountable. Each superior has definite individuals for whom he is responsible. Very often in an operational unit the command structure is informal. The leaders and the followers may be very apparent to the work group but unknown to the general management. One warewasher emerges as the "lead" warewasher for any of a multitude of reasons: All the warewashers come from the same community where the lead warewasher's family is important; the lead warewasher may be physically aggressive; the other employees may feel that he is capable of "dealing" with the manager on their behalf. As long as they last, and as long as the manager can control the total situation these informal arrangements are useful.

In many operational units there are definite formal chains of command. The restaurant director has several assistants in the maitre d', chef, chief steward. In fact, his organization structure is departmentalized, with these individuals heading their own organizational structures as managers.

9. *Introduction of the principle of exception.* Once the chain of command and organizational structure has been created the man-

ager attempts to use the structure he has created to limit his own work to those matters which are exceptional, that is, departures from routine. He tries to push some managerial functions down into the organization so that he can concentrate on those tasks that cannot be done by anyone else.

10. *Codification of the organization.* The job of organization is only complete when the structure can stand alone, independent of its creator; ideally, when the manager can hand over the organization to another manager. The ultimate articulation of the organizational structure would consist of organizational charts, a manual, operational procedures, job descriptions and specifications, employee evaluations and commentaries, and certainly, a review and up-date of procedures.

DELEGATING

A manager has to decide what he is *not* going to do as well as what he is going to do in his unit. This is seemingly a simple enough decision, yet it is perhaps the most difficult aspect of the transition from worker to manager, or from student to manager. An entire ethic militates against delegation: pride in personal accomplishment; the machismo of being better, stronger, swifter; the virtue of self-sufficiency; business seen as a competitive game; all make it difficult for the manager to share his authority. It becomes especially difficult when he realizes that he is sharing his authority but retaining all the responsibility, and even more difficult when he realizes that he is trusting someone else with his reputation and conceivably his job security.

Some individuals function best in organizations where the right to delegate has not been delegated: authority remains centralized in the single executive or the executive cadre. Below a certain organizational level the subordinate is merely an instrument of his superior without the authority to make any decisions.

Organizations without substantial delegation of authority do prosper, at least up to a certain size. At that point it becomes impossible for the single individual retaining the authority and power to competently and swiftly make the decisions necessary.

As operational responsibilities increase it becomes nearly impossible for the manager to control his unit without delegating. Vigorous enforcement of sanitary codes and the passage of the Occupational Safety and Health Act have added immeasurably to the responsibilities. So he delegates. Perhaps he can delegate upward, the food and beverage manager sees these activities as a responsibility of his office. Perhaps he can delegate sidewards; he can shift the weight to the housekeeping and engineering department heads. Most likely he must delegate downwards (the customary direction) and entrust a subordinate or a group of subordinates with the authority to make the decisions necessary to make the operation acceptable, clean, and safe.

At this point several problems present themselves. Immediately, the manager must decide what authority he is delegating. He cannot delegate authority he does not have, making this an essential preliminary determination. He may find that he has the responsibility without having the authority because of faulty delegation from his superiors, but to perpetuate his frustration is to doom the project. At each lower level of the organizational hierarchy it becomes easier for the employee to refuse responsibility.

If he has sufficient authority to make the decisions and take the actions necessary to bring the operation up to approved standards, then he has to decide whether he is delegating his entire authority to the subordinates, that is, giving them complete discretion to do what they feel is best. Or, he may establish an operational policy, for example, a plan for realizing sanitation or safety objectives over a period of time at a certain cost, and delegate only the authority to make decisions consistent with the policy. Or, he may delegate even less authority, allowing subordinates to act only within specific procedures he has established.

Even when some authority has been passed on the delegation can still fail. The delegating manager must consider a number of other elements:

1. The authority must be commensurate with the responsibility; he cannot ask the subordinate to assume tasks without giving him the power to complete them.
2. The manager has to clearly define what he is expecting of the subordinate, by what standards they will be measured.
3. He must train the subordinate in the use of the delegated authority and the job knowledge relevant to the assignment. At the very least, he must choose wisely.
4. He must prepare the rest of the unit for activities of the subordinate in his new authoritative role. He must be prepared to back his subordinate in differences with other workers or with their superiors.
5. He must follow through; that is, he must continue to survey the situation, evaluate the subordinate, encourage and aid him.

When an effort at delegation has failed, the manager should not blame the process or the subordinate but, rather, carefully examine himself. Did he choose a weak subordinate because he could not stand the thought of anyone else being competent? Did he deliberately overdelegate by giving a subordinate a problem that he himself could not handle? Did he sabotage the effort because the only way he could justify his job was by *doing,* he being incapable of *managing?* Is it a case where the delegation effort really succeeded but he wishes it hadn't because the time liberated could not be productively used by him?

DECISION MAKING

There is a critical correspondence between the level and the position of a manager and the nature of the decisions he makes. If the decisions made during a day were collected and categorized it would be apparent that high level management had made decisions which would affect the organization's future, perhaps for a period of years: decisions that deal with major fundamental policies and that involve considerable expenditures of limited resources for implementation.

It would be apparent also that the lower levels of management have made more decisions and more immediate decisions, and that the collective impact of all the decisions made by the lower management levels could have as much effect on the organizational health, future, and fortunes as many high level decisions.

The quality of decision making on the operational level is very important to the organization. Repeatedly bad decisions on the operational level affect the guest's foods, his bathroom, his recreation, his entertainment, his safety—in other words, the value and marketability of the service being offered—much more immediately than does the executive's philosophical and financial decision making.

The quality of his decision making is also very important to the manager. Unlike the executive decision, which may take years to implement and then years to evaluate in a morass of data that can be variously interpreted, the value of the manager's decision is soon apparent. In the eyes of his subordinates, his superiors, and himself he is soon "proved" right or wrong. For him, the agony of decision making is just as real as it is for the chief executive.

In any decision making, a percentage of failure is to be expected: things don't work out as the decision maker thought they should. Even when the action predicated on the decision is a success, the decision maker often has a feeling of "failure." Alternatives *not* taken are regretted; often they become more and more attractive in retrospect. Choice always occasions a sense of loss.

The objective of perfecting decision making technique is to improve the percentage of success and minimize the "regret." Each of the fundamental processes in decision making can be studied so that the decision maker brings the best possible tools to the task. He can equip himself to make routine repetitive decisions with almost 100 percent surety, and he can make decisions involving more variable, uncertain, and risky elements with, at the least, a greater awareness of his alternatives.

Methods of Decision Making

The essential process in decision making is choosing among several alternatives. When the situation in which the decision is being made does not contain many uncontrollable factors the decision is rather straight forward. Most decisions are of this type. The decision maker is right or wrong on the basis of whether he recognizes the alternative which works from the others. The method is apparent: the use of historical judgment, experience, and steering by the seat of educated pants. When the chief engineer says: "Install the drain for the tennis courts here," he has made this kind of a decision. He has made supposedly accurate assumptions based on his experience about future rainfall, the pitch of the court, the porosity of the ground, etc. The workmen building the drain also make decisions on the same basis: how much lime in the concrete, how deep should the trench be, how much gravel should be in the bottom of the trench.

When a number of uncontrollable elements are introduced, the decision ceases to be ordinary and routine, making it necessary to sophisticate the method of decision making. The scientific or logical method is used. The uncontrollable elements are recognized, but analysis or judgment is used to estimate their effect on the controllable or knowable elements in several different circumstances. To characterize the method, the decision maker "reviews" the future: "If I take this course of action, that occurrence may substantially distort the result"; "If I take this other course of action, that occurrence has less likelihood of distorting the result." If the informational basis of this review is good, and an accurate assessment made of the likelihood of distorting events occurring, the decision maker improves his chances of choosing the best alternative.

More sophisticated methods of decision making do not depart substantially from the premises of the scientific or logical method, which is treated in greater depth below. The progress in decision making technique has been in improving the informational basis of the review, and in displaying the alternatives packaged with various uncontrollable elements and the probabilities of their occurrence so that the decision maker can easily inspect them. Quantitative decision charts, or trees; simulation, computerized model building, various management information systems, applied to certain decisions, help the decision maker reach the judgment point in the scientific or logical method.

The operational manager is not usually asked to make decisions of the scope which would necessitate these additional tools. He can either make his decisions successfully with the scientific method, a pencil, and a good mind, or he cannot make them.

Deciding to Decide

Before actually making a decision, the decision maker faces two preliminary decisions, which could incidentally be approached with the scientific method: he has to decide to decide, and he has to decide how to decide.

He knows there is a decision to be made, that is, he has a sense of uneasiness about a current situation, a superior has given him a decision to make, or a subordinate has exposed a problem for him to resolve.

He may decide to make no decision, that is, to ignore the situation or pass the buck for a number of reasons. He may feel that his superiors do not want him to make the decision: he may feel that the course of action to which the decision would lead would mean too much work for him, he may foresee that the decision logically made will violate everyone's expectations. He may feel that the time for the decision has not come, or frankly that a decision cannot be made. If he realistically assesses the consequences of not making a decision which may include losing an opportunity, appearing indecisive, ceding some of his authority to the person who ultimately makes it, he can legitimately conclude that he should not decide.

Sometimes he decides to make a partial decision. He sidesteps the difficult issues, or those which would overcommit him and limits the scope of his ultimate decision to issues which he can handle.

Such ploys which might be highly undesirable in a chief executive are sometimes necessary for the operational manager whose survival depends on his organizational relationships.

Having decided to decide something, he faces a further decision: how to decide. He can make the decision alone, he can make it with a colleague, for example, another manager, he can ask a staff specialist for help, or he can involve the people ultimately affected by the decision (whatever it is) in the decision process.

Most decisions made by managers are made alone, then possibly reviewed with a colleague and conceivably put in affect by the people concerned. Lack of time, the competitive nature of management, the quasi-military organization of hospitality units limit the manager's ability to seek counsel. He makes the decision then searches for a colleague to tell him he is right; he may have to ask several but he only believes the one that agrees. He may involve the members of the unit in the decision process but he runs the risk of appearing wishy-washy, "incapable of making his own decisions" to them. Against this he must weigh the very limited contribution to actual decision making they can make. If he needs information then he can solicit it as such without involving himself in a compromising debate about its use and interpretation.

In the right circumstances, of course, both colleagues and subordinates could be very valuable; at the very least, his involving them could better dispose them to accept the decision once it is made. That the circumstances are right is in itself a weighty decision.

Factors Affecting the Quality of a Decision

Sometimes decisions are bad for technical reasons: The "facts" on which the decision was based are wrong; the decision maker did not really identify all the alternatives and missed the correct one; the alternative he chose is beyond the capabilities of the organization to implement although it is "right."

In other instances the basic logic of the decision-making process has been compromised. Frequently, the decision maker simply does not think logically. Encouraged to be creative, sensitive, and expressive throughout his school years, his thinking lacks rigor. Erroneous decisions are often based on common logical fallacies: false analogy, fallacy of accident, hypothesis contrary to fact, circular argument, undistributed middle, and so on. If a decision maker's decisions are not successful, he should start to explore, for example, the basic illogic of believing that he can schedule any workman to produce 500 units because one workman has produced 500 (*special case fallacy*); or of believing that a new menu cover is the key to his competitor's success (*fallacy of accident*); or of believing that because MacDonald's is very successful, any fast-food operation must be successful (*fallacy of division*).

The decision maker may subvert the decision-making process because of his own emotional disposition toward a particular conclusion. He makes the analysis come out the way he wants it to, perhaps for irrational reasons. He wants to fire Jones and any other alternative is wrong.

There can be a psychological influence on the decision-making process. The decision maker may want to please a superior or be a good guy to the troops to the extent of distorting the decision-making process.

As a person he may be impulsive, fearful, overly cautious, domineering to the extent of compromising his ability to decide reasonably. It is no accident that good leaders are good decision makers, and good decision makers are often good leaders. The same personality characteristics favor both activities.

A decision may legitimately be less than perfect. The ideal solution mandated by the logic of the process may be politically impossible, it

FALLACIES IN LOGIC THAT FREQUENTLY DISTORT DECISION-MAKING

Name of Fallacy	Definition	Example
Composition	A statement made of one member of a group is applied to the group as a whole.	Pizza Superbo is a very successful fast-food pizza restaurant, *therefore,* all fast-food pizza restaurants are successful.
Division	A statement made of a whole group is assumed to be true of each of its members.	Pizza Superbo restaurants are well run, *therefore,* as this restaurant is a Pizza Superbo, it is well run.
Accident	Of several qualities, the wrong one is chosen as material.	Pizza Superbo restaurants have beautiful landscaping, *therefore,* any restaurant with beautiful landscaping will be successful.
False analogy	Two objects, events, or ideas similar in one respect are assumed to be similar in all respects.	Pizza Superbo and Burger Deluxe both have labor costs of 30%, *therefore,* as Pizza Superbo has a net profit of 10% so must Burger Deluxe.
Special case	If something is true in one instance, it must be true in all instances.	When a Burger Deluxe was built next to this Pizza Superbo, business declined by 50%, *therefore,* the building of a Burger Deluxe next door always means disaster for a Pizza Superbo.
Generalization	An unqualified statement is wrongly applied to a particular instance.	Americans like Italian food, *therefore,* as Pizza Superbo offers Italian food it will be liked.
Contradictory premises	A single statement or assertion contradicts itself.	Pizza Superbo has good pizza except that they burn them most of the time.
Circular reasoning	A conclusion is justified by a re-statement of itself.	Pizza Superbo restaurants have 50% of the fast-food market in this town because of their tremendous volume of sales.

FALLACIES IN LOGIC THAT FREQUENTLY DISTORT DECISION-MAKING—continued

Name of Fallacy	Definition	Example
Begging the question	The point to be proven is assumed.	It is obvious that Pizza Superbo has 50% of the market in this town because nobody has given them any stiff competition.
Hypothesis contrary to fact	The consequences of an unfulfilled historical event are assumed.	If Pizza Superbo had just added hamburgers to its menu when it started, Burger Deluxe would have remained a three unit chain.

Figure 2.2.   Obstacles to watch for in making a decision.

may run counter to some greater organizational objective, there may be a contractual agreement which prevents its implementation.

Knowingly implementing a less than perfect decision at least effects some change in the situation, perhaps enough to create a climate for the implementation of the best decision. The manager should not fear to appear inconsistent in altering course. It is much more important to react to changed circumstances, of which subordinates may not be aware, than to buoy their spirits and pursue a seemingly consistent but erroneous course of action.

The Decision-Making Process

The decision-making process can be summarized in 12 steps.

1. Recognize a situation calling for a decision.
2. Decide to decide.
3. Decide on what to decide and when to decide.
4. Decide if decision process should be shared and with whom.
5. Identify the essential decision area, the priority, the subsuming problem.
6. Search for historical precedents, similar situations.
7. Identify all norms and standards which are relevant to the situation.
8. Consider all the "uncontrollable" elements which can affect the decision's implementation.
9. Develop alternative courses of action.
10. Weigh the alternatives.
11. Calculate the various pay-offs of the alternatives.
12. Choose the best alternative.

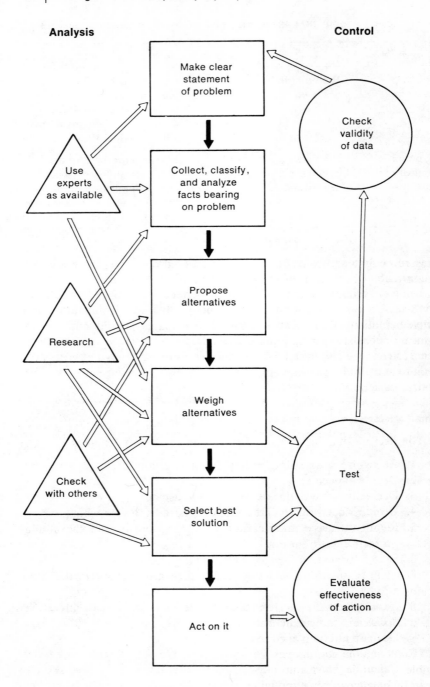

Figure 2.3. Decision making.

Recognize a situation calling for a decision. It is legitimate to decide not to make a decision. In the final analysis no action is always a postulatable alternative. It is not legitimate to ignore problems and difficult situations in the hope that they will go away.

Decide to decide. Consider scope of authority, implications of the courses of action the decision may create, moral responsibility to decide.

Decide on what to decide and when to decide. In real situations decisions are not neatly packaged. Any situation can present a score of potential decision points. Choose the ones that can be handled, sidestep others. Delaying a decision because of an anticipated change in the situation, new information coming, a change of personnel is legitimate.

Decide if the decision process should be shared and with whom.

Identify the essential decision area, the priority, the subsuming problem. The situation which brings the need for a decision to the manager's attention is not necessarily the decision area. He sometimes becomes aware of a symptom. Jones and Smith are fighting, the decision is not necessarily whether to fire them or not, it may be to undertake a course of action which will correct the situation that caused them to fight.

Search for historical precedents, similar situations. In some areas that concern the manager in the hospitality industry there is no published information, in others there are literally libraries. No one has to make a personnel decision, a make or buy decision for food products, an overbooking decision uninformed.

Identify all norms and standards which are relevant to the situation. There is enough published data in the hospitality industry to keep the manager from wasting his time and credibility advocating pie in the sky solutions to problems: advertising budgets of 50 percent to build top lines; graduate chemists to regulate dishmachine detergent concentrations; or human machines capable of single-handedly servicing 53 guest rooms.

Consider all "uncontrollable" elements which can affect the decision's implementation. Uncontrollable elements can include a late crop of tomatoes which turn potential housemen into farm workers; the opening of a fast food restaurant down the street; the closing of a nearby office building.

Develop alternative courses of action. Create plans, programs, solutions.

Weigh the alternatives. Try to see the implications of the alternatives as well as determining how they will be affected by uncontrollable events. Develop pros and cons for each.

Calculate the various pay-offs of the alternatives. Sometimes it is possible to quantify the results of alternative courses of action. Risk and cost can be balanced against potential return. When it is possible the alternative can then be rated in some fashion.

Choose the best alternative. Sometimes at this point an alternative has emerged as indisputably best. The arguments for the alternative are considerable, and the arguments against it minimal. In the event that the alternative turns out to be an unsatisfactory course of action, the potential damage is minimal.

Other times several alternatives look promising. The decision maker can choose among them on several bases: the alternative which offers the least uncertainty, the alternative which is most easily revocable, the alternative which has the least damage potential. What criteria he applies depends much more on the situation in which he finds himself in his rise through the organization than on any logic inherent in the situation.

PROBLEM SOLVING

Conceptually, and semantically, problem solving and decision making are closely related. Decision making is part of problem-solving activity, that is, decisions must be made for problems to be solved. Problem solving is part of the decision-making process. It is possible to divide situations requiring decisions into elements which are called problems, for which one seeks alternative courses of action called *solutions*.

Although interrelated, the two techniques are not identical. Problem solving is primarily directed to overcoming immediate obstacles, the nature of the solution is apparent, only the means to achieve it, and their cost need to be determined. In decision making the fundamental problems have to be discovered and the alternative solutions and their implications explored before a course of action can be chosen. To characterize it further, problem solving is short time, one shot, limited in impact.

If the operation's refrigeration breaks down just before a big weekend, a problem-solving approach is needed. The problem is clear: the food is going to spoil. The solution is equally clear: keep the food cold until the refrigeration can be put back in service. Decision making in the same area, after the problem has been solved, might address the replacement cost of the entire refrigeration system, the use of public warehousing for some food products, changes in the food production system to eliminate the need for as much refrigeration.

The solution to the problem, which might be purchasing dry ice or blocks of ice, or freezing the bulk of the food, or contacting the produce wholesaler to borrow his refrigerated truck for the weekend, *is not meant to be systemized.* The solution to the problem more than likely will not be the course of action that will be chosen when the problem has been formally addressed by the decision-making process.

Personnel problems offer a similar example of the difference between the two techniques. Jones and Smith are fighting. The problem to be solved is keeping them from continuing to fight so that the day's work can be done. Later, decisions can be made about the fault in the organizational structure that occasioned the dispute (both thought they were in charge of the crew).

Problem solving should not be substituted for decision making. Putting out fires is never a substitute for fire prevention. There is no doubt however that the problems have to be solved, the fires extinguished, before the longer term decisions can be made.

Guidelines to Problem-Solving

1. Solve the problems where the problems are.
2. Cure the symptom first.
3. Be creative rather than analytical.
4. Stretch out.
5. Accept any solution that works.
6. Make the move fast.
7. Substitute authority for rationale.
8. Make the solution work.
9. See the problem through.
10. Don't look back.

Solve the problems where the problems are. The manager has to go to the problem, he has to confront the obstacle physically if he is going to overcome it. Basically, he is relying on all his past experience to give him access to a solution. He needs the stimulation of the refrigerator full of warming food, or the data processing cards being chewed up by the machine. His presence, if he is a good manager generally, will also stimulate the workers who are standing around watching to do some thinking. Maybe they are waiting with a ready-made solution until he arrived so they can impress him.

Cure the symptom first. There is a temptation to attack the root causes of the problem, but if the problem is seen as an obstacle to the progress of the day's work, it has to be cured first.

Be creative rather than analytical. Decision making emphasizes analysis, quantification, weighing of elements to reach a solution. Problem solving requires creativity; making-do with some crazy idea until something better comes along. Why can't the window washers hand-sort the data processing cards?

Stretch out. If the problem is major and serious the manager cannot start wondering about the limits to his authority, the organizational structure, and the sensitivities of his fellow workers. The food in the refrigerator will not wait for a purchase order to be generated by the purchasing agent in response to a written request for a purchase form.

Accept any solution that works. Decision making emphasizes finding the best solution because of the long range impact of the decision. In problem solving, any temporary solution will do, so there is no need to go beyond the first one. The difference in cost between the first solution and the best, spread over the life of the solution, is minimal.

Make the move fast. A time lapse between finding the solution to a problem and implementing it allows enthusiasms for the solution to wane, union stewards start to think about work rules, other managers find uses for equipment that was going to be pressed into service.

Substitute authority for rationale. A well articulated decision can have the force of a legal brief, patiently eliminating opposing arguments. A problem solution has to be imposed before resistance develops.

Make the solution work. The solution may not be the greatest. Its only essential quality is its workability. It may need some participation by the manager to get going, and some redefining as difficulties occur.

See the problem through. The problem solving is only completed when the problem has been solved. It cannot be delegated if only because the solution has not been well articulated.

Don't look back. Once the problem has been solved the manager has to move on to whatever decision making is appropriate. He put out the fire, now he must move on to fire prevention in the future, not a reassessment of the alternative ways that the fire could have been put out.

FORECASTING

For the manager in a hospitality unit a forecast is an estimate of the number of guests who will use his unit's facilities during a particular period. The forecast is used to make preparations—material and labor —to serve adequately that number of guests.

In large operations, the front office manager issues a forecast of total hotel occupancy for a period of time, three-day and one-week forecasts are common. The front office forecast is based on a count of reservations, a count of convention guests, a count of permanent guests, an allowance for rooms assigned to staff and rooms out of service, all of which are "known," not estimated, numbers. The front desk manager also forecasts (by the same method as any other manager) how many of the reservations will not show (this figure might not be directly shown) and how many people will seek a room without a reservation. The number of guests known to be children, or singles, or tennis players or some other category of guest that might have special demands is also sometimes stated.

Starting with the front office estimated count, the other managers prepare forecasts. A manager in housekeeping has little independent

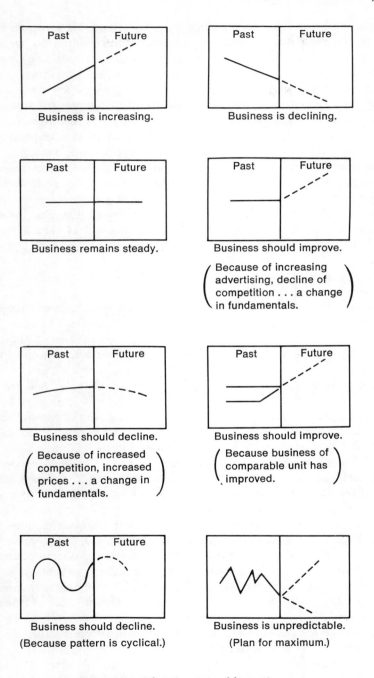

Figure 2.4. Selected patterns of forecasting.

forecasting to do, the house occupancy is essentially his forecast. Special requirements such as extra beds in rooms for children are directly communicated not abstracted from the forecast. Other managers use the front office count as a basis for their forecasting. They have to ask themselves the implications of that number of guests for their units. There may be ten restaurants in the particular operation, each managed by a restaurant director. Each has to schedule labor, requisition food, rent linen on the basis of some estimate of the percentage of people of that total number who will frequent the particular unit. The golf pro, tennis pro, or swimming pool director have to make similar judgments, although generally with less need to forecast precisely. Even in a small property, with one restaurant and one restaurant director (and no other facilities) a forecast will be necessary: how many of that total number will eat in the restaurant, eat elsewhere, not eat, eat at certain times, snack at other times, drink at still other times.

Preparing the Forecast

1. *Consult the records.* The operation should have sufficient records so that the manager can determine the general relationship between the number of people in the hotel and the use of his unit. Records might be kept precisely for this purpose. If not, he can examine accounting data, sales checks, cashier reports, etc.
2. *Consider people in the guest group to determine if they will behave typically.* Two-thousand guests belonging to a church affiliated group do not behave like an ordinary mixed group of two-thousand guests in their use of the bar facilities, nor do two thousand appliance salesmen, or two thousand single men and women.
3. *Estimate the impact of external factors.* In forecasting for sporting facilities, weather is an important external factor. In forecasting for bars—hospitality suites and cocktail parties are factors which can reduce the estimated intake. In forecasting for restaurants—banquets and outside excursions (by wives) can influence the forecast.
4. *Make the estimate.* The forecast is a judgment. If the forecaster is inexperienced he may want to allow margins for underestimating. At this point staffing, requisitioning, and ordering is done on some basis that relates the number of people and amount of material needed to the number of people to be served. (See Budgeting above.)
5. *Record the actual count.* There may be a diary form expressly for this purpose. Otherwise the manager should create one.
6. *Compare the actual count with the forecast.*

OCCUPANCY FORECAST

	SUN	MON	TUE	WED	THU	FRI	SAT	SUN
PERMANENT								
GROUPS								
A								
B								
C								
TOTAL GROUPS								
Transient w/Reservations								
Transient w/o Reservations								
OTHER								
TOTAL ESTIMATED OCCUPANCY								
ROOMS OUT OF ORDER								
OCCUPANCY %								
GUEST COUNT								
CHECK-INS								
CHECK-OUTS								

Figure 2.5. Occupancy forecast: basis for operational forecasts.

7. *Analyze the variations and their causes.* The manager re-examines the basis of his forecast to determine where the frailties of his judgment lie. Perhaps committed golfers do play in the rain. Perhaps the new generation of singles drinks more coffee than whiskey.
8. *Refine the forecasting procedure.* Make note of the new "rules of thumb" developed so that the forecast can be more precise in the future.

COMMUNICATING

Concern with the improvement of human relations in industry as the key to greater productivity, reduced turnover costs, and other direct benefits of improved morale has caused many corporations to audit the communication climate of their organizations. It is suggested that an exchange of ideas among all levels of an organization facilitates conducting business, and fundamentally motivates all employees.

Principles of Communicating

The creation of a climate of communication, and the use of communication as a motivational device are techniques which do not concern the manager as directly as the actual technique of communicating. For him, the more traditional objective of communication—getting ideas across to get something done—is more important. If he does not communicate successfully he cannot manage successfully: his ideas, orders, directives, procedural changes, plans are not implemented.

There are four basic obstacles to the achievement of the objective of a communication:

1. The communication itself is not clear, that is, the communication is inherently defective. The world's greatest expert in the field would have difficulty in understanding what is wanted.
2. The communication is not understood by the people to whom it is addressed. The communication is "too much" for the people who are listening to it or reading it, although it might be "just right" for a different group.
3. The communication is understood but resented. The communication in substance or in form creates resistance to the performance of what is desired.
4. The communication is understood but insufficient. The ultimate objective of the communication cannot be implemented because the people receiving the communication lack vital information, instruction, directives, etc.

The technique of communicating is fundamentally based on overcoming these obstacles.

MAKING COMMUNICATIONS CLEAR

Good doers are not necessarily clear thinkers, clear speakers, or clear writers. The hotel-motel industry has many craftsmen who are not promoted to manager, and many managers who are not promoted beyond minimal supervisory responsibilities because they cannot speak or write clearly.

To really achieve competence in these areas, considerable instruction in logic, composition, and rhetoric—subjects beyond the scope of this book—is needed.

At least the manager can try to follow simple guidelines to eliminate some of the gross common problems of unclear communications.

1. *Think before writing or speaking.* The objective of the communication has to be in mind before the communication is begun. An
operational communication should not be a public exploration of
a subject of concern, or a substitute for the decision-making
process.
2. *Be precise.* Specific, strong words with an unequivocal meaning are
absolutely necessary for clear communication. The greater the pre-
cision the clearer the communication. *Cook* is not as precise as
stew, fry, broil. Clean is not as precise as *scrub, mop, sanitize,
disinfect.*
3. *Be concise.* Eliminate the rhetorical packaging, make the communication as direct and as short as possible.
4. *Give ideas appropriate emphasis.* Make sure the guts of the communication are apparent to anyone. The conclusion—the action
to be done—should not be lost in the explanation.
5. *Work at communicating.* Depending on the abilities of the manager, he may be obliged to test communications, revise them several
times, rehearse them. In sum, he has to accept the responsibility
for successful communication. It is his job to communicate, not
his subordinates' job to second guess him, practice ESP, or interpret his communications for one another.

MAKE SURE THE COMMUNICATION IS UNDERSTOOD

A communication has to be customized for the receiver. A manager
may read an excellent technical article on a better method for reducing
algae in swimming pools. He understood the article so the author's communication was clear. He wants to reduce the algae in his swimming
pool. Reproducing the article and passing it among the teenage lifeguards
and pool boys would not achieve the objective of the communication:
the algae would remain in the pool, guests might be endangered by the
capricious use of chemicals, etc.

The communication has to be customized for the receivers. The communicator has to understand the abilities (and deficiencies) of the people
to whom he is communicating, and style the communication accordingly.

1. *Don't assume too much.* The manager is often communicating with
individuals of limited formal education, no job experience, a
mother tongue other than English, "short memories," memories of
convenience, limited capabilities of conceptualization and a score
of other impediments to learning. The manager has to assess the
group and communicate at its level. He must accept them as they
are, and work with what he has.
2. *Allow enough time for communication.* The understanding of the
communication is related to the amount of time spent in communi-

cating. If once over is not enough, then enough time will have to be allowed for explanations and repetitions.

3. *Communicate in circumstances that aid understanding.* People are easily distracted by job noise, by other people, by immediate pressures, by their own fatigue. While not every operational communication can be given in a tranquil conference room borrowed for that purpose, more complex communication probably has to be.

4. *Choose an appropriate medium.* Certain media of communication are appropriate for specific types of communication. An officer advancing his troops communicates successfully by yelling "Charge!" It is unnecessary for him to send written instructions. A prominently displayed "No Smoking" sign does the job if the employees read English. The content and complexity of the communication and the group to which it is being communicated, have to be related. Verbal communication, written communication, posters, displays, exhibits, signs, movies, slide shows, all have their place in operational communications. Very often several different media are required for the same communication: a talk of which people remember very little except the main subject and the tone; written instructions which can be reviewed several times; and visual ticklers in the forms of signs, posters, pictures to reinforce the important points of the message.

5. *Insure that there has been understanding.* The communicator has to face the possibility that his communication has not wholly succeeded: he overestimated his brilliance, or he misjudged the group. Within the process of communication there should be a test of understanding. He can ask the person who received the communication to repeat it or summarize it, recognizing that he may simply be getting a parrot-like recitation. He may ask questions that point to the objective: What are *you* going to *do* now? He may open the topic for discussion, listening carefully to the comments to determine the degree of understanding. He may ask one recipient to explain the communication to another person.

SELLING COMMUNICATIONS

A communication can be inherently clear, it can be understood and yet it can still fail to achieve its objectives. Put another way, communications require packaging with a particular market in mind.

1. *Communicate in a tone or fashion that is appropriate to the situation.* Subordinates will "read" the seriousness of the communicator from his tone of voice, his manner, his body actions, or his facial expression, and will act or not act accordingly. A manager can

control these communication factors and make the same content seem important or unimportant, urgent or casual, friendly or menacing, conciliatory or demanding. The attitude communicated should suit the circumstances and the communication. Even the most committed advocate of the human relations approach to management would not suggest that the manager be humorous and charming while explaining new security rules in staff housing because of widespread drug use. It is sufficient that he be matter-of-fact and businesslike.

2. *Start with what they know and accept.* The communication process is made easier by getting initial agreement before introducing the concepts that might occasion resistance. Quoting an accepted authority, using well known clichés, summarizing with popular maxims are all effective.

3. *Avoid offending in the communication.* Many times the manager is asking subordinates to do something they do not really want to do. Nasty jobs are quite common in the hospitality business: nobody wants to wash the garbage tanks. A communication is not offensive because of its substance, it is offensive because it incorporates some form of personal abuse. A communication which starts with an epithet, or includes a racial slur, or an attack on the character of an individual may lose all communicating value, as the anger, belligerency, or chagrin of the persons addressed may obscure the substantive content.

4. *Be believable.* People follow reasonable directives. They accept a manager's sincerity as witness to the appropriateness of a course of action. If any communication is going to be successful, he has to maintain his credibility with his subordinates. The manager should look people in the eye when he speaks to them. He should avoid suggesting that he is infallible. He should readily admit errors. Most important, he should communicate that he is committed to the course of action he is proposing, whether or not he originated it, whether or not he originally agreed with it.

5. *Meet challenges and challengers squarely.* The manager can lose the group by failing to answer questions, by becoming involved in some minor dispute that really is not important to the communication (although it seems to be) by allowing himself to be "beaten" by a wise guy or heckler. He should be prepared to more fully explain the substance of the communication without seeming to "defend it." If he does not need this additional material he should not use it. Overcommunication simply confuses people.

He should have stock answers to the stock gripes: not enough help; the guests won't like it; we tried it. The trick is to cut off the argument before a seeming case is made, and get on with the communication. Try counter-clichés: "I am sure you can do it"; "The marketing people say"; "Didn't that place go bankrupt?" "Times change; every now and then you have to renew your 'always'."

Challengers can be a critical problem in communication. The immediate solution is to dismiss them quickly and perhaps humorously, and then sometime later address the disciplinary problem that they represent. The heckler who asks: "Why waste our time with that?" can be asked in turn: "What's the matter, did you have an appointment to throw rocks in the creek?"

MAKING SURE COMMUNICATION IS SUFFICIENT

A communication can be understood, the people receiving it can be willing to act, but they may not know what to do, or more often, how to do it. The communicating process is only complete when the manager is sure he has left his subordinates with enough information to achieve the objective of the communication.

1. *Get some feedback.* Find out how the subordinates are going to apply what has been said. Get specific examples of their plans to implement the substance of the communication. Listen carefully to determine that they have sufficient experience or expertise to supply the "how" of the communication that has concentrated on the "what" or the "why."

2. *Measure the enthusiasm quotient.* If there is enthusiasm for the substance of the communication, there is considerable likelihood of their being able to follow through. Uncertainty about the course of action means that they are uncertain about their capabilities.

3. *Establish a mechanism for evaluation.* Establish a fairly immediate "test" that everyone can recognize, something that tells the employee he doesn't have the training or expertise to achieve the objective. The employee eliminating the algae from the swimming pool can discover he does not understand pH by testing the water as part of the chlorination program before dumping the new algicide in the pool.

4. *Follow up.* Check out the progress being achieved toward the objective. Find out what they are missing in understanding or in training.

5. *Spread the word personally.* The communication has only been sufficient if all the people concerned know about its substance. Avoid other employees learning second-hand. Confusing, misleading "he said . . ." situations result. Tell them directly.

Problems with the Spoken Word

Hospitality executives, managers, and supervisors often make speeches before public groups, potential customers, and workers. The first principle of public speaking is adequate preparation. Scrambling for a topic or a method of presentation is a direct affront to the listeners. It indicates the speaker did not care enough about them to spend a few minutes preparing himself adequately. Making an audience aware that a presentation has not been prepared or that the speaker is inadequate does not win admiration for the speaker's honesty. Rather, the audience asks, why not?

Speakers further antagonize their audiences by failing to dignify their speech by at least an effort at direct communication. They read without looking at the audience, or look to some distant point. While a speaker does not usually invite verbal comment during the speech, he is supposed to be reading their reactions so that he can emphasize points, review and summarize effectively. A speech is a dialogue not a read memorandum.

Speakers offend their audiences by stupid humor, childish anecdotes, and cuteness. The success of genuinely witty speakers, recorded faithfully by *Reader's Digest,* who entertain as they communicate has encouraged amateur speakers to attempt all sorts of unnatural humor. "Good morning" is a perfectly adequate beginning, while "Thank you" is a brilliant closing. The body of the speech should be matter-of-fact. The speaker tells the audience what he is going to say. Then he says it. He concludes by telling them what he said.

CONVERSATION

Direct conversation between two individuals of the same mother tongue would seem to present few difficulties. In reality it takes great skill to communicate fully anything more than the simplest message. Consider only how many errors are made because of misunderstood or poorly expressed verbal communications.

Faults of etiquette or breaches of good manners can compound the problem. The speaker inadvertently offends the listener, and effectively blocks the communication, or makes some remark that emphasizes their different vocational or social status. He refers to an ethnic or racial group by an unacceptable name. He causes the worker to lose face, or become defensive on some personal basis.

Sometimes the manager speaks a language the worker does not understand, even though they both speak English. Very polite people who speak several languages with equal facility, attempt to speak the native language of their partners in conversation. At a cosmopolitan gathering, one man might ask another: "What language were we speaking?" Sometimes the managerial employee has the same opportunity, although he does not have to choose between two foreign languages. In the interest of both politeness and efficiency, the manager attempts to speak in the idiom the worker understands if he can master it, or in "television" English. He says "rap" and "smoking" if he is really at home with current vernacular, and "talk" and "good" if he is not. He does not say, "proclaim" and "superlative."

Managers who actually speak the native language of foreign-born employees who do not speak English inevitably win their respect. More than being pleased at the ease of communication, they are complimented by his effort on their behalf. They recognize it as consummate courtesy that has cost the manager dearly.

INTERVIEWS

Interviews fully exercise the interviewer's sense of social amenities and courtesy. The person being interviewed is vulnerable and nervous. The interviewer can be impolite, prying, and rude, and the person being interviewed must accept him.

Courtesy and cordiality at this time is never forgotten. During the interview itself, good manners by the interviewer puts the candidate at ease. Often, skillful managers treat the candidate as a visitor or guest. For example, a polite senior executive will rise for a man or woman applying for a very junior position.

Even if the candidate is not hired, consideration of his feelings as a fellow human in an unpleasant situation reflects well on the organization. He should be told honestly why he cannot be hired immediately, he should be told that he is under consideration and why.

If he is hired, the manager should do his best to anticipate and answer the personal questions that every new worker is reluctant to ask: What should he wear, where does he eat, when is pay day, does he get a vacation the first year? Without doubt, he will eventually find out what he needs to know but it is courteous to spare him both the effort and the anxiety.

MEETINGS AND CONFERENCES

Every participant in a business meeting, even an informal staff meeting, is obliged to obey the rules of common courtesy. He must arrive on time, seat himself quietly, speak in turn, avoid angry displays and arguments, and suffer fools silently.

The chairman or meeting leader is expected to have adequately prepared himself to conduct the meeting so that it proceeds in an organized manner to some stated goal, if that goal is nothing more than dissolution when the subject areas appropriate to the meeting have been discussed. An unstructured meeting that degenerates into an amiable discussion of baseball becomes an imposition for the individual who has no interest in baseball or has another appointment.

Even normally polite individuals commit breeches of etiquette in the meeting situation. For example, some participants may bring private arguments or problems to the public meeting for the express purpose of airing them before a superior. They embarrass or bore the rest of the group. Sounding off for the boss, hogging the floor, putting down other participants, continuously interrupting disrupt the communication's flow. Criticizing, injecting personalities into comments, chatting with other individuals, talking without recognition by the leader are impolite. As well, they make it difficult for the group to complete its assignment and antagonize even the most tolerant colleagues.

MAKING TELEPHONE CALLS

When making calls, be direct; ask for the person or department you wish, then state your business. Do not "play games." As in most matters of etiquette, the individuals who merit the most telephone prerogatives do not take advantage of them. Many heads of large corporations, and some billionaires, place their own telephone calls, announce themselves by their first and last names or by their last names, and wait patiently while a junior executive's shared secretary sees if he is "in." Only the patently insecure individual juggles the telephone call so that the person called is on the line first. Ironically, he does not really win, because most people do not play the game; rather they simply see him as impolite or inefficient.

Written Communication

Most non-verbal business communication is typewritten and often from the manager's dictation to a typist. As such, the worst of it resembles a recorded impromptu speech. The main idea wrestles with numerous asides and tangential remarks under a blanket of verbiage. It seldom emerges victorious. The manager really has an obligation to himself and his organization, as well as to his reader, to either prepare himself adequately or review and rewrite.

Memorandum and internal correspondence should have as much information as possible reduced to printed form, with provision for response on the same sheet for instances when the message is addressed to an employee without a secretary. Sequential numbering for identification and some method of filing is also desirable.

STANDARD FORM FOR BUSINESS LETTER

```
                          HOTEL LUXURIOUS

                          119 State Street

                          Clinton, New York

                              11439


                                         Date Dictated

          Name of Addressee
          Title
          Company Name
          Address
          City, State, Zip Code

          Dear Mr. Last Name:

              Body of letter begins here with indented paragraph.

          Lines are skipped between paragraphs.

                                   Sincerely yours,

                                   Written signature
                                   Typed Full Name
                                   Title


          LN:BC
          (Dictated By:To Whom)
          Enclosure
```

Figure 2.6.   Standard form for business letter.

BUSINESS LETTERS

The form for a business letter is almost universally standardized. The first, and most important rule of business letter writing is not to violate the standard form. Creativity does not belong in a business letter. Other rules equally enforce the need for complete conventionality.

1. The letter should be typed on company stationery (not guest stationery in a hotel), ideally on an electric typewriter with a carbon ribbon.

2. It should be read by the manager before he signs it and corrected

by the typist, if the corrections can be made unobtrusively, or re-typed. Handwritten corrections are unacceptable.

3. The name and address of the person receiving it should appear on the letter exactly as it appears on his company letterhead and on the line beneath his signature.
4. Other than in a company letterhead, and in the salutation (Mr., Mrs., etc.) no abbreviations should be used for dates, cities, etc.
5. Most business letters will open with the formal (but not very formal) salutation *Dear Mr. Black* and close with either *Sincerely yours,* or *Very sincerely yours.* Forms such as *My dear sir* and *Very truly yours,* which must be used together are unnecessarily formal in a business letter. The recipient will wonder why they were used.
6. The envelope is addressed exactly as the inside address is written, in the precise center of the envelope.
7. Letters are signed by the executive in the space between the closing line and his typewritten full name, in dark blue or black ink. Letters signed in his name by his secretary are initialed with her initials.
8. Signs indicating carbon copies (CC) or enclosures (Enclosure) are placed directly below the identification initials: who dictated it, to whom (LN:BC), at left hand margin below signature and title. Often, in modern correspondence these initials are omitted.
9. Most business letters are typed in a standard style, as in Figure 2.6.

BUSINESS MEMORANDUM

The business memorandum has six basic elements:

1. The name of the addressee
2. The name of the sender
3. A subject matter line
4. The date
5. The body or the message
6. Routing indications for persons other than the first addressee

Inexpensive sets of forms allow a space for all of the elements, and can be printed to indicate routing—a list of names by order of "need to know," job rank, or the alphabet. These same forms permit reply and make two copies in addition to the original, one as a file copy for the sender, one as a file copy for the receiver and answerer, and one on which he writes his answer. More extensive sets allow routing without the need for reproduction.

Although, certainly, these memorandum sets are commended by their convenience, they have another less apparent advantage. They require the manager to be brief and clear. Most internal correspondence can be completely committed to a single memo, if the author has planned his communication. For the man who must read the memo standing in the middle of a working kitchen or a boiler room, its brevity is a boon.

Business titles are used for a matter of record and to help people reading the memo, other than the sender and recipient, figure out who Bob and Bill are. Initials, rather than a full signature are customary. A junior does not usually memo someone superior to his chief without either the chief's permission or, at the very least, sending the chief a memo.

While "self-defense" memos are sometimes necessary, the individual who continuously reduces clearly understood verbal instructions or discussions to memo form for the record becomes a nuisance. Deliberate vagueness in the hope that his comments will allow him to be "right" no matter what happens, more often result in his being "wrong" no matter what happens.

Stilted language marks a manager as a bore and after receiving two or three bouquets of faded roses nobody bothers to read him anymore.

3 | Management Arts

Budgeting, organizing, planning are management techniques but they are not the quintessence of management. Management is also, importantly, a generalized approach to achieving definite goals in a changing and sometimes difficult situation: a strategy.

This aspect of management demands much more art than science or logic, more talent than technique. The manager must create a functioning entity of himself and his subordinates that achieves despite obstacles, conflicts, and reversals.

Personal qualities and skills serve the manager in his effort to keep the unit together and forward moving. The hospitality manager, no less than any other manager, succeeds because of abilities in these areas:

Leading the unit
Motivating the workers
Keeping peace in the work situation
Supervising production and performance
Training a skilled cohesive work force
Cooperating with other individuals in the organization

Table 3.1 outlines some of the managerial activities that can be subsumed under these headings: leading, motivating, keeping peace, supervising, training, and cooperating.

LEADING

Before the evolution of business organizations into complex social phenomena, the ability to lead a group of individuals was thought to be related directly to a person's character traits. A man was a leader or he was a follower. Leaders were honest, ambitious, driving, intelligent,

Table 3.1.   THE MANAGEMENT ARTS

LEADING	GOAL SETTING	Standardizing Increasing Optimizing Validating
	BUCK STOPPING	
	INSPIRING	
	ACTING	Changing Reacting Responding Hurdling obstacles
	INTERPRETING	
	GOAL TENDING	Maintaining Defending
	STRETCHING OUT	Taking risks Timing Bypassing
	PRAISING	Recognizing Crediting Rewarding
	CRITICIZING	Upgrading Improving Teaching
MOTIVATING	UNDERSTANDING	Sympathizing Empathizing
	STIMULATING	Encouraging Mobilizing
	COACHING	Selling Cheering Raising job interest
	SATISFYING	Defending Involving Supporting

Table 3.1.   THE MANAGEMENT ARTS—continued

	TROUBLESHOOTING	Handling Confronting Resolving Suppressing Minimizing
	MANIPULATING	Bargaining Reconciling Zig-zagging
KEEPING PEACE	ANTICIPATING	Identifying Listening Counseling Following-up
	DISCUSSING	Bull-slinging Talking Socializing
	DEMONSTRATING	Measuring Instructing Inspecting
	ORDERING	Suggesting Requesting Commanding
	DIRECTING	Regulating Correcting Enforcing
SUPERVISING	DISCIPLINING	Warning Salvaging Firing Demoting Suspending Admonishing
TRAINING	PROTECTING EVALUATING PROMOTING	Appraising Testing Rating

Table 3.1   THE MANAGEMENT ARTS—continued

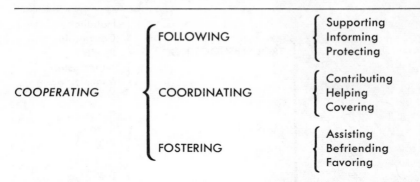

COOPERATING

FOLLOWING
- Supporting
- Informing
- Protecting

COORDINATING
- Contributing
- Helping
- Covering

FOSTERING
- Assisting
- Befriending
- Favoring

courageous, decisive, persistent, self-assured, individualistic, goal oriented, enthusiastic, farsighted, self-confident, and mature. Also they were thought of as being basically concerned with their followers, understanding, fair, sympathetic, concerned, etc. Followers were not necessarily completely deficient in these characteristics, they were simply not outstanding.

The sophistication of business organizations, technological changes, and the dilution of leadership over several strata of management has occasioned a voluminous reexamination of leadership. Modern theorists tend to limit the importance of character traits and emphasize those qualities which make an individual *effective* as a leader.

The distinction is important. In the hospitality industry and most other industries, leaders are not elected, as they may be in government or social organizations, nor do they emerge informally from the group, as they may in teams or gangs. Leaders in industry are appointed. Someone hires or promotes an individual and declares him "in charge," making him the leader. It is very likely that personality traits, certainly intelligence, drive, self-confidence have played a definite role in attaining leadership. But the individual's exercise of leadership depends on other factors as well. Personality traits, even if they could be specifically defined, would not necessarily be predicators of leadership effectiveness.

Leadership effectiveness depends substantially on an individual's doing what leaders do. That is, on an individual's acting as people (subordinates and superiors) expect leaders to act. The leader, not the follower, sets goals, establishes the standards for performance of the group, accepts responsibility for the group's performance, motivates, keeps peace, supervises, develops other people, and so on. By doing all this in fact, the individual reenforces his nominal leadership.

The leader is also a competent management technician. He plans, organizes, forecasts, communicates and generally applies management techniques so as to facilitate the work of the group. The group as such recognizes that his abilities in this area give him the "right" to leadership. It is, incidentally, this managerial ability, rather than craftsmanship or "doing what the others do" that establishes leadership.

The leader's effectiveness is also due to his ability to meet situations successfully. Leaders are flexible—in style, in choice of means, in interpersonal relationships—rather than rigid. Flexibility as such is the professionalism of leadership. An individual may be an effective leader in certain situations, those which lend themselves to his type of personality or his approach to goal achievement, but he can only be called professional—a true leader—if he can adapt to changed circumstances which require totally different approaches. Otherwise, his leadership is "circumstantial," and in other circumstances, despite his leadership performance and managerial competence, he will fail.

The hospitality industry, because of its rapid growth and diversity, offers splendid examples of the need for flexibility. Other industries, more established, more static, and more organizationally sophisticated offer more shelters for leadership rigidity.

A competent hospitality manager in the course of his career is quite likely to be the leader of diverse groups. He may at one time be in charge of a group of warewashers none of whom can be expected to stay with the organization for more than a few months. At another time he may be in charge of competent, highly skilled temperamental craftsmen. On another occasion he may be dealing with long-term clerical employees. It may be necessary to be completely autocratic with the warewashers, democratic with the craftsmen, and completely indulgent with the clerical workers, in order to facilitate the work of the group concerned in realizing *his* objectives.

In the course of his career, he may also encounter a diversity of organizational situations. In a struggling small hotel he may have to "pitch in" and catalyze some extraordinary efforts on the part of a bunch of college students. In attempting to improve the performance of a losing restaurant, he may have to hit hard at practices and procedures the group of workers finds very comfortable. In assuming the management of a group of competent but rigid professionals in a quality operation, he may have to "bargain" for what he wants done.

It is important to recognize that none of these styles of approaches is "right or wrong," rather they are appropriate or inappropriate in a specific situation. Ultimately, the leader who succeeds, the leader who is genuinely effective, recognizes the situation and adapts himself to it, so that he can direct it to the goals he has set.

Problems of Leadership

Young managers in the hospitality industry fail to be effective leaders for a number of specific reasons besides failing to act like leaders, display managerial competence, or practice flexibility.

1. *Young managers may choose the wrong leadership models.* Lack of business experience, and their exposure to leadership in other areas may prompt them to model themselves on the military officers, the coaches, and the teachers who have led them. The group, needing some other kind of leader, rejects their choice as phoney. If the young manager concentrates on "acts of leadership" and "managerial work" instead of "coming on strong," the necessary leadership style for him will become evident.

2. *Young managers may attempt to be consistent.* Flexibility is as necessary in dealing with different individuals as it is in dealing with different groups and situations. In many work units the manager will encounter three types of individuals: those who will work for no one, those who will work for anyone, and those who will work for someone. Three different managers are needed, with approaches to these groups which are totally inconsistent. The first group has to be disciplined into working by threat of some greater unpleasantness than work, being unemployed, for example. The second group has to be kept satisfied so that they remain grateful and loyal. The third group, in which the best workers are often found, has to be bargained with until an understanding is reached, explicitly or implicitly covering the degree of supervision the manager will exercise, the format of work orders, etc.

3. *Young managers may identify with the worker group.* This problem can take several forms, each dangerous: socialization, doing instead of managing, or emotionalism. Leaders who remain somewhat apart from their followers, who work at their managing, and who avoid emotional involvement succeed in both their superiors' and their subordinates' estimation.

Socialization usually leads to better morale among the workers and to lower productivity. Hands-on management results in heads-off management and the organization loses. Emotionalism, for example an effort to create one big happy family, is almost always misunderstood. Workers think that it is patronizing and reduces them to children.

4. *Young managers don't let go.* They over-supervise, over-direct, over-control. Attempting to be everywhere, they never succeed in being anywhere at the right time. Attempting to anticipate every problem, they paralyze activity. Attempting to make every decision means they make decisions after circumstances have offered their own resolution. Ultimately, the employees with half a brain quit, and the managers end up really having to think for everyone, which soon becomes impossible.

5. *Young managers can take this superior-subordinate stuff too seriously.* Leaving some groups—the family, the church, the army unit—is a momentous decision for an individual, with tremendous implications for his future life. Leaving a hospitality work group generally means that the worker gets to spend the afternoon in the park or on the beach before finding another job.

It takes incredible power of personality for a manager to create a work situation in which the worker cannot find it within himself to quit on the spot. Some young managers feel they have the ability to evoke knee rattling fear, fierce loyalty, or overwhelming gratitude in employees, and then they presume on it by pushing a man further than his sense of himself lets him go. He quits. On the spot.

A manager has to recognize the situational limitations of his leadership. If he fires people after threatening to fire them (the real pros never threaten to fire expressly) then they are not there to do the work. If he leans too hard on people, they fall over. In other words, unlike the father of the family, the clergyman of the church, or the officers of the army unit, he is a leader only if he has followers.

MOTIVATING

A successful (and hip) manager once described motivation as "different strokes for different folks" thereby at once integrating all the motivational theories of the last fifty years and rendering them all merely commentary to his remark.

Theory and Practice

Theories about motivating workers, prompting them to do the job, do it better, do it faster or do it more willingly, have ranged from those which maintained that financial reward was sufficient incentive to theories which attempt to integrate the psychological needs of the individual within the organizational objectives.

At present, the theories most in vogue, those originated by behavioral scientists, suggest that the greatest motivators are directed to satisfying worker needs beyond money compensation for his work. The arguments of the principal members of this school, Abraham Maslow, Frederick Herzberg, Douglas McGregor, Chris Argyris and Rennis Likert, are fascinating, stimulating, well-worth studying, widely quoted as management gospel, and virtually impossible for the operational manager in the hospitality industry to translate into a practical program even if he accepts their premises without reservation.

Dr. Maslow, for example, establishes a hierarchy of needs starting with physiological needs and continuing through safety and security needs, love needs, esteem needs and self-fulfillment needs. The assumption is that any need set which is satisfied ceases to be a motivator *and* that most workers are beyond the physiological security need stages. Unfortunately, many individuals in the operational manager's units in the hospitality industry work to supply their most elemental needs: immediate food, lodging, clothing, etc. In dealing with them, "higher motivators" according to the Maslow theory are of little use.

The work of other behaviorists poses other problems for the operational manager: it is largely beyond his capabilities to supply the motivators suggested. Professor Herzberg suggests that "job enrichment" is a key motivational device; Argyris wants a "fusion" of the organizational demands and the individuals needs; McGregor's system requires a reorganization of the corporate structure based on a particular theory of human work behavior. Even if the operational manager wholly accepts these theories, he can hardly supply job enrichment, a fusion of organizational demands and individuals needs, or a corporate reorganization because of his own limited authority. In sum, the thrust of these arguments has to be directed to executive management.

The best an operational management can do is recognize the essential contribution of these theories: that people are motivated by more than financial rewards and that an individual's performance may be improved by offering some other incentive.

Motivators the Operational Manager Can and Cannot Use

Motivation is the most arcane of the management arts. The operational manager is making judgments about the motives of behavior in full recognition that those motives are changing within the individual constantly, that the motive for identical behavior differs substantially among individuals, that he is dealing with used people who respond or do not respond because of past experience, and finally that he himself is limited in what he can do and in his ability to recognize what has to be done.

ACCEPTABLE MOTIVATORS

1. *Recognition.* Some communication by sign or word that the manager considers the worker a "person," and not simply a non-machine.
2. *Praise.* Commendation for work decently done, for ingenuity, persistence, effort.
3. *Improvement of Conditions.* Some operations have facilities which do not meet minimum comfort standards, and certainly not those of the Occupational Safety and Health Act: boards to keep the

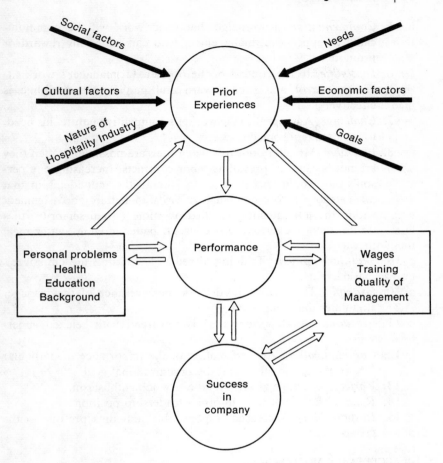

Figure 3.1 Determinants of individual work performance.

workers' feet out of inch-deep water, adequate ventilation in confined working spaces, protection against temperature extremes, etc. Beyond these necessities the manager can also attempt to improve the worker's quality of life, at least to the extent he is capable: better lodging in jobs where room and board is supplied, serviceable shoes in the proper size which can often be obtained from the housekeeping department, clothing appropriate to the weather, perhaps redeemed from the operation's lost and found department.

4. *Participation.* Some involvement of the worker in the work plan of the unit; at least, information and receptivity to suggestions and comments.

5. *Commendation.* Knowledge that good work will be communicated to upper-level management who can materially reward or promote.
6. *Discipline.* In the context of the operational manager's work situation, carrot and stick reward and punishment discipline is effective.
7. *Challenge.* An appeal to the worker's competitive nature, his need to excel, to best someone else.
8. *Incentive.* Monetary rewards when they are possible. (Often they are not because of prevailing labor contracts. Increasing one person's pay would "break the rate" for all the individuals in that job category.) Non-monetary rewards: a better job assignment within the job category, justified overtime (when seniority rules do not dictate overtime procedures), better lodging, better meal privileges.
9. *Skill-development.* Training aimed at increasing the employee's market value.
10. *Example.* The energy, hard work, perseverance of the manager stimulates the group.
11. *Freedom.* Good performance is rewarded with relaxed supervision.
12. *Communication.* An explanation of the importance of particular jobs to the group effort and the organizational goal.
13. *Variety.* A change of activity to renew job enthusiasm.
14. *Rank.* Establishment of informal leadership position.
15. *Responsibility.* Increased responsibility and thus prestige in the group.

UNACCEPTABLE MOTIVATORS

Certain motivators which may occur to the operational manager are unwise, unsuccessful, or illegal.

1. *Promises that cannot be kept.* In motivating, the operational manager has to know his own authority: Can he really promote, provide bonuses, etc.? A certain tactical advantage may be gained by false promises, but the end result is disastrous: a total loss of credibility.

2. *Two-fisted management.* Physical force, or the threat of physical force, cannot be used as a motivator.

3. *Goods and services.* In general, operational management must have expressed permission to offer workers food, drink, lodging, use of facilities, tickets, or other goods or services the operation sells. When an operational manager gives a worker an alcoholic drink because of some effort on his part, the manager has usurped executive policy-making functions.

4. *Compensatory time off*. A worker can be given time off with pay if the general personnel policies of the organization permit this practice. He cannot be given time off instead of pay.

5. *Insult*. Young managers frequently use abusive language to prod workers. Almost immediately the problem becomes a lack of vocabulary. After the second parcel of epithets has been delivered the manager has lost his ability to motivate; he amuses the worker.

6. *Privilege*. A worker permitted to leave early or come in late because of some special effort or as an inducement to special effort, tends to see this as a continuing right that cannot subsequently be withheld.

7. *Higher motivators*. Often, the best an operational manager can do is make a case to a superior manager for the worker's gaining: merit increases, participation in wage incentive programs, promotion, or formal training.

8. *"Personal" motivators*. It generally costs a young manager about a hundred dollars before he realizes that his little gifts to employees, his small loans, his occasional purchase of cigarettes does not do him much good. Unfortunately, he is usually being generous to those employees capable of "working" him rather than to those employees who are capable of working. However expert a manager may be, many of his subordinates greatly exceed him in "street knowledge," a sort of rudimentary practical psychology which lets them divine a soft touch.

KEEPING PEACE

Managerial breast beating has become fashionable in the hospitality industry now that it is concerned with building genuine career opportunities as motivators for workers. Some managements accept the blame for past personnel failures such as low productivity, high turnover, absenteeism, percentages of employees quitting during the work periods, and so on.

Certainly the organizational structures created by management, and management's personnel policies have been substantially to blame, but two other factors have to be considered. 1) The employee willing to work in those structures, and with those policies expects to quit and be absent: he is not committed to this work as a way of life. 2) Problems within the group of workers account for at least some of these problems.

While executive management can take the position that the fundamental problem is still addressable by management—better structures and policies will attract better workers and create better workers and thereby reduce the intra-group conflict—the operational manager, at least for the foreseeable future has to address the symptoms.

"Shorty," a houseman, is being physically abused by the rest of the crew. Ideally, the manager would be able to address the problems of the rest of the crew, somehow relieve their frustrations, and productively channel their aggressiveness so that they did not "have to" abuse Shorty. However, being neither the owner of the hotel, a trained psychiatric worker, or a lay missionary, the manager "solves" the problem by transferring Shorty to the health club where he works alone. Of course, he did not solve anything, he kept the peace.

Peace keeping may occupy a significant part of a manager's day when he is in charge of certain operational units. It also figures considerably in his planning, scheduling, organizing, and work assigning. He tries to anticipate trouble, avoid it, and finally to contain it when it does occur.

Anticipating Trouble

Managers who stay at their desks and shuffle their papers cannot anticipate trouble. They don't see the horseplay or wisecracking that usually precedes more cruel aggressive behavior. They don't see the cliques form on racial, ethnic, or religious lines. They don't see the group isolate an individual at lunch time.

More important, they cannot cultivate a relationship with any of the employees and therefore lack an informal conduit for information from the group and to the group.

Managers who manage on the job, in the dishroom, on the loading platform, in the stock rooms, in the boiler room, learn to recognize the telltale signs of an impending malfunction in the group. Just as the chief engineer can hear subtle changes in the rhythms of his motors, the manager can detect changes in the rhythm of group activity.

The chief engineer does some preventative maintenance, and the manager applies some positive motivators, makes personnel changes, re-schedules or reassigns work, and in sum, does preventative maintenance on the group structure.

Avoiding Trouble

Dissatisfaction, conflict, gripes, complaints are an inevitable product of men working together. The manager avoids the problems this may produce—lost productivity, turnover, absenteeism—by providing legitimate outlets and working at reducing their causes.

Accessible management is the key. A manager who listens attentively and considerately can blunt the impact of the problem (which he may not be able to solve) by letting the man blow off. The worker does not have to take the problem back to the job and destroy five or six cases of lettuce to get even, or break a machine to feel good, or abuse some fellow worker to exercise his machismo.

Management also has to accept workers as they are. Most crews function best with a moderate amount of tension, or pressure to achieve. Part of their motivation is the relief of the tension or the pleasure of relaxing after the challenge is met. If the manager sets the pace too fast, or makes the goal utterly unattainable, the unit begins to self destruct. At that point he has to release the tension ("Okay, everybody take five, let's have some coffee.") and allow the members to regain their composure. Otherwise, someone gets hurt or a machine gets broken, which is the easiest way for the worker to release the pressure: Cases of canned goods being passed in a line of men start getting hurled from one man to the other, a fork jams the conveyor chain on the dish machine, a floor waxer mysteriously rips up its own wire.

The manager sometimes has to make compromises with attitudes he personally finds distasteful. He encounters individuals who will not work together or in a superior subordinate role because of racial, ethnic, or social bigotry. He cannot successfully reform them, rather, he avoids the problem by not precipitating the confrontation.

Handling Trouble

The manager's principle concern is the continued productivity of the unit. When trouble occurs: arguments, fist fights, generalized yelling and screaming, work is stopped while workers stream into his office. His first concern is to try to get everyone back to work. His second concern is to somehow resolve the dispute so that it does not reoccur. His third concern is addressing the fundamental problem as well as he can.

The necessary steps are rather simple. The noncombatants, who are thoroughly enjoying this break from the work routine, and the combatants are separated physically: "You guys get on with stocking the freezer while Joe, Bob, and I find out what this is about." The second step is to separate the combatants: "Okay, okay, that's enough, why don't you get a cup of coffee, Joe. I'll talk to you in a moment." Deprived of their audience and therefore no longer in danger of losing face or able to make points, the combatants generally calm down.

Joe gets his cup of coffee, Bob sounds off to the manager. Then Bob gets his coffee, and Joe sounds off. Sometimes the manager is actually able to listen to both sides and make some sort of acceptable, equitable decision. Most of the time, he succeeds best by separating the disputants for the remainder of the shift or permanently, hoping perhaps, that they will settle the problem themselves on their own time.

Sometimes this solution is grossly unfair to a particular individual. For example, a chef and a waiter are arguing bitterly. Sending the waiter to work in the linen room, or sending him home, or transferring him to another unit may be unfair, especially if he was "right" in the dispute. Faced with the prospect of losing the waiter or losing the chef, the manager has only one immediate choice. There are ten waiters, there is one chef. The need to keep the unit functioning makes it necessary to take the expedient course in the hope that the other waiters will not become aggrieved because of its unfairness. Sometime later the "problem" of the chef—his attitude, his generally counter-productive behavior—has to be addressed.

SUPERVISING

Supervising can be a manager's most difficult activity. He is functioning under tremendous pressure: downward pressure to produce from the higher levels of management, upward pressure from his subordinates to allow them to go their own way. In a sense, his supervisory activity is the interface between the organizational demands and the workers' individualities.

The operational manager is indeed the middle-manager, obliged to meet the demands of higher level managers and sympathetic to the workers' problems in meeting those demands.

Effective supervision is a delicate balancing act by which the manager tries to reconcile what must be done, what the workers can do, and what the workers are willing to do.

In common with much of the manager's work, how exactly he will supervise will depend entirely on the situation. Some situations demand a prison warden's intensity, others a cheer leader's enthusiasm. In most situations, however, the manager makes his supervisory contribution by establishing some standard of quality or production, very often by demonstrating it, by articulating what is expected of individual employees in a given time period, by staying on the job to insure performance, and by correcting employees whose behavior or quality of performance jeopardizes the group effort. He demonstrates, directs, surveys, and disciplines to the extent and intensity that the situation demands. Problems occur because he is very often making on-the-spot judgments in areas where there are no really satisfactory answers.

Demonstrating the Job

Sometimes employees have to be shown how to do a job. They have to be instructed, trained or taught. While these are certainly managerial activities, more often, the manager finds it necessary to establish the standard for the job for people who fundamentally know how to do it. The crew is to clean and polish a ballroom floor. How clean should it be? How long should the cleaning take? How bright should it be when the job is done? The supervisor is the conduit of the operation's standards to the employee. As it is often extremely difficult to articulate these standards, he becomes the standard by remaining on the job, or by demonstrating the production of an acceptable sample.

Every operational manager spends a good deal of time demonstrating: this is how brown *our* french fries should be, this is how *we* fold a napkin here, this is how *we* make a brandy alexander. If the employee is well motivated and skilled in his particular craft—fry cook, waiter, bartender—the demonstration itself becomes sufficient job directive.

Directing Employees

For some employees and some jobs no specific direction is necessary: what has to be done is obvious, and they are sufficiently motivated to do it. A switchboard operator for example should not have to be specifically told what to do. A trained operator, familiar with the operation, will not have to be told expressly to answer incoming calls and to place outgoing calls.

In other operational situations, especially those in which tasks vary from day to day, or where there is a variety of activities to which a particular employee might be assigned, there is a need to specifically direct the employee. A great many hospitality operations have crews operating on this basis: restaurants, receiving and stewarding areas, clerical, engineering, landscaping, recreation and sports departments.

How exactly the manager will tell the worker what he must do, will depend on the general climate of the situation, the result of their experience with one another. The manager may simply have to outline the unit's activity for the day and, in a generally cooperative atmosphere, the workers will fall into place and do a fair part of the job.

He may have to introduce a little more formality into the process by specifically suggesting that a worker do something: "I think it would be a good idea if Joe got started on that liquor room inventory."

He may have to be somewhat more formal: "Joe, would you get started on the liquor room inventory."

In each of these instances he can be very precise, with a consistent tone: "after lunch we'll see about those invoices" or "that should take you until about lunch, then you can see what you can do about those invoices" or "get done by lunch time because I want you to work on the invoices this afternoon."

To this little scheme indicating the intensity of directing, extremes can be added: participative directing, and short directing. The manager practicing participative directing tries to involve the worker in the decision about what has to be done. With very professional, generally well-motivated employees this approach is successful.

Short-directing is the opposite extreme. Instead of telling the employee the whole order, the manager divides it into explicit commands covering a very small time period, "Joe, count the bottles on this shelf, and then get back to me."

Surveying

The manager has to decide how closely he will watch his subordinates actually working. Obviously, the intensity of his supervision can vary from watching them as much as he possibly can, to simply checking back with them at the end of some period.

In a single crew doing a single job, there may be individuals who prosper under both of these extremes: people who cannot work under scrutiny, and people who must be watched constantly. Sometimes there is no answer. Other times the manager can resolve his dilemma by putting the self-motivating worker in charge of the potential slacker, or by giving those workers who need no supervision jobs where they can work alone.

Many young managers tend not to supervise enough. They assume the job will get done because everyone understands what has to be done, and has the necessary skills. Also, they try to avoid the nasty confrontations that direct supervision occasions. It is tedious, unpleasant, frustrating, to hammer away at an individual or a crew; sometimes it is the manager's job.

Disciplining

A distinction is sometimes made between "positive discipline" which helps the worker "reform from within," and "negative discipline" which is aimed at punishing the worker in the hope that he will not invite the punishment again, and at deterring other workers who see him punished. In practice, positive and negative discipline tend to describe stages in a program of discipline applied to a particular worker. When a worker departs from company policies by arriving late, or does not meet company standards of production or quality, the manager usually counsels him. There may be mitigating circumstances: his ignorance of the rule, his failure to understand the procedure, and in a sense this indicates a management fault in communication or training.

The second instance, a reoccurrence of the same problem, or a second problem with the same worker usually occasions a more formal approach. The worker is admonished. He is told essentially that manage-

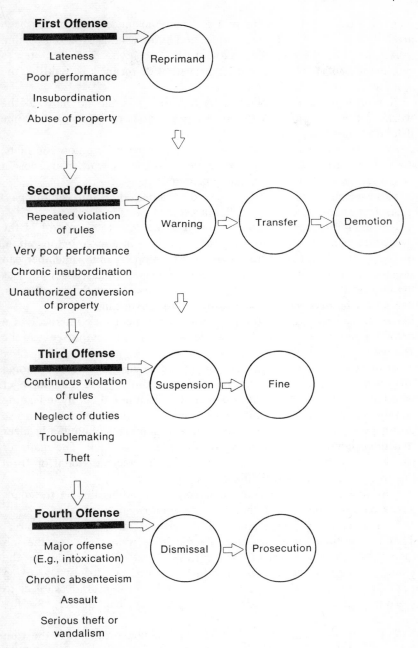

First Offense

Lateness

Poor performance

Insubordination

Abuse of property

Reprimand

Second Offense

Repeated violation
of rules

Very poor performance

Chronic insubordination

Unauthorized conversion
of property

Warning → Transfer → Demotion

Third Offense

Continuous violation
of rules

Neglect of duties

Troublemaking

Theft

Suspension → Fine

Fourth Offense

Major offense
(E.g., intoxication)

Chronic absenteeism

Assault

Serious theft or
vandalism

Dismissal → Prosecution

Figure 3.2. Levels of disciplinary action.

ment no longer recognizes any mitigating circumstances; that he has been around long enough to know the rules and know what is expected of him.

At this point the discipline ceases to be "positive." The next step, a reprimand which may be written or verbal is meant to "punish" the worker by striking at his pride.

A reprimand can be followed by a warning, a second blow to the worker's pride and a frank threat of more serious punishments to come if he does not "shape up."

After the warning, or in some situations governed by union contracts, a series of warnings, a disciplinary action is taken. A worker may lose a privileged position, he may actually be demoted.

More seriously, he may be suspended for a period of time without pay.

And, ultimately he may be discharged.

It is likely that the operational manager will lose total control of the procedure as it becomes more serious, especially in a large organization, or in an establishment with an employee's union. A union member can seldom be summarily dismissed except for very serious causes such as fighting on the job, intoxication, or theft. And even in these instances, proof may be necessary for the dismissal to be sustained.

In a large organization, the personnel department may intercede at a certain point in the procedure to determine if the employee can be salvaged.

In most organizations, the disciplining procedure on the operational level is much more subtle than this outline would suggest. The manager who has the respect of his subordinates can discipline them by indicating simply that they have fallen in his esteem. The skillful manager can use group pressure to discipline, essentially by making it abundantly clear that the other workers are taking up the offender's slack. The manager can withdraw positive motivators from the specific individual or from the group in an effort to stimulate group pressure.

Initiating a formal procedure is generally an admission on the manager's part that he cannot "handle" the employee.

Young managers make some rather critical mistakes in this area. They fire or threaten to fire more people in their first year on the job than they will in the rest of their careers. Most of the employees the young manager in the hospitality industry encounters do not fear being fired. In a mobile, affluent society, in an industry constantly subject to seasonal demands, jobs are always available. They can answer, "So, fire me," and they can go.

Young managers also tend to ignore disciplinary problems in the vain hope that they will go away. A man who misses a day's work without notice and without communication during that day is going to continue to miss work again unless he is disciplined. It is very difficult for the young manager to make an older worker, perhaps someone who has been with the organization longer, personally accountable, but it is necessary for the functioning of the unit.

Young managers also tend to take the "blame" for disciplinary problems. Influenced by the human relations managerial approach they look for the underlying causes of the problem and tend to disregard the problem which is manifest. An individual's background makes it hard for him to accept the regimentation of a regular job, but unless the manager's budget somehow includes a fund for social action, the worker must be made to conform, or be dismissed.

Young managers tend to lose perspective when confronted with disciplinary problems. They become emotional: either aggrieved or inordinately angry. They are disappointed or disillusioned. In essence, they bring the ethic of other groups, the family, the team, the army unit, to the work group when in fact it cannot be transplanted. A worker storms into the manager and tells him that he can take the job and shove it down his throat unless the manager does such and such. The manager may indeed horsetrade. He may simply let the man blow off, which is what he wanted to do. Or, the manager may calmly recognize that he has a big throat with nineteen jobs already in it, and he seems to be breathing normally.

TRAINING

A great deal of the manager's success at motivating people and at building morale in an operation depends on the opportunity the operation offers the employee for promotion and advancement. The employees work better and are happier if they are improving their skills, learning new ones, and advancing in the organization. In addition to the obvious benefits of well-motivated and contented employees, training programs provide the operation with the precise skills it needs. Training on a day-to-day basis most often involves teaching skills that are immediately usable, or at least usable in the immediate future. The busboy who learns how to serve from a platter may be able to help on a station that weekend. The dishwasher who learns how to open clams may be able to substitute for the pantry man at the next banquet planned. Even semi-skilled work, which is learned on the job, should be programmed. The service routine of the busboy, for example, should be analyzed and presented clearly to the new employee: setting the table, removing soiled dishes, cleaning linen, filling water glasses, serving butter, offering breads, keeping service stands cleared, and other tasks should be discussed and demonstrated, and, if possible, presented in written form. Allowing the employee to simply learn by his mistakes greatly extends the period of learning to work efficiently.

Training in a hospitality operation should always be responsive to the needs of the operation. No responsible operational manager initiates a training program unless the graduates of the program will be useful to the operation.

For example, a manager might find that there is a consistent problem in electrical maintenance, even with a competent electrician working as supervisor in the operation. Examination of the operation's electrical system records indicates that there have been excessive emergency repairs, motor burnouts, daily complaints of shorts and shocks, etc.

A survey of the personnel files indicates that part of the problem is a lack of knowledge of electrical circuitry by most of the mechanics. The electrician supervisor cannot be expected to fulfill the maintenance requirements of the operation alone, or with mechanics of the level of competence now employed.

There are three major alternatives: (1) hire an outside electrical contracting firm to do routine maintenance; (2) hire competent electricians; or (3) train the mechanics already employed by the operation and already charged with electrical maintenance.

An outside firm will probably have to be hired to solve the immediate problem. Hiring competent electricians provides a satisfactory alternative if the mechanics already on the job can be dismissed readily. Training mechanics who cannot be dismissed (because of labor contracts) offers a long-term economical solution.

Several of the maintenance mechanics are selected for training, and a program is established. The chief electrician, who is competent although overworked, is the logical choice to teach.

Management should prepare the teachers with an instructional session. The expertise of the supervisors should be assumed and the session begun with a discussion of the necessity for training the workers effectively. It might be demonstrated that the old way of learning—by trial and error —is not producing satisfactory results. The trial takes too much time and the errors are too expensive.

Management can profit by some feedback from the individuals who are involved in the actual operations. Part of the problem for the electrician supervisor might be an inadequate inventory of electrical supplies and parts.

Perhaps a recurring problem in the housekeeping department has been frequent guest complaints about the quality of guest-room cleaning. The supervisory employees in this department are well aware of the importance of guest satisfaction in generating repeat business. Training for better cleaning of bathrooms does not have to be elaborately justified beyond the simple economic truth.

Establishment of the Training Program

Some problems will require a long-term training commitment on the part of management, the supervisors and teachers, and the employees. The electrical training program will require the rescheduling of the employees involved so that they can work under the direct supervision of the chief electrician.

It may be necessary to spend several weeks orienting the men so that they will understand the elaborate system of safety devices, fuses, and circuit breakers that protect the electrical system. They must be able to identify the various parts of the circuitry. Then they can proceed to the actual instruction sessions: thermal overload protection devices, electrical contactor maintenance, the use of resistance and insulation testers, and troubleshooting and electric circuit.

The more limited problem of dirty guest bathrooms can be dealt with quickly. The employees may simply be coached in the proper cleaning techniques by the supervisor, and then asked to demonstrate their proficiency. Sometime later a reinforcement session might be scheduled to discuss the progress made and the possibilities of improvement.

In either case, the employees have been made aware of a goal for the training: a desired performance level.

There should be some method of evaluation. The electrical maintenance program may include a written examination that includes everything the trainee should know at the end of the program. The program should be structured to prepare the trainee for evaluation. The bathroom cleaning sessions can be evaluated by inspection, using a standard check list.

TRAINING TECHNIQUES

Depending on the difficulty of the subject and the needs of the operation, any of numerous techniques for training may be chosen. In actual practice, operational departments of hospitality establishments use every technique from the simplistic, but effective, Job Instruction Training procedure developed in World War II to programmed instructional materials that require elaborate audiovisual devices.

The Job Instruction Training procedure includes the following:

Step 1. Prepare the worker to receive the instructions; put him at ease; explain the job and find out what he already knows about it; get him interested in learning the job; place him in the correct position.

Step 2. Present the operation; tell him, show him, illustrate one important step at a time; stress each key point; instruct clearly, completely, and patiently, but no more than he can master.

Step 3. Try out his performance; have him do the job and correct his errors; have him explain each key point to you as he does the job again; make sure he understands; continue until you know he knows.

Step 4. Follow up. Put him on his own; designate to whom he goes for help; check frequently and encourage questions; taper off coaching and close follow-up.

PROGRAMMED INSTRUCTION

Programmed instruction books are available for a number of areas. The books offer a carefully constructed discussion that breaks the subject down into small bits of information. The instruction book uses a question-and-answer and immediate-correction approach. Several manufacturers of cleaning products offer this type of training device for equipment cleaning and maintenance. The federal government and a number of large manufacturing concerns offer similar materials for structural, electrical, and mechanical maintenance training programs.

Both workers and supervisors should be encouraged to take advantage of any available formal training. For example, the increasing public awareness of ecology and related problems has caused a mushrooming of courses on sanitation. Community colleges offer basic sanitation courses. There are management seminars sponsored by state and national restaurant associations. Sometimes local health departments sponsor clinics and courses.

IN-SERVICE TRAINING

In addition to training programs directed to specific needs, an on-going training program that involves most workers has certain dividends. Career goals can be inspired in some employees. The operation does not need to rely on "indispensable" craftsmen because other workers learn the job.

There are at least five definite phases in an in-service training program with general objectives:

1. Orientation and training of new employees for specific jobs.
2. On-the-job training and person-to-person discussion with the supervisor on a continuing basis in order to guide the employee to a more satisfactory job performance.
3. Weekly formal training sessions with the immediate supervisor. Each group should include five to eight individuals. All employees should attend at least once a month.

4. A general monthly staff meeting to show training films; to introduce and demonstrate new methods, procedures, supplies, and equipment; and to review progress and performance.
5. A supervisory development program to offer instruction in training and dealing with employees, to provide training in supervisory skills, to promote professional organizations, and to discuss professional periodical literature.

Table 3.2. ADVANTAGES AND DISADVANTAGES OF TRAINING METHODS

Method	Advantages	Disadvantages
Coaching by other workers	Learning situation is realistic. Actual performance is possible.	May be resented by both trainer and trainee. Tends to perpetuate bad practices as well as good.
Job rotation	Increases understanding of total operation and interrelationship of jobs. Adds variety to worker's job.	Can disrupt work routine. Difficult to administer fairly.
Planned reading	Economical. Allows worker to proceed at his own pace. Readings can be chosen with particular person in mind.	Difficult for worker to apply general concepts or procedures to actual job. Learning skills may be poorly developed and worker may become frustrated.
Self-teaching courses	Specialized courses can be provided. Worker proceeds at own pace.	Self-discipline may be absent in worker.
Lecture	Economical. Familiar. Suitable to large groups.	Little opportunity for communication. Evaluation of learning experience difficult.
Meeting	Information is pooled. Good communication possible.	Time consuming. Practical only with small groups. Tends to wander from subject.

COOPERATING

In the hospitality industry, sustained revenue-producing activity is usually the result of a group effort. The productivity of the group depends as much on its functioning harmoniously as on the particular talents of the individuals in it. It is almost impossible for the highly skilled but abrasive individual to make a long term contribution, in dollars and cents, to the organization. He may make sales but virtually eliminate the possibility of repeat business by so alienating the people involved in servicing his sales that they displease the customer. An absolutely brilliant cost analyst may be unable to implement his cost reduction procedures because of the resistance he creates on the operational level. A fine chef may not be able to produce acceptable meals because he cannot do everything himself, and yet his attitude stimulates only the most meager effort from his assistants.

Individuals' careers, like corporate revenues, can be limited by the basic failure of the individual to successfully work with the other members of the group.

The individual who works well but prevents other people from fully functioning has considerably diminished his worth to the organization. The manager who personally causes an increase in labor cost by stimulating only mediocre productivity, or by increasing turnover, tardiness, absenteeism, or grievance actions has failed in an essential part of his job. The individual who cannot work with his superiors, obviously will not enjoy their favor.

The study and application of standard motivational procedures is only a partial solution for the individual whose group relations are stressed. He cannot "motivate" his peers nor "morale build" among his superiors. Likewise, even when these techniques are properly applied to relations with subordinates, they do not necessarily work for him.

The individual, as an individual, must establish a successful human relationship with the other members of the group. Numerous bases can be postulated for this relationship; there are men who are fathers to their subordinates, sons to the superiors, and brothers to their fellows. Others become non-belligerent eccentrics who manage to divert their colleagues' attention from their personality problems with the red herring of their idiosyncracies. But these are special cases, rare instances of successful accommodation in unusual circumstances.

Most people who succeed, succeed much more simply: they recognize that certain behavior is expedient. Whatever their inner feelings and problems, they find that a façade of conventionality, etiquette, manners, courtesy, and politeness saves them the bother of having to relate specifically to each individual with whom they work. Because their actions and speech are conventional and ordinary, they are understood as what they are. There is no need for subjective interpretation. When the individual who says "Good morning" to everyone says "Good morning" to anyone, no one has cause to wonder what he meant by that.

Most extremely successful executives have learned this lesson: they are unfailingly mannerly. While their own personalities may range from bonhomie to ducal aloofness, they are basically polite. Unlike the middle-level manager or the junior executive, they are as likely to address a dishwasher as *sir,* as the chairman of the board. They couch all their remarks as suggestions ("What do you think of a long-term forecast on the Los Angeles market" or "Let's try to keep the receiving gate closed.") and they are appropriately interpreted by the person to whom they are addressed as commands, requests, suggestions or observations.

While it may seem that relationships founded on impersonal cordiality rob the manager of a measure of fulfillment in his work, it is more efficient as well as personally and professionally profitable to have cordial relations with everyone based on conventionality, rather then to have love affairs on the one hand and feuds on the other. At the very least, some of the pandemic problems of business are avoided: backstabbing, politicking, internal sabotage, status plays, and professional (and personal) paranoia. Involvement, commitment, and devotion to work are marvelous attributes in a manager, but there is a great deal to be said for the individual who does his job efficiently, works well with his colleagues and then goes home without entangling the entire operation on the protuberances of his psyche.

Common Sense

Most people do not know that the caller, not the called, should end the conversation, nor are they bothered by others of the minutiae that offended people in more courtly times. Much more apparent to people today are personal attitudes and bad habits that cause friction among colleagues.

If every employee had a personal suggestion box, few of the comments would concern business matters. They would be filled with an accumulation of minor offenses and small suggestions that seem singularly insignificant but are collectively important to the harmony of the group.

COMMON DON'TS

1. Don't litter other people's work areas.
2. Don't backslap or otherwise touch people.
3. Don't borrow another's staff without permission.

4. Don't borrow equipment or use other people's desks or telephones without permission.
5. Don't jump into the conversations other people are having with superiors or guests.
6. Don't discuss salaries or the cost of possessions.
7. Don't gossip.
8. Don't respond vaguely when unable to make a decision.
9. Don't jump in the chain of command, i.e., go over your boss's head.
10. Don't put on or tease other employees.
11. Don't brag or show off.
12. Don't become overly familiar.
13. Don't chatter.
14. Don't over-decorate the office.
15. Don't form or participate in cliques.
16. Don't complain.
17. Don't discuss personal problems; mention personal triumphs briefly if at all.
18. Don't borrow money or ask for personal favors.
19. Don't involve other workers in personal errors.
20. Don't get angry or impatient.

COMMON DO'S

1. Be positive, receptive, and helpful.
2. Dress appropriately for the job, and stay dressed: jacket and tie unless it is appropriate to work in shirt sleeves.
3. Praise publicly, criticize privately.
4. Be scrupulously polite: greetings to everyone, thank you's, please's, etc.
5. Be specific in requests and orders.
6. Accept responsibility for the errors of subordinates and colleagues.
7. Do the work.
8. Have only one "personality" for superiors, subordinates, and peers.
9. Be careful not to offend racial, national, or sexual minorities.
10. Try to limit offensive personal habits, for example, cigar smoking.
11. Sit properly, walk alertly.
12. Talk modestly, quietly, and without swearing.
13. Give credit to subordinates and colleagues for their ideas.
14. Obey company rules, even if rank precludes their enforcement.
15. Be punctual, especially when rank obliges the visitor (or visited) to wait.

16. Control personal phone calls, visits, and privileges for family.
17. Remember names of subordinates and colleagues.
18. Respect other individual's private obligations, avoid detaining them or disrupting days off and vacations when possible.
19. Maintain business and personal confidences.
20. At least seem to approve of baseball, motherhood, the flag, and lunar exploration, and to disapprove of drug use, open marriage, hurricanes in Texas, and the boll weevil, so that energy and passion are not dissipated in fruitless argument.

Relations with Superiors

The tremendous growth of the hospitality industry and its potential for growth in the immediate future helps temper the subordinate's aggressiveness and keeps superiors from viewing their juniors as enemies who have not fully revealed themselves. It is possible for a senior manager to help train a subordinate without his fearing that he is preparing his replacement. There is another unit being built somewhere.

Manners in the hospitality industry between superior and subordinates are therefore somewhat more relaxed than those in general business. Necessary formality with the public also tends to make compensatory informality within certain bounds more permissible.

The few notable exceptions are confined to the "old school" European or European-trained hotelmen who insisted on their privileges. For example, most executives, managers, and supervisors within two or three "rungs" of each other on the "career ladder" use first names in private and last names in public and before subordinates. It would be unthinkable for a junior employee to call a continental maître d'hôtel or chef by his first name. Even superior officers hesitate and sometimes preface their first names with "mister" or use their last names alone, which is as informal as European gentlemen who have not known each other as boys ever get.

Informality should not be confused with bad manners or denying a superior his, or her, earned and merited prerogatives. At the very least, the junior employee should respect certain basic executive privileges:

1. The superior sets the tone of the relationship. He, or she, starts calling the junior by a first name and expressly invites him, or her, to reciprocate.
2. The superior initiates social contacts by first inviting the junior (and perhaps his, or her, spouse) to dinner or cocktails.
3. The junior rises when conversing with a standing superior, and stands until invited to sit when speaking with a seated one.

4. Appointments, telephone meetings, conferences are made to suit the superior's convenience.

5. The junior employee avoids using the superior's office, secretary, lunch table, car, golf clubs, etc., unless specifically invited to do so.

6. When possible the junior "honors" the superior by allowing him, or her, to pass through the door first or seat himself, or herself, at table.

7. The junior avoids imposing on the superior's time, even when their relationship is informal. The superior's time is considered more valuable (and is more valuable on a dollar basis). It is economized first.

8. The junior respects the chain of command. He, or she, does not jump executive levels, no matter how informal the entire operation is. The junior does not plot with other officers.

9. The junior employee keeps the superior informed so that he, or she, seems competent to superiors, and the junior has the advantage of comments, criticisms, and support.

10. The junior employee respects the superior's authority and area of concern. He, or she, does not whittle away at the superior's job function.

Relations with Colleagues

Any relationship with a colleague, an employee on the same job level, must have a certain duality. The colleague is first of all a co-worker, the good of the organization depends on his success. Yet it must be accepted that he is also a competitor even if he is in another department. The general manager of a hotel may have a background in accounting or in food and beverage; the president of a restaurant chain may have started as unit manager or a commissary purchasing agent.

The most successful course for the individual is the one which benefits the organization most. Overly aggressive managers seem to forget that their superiors are fully aware of the situation. They have been the route. Necessarily, they do not look kindly on actions which reduce productivity or profitability, it reflects on their performance. Nor are they anxious to welcome to their level anyone who has shown too much fang at a junior level.

The best approach to co-workers seems to be a mixture of absolute cooperation, cordiality, and general aloofness. Colleagues present the biggest problem when they are no longer colleagues but distant subordinates who presume on personal relationships that began in the storeroom or in the little bar on Tenth Street. As well, there is always the possibility that a "friend" is an enemy who has not been discovered. *He* may not be playing by the same rules. For example, co-workers competing for an immediate or distant promotion have stolen ideas from each other, fed each other wrong information and exploited personal problems of a colleague for business leverage or blackmail. Regrettably, but inevitably, friendship founders when one or the other friend prospers. A cordial, proper, business relationship seldom can endure 40 years and stretch from the board room to the boiler room.

Relations with Subordinates

It is almost universally accepted, at least intellectually, that all employees should be treated like "people" no matter what their pay rate or their job. It is possible to radically misinterpret the wide acceptance of this approach. It does not mean that all employees are the same, i.e., that all people are the same, or that managers and supervisors must be buddies with their subordinates or share their decision making. To the hospitality manager who applies it successfully, it means that the employee's sense of himself as an individual of worth, dignity, and personality must not be placed in irreconcilable conflict with the demands of his job.

The manager's role in dealing with his subordinates, in talking with them, in defining their jobs, and in evaluating their performance is always to allow them to remain something more than "nothing." A man can believe himself poorly paid, overworked, generally abused and maligned (he may be making four-thousand or 40-thousand dollars) and still keep on working well. When he comes to the realization that he has ceased to "be" and become "nothing," he quits, or loses vast chunks of productivity.

4 | Management Concerns

The actions of the operational manager in his day-to-day management of a hospitality unit can have considerable implications for the organization in four significant areas: employee relations, legal affairs, public relations, and labor relations.

Although the operational manager does not make policy in those areas or have ultimate responsibility for them, what he does on the operational level can result in either cost economies or extraordinary costs.

He contributes to good employee relations by creating and maintaining a "high level" of morale which tends to result in increased productivity and lower general labor costs.

He avoids entangling the organization in legal actions which may result in costly judgments against the company.

His role in public relations includes protecting the company's reputation—which is its principal commodity—and making whatever positive contributions he can toward promoting it as a service oriented establishment.

In the area of labor relations, he guards the company's interests and avoids compromising its bargaining positions.

EMPLOYEE MORALE

Many hospitality units have poor morale: as a group, workers are generally unhappy about their jobs, their job conditions, and their organizations. The symptoms of wide spread low morale are apparent: high rates of turnover and absenteeism, little respect for supervisors, low general output, lack of cooperation among workers, numerous disciplinary difficulties, general tardiness, derogatory comments about management (often to management), indifference to health and safety rules, and conflict among workers. These problems cost operations significant sums. Turnover, for example, at the least generates recruitment and training costs.

In attempting to improve morale, the operational manager encounters a number of problems. He cannot address many of the fundamental factors which generate poor morale. Most studies of group morale indicate that job security, opportunity for advancement, job interest, working conditions, promotional opportunities, and wage benefits, are among the most important morale factors. In most instances the operational manager has little or no control over these. An entire restructuring of the organization in which he works, based on technological advances that are now being introduced could genuinely achieve progress in these areas. However, he cannot make the decision on organizational structure or on major capital investment in labor-dignifying machines and systems.

The operational manager, in making an effort to improve morale as well as he can, may face further difficulties. The success of his efforts depends largely on the group of people with which he starts. Personality factors, conditioning of the persons before employment by his company, and outside conditions may limit his success.

Many hospitality jobs have been designed to be simply routine. Ultimately they become boring. Others involve heavy physical labor. The individual who is not emotionally or physically suited to this type of employment is hardly going to approach it with a cheer leader's enthusiasm and good spirits no matter what the operational manager attempts.

At the moment, the labor pool from which the hospitality industry draws many of its workers includes individuals who have been badly battered by life's vicissitudes. The somewhat feeble morale builders in the operational manager's repertory often prove inadequate to revitalize them. As regrettable as this is, the operational manager in his very defined role, has little choice but to accept it.

Outside conditions also exert a powerful influence on the individual's on-the-job morale. While the argument might be advanced that many of these situations have been created or aggravated by conditions experienced by the individuals over a lifetime of unfulfilling labor, the operational manager currently employing the individual must simply recognize the symptoms as the sum of his problems (addressing the root causes are beyond him). Operational managers will encounter individuals with numerous social problems: sickness, alcoholism, drug addiction, emotional problems. There is little he can do to uplift spirits on the job sufficiently to overcome difficulties of this magnitude.

There is still a further obstacle to the operational manager's morale building efforts. Higher level management may maintain that there are other more important priorities for the manager, namely cost reduction, control, direct supervision, and managerial functions, such as planning and budgeting. High morale may be seen as only one possible motivator among others—with others such as direct monetary incentive to individuals considered more powerful. Or, it may be suggested that a "happy" crew is not necessarily more productive. The public squabblings and grieving of successful sports teams is often chosen as an example.

Within the limits of his capabilities the operational manager in a hospitality unit should make some effort to improve morale. At the very least it will make his own job more pleasant. He has an obligation to avoid worsening it.

Morale Builders the Operational Manager Can Use

The operational manager has to choose those morale builders which will work in his particular unit at a particular time. The morale of a group of college students working on their summer vacation might be raised if the manager should form a softball team for after-hours recreation. It is unlikely that this device would work with a crew of seasonal housemen or night auditors. Likewise by limiting his supervision of a group of bakers he might raise their morale considerably, but for him to employ the same technique with a group of warewashers would be disastrous whatever the effect on their morale.

The list that follows, therefore, should not be considered the outline of a morale building campaign.

1. Positive management attitudes
2. Limiting supervision
3. Selection of employees for inclusion in group
4. Good orientation procedures
5. Institution of an effective grievance mechanism
6. Employee participation in managerial decision making
7. Institution of firm ground rules
8. Keeping employees busy
9. Raising work interest
10. Employee counseling
11. Recognition of employee efforts
12. Communication
13. Creating job titles
14. Changing work assignments
15. Treatment of employees as individuals
16. Development of social aspects of the job
17. Rest periods
18. Protection of employee sensitivities

19. Monetary incentives
20. Good management

1. *Positive management attitudes.* Poor morale on the part of the manager rubs off on the group. While it is unlikely that a bubbling, enthusiastic manager can uplift the group on that basis alone, a grouchy, sarcastic, impatient manager is a definite depressant. It is to be hoped the operational manager's superiors will be concerned with his morale. If they are unsuccessful in raising it, he still has the obligation to seem enthusiastic, at least until the day he quits.

2. *Limiting supervision.* Grown men are a great deal more happy when they are not watched. Fundamentally, the manager has to weigh the productivity gained by their improved spirits with the productivity lost because of diminished surveillance.

3. *Selection of employees.* In many operational situations the manager does not hire his own crews. The personnel department sends him workers according to a projection of his needs. As the attitude of particular individuals will affect the morale, morale factors—to the extent he can control them—should be made part of the job specifications the manager sends to the personnel department. More informally, he should vigorously protest the personnel department's assigning him a manifestly unsuitable individual. An individual with the smell of a goat, the manners of a vulture, and the work ethics of a hyena may have been the only person available to personnel, but the manager should find out.

4. *Good orientation procedures.* The morale of new employees is bouyed by knowing about the company, their jobs, what's expected of them, what they can expect, when they eat, when they rest, where they put their coats. Information during the first few hours gives them some control of a basically fearful situation. Their initial reaction to the company at this critical point colors their feelings about it for a considerable period.

5. *Institution of an effective grievance mechanism.* There may be a legitimate way for employees to let off steam, try to right real or fancied injustices, and make a case for themselves in disciplinary procedures. The operational manager's willingness to listen and to render judgment fairly is a necessity. The organization should also have a mechanism, instituted by higher level management, through which the employee can seek redress for the manager's action or another hearing for a problem the manager cannot address.

6. *Employee participation in managerial decision-making.* While it may raise the morale of employees to feel they are participating in the decisions that affect them, the manager must be very careful to limit their participation to those matters which do indeed affect them. The danger

is in the manager's ceding his legitimate functions to an employee group which is neither qualified nor responsible. Staff meetings and daily briefings are among the morale builders of this type.

7. *Institution of firm ground rules.* People are happy at work if they know what they can do and what they cannot do. Simply, they are not menaced by the unknown and their spirits are better. They gain control of the situation and can organize themselves emotionally to deal with the job.

8. *Keeping employees busy.* Workers kept busy at work that at least seems somewhat meaningful do not have the time to contemplate their misfortunes. The time passes, there is a meal break, and then there is quitting time.

9. *Raising work interest.* Very often, as hospitality jobs are now structured, it is impossible to make the work interesting. It is supposed to be mechanical and routine so that training can be quick and effective. Weeding flower beds, washing dishes, polishing ballroom floors, posting guest charges, and a hundred other hospitality jobs are not particularly entertaining. Sometimes the manager can inject some interest into a job by explaining its importance, by setting job standards high enough to be challenging, by asking a worker to beat his own or somebody else's record.

10. *Employee counseling.* Very often the manager finds himself listening to an employee's personal problems. He asks the employee why he is late, hoping that the man will say that the bus was late and he does not expect it will happen again. Instead, he hears a story that seems to involve a sick baby, a midnight stabbing, and several individuals whose actual roles are not immediately apparent.

He hears about deserting husbands, runaway children, mortally sick in-laws, broken love affairs, mutilated puppies, the problems of minorities, the cupidity of landlords, the insensitivity of hospitals, and the general barbarism of a world he does not really know.

Often the manager is young, completely inexperienced in most of these matters, and conceivably as personally impotent as the employee unburdening himself. The operational manager builds morale in his group by listening, sympathizing, and attempting to act as liaison with some person or agency competent to deal with the problem.

There is the hope that the act of talking will help the employee organize some solution of his own. Sympathy of the "my gosh" and "how terrible" variety is at least comforting on a personal basis. Referring the individual to a social agency or a governmental body might provide him with genuine counseling and real help. Any activity beyond these three basic efforts is usually a disaster for the manager and the employee.

11. *Recognition of employee efforts.* The operational manager builds

morale by recognizing the importance of the individual's contribution to the organization as a whole. He makes the man's work meaningful by complimenting him on it, praising him, by crediting him with a good effort.

12. *Communication.* Communication has been amply discussed as a management technique in Chapter 2. In addition to promoting efficiency and effectiveness, it serves as a positive morale function: people are happy if they have some idea of *why* they are doing some particular task. A group of workers, hip deep in rubble, work with better morale if they know that that is where the new computer room is being installed.

13. *Creating job titles.* Certain hospitality jobs have such low social status that the only possible way to dignify them and make some bid for social prestige is to abandon the old title and promote a new one. Warewasher, for example, is more exact than dishwasher and slightly less deprecatory. "Serviceware sanitization machine operator" sounds more prestigious but is complicated and confusing. The danger of course is that a ridiculous title makes the man ridiculous. Genuine morale building on this basis will have to be part of a mammoth effort to redesign the jobs themselves. Operational managers might try *roomkeeper* instead of maid; *salesperson* instead of waiter; *room counselor* instead of front desk clerk; *assistant sales person* instead of busboy; *service attendant* instead of bellboy, and so on.

14. *Changing work assignments.* Often it is possible for the operational manager to rotate jobs within a crew so that the work is more fairly distributed, a morale builder in itself, and so that the boredom is relieved.

15. *Treatment of employees as individuals.* In hospitality units with high turnovers, seasonal layoffs, and constant absenteeism, a manager may develop the attitude that the workers are inferior machines; machines because they perform robot-like jobs, inferior because they tend to break down often, complain, and occasion considerable paperwork. If he can fight this tendency, the operational manager can raise morale. The most important step is remembering a man's full name and addressing him properly: machines don't have names of their own. Second best is calling him "Sir" when his name is not known.

16. *Development of social aspects of the job.* Before beginning a program that develops the social aspects of the job, the operational manager will require some policy directives from higher level management. Some organizations encourage bowling teams, picnics, or group outings, and some do not. Some organizations will both permit and sponsor these kinds of activities.

At the very least, the operational manager can try to build cooperation and friendliness among the workers. Finding them a decent place to eat together is a start.

17. *Rest periods.* In general, workers are more productive and their spirits are better if they have some rest periods in the course of their work, even if it means that they have to pace themselves faster to make up for the time out. At least the operational manager should experiment with rest periods, coffee breaks, or beer breaks to determine if he can build morale and productivity by this means.

18. *Protection of employee sensitivities.* The fundamental rule in this area is: "Praise in public, criticize in private." Humiliated workers quit, or they slow down, or they bust machines, or throw out heads of lettuce with the trash. There are also a host of specific sensitivities for which the manager can develop an awareness: ethnic and racial groups sometimes have a different cultural perspective; older workers and women workers sometimes react differently to directives from management.

19. *Monetary incentives.* In most circumstances the operational manager requires the permission of higher level management to establish monetary incentives related to job performance. Such incentives, even if the sum involved is small, work both as a powerful motivation and as a morale builder. The worker is specifically stimulated to achieve—the monetary incentive functions as a motivator—but of equal importance is the need to give his work some personal meaning. He is working toward a personal objective, not just the abstract organizational objectives established by the manager: his morale necessarily rises. Possibly the group morale is improved by the game-like aspect that a monetary incentive adds to the work. Even polishing glasses or something equally tedious can be more enjoyable if there is a fun way of keeping score. Incentives can be tied to increased sales, for example bottle bonuses for liquor sales, or to reduced costs, for example lower chemical utilization in cleaning projects, or to cost cutting or profit building suggestions themselves.

20. *Good management.* People like to be part of a winning team even if their particular roles are not glamorous. The manager who succeeds, who prompts his unit to succeed, encourages a certain pride among the workers. They share his triumphs just as they experience difficulty and uncertainty because of his failures.

Good management as well limits some of the activities that make hospitality jobs so devastating to morale. Good labor utilization is good management; it also means that a tedious job may be eliminated or shortened and the worker freed for more interesting work. Good planning is good management; it also means workers are not involved in ludicrous tasks such as stacking, unstacking, and restacking a pallet of case goods three and four times in the same day.

LEGAL CONCERNS OF THE OPERATIONAL MANAGER

Overzealous and ignorant operational managers can subject their operations and sometimes themselves to fines because of their violation of statutes and governmental regulations, and to costly civil judgments because of their inappropriate actions, or failures to act when action was necessary.

It is not upon the subtleties of the law that the operational manager runs aground, i.e., distinctions between a tenant and a guest, or improper application of an innkeeper's lien, or similar matters usually pursued at higher executive levels with the aid of an attorney. Rather, his problems occur in day-to-day relationships with guests and employees and in day-to-day operations. He makes an error in judgment that makes the operation vulnerable. Ninety-nine percent of legal problems on the operational level occur because a manager or an employee for whom the manager (and hence the operation) is responsible made one of the following mistakes:

1. Refusal to admit an individual who qualifies as a legitimate guest.
2. Ejection of an individual who has the right to be on the premises.
3. Causing injury to a person because of negligent operations, negligent supervision, or failure to adequately maintain the premises.
4. Failure to protect a guest's or non-guest's person.
5. Violation of a guest's rights.
6. Negligence in protecting a guest's property.
7. Violation of governmental regulations concerning the public health or safety.
8. Violation of governmental regulations concerning employment practices.
9. Entering into a contractual relationship prejudicial to the operation's interests.
10. Violation of the body of law governing the hotel-guest relationship.

Refusal to Admit an Individual Who Qualifies as a Legitimate Guest

Hotel and motel operations have a fundamental obligation to accept all individuals seeking accommodation for lawful purposes and able to pay for it, up to the capacity of the establishment, as they apply for that accommodation.

Commonly, operational managers err: when they falsely state that the operation is full, in order to discriminate on the basis of age, sex, race, creed, or national origin; when they promulgate rules or regulations that are discriminatory.

In practice, a hotel with rooms available must accept any individual willing to pay no matter how he looks, how he talks. The hotel may refuse accommodation on limited grounds: accommodations are full; inability to pay; intent to use the premises for immoral or illegal purposes; or unfitness to be received.

Inability to pay must be demonstrated, it cannot simply be supposed by the person receiving the traveller. If the person is asked to pay in advance and refuses, then, and only then, can the operation refuse to receive him on this basis.

The hotel can refuse a person who is obviously going to use the premises for immoral purposes—a prostitute, drug dealer, gambler—because of its obligation to protect its other guests.

Unfitness to be received must be construed as gross unfitness, totally objectionable behavior, a completely repulsive appearance and demeanor. It is not a criterion to be applied lightly. A traveller who is slightly drunk but no menace to himself, the property, or anyone else has to be received. An individual who has been backpacking in the national forests and arrives smelling of more than the great outdoors has to be received. Sleeping off a drunk (instead of driving home) or bathing and shaving are legitimate uses of hotel accommodations.

Ejection of an Individual Who Has the Right To Be on the Premises

The grounds on which an individual may be ejected from the premises are fairly straight forward; it is the pursuit of the hotel's rights in these matters which occasions the difficulty. Except when the matter is urgent —other guests are being menaced—the operational manager should seek counsel with executive management or the operation's attorneys before acting on his interpretation of the law.

Common grounds for legal ejection include: wrongful refusal to pay a bill; objectionable conduct; use of facilities for illegal business; annoyance of other guests; serious illness or a contagious disease.

Ejection is generally accomplished by asking the guest to leave. When the guest does not comply, *reasonable* means may be used to remove him. As well, ejection must be accomplished in such a fashion as not to subject the guest to public humiliation. An operational manager cannot, in other words, physically assault a guest in removing him because he did not pay his bill, although he can restrain a guest who is being ejected for beating other persons. Application of any force requires careful consideration and consultation, if at all possible.

Ejection for illness is another problem-some area. The decision should not and need not be made on the operational level. In principal the hotel can eject the guest but it must insure that the person will be reasonably cared for and safe. Obviously, both medical and legal collaboration are necessary.

An attempt to eject guests for other reasons than those listed is dangerous. For example, an individual is not obliged to enter and leave a hotel at the hotel's convenience, dress in a certain fashion, or remain tranquil when hotel service for real or fancied reasons disturbs him.

Causing Injury to a Person Because of Negligence

A person who is injured on hospitality unit property must demonstrate that the operation failed to exercise reasonable care and that the failure was primarily responsible for the injury, before damages can be collected.

The obligation of the operational manager in this matter is to keep the operation safe. Chapter 11 discusses guest and employee safety. If a person is injured, certain limitations on the hotel's liability may relieve it of some or all of its responsibility, but the matter will *not* be adjudicated by the operational manager. If the manager is aware of a menace to the public safety, he must move to correct it, whatever its cause and whomever it is menacing.

The operational manager's conduct when a guest has fallen ill or had an accident can be construed as negligent if he has failed to take actions that could be reasonably expected of a prudent individual. He is not expected to undertake medical treatment, in fact, he should not attempt it, but he is expected to call a physician. He is not expected to move a person to a guest room from the scene of an accident, generally he should not move the person at all, but he is expected to protect the person from further menace, for example, from the collapse of the rest of the ceiling.

Failure to Protect a Guest's or Non-Guest's Person

Operational procedures should not potentially menace a guest. Quite obviously, if a public stairway is poorly maintained and a person is hurt the hotel has been negligent. This same principal extends to conditions which are not inherently dangerous but have the possibility of a danger that a reasonable person can foresee. For example, hotels have been held liable because guests have injured third parties under conditions that the management could foresee. Conventioners have injured passing strangers with objects hurled from windows: the courts held that hotels are aware of the activities of the conventioners and failed to take adequate precautions for the protection of passing strangers.

An operation which books a rock-and-roll group can expect a crowd of excited fans. It has an obligation to control the crowd adequately to protect other individuals from being trampled. A hotel has an obligation to protect guests in a swimming pool from the rowdy conduct of other guests.

Violating a Guest's Rights

The hotel guest has certain basic rights which cannot be violated: privacy, freedom of movement, freedom from assault, freedom from battery.

The concept of reasonableness governs the hotelman's access to a room which he has rented. He cannot capriciously or unnecessarily disturb the guest's quiet enjoyment of the room. He can enter a room to clean it, repair it, protect guests of other individuals, protect the hotel's property, prevent a crime, or enforce reasonable regulations (for example, a prohibition against cooking in rooms). In most cases he is expected to announce himself either directly or by telephone before entering.

FREEDOM OF MOVEMENT

A hotel cannot detain a guest unless he gives his consent or unless there is reasonable suspicion that a crime has been committed by the individual. In the latter instance, the hotel will have to demonstrate that the detention was reasonable on the basis of sufficient proof for the action. If the person wants to leave, the hotel must either release him, or call the police to arrest him.

If the individual is arrested under a warrant sworn by the hotel manager, and the warrant in a subsequent legal proceeding is declared void, then an action may be commenced for false arrest. Restriction of a person's movement without considerable grounds is an essentially dangerous action.

FREEDOM FROM ASSAULT

Guests have the right to protection from the threat of physical violence when there is the immediate possibility of that attack occurring. Employees cannot menace guests.

Guests also have the right to be free of other assaults such as humiliating and insulting treatment. A failure in this area may make the operation actionable.

FREEDOM FROM BATTERY

If assault, or the threat of violence, is actionable, then obviously the violence itself is. While physical force is permissible when it is appropriate, for example in preventing a guest from injuring himself or another person, it becomes battery when the force used exceeds the minimum the situation requires.

Negligence in Protecting a Guest's Property

Historically, innkeepers have been absolutely liable for the property of a guest within their premises except when the guest himself has been negligent, or the property was lost through an act of God (storms, earthquakes, and the like) or the action of enemy soldiers.

In many states, this absolute liability still applies. In others, it has been limited by statute, the basis of the notices often posted on room doors. As the statutory law is essentially against the thrust of common law, courts have tended to be very rigid in interpreting the statutes so that the *guest* can take full advantage of those aspects of the hotel's liability which have not been limited by the statute. If the statute specifies a limitation of liability on certain property, it can be construed that there is no limitation of liability on other property.

As a matter of practice, the operational manager must function as though the operation had absolute liability for a guest's property, as negligence can cause the hotel to lose its statutory limitation of liability.

Violation of Governmental Regulations Concerning the Public Health or Safety

Governmental bodies ranging from the local fire department to the federal Occupational Safety and Health Administration have jurisdiction over aspects of a hospitality establishment's operation. Conforming to these various statutes, codes, and regulations is essentially the operational manager's responsibility although he may need permission or collaboration to institute systems changes or purchase specific equipment to conform. A comprehensive list is virtually impossible as regulations vary from area to area. The manager should investigate the following areas to determine what specific laws apply to his operation, and then assess the operation to determine how well it complies: building, health, and fire codes; safety codes for workers and the public; kitchen sanitation, food handling, and food production equipment codes; codes governing the serving of alcoholic beverages; codes governing the construction and use of sports facilities, especially swimming pools; codes governing environmental sanitation, garbage disposal, littering, noise.

Violation of Governmental Regulations Concerning Employment Practices

Discrimination in hiring on the basis of sex, age, race, creed, color, or national origin is expressly forbidden. By extension, employment practices, for example, the assigning of work, hiring, and laying off, cannot be discriminatory. Every potential worker must be judged on the basis of his job related qualifications. Each employee must be dealt with only on the basis of job related abilities and characteristics.

Courts have also protected the employee's freedom of conscience and freedom of expression. For example, an employee may not be fired because of his political views or his refusal to attend a worship service.

Problems for the operational manager occur when the implications of the statutes are considered. For example, questions on an application blank may be unlawful when the information they solicit tends to cause discrimination against minorities. Information on arrest records, credit records, or garnishment records may be construed as discriminatory, as minority groups tend to have more irrelevant arrests, less credit standing (being poorer as a group), and a more considerable history of garnishments. Height and weight requirements may have the same effect, as some minority groups are physically smaller. The question can only be asked when the requirement is a bona fide job qualification, for example, the sex of a health club attendant.

Another recurrent legal problem for the operational manager concerns the general employment practices code under which his company is operating. There are federal and state regulations governing minimum wage and working conditions, the employment of minors and women, with which the operational manager must become familiar, especially in the absence of a personnel department. As state regulations differ radically, it is impossible to give comprehensive guidelines. The manager should be aware of posting requirements for regulations, the laws governing computation of overtime, the laws governing employment of individuals still in school, curfew regulations for minors, proscribed occupations for minors and women, regulations governing rest periods, meal breaks, and occupations which require standing.

Entering into a Contractual Relationship Prejudicial to the Operation's Interests

The authority to enter into certain types of contractual relations, either verbal or written, is sometimes expressly given an operational manager. He is told, in writing or orally, that he can purchase certain items, contract for certain services, and obligate the organization in certain ways. Beyond this expressed authority may be an implied authority covering those contractual relationships not expressly indicated. The other party in a contractual relationship may also assume "apparent authority" when a contractual arrangement is concluded with an individual who has neither expressed authority or implied authority but seems to.

The operational manager is thus in a position to involve his company in a contract which is prejudicial to its interests. Under certain circumstances, the contract will be binding on the company, and the company will have no immediate recourse except to honor it, and then perhaps take action against the operational manager who exceeded his authority. In other instances, the other party to the contract, unable to oblige the company to honor an unauthorized commitment, may hold the operational manager liable.

There is the possibility of problems occurring in the purchase of goods or in the sale of hospitality services, but difficulties in these areas are unlikely. Hospitality products are seldom especially produced and, as damages are limited to the losses actually suffered by the parties, liability in this area is limited. As well, the company usually can legitimately cancel an unauthorized purchase.

In the sale of hospitality services, it is generally accepted, if not explicitly stated, that a sales representative's promises only become contractual material when they are approved in writing by higher level management.

In purchasing services, such as those of a swimming pool cleaning company, exterminator, or glazier, the operational manager is more vulnerable. In all probability he has either obligated the company or himself to pay for services he orders.

For the operational manager, a reasonable program for avoiding this kind of problem should include an expressed statement of authority by management, the use of written agreements for all purchases, and consultation with higher level management and company attorneys when the contract is complex or extensive.

Violation of the Body of Law Governing the Hotel-Guest Relationship

In addition to its basic obligations to receive the public and to provide for the protection of the guest's person and property, the hotel has additional obligations that are the responsibility of operational management. A guest must be provided with adequate sleeping facilities and sufficient food of a reasonable quality if the hotel is American Plan. Adequate provision must be made for a guest's baggage.

In sum, reasonable care and facilities, consistent with the nature of the establishment, is expected, and it is the responsibility of the operational manager to meet these expectations.

PUBLIC RELATIONS

No one would dispute that the operational manager's first responsibility is to contribute to his organization's profits. Social responsibility and accountability are among the philosophical concerns of the corporate managers not the individuals involved in day-to-day operations.

The operational manager, however, must be wary of shortsightedness in his pursuit of profits for the organization. Optimum profitability for an organization is not necessarily identical with the highest immediate profit. Sometimes immediate profits are limited in the interest of long term profitability. Sometimes immediate efforts have no direct dividend but in the long term improve the profitability of the enterprise.

Operational managers have a number of concerns which, if they do not compromise profits seem to have little relationship to them. In fact, the relationship is indirect and long term but important. The quality of an organization's public relations—community relations, communications, media relations, ethical business behavior—ultimately affects profitability. An operation which has built considerable community good will finds the community willing to extend its deadlines for the operation's reduction of the pollutants in the air vented from its charbroilers. An operation which has cooperated with the media for a period of years, finds the media willing to minimize unfavorable publicity because of a suicide or labor action. An operation known for its ethical business behavior finds this behavior reciprocated by suppliers and competitors, and, as well, a positive factor in attracting business.

Even in organizations that have a public relations department, public relations is an operational manager's responsibility. The public encounters the operational manager, and, unaware of the niceties of corporate organization, identifies his behavior and actions as the company's public relations policies.

Community Relations

Good community relations are founded on the personal participation of the manager in the community; good communications about the company to the community; cooperation in community efforts; and a positive community image.

PERSONAL PARTICIPATION

Operational managers should make an effort to participate in educational, religious, fraternal, and social organizations. Their management skills and personal energies are seen as a corporate contribution to the community. They are able to learn something of the community and its reactions to the company's business activity, and they are able to personally communicate the company's perspective on controversial issues.

A major resort, for example, may seem to be fundamentally alienated from the small farming community in which it is located. In addition to being of personal service to the community, the operational manager can also make the case for the resort as an employer of local people, and as a source of additional income for much of the populace because of the money it and its guests spend at local enterprises.

COMMUNICATION

A great deal of a hospitality operation's continuing patronage can come from local sources: referrals by local businessmen and community leaders. As they are unlikely to be patrons of more than restaurant facilities, the operational manager should make an effort to acquaint them with the facility. Tours, use of facilities for outings, school trips, and other such accommodations, develop a community understanding of what the operation has to offer.

COOPERATION IN COMMMUNITY EFFORTS

It is good business to lend facilities and resources to community groups for two reasons: (1) members of the community group can become cash customers for the same facilities and (2) the operation can show its social consciousness in areas where it may some day be vulnerable to regulatory action.

The first reason is almost self evident. The people involved in charity affairs are usually sufficiently prosperous to pay for weddings, debutante balls, and other social events. They are also generally the decision makers for corporate entertaining and meetings.

The second reason is equally important. Hospitality operations are a mixed blessing to many communities: the community likes the business generated but is concerned about ecological damage, overcrowded roads, litter generated, undesirables brought into the community, etc. A hospitality operation that makes positive efforts in the areas in which it is vulnerable blunts criticisms that may lead to regulatory action. For example, fast food operations should sponsor clean up campaigns and beautification programs. Large resorts which dump seasonal labor on the community should make a special effort to cooperate with training programs for the disadvantaged. If it is beyond the operational manager's authority to participate or initiate programs of this order, he at least has the responsibility to make a case for corporate management.

POSITIVE IMAGE

Hospitality operations may suddenly find themselves fighting zoning boards, health departments, or building departments, because they unnecessarily offended members of the community. Often the offended community overacts, and the regulations it enacts cost the company much more than the preventative maintenance of community relations that would have avoided the offense. For example, a restaurant's exposed garbage cans offend its immediate neighbors. An ordinance is passed which prohibits outdoor holding of garbage and rubbish. The operation must then buy a compactor, a bottle crusher, and a garbage disposal and renegotiate its contract with the rubbish carter so pick-ups are made during the restaurant's open hours. These costs could have been avoided by recognizing the image problem before the neighbors did and building a simple fence around the garbage cans.

The behavior and attitudes of personnel in the community can occasion the same type of retributive action and can be avoided by a little common sense before the problem escalates. For example, a resort operation with considerable convention business systematically lays off workers during slow periods. Often these workers create a public disturbance in the neighboring village. Finally, the community reacts by systematically arresting everyone who looks like a hotel worker on charges of disturbing the peace and vagrancy. To say the least, the resort's recruitment efforts and personnel scheduling are disrupted. Bussing the workers involved back to the metropolitan area from which they came and to which they really want to go, would have avoided the problem.

Communications, Media Relations

The operational manager of a hospitality property and the local television, radio, and press reporters can establish a give-and-take relationship that is not necessarily based on free drinks and dinners. The operational manager can provide the media with legitimate news, feature stories, notification of celebrity visits, and assistance in covering public events such as political press conferences, meetings, or conventions and product launchings held at the hospitality operation.

In turn the media can agree to communicate company news of promotions, special events, and employee efforts to the community at large. As well, it is likely that when the operation experiences a crisis such as the suicide of a guest, a narcotics bust of an employee, or a labor action, the elements unfavorable to the operation will be treated objectively. Often goodwill created through cooperation with the media keeps the operation's name out of the news: it is identified as a local restaurant, or a mid-town hotel.

Ethical Business Behavior

Ethical standards are largely subjective. It can only be asked that the operational manager in a hospitality organization be intelligent in his subjectivity, and that he carefully equate short term gains against the risks that they involve. The most considerable risk is the possibility of exposure. A well-known ice cream company was recently accused of falsifying records so that products with higher than acceptable bacteria counts could be sold. The managers involved, some of whom face prison terms, appear monumentally stupid when the damage done the company in dollar terms is compared to the few dollars gained.

Sharp dealing even when not actually dishonest is inconsistent with the long term profitability of a service organization. Customers arranging weddings, social events, or conventions are usually totally unequipped to specify what they want. The sharp manager can make a killing but can also wound his future sales rather badly.

Unfair competitive practices, even if they do not become known to governmental authorities, always become known to other individuals in the hospitality industry. The manager loses the cooperation of his peers and their assistance when his freezers break down, his chef quits, or he disastrously overbooks.

Customers attracted by misleading but not quite fraudulent advertising may swell one week's sales figures, but the most expensive advertising campaign hardly compensates for the bad image of the operation the customers pass on to the community.

Unethical behavior that is observed by employees, peers, and superiors makes the observers question the manager's dealings, and may ultimately erode his position in the organization.

Finally, unethical behavior is dysfunctional because of the damage it does the individual. Few people are sufficiently oblivious of conventional morality to violate it without anxiety and regret, and they thus lower their own productivity and personal morale.

The operational manager contemplating a course of action which he recognizes as unethical might ask himself some critical questions:

What risk does exposure bring? Is it worth it?

Will I regret this action, even if it is successful, every time I think of it?

How would people whose opinion I value—family, friends, superiors —react to knowledge of this decision?

Does the contemplated action violate general standards of sportsman-like behavior, the ten commandments, or the precepts of the free enterprise system?

What would I do if somebody did it to me?

LABOR RELATIONS

Many of the millions of people employed in the hospitality industry in over 600 thousand different establishments are not members of a labor organization. There are some workers, however, especially in the larger hospitality organizations and in those organizations associated with enterprises which are unionized, for example the food service in an industrial plant, who do belong to a union. The union functions as the workers' bargaining agent and negotiates a contract with management on their behalf.

Fundamentally, the operational manager's activities, responsibilities, and concerns are no different whether the workers are members of a union or not. Management always retains the right to manage the enterprise. The operational manager in a union establishment is still in charge of his unit, he still makes the operational decisions, he still has the ultimate responsibility for its functioning.

As far as the operational manager is concerned, the difference between managing union workers and non-union workers essentially is found in two areas, neither of which need be particularly troublesome: management decisions that directly affect the worker; and the handling of worker grievances.

Management Decisions that Directly Affect the Workers

Workers form unions in an establishment so that they can effectively negotiate their rates of pay, working conditions, hours of employment, overtime, vacations, and benefits. After the union has been recognized by management, negotiations are begun and a contract formalizing an *agreement* about these matters is signed. It is important to recognize that both parties have agreed to the terms of the contract: it represents management's intentions and rights as well as the workers'. From the operational manager's perspective it is a management policy statement as well as a union document.

Some of the clauses of the contract limit the operational manager's authority in the same way that any policy formulated by upper-level management may. It tells him what he may do, and what he may not do. In this instance, the thrust of these directives concerns those basic areas of the worker's concern: wage rates, overtime, vacations, working conditions, etc.

Although the operational manager may have been consulted during the course of negotiations, and thus helped to formulate the contract, his basic task is to implement it. Perhaps the contract says that workers will be given overtime on the basis of their seniority, that is, their length of service with the company: when there is overtime to assign, the operational manager follows his instructions and assigns overtime to the most senior worker. The contract says that the senior workers have their choice of shift: the operational manager follows the contract and gives the senior workers their choice of shift.

Obviously, the contract limits some of his flexibility in organizing, planning, and scheduling, but the operational manager has little choice in the matter. He does not "beat" the contract. He follows the directives of upper-level management. While contracts differ in their specific stipulations, it is entirely safe to say that the operational manager avoids most labor problems by understanding the terms of the contract and simply abiding by them.

It should be remembered that the contract limits the manager only in areas which affect the workers and not any others. A manager's authority to act is unaffected otherwise. He closes, he opens, he refuses customers or accepts customers, he sells the product or gives it away and he remains accountable only to his superiors as long as he respects the specific labor related directives of the contract. He might decide that only three workers are needed to take care of business that everyone else in the unit thinks will require ten. The contract might provide that senior workers will be given work first. As long as he respects seniority in laying off the seven workers, that is, he retains the three most senior workers and does not schedule the junior workers, he is conforming to the provisions of the contract. If the decision is wrong, he has to explain himself only to his superiors. (If the decision is right he explains himself to no one.) Nowhere in a union management agreement does it say that managers have to be smart: just that they have to follow the contract.

Handling Grievances

Most contracts contain an agreed upon procedure by which the worker's grievances (formal complaints)—about his working conditions, disciplinary actions, assignment of overtime, seniority rights, etc.—will be heard and weighed for their merit. The worker formalizes a complaint and either discusses it directly with the operational manager or discusses it with the union's representative in the unit, who then may discuss it with the operational manager. The union representative or steward is most often a worker, still working, who has been elected by his fellows to act as their spokesman. The operational manager cannot tell the workers to come directly to him, but he certainly may discuss their complaints with them without union permission and try to avoid a formal grievance. In most instances the operational manager keeps the union steward informed of at least the disposition of a grievance. In most instances the union steward and the operational manager have cordial dealings entirely governed by their fundamental manager-worker relationship.

Really professional operational managers avoid the initiation of a grievance procedure by conducting fundamentally fair dealings with the workers who come to them with whatever problems they have, expecting

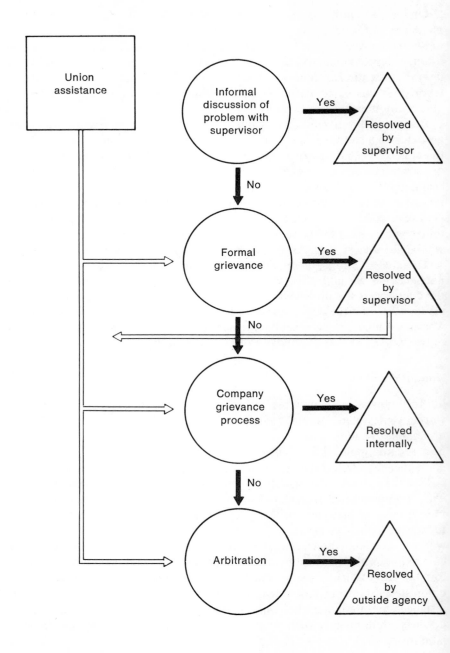

Figure 4.1.   Steps in the formal grievance procedure.

a fair deal, although not necessarily a decision in their favor 100 percent of the time.

If the worker makes a complaint to his steward, the steward may simply discuss the matter with the worker and convince *him* that he has no gripe. If the steward pursues the matter, it is either because he is convinced that some injustice has been done the worker, or because he feels obliged in the particular circumstance to champion the worker, right or wrong. The steward, being an elected official of the union, must necessarily be a partisan politician at times.

When the matter is pursued, by either the worker or the steward, the operational manager is obliged to make a decision. He may examine the facts, investigate the matter and determine that the worker is correct. The manager himself is wrong: it is apparent from the terms of the contract that he erred. He did not respect seniority in regard to overtime, or scheduling. He corrects himself: he admits he is wrong, tells the parties concerned promptly and makes the necessary adjustment. He gains generally by admitting his occasional fallibility.

If the manager feels that he is entirely correct and that the terms of the contract explicitly support him he makes his decision accordingly and then tries to sell the steward and the worker on the correctness of his judgment. Most often he succeeds; the grievance is pursued no further.

If he is uncertain, after investigation and study, he can then consult someone in upper-level management or someone in the personnel department. He should not make a hasty decision.

For most operational managers, deciding to decide is a continuing problem. They must make absolutely clearcut decisions themselves and relatively quickly or they are abandoning their management functions. On the other hand, there is a natural tendency to want to consult with someone else so that the problems and most of a protracted grievance procedure are avoided.

The manager should decide independently when the matter concerns the literal terms of the contract. In general, he should involve higher level management when the problem requires him to interpret a clause of the contract because the matter is not explicitly treated. For example, the contract may state the senior workers should be given their choice of shift. When a junior worker and a senior worker are disputing this matter, the manager's decision is quite clear: the senior worker gets the choice. He makes the decision himself. On the other hand, does that clause of the contract mean that the senior worker can switch shifts every week or every day, or does it mean that he can elect a shift and be expected to maintain his decision for a reasonable period of time? The manager confronted with this problem would wisely seek assistance, for whatever decision he makes becomes a precedent on which future decisions must be based.

If the area of decision is not covered by the contract explicitly, the manager is interpreting the contract. Legally and contractually he is speaking for the company; his decision becomes the applicable policy in this area.

When a manager makes a decision on a grievance, it is vital that he respect the worker's and the union's rights in making the grievance. If the grievance is pursued, when it is unfavorable to the worker, first to the upper levels of management, and then to an independent third party called an arbitrator, *how* the operational manager handled the grievance is quite as important as his disposition of it.

Most operational managers keep records of the grievance—the facts, their investigation of the facts, and their decisions—so that they can demonstrate that they attempted to make a fair decision. As well, should the matter come to arbitration, a written record provides the operational manager with an accurate statement of the facts, should his recollection fail him when he is called upon to testify.

Some Guidelines for Promoting Good Labor Relations

The operational manager has little to say about the formulation of a contract between management and a union. He has a great deal to contribute to the climate in which subsequent negotiations and the adjudication of grievances will take place. As far as the workers and the union steward are concerned, in his unit he is the management. The contract, the labor laws of the United States and of the state in which the company is operating, and good common sense dictate the course of action he should pursue. The following guidelines can lead to good labor relations:

1. Do not attempt to influence workers in any way concerning their relationship with the union.
2. Do not attempt to interfere with the performance of union activities such as chapter meetings, or with the contractually established activities of the steward in collecting dues or soliciting memberships during his working hours.
3. Do not discriminate in any way against an employee for being a member of the union, for filing a formal grievance, for participating in a grievance proceeding (as a witness), for participating in a labor action or strike.
4. Do not attempt to circumvent the steward in his relationship with the workers or attempt to undermine or weaken the union.
5. Attempt to follow the spirit of the contract rather than the letter when the intentions of management are clear. Battling with tech-

nicalities instead of a solid reasoning will simply invite the union representatives to "Mickey Mouse" operational managers in return.

6. Attempt to establish a working relationship with the steward so that communication is easy. The operational manager cannot share the decision-making process with the steward but he certainly can keep him sufficiently informed so that grievance situations do not occur. Complaints, before they become formal grievances, can be fielded by an informed steward.

7. Solve the workers' problems and address their complaints even when the problem does not have the legal or contractual substance of a grievance. It may be obvious that neither the operational manager, the upper level management, or an arbitrator can rule in the worker's favor. The man still has a gripe; the operational manager promoting good labor relations (and high morale) at least tries to address the problem. Management does not necessarily win because the worker cannot.

8. In dealing with workers, stewards, and other union officials do not become emotional. Rash actions or ill-considered decisions commit the company as well as the operational manager.

9. Protect the human dignity of the worker, and the prestige of the union steward by allowing them a graceful way of accepting an unfavorable decision. Make whatever minor concessions can be made, explain the logic of the decision and its appropriateness, recognize the sincerity and merit of their arguments—without necessarily altering the fundamental decision.

10. Anticipate problems and correct them before they become the substance of a complaint. Address complaints before they become grievances. The existence of a contract and grievance machinery in no way relieves the manager of his responsibility to interact with the workers under him, or his obligation to keep the operation running smoothly.

5 | Management of Work

The phenomenal growth of the hospitality industry to its present status as a major segment of the American economy has been due to high volume and cheap labor. For years there were plenty of customers for a limited number of guest rooms and restaurant seats; and an abundant pool of inexpensive labor. Until recently, it was possible to achieve acceptable revenues without giving too much managerial attention to either competition or the cost of labor. Customer accommodation and other cost factors, such as food cost, were stressed.

The briefest experience in the modern hospitality industry will amply demonstrate that growth predicated on high volume and cheap labor is no longer possible. Competition has increased considerably, driving the occupancy rates for hotels down and limiting the volume potential of restaurants. The minimum wage has taken mighty leaps in the past few years and will surely reach $3.00 before 1980. As well, there is every possibility that the tip credit which allows the operation to pay a gratuity employee less than the minimum wage on the assumption that he is receiving at least that sum in tips will vanish. Increases in employer contributions for benefits such as social security and a decrease in the work week resulting in more time-and-a-half overtime pay for forty hours work can also be safely predicted.

INCREASING THE PRODUCTIVITY

Future growth of the hospitality industry will have different impetuses, thus managerial priorities must also change. Aggressive marketing, control of cost factors other than labor, and better general management can provide a partial solution. In the operational unit, however, from the front desk to the snack bar, the main managerial emphasis must be on productivity: an increase in the amount of work done for the amount of time or dollars spent doing it. A dollar spent on labor will have to result in more sales dollars.

Today many front desk clerks, cashiers, waiters, countermen, utility men, cooks, bellmen, and room maids, still service the same number of customers they serviced 25 years ago. Their wages have increased both absolutely and as a percentage of sales dollars but their productivity has not. In very many instances, if employee productivity is expressed in terms of the labor dollars the operation invests for the sales dollars it receives, their productivity has declined. There are several explanations for the declines. Competition has limited the possibility of increasing prices to the customer to neutralize the increased costs. The volume of the operation has declined so that its basic labor costs have become relatively more expensive. Even when a hotel has 10-percent occupancy or a restaurant fills only 10-percent of its seats certain employees must be present, as "positions" must be manned. In periods of high volume this basic cost is spread over a considerable number of sales dollars. When volume has declined, each sales dollar must bear a larger portion of this "fixed" employee cost.

Employee productivity has thus become a major hospitality management concern. Since it is unlikely that management can pay specific workers less, when it is already paying the minimum wage, management has to seek ways of improving their output.

Capital investment in equipment has provided part of the answer. The small computer systems designed for front desk and night auditing functions greatly increase the productivity of the night auditor by allowing him to assume the workload of several other people. The operation saves the cost of their labor less the cost of the computer system. Even simple kitchen machines, such as vertical cutters, slicers, and potato peelers increase the productivity of workers using them. The operation saves the cost of the utility workers the machine replaces.

Unfortunately, the size of many hospitality operations limits their exploitation of labor-saving equipment. The cost of the equipment exceeds the savings they can anticipate. A vertical cutter does not "pay" for itself unless it is used several hours a day. Even very large operations cannot hope to find a complete technological solution to the problem of labor productivity. They can make more use of equipment, from automated window-washing machines to silver-sorting systems, but they too are limited by the present unavailability of labor-saving equipment for many tasks and the particular nature of the hospitality industry.

Robots capable of sorting linen or setting up banquet rooms are not available. Scores of hospitality jobs still have to be done by people. Even if there were a machine invented for a task the customer would not necessarily be pleased by being mechanically served: machines don't smile or say good morning.

The nature of the hospitality business also precludes numerous machine solutions. Faced with similar problems, industrial companies have automated. A hotel or restaurant, unlike a factory, has little capability of adjusting its product runs to promote the efficient use of its facilities. Guests check in during the late afternoon and evening; they check-out during the morning; a factory can schedule its production on a twenty-four hour basis. Restaurant customers require the product when they are hungry, generally in the morning, at noon, and in the early evening; a factory can produce and store its product. Machine utilization is certainly a partial answer, but only that.

In the foreseeable future, the greatest increase in worker productivity in the hospitality industry will come from the intensive management of work. Management, especially operational management, addressing the problem of labor efficiency can increase productivity. There are some techniques and concepts that can be borrowed from industrial managers faced with a similar problem, however, the basic thrust of the operational manager's effort is in applying systematic attention to the problem. Thinking productivity, wanting productivity, and then examining procedures and jobs with that perspective has results. In fact, it may well be that an unacademic informal approach will be more successful than an attempt to impose the rigorous techniques of the industrial efficiency expert on the hospitality industry. Much in the repertory of the industrial "time and motion" man presumes the routine repetitive work of the assembly line. Although many hospitality jobs are routine and repetitive, there are many that can be improved, but are not repetitive.

The Operational Manager's Productivity Program

After an initial step—work study—the operational manager can explore four other basic avenues for improving the productivity of his unit.

1. Work study
2. Labor utilization improvement
3. Work design improvement
4. Method improvement
5. Increased worker efficiency

1. *Work study*. The fundamental procedure in attempting to improve productivity is necessarily to assess it. Whether the operational manager is attempting to increase the number of sandwiches his cook produces or decrease the number of trips the laundry truck makes, he has to study the current procedure and express its current productivity if he is going to be able to improve the procedure and measure the results.

2. *Labor utilization improvement.* Certain aspects of improving productivity are almost entirely within the manager's control. He can budget more efficiently the labor units he expends.

3. *Work design improvement.* Planning is basically a managerial function. Good work plans result in increased worker productivity. As well, the manager can create a work system of men, machines, and methods that maximizes the unit's productivity.

4. *Method improvement.* Many of the procedures and techniques used in hotels and restaurants were developed during the period of inexpensive labor. Essentially they are wasteful even when the workers are working with full effort. Today they have to be re-engineered.

5. *Increased worker efficiency.* The manager has at least partial control over a number of factors which either promote or diminish human productivity. These factors range from the proper use of the human body to the physical conditions of work.

WORK STUDY

In industrial corporations, work study is an extremely rigorous and expensive activity demanding trained personnel and expensive equipment. Rates for workers, prices for customers, and decisions on capital investment are all based on the results of the study. In the hospitality industry, work study need not be as formal; any attention to the management of work after these years of neglect will have positive results. On the operational level especially, work study can simply be defined as "work cost awareness," a recognition that any product or activity is costing labor dollars.

A very simple program of study by the operational manager as part of his daily routine will give him ample insight into those areas which can be improved. The operational manager need only have some idea of where the problems are in the hospitality industry as a whole, some recognition of the signals of low productivity, and some knowledge of the techniques for examining productivity to isolate priority targets for productivity improvement.

Where the Problems Are

In the hospitality industry, the lowest productivity is associated with the lowest paying jobs. The wages of the individual warewasher, utility worker, yardman, pool boy, or bellman may be low, but the cost of the functions they perform is expensive. The operation is paying a staggering sum to have its linen delivered to the maid's closets or its garbage raked. In the most general terms, the major productivity problems involve the minimum wage worker: anything he is doing deserves examination.

Within this group those workers who are *not* hired or fired as the volume of the operation increases or decreases should be the first object of the manager's attention. The cost of labor for workers whose jobs are created by increased volume can at least be considered part of the cost of sales. Workers who are employed regardless of volume are a fixed cost and hence much less productive over the course of a year in terms of sales dollars.

The second thrust of a problem search involves the manager in an examination of the operation itself with a productivity perspective. Systems and procedures were created when productivity was not a managerial concern. These traditions have to be examined by the operational manager. He is looking for gross inefficiencies: jobs without real functions such as saladmen hired for a menu which no longer exists; clumsy procedures such as double-handling goods being received by unloading them on the receiving dock from the truck and then loading them on flat trucks; evidences of poor planning such as crew scheduling to a standard number irrespective of volume; equipment placements that generate a great deal of walking, and so on.

Recognizing Productivity Problems

Very often the operational manager already knows of productivity problems but he does not recognize them as such. Labor cost as a percentage of sales *can be* an indicator of low productivity. A high labor cost relative to the operation's past performance can be indicative of a productivity decline. It may also simply indicate that volume has declined or that the wage rate has increased, meaning that there has been no change in real productivity, only a change in the indicator. Likewise, if productivity seems to have improved it may simply mean that there has been an increase in volume or a rise in prices.

As well, the labor cost percentage as a measure can be deceptive because it represents an average. A month's labor cost is the average of 30 days, and conceivably 720 hours of operation. High productivity periods and low productivity periods may have balanced each other, and the labor cost percentage will not reveal that there has been considerable low productivity. A labor cost percentage on a daily basis would be much more indicative.

The severest limitation on labor cost percentage as an indicator is the absence of any industry standard. Hospitality operations are too diverse for any particular percentage to be given as a benchmark of good performance. Labor cost percentage is useful only when it is coupled with other indicators and related to the operation's past performance.

PRODUCTIVE MAN-HOURS PER DAY

Department/Employee	(1) Productive time per 100 customers	(2) Number of customers per day divided by 100	(3) Productive time per day (1) x (2)	(4) Actual time per day	(5) Performance (3) ÷ (4) x 100
	Man-hours	Number	Man-hours	Man-hours	Percent
Total					

Figure 5.1.   Productivity ratios: a form for determining productive man-hours per day.

WAITRESS PRODUCTION CHART

Waitress Name (1)	# Hrs. Worked (2)	Total Sales (3)	Sales per Manhour $(3 \div 2)$ (4)	Total # of Customers (5)	Average Customer Sale $(5 \div 3)$ (6)	Comments: Re Legibility, Errors, Suggested Selling, Etc. (7)
TOTAL FOR THIS DAY'S CHECKS						

Figure 5.2. Analysis of waitress productivity in terms of sales dollars and customers served.

Productivity ratios give the operational manager more information with which to work. The cost of activities is expressed in terms of the results of those activities. If a waitress serves 64 customers in an 8-hour period, then her productivity ratio is 1 man hour for every 8 customers. If her sales during that period are examined, they can be compared with her cost to the employer (wages and benefits) to produce a ratio of labor cost to sales dollars. Very often the operational manager can arrive at these ratios by an analysis of the operation's records. Records kept for other control purposes can indicate the labor cost for producing catering boxes, or preparing vegetables for dinner, or handling "packages" in a storage facility, etc.

Some jobs which can be improved cannot be measured in this manner. A worker charged with inspecting the operation garbage for silverware is not more or less productive as he retrieves more or less silverware. He is optimally productive when he has not *missed* any silverware, or has retrieved *all* the silverware in the garbage even when there is only one piece retrieved. The decision factor here involves the cost of control—whether the silver he retrieves is worth more than his salary—not the productivity of the individual.

Productivity indices do not always have to be quantifiable. Worker complaints that a procedure is unduly tiring or "stupid" can often indicate that it is inefficient. People are generally willing to do a day's work; people generally want their work to be somewhat meaningful. If a particular procedure is generating complaints or inordinate turnover it may very well mean that it is poorly designed or unnecessary. The worker need not have the solution; he can simply point to the problem.

Perhaps the best indicator of low productivity is common sense observation. If the manager sees that well-motivated workers are often idle, or that good workers are often snowed under by work loads, or that people in his operation are constantly walking around getting and fetching, he can be sure that he is unnecessarily losing labor dollars.

Techniques for Analyzing Productivity

Having isolated some possible productivity problems in particular jobs or particular procedures, the operational manager's next step is analysis. He takes the job or procedure apart to determine to what extent it is inefficient and what particular aspects of it are inefficient. If a man is washing greens for salad and the operation needs the salad, the procedure is necessary. (If the salad were not necessary as a menu item then general productivity would be raised by eliminating it.) The task of the operational manager is then to examine the procedure step by step to see if each step is necessary, to examine the worker's activity to see if it is wasteful of energy or time, to examine the process in the context of the whole operation to see if the process is being facilitated or impeded by other activities such as the delivery schedule of the produce, or by physical facilities such as the limited availability of salad-washing sinks.

Expressed more formally, the operational manager is analyzing the process, the man-process and work activity. He can then address the process with method improvement techniques, or address the man-process with efficiency measures, or address the work design or labor utilization improvement, whichever is necessary.

In each instance, the analysis consists of dividing the whole procedure into its components. In analyzing the process, the operational manager lists the steps necessary for the operation and then classifies

LABOR ANALYSIS SHEET

DEPARTMENT _____ DAY _____ DATE _____
(OR SECTION)
(OR EMPLOYEE CLASSIFICATION)   PERIOD: _____

TOTAL SALES (OR PRODUCTION UNITS) _____
TOTAL CUSTOMERS   _____
TOTAL LABOR COST   _____

PERIOD HOURS	SALES PRODUCTION (1)		CUSTOMERS		LABOR (2)	
	Dollars/Units	Percent Total	Count	Percent Total	Cost*	Percent Total
6:00						
6:30						
7:00						
7:30						
8:00						
8:30						
9:00						
9:30						
10:00						
10:30						
11:00						
11:30						
12:00						
12:30						
1:00						
1:30						
2:00						
2:30						
3:00						
3:30						
4:00						
4:30						
5:00						
5:30						
6:00						

(1) Dollar Sales or Units Produced, ex: dishes washed, burgers made
(2) Computed for each 1/2 hour paid by totaling number of workers in each job category present times rate (for 30 minutes) for each category: totaling category totals.

Figure 5.3. Labor analysis.

them as productive or non-productive, that is, as advancing the process from one stage to another or not advancing it. In formal process analysis this consists of arranging the steps in five categories: operation, movements, delays, storages, and inspections. Once analyzed, the process can be improved by combining operations, reducing delays, or eliminating steps.

In analyzing the man-process, the operator again tries to identify the component elements of the procedure. His task is made more difficult because of the multiplicity of brief actions involved in a minute of a man's work. A procedure such as washing produce may legitimately take 3 hours and be comprised of only a dozen major steps (to be reduced to ten) but a man involved in the same process may be moving constantly for the three hours with every movement of both his hands representing a step in the process. Although it is surely possible to analyze the man-process completely, it demands special training, often special equipment such as film, cameras, and a rather considerable investment in time. For the operational manager, a more reasonable approach is to identify those movements which are in gross violation of the rules of motion economy and attempt to correct them.

Work activity analysis can be most rewarding for the operational manager. In this instance, the operational manager is trying to determine what percentage of the time the man, or the man and machine or man and facility system are productive. If the man is not productive for a significant percentage of the time, then this problem has to be addressed by better equipment, better work design, or better facilities organization.

The basic study procedure is to clearly focus on a particular activity and then make numerous random observations of the work location, noting whether or not the activity is being performed. The presumption necessarily is that the man would work if he could. If a man loading a truck is observed a thousand times at random intervals during his working hours and is found to be idle 300 times because there is no produce to load, then he is only 70-percent productive. It can be statistically assumed because of the largeness of the sample that he is idle 30 percent of the time and working only 70 percent. Likewise, if the activity of a cook is observed on a similar basis and he is found to be walking— getting and fetching—30 percent of the time, then he is being only 70-percent productive in the sense that only 70 percent of his time is directly devoted to preparing the food.

As the operational manager need not demonstrate statistical validity, he can limit his sample and be more arbitrary in his time of observations so long as he is able to come away from the analysis with some idea of both the man hours lost and the reasons for the loss.

The nature of many hospitality jobs and procedures almost demands that these analytical techniques be combined. Many workers perform

Productive and Actual Restaurant Employee Man-Hours
per 100 Customers

Department and activity	Production time per 100 customers	Actual time per 100 customers	Per-formance index
DIRECT LABOR			
Meat and Vegetable:	Man-hours	Man-hours	Percent
Preparing meat and vegetables___			
Cooking___			
Filling orders___			
Cleaning stations___			
Walking loaded___			
Walking empty___			
Miscellaneous work___			
Unavoidable delay___			
Nonproductive___			
Total (or average) meat and vegetable preparation___			
Salad:			
Preparing salads___			
Assembling salads___			
Cleaning stations___			
Walking loaded___			
Walking empty___			
Miscellaneous work___			
Unavoidable delay___			
Nonproductive___			
Total (or average) salad preparation___			
Warewashing:			
Washing dishes___			
Washing pots and pans___			
Wrapping silver___			
Cleaning stations___			
Walking loaded___			
Walking empty___			
Cleaning kitchen___			
Cleaning dining room___			
Miscellaneous work___			
Unavoidable delay___			
Nonproductive___			
Total (or average) warewashing___			

Continued

Figure 5.4.   A profile of productivity for an entire operational unit.

Productive and Actual Restaurant Employee Man-Hours
per 100 Customers

Department and activity	Production time per 100 customers	Actual time per 100 customers	Per-formance index
DIRECT LABOR	Man-hours	Man-hours	Percent
Customer service:			
Walking loaded			
Walking empty			
Serving customers			
Clearing table			
Setting up tables			
Picking up orders			
Miscellaneous work			
Unavoidable delay			
Nonproductive			
Total (or average) customer service			
Bar:			
Filling beverage order			
Making change			
Walking loaded			
Walking empty			
Washing glasses			
Clearing bar			
Miscellaneous work			
Unavoidable delay			
Nonproductive			
Total (or average) bar			
Total (or average) direct labor			
INDIRECT LABOR			
Storeroom attendants			
Cashiers			
Housekeepers and repairmen			
Managers			
Total (or average) indirect labor			

a multiplicity of tasks which cannot be studied by any one method. The manager develops a sense of the operation and notes the important aspects of the procedure and the worker's activity so that he can attempt to improve them.

LABOR UTILIZATION IMPROVEMENT

The individual operational manager after completing a study of the productivity of his unit usually has some idea of the cost of excess labor to his operation. It can be a staggering figure. In several "successful" operations studied, if the excess labor purchased could be eliminated the profits would triple. An individual operation may have a labor cost of 30, 40, or 50 percent in excess of its true needs.

A considerable part of the excess cost may be generated by bad management practices. The problem is not so much in the individual worker's productivity or the system's ability to produce but in the misuse of labor, improper labor scheduling, and poor control of labor costs.

Management failings in this area can be broadly categorized as concerning:

1. Organization
2. Scheduling
3. Personnel policies
4. Cost analysis

Organization

Organizational errors result in excessive labor costs: too many jobs are created, jobs are overspecified and job categories are made too rigid.

The first step in organizing a hospitality unit or reorganizing an existing unit is a listing of the personnel needed for the operation based on the manager's estimate of the potential volume (in sales or in work load) of the unit. The manager estimates the jobs and the number of people needed in each job category. For example, he might list: *front desk clerks, 2;* or *hatcheck girl, 1,* and *cigarette girl, 1.* A rough job breakdown before him, the manager asks himself if each of the jobs is necessary or if any can be eliminated. Can the potential sales of the dining room really justify both a hatcheck girl and a cigarette girl?

If the job cannot be eliminated, can it be combined with another job so that the need for the employee is eliminated and the work still done? Is the second front desk clerk necessary or can the night auditor function as both a night desk clerk and a night auditor? Is the service bartender necessary for lunch or can the waiters get cocktails from the lounge bar?

When there is no way of eliminating the individual or the job, the manager tries to downgrade the job. Many hospitality jobs are over-specified. Just as the operation pays for goldplating in materiel purchases (Chapter 6) it pays for personnel qualities it does not need. Some job specifications for fairly undemanding jobs are so overwritten that the Secretary of State would have difficulty qualifying. In many operations expensive dining room captains can be seen taking reservations, and food and beverage controllers reconciling registers. While the quality of service and the standards of the operation should not be compromised, there is a definite need to accurately categorize a job so that the person with the minimal qualifications and rate can be hired.

For his own convenience, the operational manager sometimes makes the job categories in his unit too rigid: it is easier to write schedules and complete payroll. Suiting his convenience becomes costly to the operation when an employee cannot be used to avoid overtime in another section. Although there may be union imposed limitations on the manager's ability to combine jobs, he should at least build flexibility, to whatever extent he is permitted, into his organizational structure. In most instances, it is the manager's desire for nice neat organizational charts and work schedules that are costly, not union restrictions. The only real limit on this kind of an effort is the ability of the employee to produce acceptably in a variety of jobs.

There is also a reluctance on the part of operational managers to use part-time workers and transient workers because of the managerial effort involved. There is a tendency rather to build up a crew of regulars whom the manager can "count on." Meaning more precisely, a crew which he does not have to supervise as closely. Unless the manager can demonstrate that part-time workers or transient labor cost the operation more because of their lower productivity, poorer production, or greater waste, he has an obligation to keep no more than a bare-bones skeleton crew on the full-time payroll.

Scheduling

There is exactly one major principle for the effective scheduling of personnel: schedule the workers when the work is. As obvious as this seems, it is almost never applied. Most hospitality workers are scheduled in continuous shifts which begin and end at fixed times. Everybody in the kitchen reports at 7:00 a.m. and leaves at 4:00 p.m. There is thus the presumption that they can work continuously throughout the day.

The workload in that same period however may be distributed in an entirely different pattern. If the cooks of the kitchen are considered, it may be heaviest at the lunch period from 11:30 to 2:30. If the dishwashers are considered it may be heaviest from 12:30 to 4:00 p.m. The manager does not notice any problem because he has staffed for the heaviest period. He has enough cooks at noon and he has enough dish-washers after lunch so everything is "running smoothly." In fact, he is paying personnel for doing little or nothing for a good part of the day.

If the problem is extended to the entire work day or to the work week with the manager consistently staffing for the peaks of business such as dinner on Friday and Saturday nights, the cost to the operation is horrendous.

The basic premise of good scheduling is first to analyze the work load and determine the hourly pace of activity. The manager makes a time schedule or a graph and notes how many customers reach the front desk, or how many guests use the swimming pool, or how many sand-wiches are being made. If he has done some productivity analysis he should have some idea of how many customers a clerk can accommo-date, how many sunbathers a cabana boy can service, how many sandwiches a cook can produce per hour. He has a time standard. It then becomes a fairly simple matter to determine how many clerks or cabana boys or cooks he will need during a given hour. He can make allowances for individual productivity rates, for personal needs, for coffee breaks and still relate the number of people needed to the work load. If his time standard has been based on a normal worker's pace during a full work-ing day, the manager will be correct in his scheduling.

The best way to schedule on a work load basis is to consider the labor in terms of "slots," not individual workers. A need for 5 clerks at 7:00 p.m. means that there are 5 slots to fill at 7:00 p.m., ignoring for the moment that Jim, Pat, Bob, Bill, and Fred are desk clerks. The slots are indicated on the schedule so that labor scheduled corresponds to the work to be done. When the schedule is finished it may be apparent that five individual schedules have been written, each with a different starting time and quitting time, and perhaps each with a different num-ber of scheduled hours. There may be only 3 continuous hours when all 5 slots appear, otherwise during the day 1, 2, 3 or 4 clerks are needed. This schedule would represent the complete utilization of the labor purchased.

The manager cannot always achieve full utilization because his ability to schedule personnel exactly when he wants is limited. A union con-tract may mandate that a worker be given no less than five hours work if he is called in. If one of the slots scheduled were only 4 hours, a non-productive hour would have to be added. A valuable, hard-to-replace worker might not accept a certain starting time. Adjustments to suit contractual obligations and personal needs are made at this point, after the schedule has been developed, so that at least the man-ager is aware of his alternatives.

Seeing the schedule with this perspective not only results in stag-

SLOT SCHEDULING LABOR
(WORK SHEET)

DEPARTMENT: _____ SHIFT: _____ SECTION: _____

DAY: _____

	HOUR PERIOD:				MON.									TUES.									
		7	8	9	10	11	12	1	2	3	4	5	8	9	10	11	12	1	2	3	4	5
1	FORECAST FOR HOUR:																					
2	ACTUAL PER HOUR:																					

3	JOB CATEGORY ( )	4 STANDARD																					
	SLOTS																						
	1																						
	2																						
	3																						
	4																						
	5																						
	6																						
	7																						
	8																						
	9																						
	10																						

1. Forecast of either dollar volume, units of production, or customers.
2. Actual operational data: volume of dollars, units of production, or customers to be completed afterwards.
3. Job category such as waiter, cook, utility man, etc.
4. Standard of labor productivity such as: 1 waitress per 10 customers per hour.
   1 waitress per 100 dollars volume.

Using worksheet: Divide forecast figure by standard for each hour. Make X in vertical column under hour number for each worker needed in that hour to accommodate business. When worksheet is complete, slot schedules can be read across on numbered slot, complete with workers' names.

Figure 5.5. Slot schedule worksheet: Workers are scheduled as labor units. Schedules evolved are then assigned to particular individuals.

gered scheduling of employees, which is generally more productive, but actually allows the manager to reduce full-time crews. The extra slots on the schedule can be filled with part-time workers, if they are available, just for the peak periods. Or perhaps it makes sense to pay one individual overtime for a limited period each week because his extra hours cost the operation far less than maintaining a full-time person at the regular rate when he is only really needed for a short time. Overtime may be a nasty word in some operations, but it certainly makes more sense to pay a worker time and a half for 2 hours' work, than to pay another worker straight time for 8 hours.

A schedule which is related to the work load also allows the manager to schedule split shifts when this practice is permitted by labor agreements or local labor laws. Instead of hiring one warewasher for dinner and another for lunch, a total of 16 hours, the manager whose schedule reveals that a man is only needed 4 hours each meal, schedules one man to work during each period. The man may work "8 over 12" that is, 8 paid hours during a total period of 12 hours. Quite obviously the manager can afford to pay a substantial premium to the employee and still reduce his labor costs.

If the entire unit is scheduled so that there is a correspondence of workers scheduled to work load, it may become apparent to the manager that he can construct 8-hour continuous days for some workers only by having them work in several sections. The front desk clerk for example may spend 4 hours in the night club as host. A warewasher may work on vegetable preparation and then as a warewasher. When the workers are adaptable, and jobs are not too diverse, this method of scheduling is more beneficial than scheduling part-time workers because of reduced administrative costs.

Sometimes managers need to prepare a "short" or "interval" schedule for each employee instead of a weekly schedule that indicates starting times. The short schedule tells the worker what he should be doing at definite times each day. It is less confusing for the individual than a master schedule for the entire unit with a multitude of starting times and symbols representing work sections.

A schedule has to be seen as a management tool for effective labor utilization. It has to be changed to respond to any changes in work load. Even good stagger schedules making use of split shifts and part-time workers cannot be used routinely from week to week unless business is identical each week.

Personnel Policies

The quality of supervision, the efficacy of communication, the success of morale building and many of the other significant aspects of management which have been discussed in prior chapters have a considerable impact on worker productivity. If the operational manager is generally effective he will be able to limit these rather potent productivity inhibitors: turnover, absenteeism, and tardiness.

Turnover can increase the overall cost of labor. A worker must be hired to replace a worker who quits or is fired. Necessarily, this means the additional cost of recruitment and personnel administration. It also means that the worker has to be trained in his new job with a resultant loss of productivity on his part while he is being trained and while he is mastering the job. Perhaps more importantly, it means a loss in productivity for anyone who is involved in his training or supervision. New workers are also likely to have a higher percentage of error, waste, and breakage. Although many hospitality jobs have been designed to allow the easy replacement of one unskilled worker with another, thereby making the dollar cost of turnover somewhat less for the hospitality operation than for the industrial corporation, some cost is obviously incurred. It may only be the indirect cost of maintaining a personnel office staff. However, the cost is indisputable.

Any of the morale builders and motivational aids suggested in Chapters 3 and 4 will work to some extent to limit turnover.

Absenteeism presents another problem. At the very least, the hospitality unit's performance is compromised when other workers have to stretch out to cover for the absent worker. Absenteeism can have an even greater effect on general productivity indices. Managers faced with considerable absenteeism tend to overstaff, seriously compromising the unit overall productivity. Morale building and discussion with the worker of the importance to the group of his efforts may help reduce the problem.

Many hospitality workers are not particularly susceptible to an appeal for team spirit. Operational managers who avoid the problems of absenteeism successfully find that the best approach is to plan for it. Workers are cross-trained so that productivity and quality are not unduly compromised. Back-up systems are developed. A shadow crew is cultivated in other departments so that the operation manager can snag a replacement worker as he goes off the shift. Finally, the operational manager tries to find out when the worker is leaving, or when he needs "a few days off." If the operational manager does not pretend that a 50-year-old warewasher is on the threshold of an ennobling career in the hospitality industry, the warewasher will not. He can be asked when he intends to leave; "The job is yours as long as you want it, just tell me a couple of days before you take off, okay?" If the worker obviously considers the fruit of his labor as a measure of how much fruit of the vine it will purchase, then the manager can schedule him for a couple of days off to recover his emotions—at every pay day. If the operational manager is realistic he can schedule tightly and still avoid the penalties of absenteeism. Naivete is the principal problem here, not the absenteeism.

Tardiness has to be dealt with seriously: the integrity of the schedule is being attacked. Often the manager is being tested. Some form of immediate discipline ranging from a reprimand for the first offense to a "docking" of pay for repeated offenses is in order. At the same time, the operational manager should reconsider the schedule, perhaps the employee knows something he does not. If it means that they will have to rush through their work, most workers will not arrive late.

Cost Analysis

Decisions involving labor utilization can only be properly founded in a constant awareness of the cost of labor. Overtime becomes excessive when the manager scheduling the workers does not consider that there is a radical change in his costs when a worker works a seventh day, or more than the regular work week. Labor costs build when the manager does not recognize that a tip credit can make a gratuity worker less expensive even at overtime than a straight time minimum wage worker.

The allowable deductions for room and board and for board alone can affect the basic costs of the worker to the operation. As they differ substantially from one area to another and in cost to the operation from one operation to another, generalization is difficult. It can be said that deductions should be a factor when the manager is scheduling or even hiring. The ability to pay lower than minimum wages to students and special dispensations from the local minimum wage laws for certain classes of hospitality operation can also affect basic labor costs.

The manager must clearly identify, by his rate, every category of worker likely to be in his unit and should be able to compute the real cost to the operation under various conditions of employment: overtime or straight time, room and board, board but live-out, no room and board deduction, student or non-student pay, gratuity or non-gratuity. Combinations of these factors result in pay rates which are dramatically different. A room and board gratuity student minimum wage worker might have a cash rate (money which will be paid the worker) of only 52 cents an hour while a no deduction non-gratuity, non-student minimum wage worker will cost the full $2.30 minimum wage. Both are minimum wage workers. As these examples are based on regulations that are constantly convulsed by change and confused by overlapping federal and state statutes, they should not be assumed to be generally

PAYROLL ANALYSIS

MONTH_____   WEEK ENDING_____

JOB CLASSIFICATION	DOLLAR PAYROLL								MAN-HOURS							
	LAST MONTH		THIS MONTH		LAST WEEK		THIS WEEK		LAST MONTH		THIS MONTH		LAST WEEK		THIS WEEK	
	EST.	ACTUAL	EST.	ACTUAL	EST.	ACTUAL	EST.	ACTUAL	EST.	ACTUAL	EST.	ACTUAL	EST.	ACTUAL	EST.	ACTUAL

Figure 5.6. Payroll analysis form for controlling cost of labor.

applicable. The lesson is applicable: the manager has to know the rate of specific individual employees. If he has difficulty in keeping apprised of the law, the accounting office of the operation, or the personnel department, or the State Department of Employment can assist him. After determining the employee's wage rate he then has to compute the cost of benefits (including paid holidays and vacations) which can add as much as 20 or 30 percent to the wage rate.

It is only by knowing the real cost of labor to the operation for a particular process or function that the manager can decide among the several alternatives which are possible in many hospitality operations using labor in the "traditional manner," purchasing the labor from an outside source, or buying a labor-saving device.

Although there may be decision factors other than the cost of labor in these choices (see Chapter 6), labor is certainly a principal factor. Should the operation rent linen from a laundry or process the linen within the hotel? Should the operation buy a particular food product ready-to-cook or ready-to-serve or make it from scratch, almost from scratch, or from prefabricated components? Should the operation peel potatoes by hand? Peel them by machine? Or buy them peeled? The basis for all these decisions is an accurate knowledge of the productivity of the workers, specifically the standard (amount normally produced in a given time) and the real rate being paid the workers involved. Then the operation's real cost for the procedure can be compared with the cost of outside performance or machine performance.

WORK DESIGN IMPROVEMENT

The fundamental task of the manager is to keep the unit's employees working continuously and productively throughout their scheduled working time. If a worker is idle because "there is no work" or forced to spend part of his time unproductively, the manager, not the worker, is at fault. The manager's observations of man-hour productivity can reveal the extent of the problem. Sampling the unit's activity by repeated observation can show that workers spend a considerable amount of time waiting for supplies, waiting to start one phase of a process while some other worker completes a prior phase, waiting for equipment to be available. Sampling can also show that a good deal of the worker's time is spent in non-productive activity, although certainly he is "working." Instead of actually performing the job for which he was hired, a worker spends a considerable amount of time gathering supplies, preparing to work, moving his product from his work space and so on. Even a single aspect of this non-productive activity can occupy a significant fraction of a worker's day. If the time that cooks, waitresses and janitors

LABOR COST PROJECTION

JOB CLASSIFICATION	1 REQUIRED DAILY HOURS	2 ANNUAL WORK HOURS REQUIRED	3 ANNUAL HOURS ACTUALLY WORKED	4 PERSONNEL REQUIRED (Col. 2 ÷ Col. 3)	5 AVERAGE ANNUAL COST*	6 TOTAL COST (Col. 4 x Col. 5)

TOTAL _____

*Wages plus benefits

Figure 5.7. Labor cost projection on an annual basis: foundation for budgeting and expense forecasting.

spend walking is calculated, the manager may discover that they are losing 25 to 30 percent of their day in walking alone.

The time lost either in waiting or in unproductive activity has a manifest impact on the productivity of the unit. The workers are being paid during these periods, and that pay must be apportioned over the productive periods of the work day. If a worker earns $2.30 an hour for an 8-hour day but is only working productively for 6 hours, his labor cost for work actually done has increased more than 30 percent.

Work design improvement on the operational level has two important thrusts: better planning of work to reduce idle time and better organization of work system to reduce unproductive activity.

Better Planning

While food production provides many dramatic examples of planning failures resulting in idle workers, the problem exists in every hospitality department. Clerks wait for charge control forms from various units so that they can post guest bills. Maintenance men wait until a fork lift becomes available so that they can install a ventilation system. Groundsmen wait for the dew to evaporate so that they can mow lawns. And certainly, sauce cooks wait for butchers to finish the meat order and pantrymen wait for the produce to clear the receiving area.

REAL-TIME PLANS

Although the manager may have planned these activities carefully he has not given his plans an essential dimension: real time. Perhaps everyone concerned knows *what* has to be done and *how* it should be done, but the essential element *when* has not been considered adequately. If any activity is considered as a series of steps, some steps *must* precede others, some steps can be performed at the same time as others, and some steps *may* be performed before or after others. The meat for the stew *must* be butchered *before* it is cooked. The stock for the stew *can* be prepared *before* or *while* the meat is being butchered. The garnish vegetables *may* be prepared *before, during,* or *after* the butchering or the cooking of the meat. The efficient plan reflects these considerations: the meat is scheduled to be butchered so it is ready when the cooks are ready for it. The stock is started so that it is ready by the time the meat is butchered. The vegetable production is scheduled so that the vegetables are ready when the stew is ready; before the production of the stew or during the production or after the production; whenever the time is available because the vegetable production is not critical to any other step.

It is virtually impossible for the manager to consider the total func-

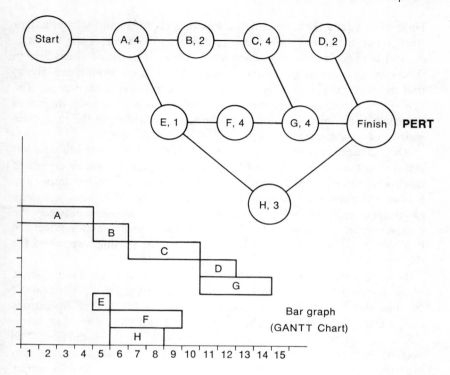

Job	Duration	Job which must precede it.
A	4 hours	. . . . .
B	2 hours	A
C	4 hours	A, B
D	2 hours	A, B, C
E	1 hour	A
F	4 hours	A, E
G	4 hours	A, B, C, F
H	3 hours	A, E

Note: E could be started any time up to the sixth hour without delaying project. H could be started up to the twelfth hour without delaying project, etc.

Figure 5.8. Eight jobs scheduled by PERT and GANTT charts.

tioning of his unit with this much detail. Only a computer planning system such as the PERT/CPM (Program Evaluation and Review Technique/Critical Path Method), used first to develop the Polaris missile and now used for planning large industrial projects, can effectively handle such detail completely. The operational manager's responsibility is trouble shooting the unit's activity for real-time problems.

He tries to isolate those tasks that are critical to others and schedule their start so that there is adequate time to complete them before the activities on which they depend are scheduled to begin. He tries to schedule in the same time slot those activities that can be done simultaneously so that the total time necessary to complete the process is shortened. The process of preparing lunch to be ready at noon is obviously shortened if the spaghetti sauce, the soup, and the stew are started at the same time instead of in a series.

The manager also tries to fill the worker's time by tentatively scheduling non-critical work. It would place undue pressure on everyone if tasks were to be completed exactly on the deadline for their completion. Rather, the manager schedules non-critical tasks to fill in whatever slack or margins exist in the schedule. For example, the time between the completion of preparation for lunch and the actual lunch service can be spent in making puff-paste hors d'oeuvres, or peeling vegetables for the next day.

Much of this concern with real time was part of the common sense of the hospitality craftsmen. Traditionally, the manager did not "think" for the chef or the head of maintenance. As hospitality operations evolved to place more emphasis on equipment systems using semi-skilled labor, brains as well as skilled hands were eliminated. The present workers in a chefless kitchen may have no sense of the real time imperatives involved in foodservice. The manager has to supply them, as well as the operational plan.

EQUIPMENT UTILIZATION

He also has to consider the equipment utilization. Often workers are not waiting for a step in a process to be completed, they are waiting for a piece of equipment being used in another procedure to become available. Use of equipment, like time, has to be planned. In this instance, the activity of the entire unit over a period of time has to be considered, not just individual steps in a single procedure. The separate single procedures are linked by common equipment utilization. The making of rolls can proceed independently from the preparation of meat loaf if the operation has enough mixing machines and oven space to allow the mixing of dough and the grinding of the meat, the baking of the rolls and the cooking of the meat to be scheduled simultaneously. When there is only one mixer, and one oven, the two procedures have to be coordinated so that each can proceed without a delay occurring in the other.

As the piece of equipment is the key, its use is scheduled. Constructing a chart with time intervals, for example the hours in a shift, across the top and the equipment being considered along one side, allows the various procedures using the equipment to be plotted so that they do not overlap.

If the mixer must be used for both rolls and meat loaf, the total time for these procedures and the actual mixing time in each procedure is determined. Then the total procedure time is marked on the chart along with the time scale, with the mixing time clearly indicated perhaps by a slashed line or second color. When both procedures are plotted it becomes obvious that within the total time available for the use of the machine they can be started earlier or later so that the two mixing periods (plus a clean-up period between them) do not overlap.

When total required machine time exceeds total available machine time, the manager has to either change the method to utilize another piece of equipment or change the procedures so that there is a scheduled delay or a reordering of steps. The meat, for example, may be chopped in a vertical cutter, or the roll dough may be mixed earlier and held in a retarder.

The problem exists in departments other than the kitchen. In most hospitality operations the use of rolling carts and trucks, banquet tables and chairs, floor machines, wet/dry vacuum cleaners, and other multi-purpose equipment has to be carefully scheduled to avoid delays.

Better Organization of the Work System

A work system consists of men, machines, and material functionally interacting. Many hospitality activities are based on a work system of one kind or another: the racking of rooming slips, the washing of dishes, the distribution of linen, all involve men, machines, and materials in interdependent relationships.

A better organization of the work system speeds the work and increases the productivity of the system by limiting delays within the system and transportation time or costs between elements of the system. If the system is considered to be a series of stations through which the work passes, then the object of work design is to limit the time the work spends in each station and limit the time between stations. Detours, slowdowns, bottlenecks, dams, by-passes, cloverleaves, pit stops, traffic jams, or lane closings, which describe conditions of impeded flow in other situations, all have their parallels in work systems. The manager can eliminate some of the impediments to the flow of work in his particular unit by the application of 10 basic organizational principles. Other problems that he may discover will require major capital investment to improve: electronic data-processing equipment, mechanized materials handling equipment, or structural changes in the facility, and this will require the collaboration of higher level management.

Keep work flow moving in one direction. The work should move in a short straight line. For example, a maid cleaning a bathroom may be observed to be backtracking, crisscrossing, changing direction as she moves from the sink to the bath to the towel rack, etc. If these changes of direction are eliminated by better organization through a reexamination of the sequence of procedures, the work is speeded.

Make work centers as close to self-sustaining as possible. Getting supplies and preparing to work are non-productive. The sandwich station in a kitchen is usually a good work center because it is self-sustaining. Other stations may require that the cook charge all over the kitchen. These should be re-engineered. A work center need not be fixed to be self-sustaining. A properly equipped janitorial cart used for cleaning public lavatories is a good example of a mobile self-sustaining work center that saves endless time. Consider: the at-handness of raw materials, in-process storage, storage of finished products, and waste disposal.

Design the work center around the human element of the system. It is possible to customize the equipment and to modify the materials. It is virtually impossible to re-engineer the humans involved in a system. This rather obvious proposition is frequently violated. Only a phenomenal athlete can place dishes in the conveyor of a flight type dishwasher so that the machine is operating at full capacity.

Limit the length of dense work flow. Most facilities are used for several purposes, that is, the same elements are used in several different systems. For example, a particular room may be used for both bar and foodservice: a beverage service system and a foodservice system are functioning. The arrangement of the elements in the facility—the service bar, the refrigeration, the cashier, etc.—should correspond to the service with the most activity, or densest flow. Compromises are often necessary in work systems: the equipment needs of the breakfast service in a kitchen may not exactly correspond to the dinner needs; the night auditor and the cashier share the same station, etc.

Handle products, raw materials, and work in bulk. Work of any type should be organized in batches so that the preparation time necessary to do the work is spread over a greater number of units. It is more efficient to shampoo ten upholstered chairs at once, than ten chairs one at a time.

Gang produce. Assembly line techniques and mass production can be applied to many hospitality operations very effectively. In the kitchen, preparation for meal service is too often influenced by the organizational system used for the meal service itself. A dozen cooks independently work at the positions they will occupy during the meal service. Six batches of chopped onion are prepared, 6 batches of chopped parsley,

8 pots of melted butter. A more efficient system would organize the production so that preparations are consolidated. As well, the labor of all the cooks could be used systematically. Ten men in an hour can assemble many more chef salad bowls, than one man working for ten hours, no matter how well organized he is.

Use machines instead of men. When an operation owns a machine, it is undoubtedly more efficient to use it than a man. Even if the machine is "slower" the cost of operating the machine for an hour is fractionally that of a man-hour and the man is liberated for other work. The manager often has a selling job to do: The worker has to be convinced that a crepe machine producing 6 crepes a minute is more efficient than a cook who produces 24 in the same amount of time but at much greater cost.

The case for the purchase of a machine can be made on the same basis. In addition to operating costs, acquisition costs have to be considered.

Assign the unavoidable non-productive work to the cheapest labor. Because many facilities are used for several purposes, a completely functional design is rare. Some transportation of work and change of work flow are almost inevitable. At this point the manager can decide *who* is to handle the transportation. While kitchen runners, plumbers' helpers, and barboys can be excessive cost items, it is reasonable to attempt to let a cheaper worker do the walking, lugging, and hauling.

Position elements of the system so that the process sequence is respected. Large offices are frequently arranged inefficiently because the arrangement of desks and cubicles is governed by status among employees rather than process sequence. A piece of paper being processed, for example, a purchase order, crisscrosses among the desks because the third person who should see it is also the most senior clerk and merits the desk near the window.

Clean dish storage is placed near the start of the dishwashing line instead of the end: the glasses in the bar are the length of the bar away from the ice which is near the register, an unnecessarily out-of-process sequence.

Build flexibility into the design. The use of facilities for several purposes and the ever changing nature of the hospitality business suggests that equipment be easily moved if not out and out mobile. Placing machines on wheels, or rolling carts—with some provision for anchoring the machine when it is in use—allows different configurations of equipment used as part of different systems or by different people. A frying station for example might be arranged quite differently when it is being used for processing veal cutlets during a preparation period and processing French fried potatoes during a meal service. Likewise, a left-handed cook might require an entirely different arrangement from that of a right-handed cook to operate at full efficiency.

METHOD IMPROVEMENT

In many respects, the techniques and concerns of the manager in attempting to improve the method by which a particular task is performed parallel his approach to work design. In method improvement the target is smaller. Instead of attempting to upgrade an entire function or the activities of an entire unit over a period of time, the manager is concentrating on a single particular task.

There are five basic steps in any work improvement program.

1. Pick a job to improve
2. Analyze the job in detail
3. Question every detail
4. Develop a new method
5. Implement the new method

Although each step involves both the manager and the worker using the method, there is a change in the degree of participation as the program progresses. Ultimately, the worker and the manager must cooperate to implement the new method. Selling the workers on the new method is a hidden sixth item in the program. In no other area is there so much resistance to change. The most loyal, cooperative, and skilled workers resist a method change. In fact, it is far easier to introduce a new system to workers who do not know that they are not supposed to do it that way than to alter the traditional methods of experienced personnel. Some of the most productive hospitality operations in the country deliberately hire unskilled workers rather than professionals so that only their methods are known to the worker. One young cook produces 5 or 6 hundred dinners single-handed, warewashers process the dishes from 4 thousand dollars worth of business because nobody ever told them they were not supposed to be able to do that, *and* they were given a productive method.

Frequently, workers who have been "convinced" revert to the old method in small stages, hoping that the manager's reluctance to confront them over "trivial" details will let them continue to subvert the method improvement. In some work climates the employees actually sabotage the testing and the implementation of the new method.

There are fewer problems with methods improvement if there is a general spirit of cooperation between the workers involved and the manager. Early participation also allows the particularly adroit manager to convince the workers that it was their idea all along and he is just helping with the details.

In tense circumstances where more cooperation and participation are impossible, supervision and strong discipline serve instead.

Pick a Job to Improve

In the course of observing the operation with increasing productivity in mind, the manager sees jobs which simply seem to be tedious, wasteful, or involved. He does some quick calculations and discovers that it is costing the operation a proverbial fortune for some tasks that do not really contribute significantly to the success of the operation. If the job cannot be eliminated (Do we really need napkins folded into viking ships?) he targets it for method improvement. Cleaning the chandeliers in the main lobby of a hotel might be a good illustration. In this particular situation, the floor cleaners must wait until the chandeliers are cleaned before beginning the floors; the work involves 2 men for 3 hours; often some of the hanging pendants are broken; the job is seldom done really well. It has all the elements of a job for which method improvement is needed. It is a bottleneck in the general functioning of the unit, a labor intensive procedure, expensive because of the material lost, and generally inefficient.

Analyze the Job in Detail

The job being targeted has to be observed repeatedly so that all the facts about the present method are known as well as the particular job's interactions with related tasks.

If the employees cleaning the chandeliers were watched carefully and every detail of their work noted, some of the problems of the method would become apparent. The employees go up and down ladders numerous times. They are constantly shifting drop cloths in a usually unsuccessful effort to protect the floor. They must make several trips to a custodial closet to rinse rags, etc.

Question Every Detail

Once the job is broken down into its component steps they can be examined. Some formal method might be considered by which those steps not directly related to the purpose of the activity—washing the chandelier—are isolated. Or the manager may simply question each detail, by asking himself why, precisely, it is necessary.

Is it necessary to ascend and descend the ladder? Why? Are drop

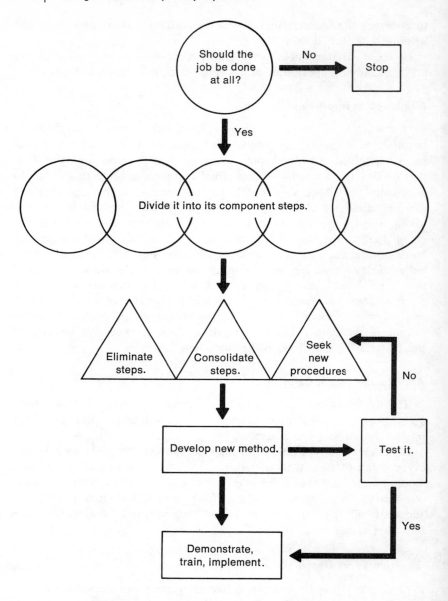

Figure 5.9.   Method improvement step by step.

cloths the only method of protecting the floor? Is there an alternative to washing, rinsing, and drying every pendant with a succession of cloths? Can more accessible water be supplied? Does it have to be done at that particular time of day? Who originated the present cleaning method? Who is doing the job? What alternative methods have been explored?

Develop A New Method

Some of the answers to the questions posed will be productive. Others will lead nowhere. The new method evolves from the weighing of several different alternatives for each step of the process. Activities are combined. The sequence of steps is altered. Techniques are borrowed from other tasks.

In this hypothetical example, there are several opportunities for

```
                    METHOD IMPROVEMENT ANALYSIS

    DEPARTMENT_____ DATE_____ BY_____

    Procedure Studied:_____
    Work Done By:_____
    Equipment, Tools:_____Classification:_____Rate:_____

                          COMPARISON
    _____
           PRESENT METHOD              PROPOSED METHOD
    _____
                        Standard                    Standard
            STEP BY STEP    Time  Cost    STEP BY STEP   Time  Cost
    1.                              1.
    2.                              2.
    3.                              3.
    4.                              4.
    5.                              5.
    6.                              6.
    7.                              7.
    8.                              8.
    9.                              9.
    10.                             10.
                 COST                         COST
    Labor:_____      Labor:_____
    Materials:_____      Materials:_____
    Misc:_____      Misc:_____
       (Energy)_____         (Energy)_____
    TOTAL_____      TOTAL_____

        ESTIMATE OF SAVINGS          COST OF CHANGE
    Cost of Old Method_____           Acquisition  Annual
    Less Cost of New Method =_____  Equipment_____
              X                     Installation_____
    Yearly Repetitions_____    Training_____
              =                              First Year  Yearly
    Annual Savings_____    Total Cost_____

        SAVINGS FIRST YEAR
    (Annual Savings Less Cost of Change First Year):_____

        ANNUAL SAVINGS
    (Annual Savings Less Annual Cost):        _____

        OR
    CHANGE "PAYS FOR ITSELF"              _____MONTHS
```

Figure 5.10. Form for determining cost of implementation and savings gain of a proposed method-improvement plan.

change. If the pendants could all be dampened at once, several steps would be consolidated. The sequence of procedure could be changed, eliminating unnecessary trips up and down the ladder. The major problem is finding a way of applying the water and detergent solution and then capturing the water as it falls from the pendants, without damaging the pendants and without soaking the rug underneath.

A light-canvas umbrella can be suspended inverted under the chandelier. An outlet from the umbrella will lead to a hose running directly into a bucket on the floor. The water and detergent could be sprayed over the pendants from an air compressor. Then the pendants could be rinsed and air-dried.

Implement the New Method

Before the new method can actually be implemented several tests of it are necessary. Will the air compressor blow the pendants off the chandelier? Is the canvas umbrella waterproof? How big should the umbrella be? Before the manager can introduce the workers to the new method he has to experiment fully. Because of the organizational climate in most hospitality operations, the method has to work the first time it becomes standard operating procedure.

When it has been perfected, several demonstrations for the workers are probably necessary. The operational manager has to train them, convince them, and then finally supervise them until the new method is accepted.

INCREASING WORKER EFFICIENCY

In giving his attention to increasing the productivity of the operation by better labor utilization, work design, and method improvement, the manager should not ignore the possibility of improving individual worker performance. In addition to using motivational devices, morale building, and training, which have been discussed in previous chapters, the manager can teach the workers how to work smarter, with less fatigue, and he can attempt to create a work environment that favors human efficiency.

Working Smarter

Both the operational manager and the average worker should ask themselves two essential questions:

1. What does the exceptional worker do that the average worker does not?
2. What does the below average worker and the average worker do that the exceptional worker does not?

In other words, what are the secrets of the exceptional worker and the mistakes common to both average and below average workers, but exaggerated in the below average worker?

Even the most casual consideration of the work habits of the unit's employees will demonstrate that the difference among workers, with productivity, the quality of workers, and personal fatigue as standards, fall into three major categories.

1. Good workers plan their work.
2. Good workers use their equipment properly.
3. Good workers know how to use their bodies and how to pace themselves.

PLANNING THE WORK

A good work plan for an individual has several elements: there is a logical sequence to the performance of the task; tools are placed near their point of use; trips for supplies and equipment are minimized; there is adequate preparation for the job. If the worker cannot develop an effective work plan for himself, the manager must supply it. Managers must teach experienced "housewives" working as maids the efficient method of making a bed. At home they crisscross from side to side, tucking in each article of linen. For increased productivity in the hotel situation, they are taught to place all the linen on the bed from one side, and then tuck it in once.

Even experienced workers in kitchens do not understand the importance of "set-up" or *mis en place*. To make it easier for the worker to actually perform his job, the manager often has to push the worker to process items to the greatest possible extent. Otherwise, people are chopping parsley and cutting lemons with great energy expenditure during the meal service. Almost every hospitality worker can profit by strong preparation during the slack periods so that guest service or job performance can be accelerated during the busy periods. The manager should convince waitresses to pre-prepare a number of guest checks with the heading information complete except for the number of covers, and convince the head bellman to tab index a telephone book so that he can find the section listing movie theaters or dry cleaners easily, and so on.

USING EQUIPMENT PROPERLY

If managers were to instruct workers in 10 basic principles of equipment utilization much lost productivity would be regained.

1. *Have the equipment at hand.* The very least amount of time should be spent reaching and fetching. Workers leave the supplies

or equipment for a sequential operation all over the work center instead of arranging them so that they are handy and in order of use.

2. *Use the right tool for the job.* Putty knives make bad screw drivers, ladles make bad pot hooks, french knives make bad bottle openers, steak knives make bad bar tools but workers throughout the industry try to use them.

3. *Follow the manufacturer's instructions.* The worker does *not* know more about the device or machine than the manufacturer. He has to follow the instructions for use, preventive maintenance, and repair. Sometimes it is necessary for the manager to have the appropriate portions of the manufacturer's booklet made into *large* signs.

4. *Work with the tool, not against it.* A french knife is meant to be used with the point in a fixed position on the cutting board, a carving knife is meant to be parallel to the cutting board, yet workers use them both similarly. A corn broom is meant to be used with a side to side motion, a dust mop is meant to be pushed along the floor in a straight line, yet workers use them both similarly. There are hundreds of instances where the use by the workers turns the functional design of the piece of equipment against its efficient use.

5. *Take care of the equipment.* Improper handling or a failure to provide preventive maintenance and abuse quickly reduces the efficiency of the tool.

6. *Don't make work.* The careless use of tools can generate more work than they save. A vacuum cleaner even with bumpers can mar baseboards and furniture. A mixing machine can spatter 50 square feet of kitchen walls.

7. *Customize equipment when possible.* The manufacturers of equipment do not always have the operation's exact lend use in mind. For example, a squeegee can be cut to exactly accommodate bathroom mirrors. A patch of abrasive material can be sewn on the back of mops so that gum can be scraped from floors. A metal spoon and fork combination can be cut from a standard kitchen spoon for cafeteria-line operations. The side of a kitchen spatula can be sharpened so that the grilled cheese sandwiches can be handled and cut with the same tool.

8. *Use equipment, not muscle.* The manager has to convince the worker to forego feats of strength and exhibitions of maculinity in lifting and hauling. When equipment has just been introduced, he may have to convince the worker that it does the job just as well as the old french knife or the mop and the bucket.

9. *Don't push the equipment.* Vacuums don't work properly unless the bags are emptied. Deep fat fryers take a certain maximum charge of product. Lawn mowers cut grass of only a certain maximum height.

10. *Choose the equipment to suit the worker.* The manager has more responsibility in this area than the worker as he influences purchasing. Two proportionately built individuals, one 5'3" and the other 6'1" are not going to be equally comfortable or equally efficient working with the same sized mop head, broom handle, french knife, table tops, mixer controls or even work station. While only limited adaptations in permanent equipment can be made for particular individuals, some modification can usually be made. Tall cooks can work on piled cutting boards to bring the table height to their level, short cooks can be given small, sturdy, moveable platforms. Personal and small equipment is available in enough different sizes and weights so that individuals can be accommodated.

USING THE HUMAN BODY EFFICIENTLY

The rules of motion economy are patently obvious. It makes sense to try to use both hands instead of just one, or work with the motion that requires the least expenditure of energy such as a finger motion instead of an arm motion. Unfortunately, retraining workers in proper motion economy is as difficult as attempting to teach elephants to waltz. Even when the effort is successful the result is unnatural and clumsy.

Prior training, habits, and the carry-over effect of other activities, from lounging to sports, have a stronger influence on the hospitality worker than the manager's brief instruction. Often hospitality workers in high turnover jobs are simply indifferent. It is easier for a worker to wash a table with two cloths and smooth, symmetrical, rhythmic motions than it is for him to use one cloth and a back-and-forth motion. From his perspective, perhaps rightly, the worker reasons that he is going to go home at 8:00 no matter how he works, and that *thinking* about washing tables *and* washing tables is harder than just washing tables. In the actual work situation, it is difficult to convince workers to follow a work system designed by someone else; dishwashers quit when they are told to stack dishes dirty instead of racking them directly from bus boxes. It is doubly or triply difficult to try to choreograph their movements.

The manager can still improve the utilization of the worker's body by arranging the work center so that the more economical motions are favored. If sinks are fitted with foot treadles that regulate the water the employee is obliged to use his feet to turn it on and off. If garbage chutes are built into kitchen work tables, the worker cannot avoid using gravity to move the waste from the work area. If food items for assembly are placed on a revolving table in front of a narrow assembly area, the worker will find it harder to contrive his own system than to follow the obvious efficient one. If a rolling cart has fixed wheels on the two corners of one side, and wheels that turn 360 degrees in ball bearing sockets on the opposite side, there is only one way a sane person can push it.

Four basic rules of motion economy can generally be applied:

1. Put both hands to work.
2. The path of all motions should be natural and smooth.
3. Motions should be as simple as possible, involving the least body movement to get the job done.
4. Devices and equipment should be used to free hands.

Work Environments that Favor Human Efficiency

A physically comfortable worker works more efficiently. As well, he experiences less fatigue because he is not expending energy in fighting the environment. In other words, in a favorable environment, he can be more productive and work at a productive pace longer.

Both concern for productivity and the Occupational Safety and Health Administration rulings prompt designers to create favorable working conditions in new properties. Older hospitality facilities, although in general compliance with the law, are often environmentally deficient. In many instances, wholesale correction of the problems would demand considerable capital investment. Rather, managers and workers have to resort to "housewifery" to make the circumstances of work more bearable. Four environmental factors should be considered: atmosphere, light, sound, and structural properties.

Many kitchens are too hot, too humid, and inadequately ventilated. The proper conditions should range between 55–77 degrees F temperature, with 50% relative humidity and an airflow between 1–3 feet per second. Adding fan units to increase the circulation of air, insulating pipes carrying steam or hot water (for energy conservation purposes as well as comfort), evacuating steam from dishwashers, and other relatively minor measures can improve many facilities inexpensively.

Illumination in many older properties is insufficient for manual work, reading controls, or the daily paperwork. On the other hand the general lighting can be painfully bright. The electric company can be extremely helpful in both conserving energy (see Chapter 6) and correcting illumination.

Excessive noise is fatiguing. Many operations which have grown beyond their original facilities locate offices and work areas adjacent to compressor rooms, loading docks, metalworking shops, and other noisy areas. The problem is not easily addressed; genuine sound-proofing can be expensive and can restrict ventilation. Rescheduling of one activity so it does not coincide with the other often is the best answer. An examination of the property with this perspective may produce storerooms in quiet areas: perhaps an exchange of some kind can be made.

Deficiencies in the structure such as slippery floors, bumps in floors, narrow aisles, sloping work surfaces often present a safety hazard and a productivity problem. Those conditions which are unsafe must be corrected. Other structural problems can usually be eliminated by ingenuity and some modest reconstruction. Ramping over bumps is usually cheaper than repairing uneven floors. Covering slippery areas with slip-resistant deck boards is less expensive than resurfacing. Uneven work surfaces can be bridged fairly inexpensively. Narrow aisles call for narrow carts, ceiling obstruction and cramped work areas for small workers.

When the environmental conditions cannot be substantially improved an effort should be made to reduce the worker's fatigue. Frequent rest breaks during the course of the day improve overall productivity. Some measure of self-pacing can be allowed individual workers so that they work at a rate more personally suitable for conditions. A decent rest and meal area, nourishing and appealing food also help workers deal with fatigue, both mental and physical.

Frequently some productivity improvement can be made by attention to the worker's clothing. Certainly, adequate coats should be supplied for jobs in the refrigerator and freezer. Protective boots minimize the problem of wet floors. Protective aprons, ear plugs, headbands, wristbands, gloves, and support belts can make the worker more comfortable in many circumstances. In conditions of high heat, the manager can make available salt tablets and glucose-rich candies, as well as ample potable water.

6 | Management of Materiel

Management attention is traditionally devoted to three areas: men, money, and materiel. In the hospitality industry the elaborate and necessary attention paid personnel problems and labor utilization on the one hand and control of operations on the other sometimes obscures management's third concern: management of materiel. The operational manager can improve the profitability of his organization by the exercise of management in the purchasing, ordering, and storing of supplies, the care of the building housing his operation and its equipment, and in the utilization of energy. Cost excesses in these areas are often unnoticed. They tend to generate relatively small day-to-day losses that lack the sudden significance of a rise in labor cost percentage, an irreconcilable cash drawer and register tape, or a refrigerator full of rotten produce.

Ten dollars a day lost because of a poor purchasing specification, the cost of an overstocked item, the accelerated deterioration of the facilities or equipment, or the imprudent use of electricity is as surely $3650 a year lost as is this same sum in unneeded overtime or poorly scooped ice cream or pocketed bar revenues.

In many operations, even those that have maximized the use of their labor and honed operating cost percentages to a fine edge, poor materiel management accounts for much more than 10 dollars a day. One prominent hospitality consulting firm has made its substantial reputation precisely in this area. Although it offers feasibility studies, method engineering, facilities design, control systems, and financial reporting, it is for its ability to improve hospitality management by examining costs that were *always* assumed to be proper, by cuts and slashes at the fat in specifications, inventory procedures, equipment replacement programs, and utility bills that it is best known.

Operational managers can have a special stake in certain aspects of materiel management. It is unlikely that the operational manager will have the opportunity or authority to make a tremendous "buy" in the wholesale meat market, or be able to speculate successfully in the commodity market or design a new wing of rooms for maximum operating efficiency. If he is going to make points for the operation and for himself in the management of materiel it will be at the operational level: reduced day-to-day costs.

PURCHASING

Basic purchasing principles and control systems, and the purchasing procedures for specific products have been articulated in a number of excellent books. It would be impossible and of no real service to repeat them here in a book devoted to wider areas of operations management. Rather, two important managerial concepts are often lost in the volume of material devoted to preparing bids and recognizing ripe avocados: value analysis and make or buy analysis.

Value Analysis

As a concept, value analysis is quite simple: reduce costs by eliminating the gold plating in the products purchased. If a quality or attribute of a food product, cleaning substance, or supply is not needed then the product is costing more than it should, that is, the same product without the gold plating—the unnecessary feature—should be purchased.

In application, value analysis can become extremely complex, as a rather complete knowledge of how the product is used (what qualities are required) and the alternative products in the market—(what is available) is needed. Every product used in the operation can be value analyzed, but generally managers concentrate on those items that represent high dollar value as used. The essential process is to look at the product and its use to eliminate the overspecification. As food products in most operations represent considerable dollar volume of products purchased they present the most profitable example of this procedure.

VALUE ANALYSIS OF FOOD PRODUCTS

For any food product the manager can test 12 elements for appropriateness to his production and preparations:

1. Quality
2. Size
3. Type
4. Format

5. Packaging
6. Proportion
7. Unit of purchase
8. Brand
9. Customization
10. Uniformity
11. Trim
12. Processing

Quality. The quality element of a food specification includes color, grade, appearance, ripeness, condition, etc. A difference in quality does not necessarily mean a difference in fitness for eating or in ultimate quality on the customer's plate. For example, Grade C eggs have the same functional properties, healthfulness, and nutritional value as Grade A eggs. They cannot be used for sunny-side-up eggs because they don't look as nice, but they can be used in baking and cooking.

Grade C chickens or Parts Missing chickens, turkeys, and ducks have been damaged in processing, but how many operations serve whole chickens, ducks, or turkeys. When the customer eats a fried chicken leg or a turkey pot pie he can have no idea of the attractiveness of the fowl before it was prepared.

Size. For many items sold by the *piece,* a difference in size can mean a difference in cost per *unit of measure.* It pays the manager to maintain flexible specifications. For example, sometimes it may pay to purchase larger lemons for bar use as twists and sometimes smaller lemons. A 110 lemon yields about one third more twist than a 165. Although he is buying lemons by the piece (a case of 110 pieces), he really should be costing the "square inches" of lemon peel. Likewise, eggs for cooking can be purchased economically either as large or medium, depending on the cost per ounce of egg.

Sometimes the manager finds that he has overspecified by specifying a small size. Certain items, especially fruits, are cheaper on a cost per piece basis, in larger sizes, because they cannot be sold in supermarkets to home managers.

Type. Overspecification can occur when a manager does not clearly identify the functional properties needed in an item used in a preparation and chooses a type, variety, or formulation of product that offers much more than these specific functional properties. For example, parsley is used for decoration instead of chickory, which is often much cheaper per garnish sprig. Parsley has many properties that chickory does not, among them, texture, aroma, "chopability," but none of them is needed here. A manager may specify table quality salt for cooking use when in fact the property that makes it more expensive than bulk salt, its resistance to caking, is not needed.

Format. Many products are offered in different forms that differ considerably in price. For instance, olives may be purchased as broken "salad" olives instead of perfect individual pieces. Pieces of canned fruit are available.

Sometimes distinctions among formats are more subtle: costing a "sandwich loaf" and a "pullman loaf" on a per slice basis can be a revelation.

Packaging. Packaging costs money both for materials and for labor. The manager might ask himself if he really has to buy potatoes and tomatoes wrapped in paper, vinegar in gallons, sauces in boilable bags, etc. Often he is paying for the materials and labor of the purveyor and for additional labor to unwrap the product.

Sometimes it is also possible to eliminate the cost of cartons, crates, barrels, and boxes, either by returning them to the purveyor, supplying him with transfer containers, or by selling the packaging.

Proportion. When a manager purchases a manufactured product, for example, a soup base or a salad dressing or seasoning salt, he must clearly identify what ingredient of the several that make up the product he wants to purchase and cost it. For example, buying soup bases which contain mostly salt and very little flavor elements is an expensive way to buy salt. A higher priced base can have a lower cost for flavoring. If a manager wants "gelatin" he should not be buying a gelatin dessert which contains mostly sugar.

Unit of purchase. Even experienced managers overspecify in this area. While they effect economies by bulk purchasing some items they do not completely investigate all their alternatives. For example, juices are available in #10 cans at a considerable savings over #5 cans. Condiments such as ketchup, steak sauce, pepper sauce, worcestershire sauce are bought for cooking in table-service units or consumer sizes when they could be purchased in bulk.

Sometimes, bulk buying can be more costly. The manager purchasing products in 55-gallon drums must include in his calculations a considerable amount for handling the drums and for hand pumping.

Brand. Certain companies have unique formulations, especially high standards of manufacture, and specialized sources of ingredients. Others are really relying on packaging and advertising to establish their product's identification. The manager who has specified by brand must ask himself whether he cannot obtain the identical product less expensively from a local purveyor or a supplier to manufacturers.

Customization. A manager tends to assume that a purveyor can perform a processing operation at a lower cost than he himself can, even when a reasonable profit is added. When the processed product has a considerable market this is probably the case: The purveyor can afford a system or machinery that is more efficient.

When the manager is specifying a custom process, however, for example the frenching of lamb chops, he may be generating excessive costs because the purveyor is ill equipped to meet the specification. A highly paid butcher may have to be taken from a meat processing line where he is very productive to do the work of the semi-skilled worker whom the purveyor does not normally employ. On the other hand, the manager usually has this kind of general kitchen labor.

Any specification which is not being mass-produced by the purveyor is likely to be excessively expensive.

Uniformity. Nature is not neat. Somebody has to sort tomatoes, potatoes, carrots, beets, turnips, etc. When the manager can change a specification from a finite dimension to a "field run" he effects considerable savings. He can economize to some extent by broadening any specification. Certainly, all specifications for vegetables for soups, casseroles, purees, and the like should be very carefully examined for excessive uniformity demands.

Trim. Trim of meat is a particularly subtle area of overspecification. Specification of trim is primarily for control. The manager who has specified a 10-inch trim on ribs of beef is primarily concerned with maintaining a standard by which he can compare price per pound of whole ribs. The functional properties of the ribs are not affected by the extent of the trim. The standard per se, does not have a special virtue.

If he specified and accepted less trim, the price per pound of the ribs would go down. Overspecification occurs when the manager demands such extensive trim that the purveyor has by-products which cannot be marketed. Or it occurs when the manager has "given" the purveyor by-products whose value to the manager exceeds the total difference in cost between the trimmed and untrimmed piece. For example, the manager may cause "hamburger meat" and fat to be trimmed from a piece, reducing its cost by $3.00, when if he accepted the trim he might have gotten hamburger for which he has to pay the same purveyor $3.50 and fat which he could sell for $.25 or utilize instead of vegetable oil worth $.75 as a frying medium. Some consideration necessarily must be given the labor involvement in trimming but overspecification of just this type exists when managers do not carefully analyze their trim specifications in relation to changing market prices for by-products and thus miss opportunities for cross-utilization of products.

Processing. Testing the appropriateness of degree of processing obliges the manager to be completely familiar with his costs of operation. Cer-

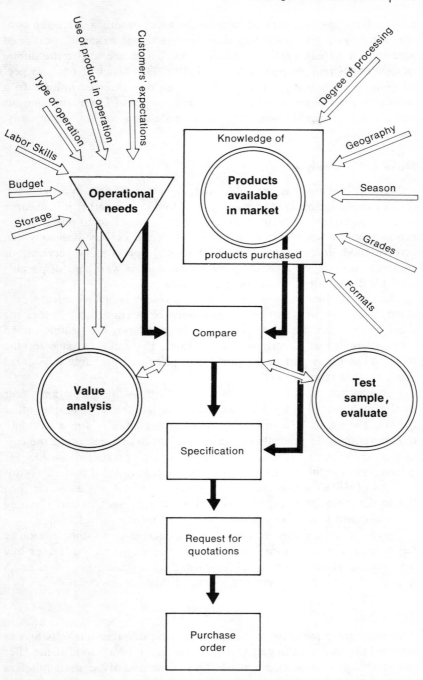

Figure 6.1.   Purchasing decisions step by step.

tainly, there are instances of overspecification, where a manager consistently buys more processing than he needs, for example, portioned meats when he can portion them for less. There are also more subtle factors which require purchasing flexibility: how much it costs to peel an onion and chop it; how much it costs to buy chopped onions. In a volatile market situation with an irregular supply of labor, the analysis and buying decisions would have to be made on a weekly, if not daily, basis.

Make or Buy Analysis

Make or buy analysis like value analysis is more simple in articulation than in implementation. The manager has to decide whether it is cheaper to make a product or perform an operation in house or to purchase the product or the service from a purveyor. Make or buy decisions can involve food products (and most often do), or laundry services, or contract cleaning, or a choice between permanent ware and disposable ware for dining room service or guest rooms.

The cost to the operation of the labor involved is always a factor; for example, in washing the guest room linen or peeling the potatoes the manager pays for the labor directly. If he purchases the product, linen from a laundry or already peeled potatoes, the manager pays for the labor indirectly as part of the purveyor's price and probably pays for a profit on that labor as well.

Labor is not the only factor and the difficulties in calculation occur as the manager is obliged to *accurately* weigh the cost of the other factors. He might be considering on-premises laundry for a 100-unit motel averaging 75 percent occupancy. He has to first determine the cost of having the linen, bath towels, bath mats, etc., processed outside. He then has to determine what equipment he would need and how much this equipment will cost either by direct purchase, rental, or lease. He then has to determine the cost of utilities for the machines, water, cleaning materials, and labor. He can then compare the two sets of figures.

The decision to make or buy a food product, in effect, the decision to buy a particular product at one degree of processing and finish it, or buy it at a more advanced degree of processing for a greater price and finish it, even more fully illustrates the nature of this calculation.

MAKE OR BUY ANALYSIS OF FOOD PRODUCTS

A manager considering goods processed by different methods and to different degrees is ultimately trying to determine which food items offer the most cost-reduction potential. This is necessarily a determination peculiar to each operation: With the exception of items like salt and sugar, no processed product can be universally guaranteed to cost less than the cost of producing it on the premises in some fashion.

There are ten major cost factors for him to consider:

1. Cost of production
2. Cost of labor
3. Cost of storage
4. Cost of inventory
5. Cost of equipment
6. Cost of space
7. Cost of management
8. Cost of service
9. Cost of processing
10. Cost of availability

1. *Cost of Production.* If preparation from raw materials is being compared with a finished product, it is extremely important that the manager compare edible portions. He cannot, for example, compare the purchase price per pound of raw asparagus with the purchase price per pound of frozen asparagus, as 30 pounds of raw asparagus are required for every 15 pounds served. In other words, the cost of the raw product, for the purposes of this determination, is twice the purchase price. The real cost of the product has to be determined for all raw and partially processed products when they are compared with products with any greater degree of processing.

2. *Cost of labor.* The cost of labor has to cover all labor involved in handling the item, including ordering it, moving it in the operation, and preparing it. The most considerable labor cost may not always be preparation. For example, the manager might be determining whether to buy portioned orange juice or orange juice in quart containers. Handling is the biggest cost factor. It might be determined by dividing the number of packages handled by the total cost of handling all packages.

When cost is being determined by analyzing the time individuals with different work rates spend in preparation, care has to be taken that cooking times or preparation times are not confused with actual labor involvement. It may take 5 hours to cook a stew, but it does not take anyone 5 hours of labor. There must be a compromise figure that reflects what a man can actually produce during his entire shift.

When the manager is comparing peeled potatoes and unpeeled potatoes, the calculation is much more straightforward: A man earning a certain amount peels a definite amount of potatoes an hour. The cost of peeling the potatoes per pound is his hourly rate, plus benefits, divided by the number of pounds peeled.

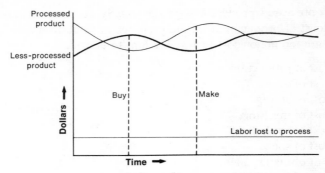

"Make" when cost of less-processed product plus cost of labor is less than cost of processed product.

Figure 6.2.   Cost figures graphed to aid in make-or-buy decisions.

3. *Cost of storage.* Cost of storage involves the cost of the equipment plus the cost of receiving and storage, shrinkage, loss to vermin and theft, record keeping, cost of electricity for refrigeration and lighting, and cost of maintenance of equipment.

Although the total cost of these items might be determined on an annual basis, turnover of items is another factor. For example, if a freezer that holds 1,000 pounds costs $300 a year in maintenance, depreciation, and electricity, it makes a rather considerable difference in the storage cost per pound of product if the freezer is turned over one time a year (33¢ a pound) or ten times a year (3.3¢ per pound).

This item may or may not be a plus in the processed food column. Frozen processed foods require less space than the same number of edible portions of fresh food (for example, carrots), but they must be kept frozen, which is more expensive than keeping them refrigerated, much more expensive than keeping them as canned carrots, and very much more expensive than keeping them without refrigeration. On the other hand, all factors considered, canned carrots (per edible portion) may be more cheaply stored and handled than sacks of carrots.

4. *Cost of inventory.* When a food operation buys for its own use and not for resale it commits some of its operating capital to the purchase. An involvement of $10,000 in a processed food inventory on an annual basis adds the amount of interest lost on that sum to the cost of the product. On the other hand, fresh products may be paid for as they are used.

5. *Cost of equipment.* Cost of equipment is a major consideration when the manager is thinking of converting to a convenience system that requires new equipment, or when he is deciding between a conventional production system and a convenience system. Necessarily, the cost of the equipment (initial purchase price, utilities, and maintenance and

repair, divided by anticipated life) has to be assigned to the items prepared.

For example, in a newly installed kitchen which is convenience-food oriented, an entire preparation system may be unnecessary if no un-processed foods are going to be brought into the operation. However, a convenience system might require an investment in racks, thawing re-frigerators, and special reconstitution equipment. This investment must be reflected in the portion cost.

6. *Cost of space.* Unless the manager proposes to convert an operation to a total convenience system and then use the space saved to produce additional revenues, cost of space is only a consideration in new con-struction or installations. Here the savings in construction costs, capital investment, and potential revenues can be considerable with a conve-nience system. As an item's state of preparedness advances to ready-to-eat, it requires less space to hold and to prepare. The difference in space requirements for a conventional kitchen, or a back-of-the-house arrangement, or a finishing kitchen can be of four, five, or more mag-nitudes.

7. *Cost of management.* Among the costs of running a conventional kitchen, the following must be considered: the supervisory personnel, the accounting and auditing personnel necessary for an operation that orders from numerous purveyors, and the more knowledgeable receiving personnel.

For example, if all other factors are equal, someone must still hire the five onion peelers, supervise them, and conduct all the different move-ments of raw and partially processed onions.

8. *Cost of service.* Cost of service can be a considerable factor in some instances. The necessity of maintaining a slicing station on a cafe-teria line when a whole ham is used adds to the per-portion cost of the ham. The savings in purchasing bulk packs of food instead of pre-portioned food may be offset by the additional cost of personnel on the tray-make-up line.

9. *Cost of processing.* Cost of processing, in addition to the cost of utilities, also includes the cost of water and of garbage removal per pound. Admittedly, most of the time this is a minor consideration, but on occasion it becomes a primary factor. For example, the cost of garbage removal from a rooftop restaurant may prompt its manager to use nothing but convenience foods.

10. *Cost of availability.* Any disruption in the production routine can be an expense. If a raw food item is late in arriving, personnel may be idle while waiting for it. If a convenience item becomes unavailable or simply does not arrive, the emergency preparation procedure to replace it from scratch or from semiprocessed ingredients may wipe out months

of profit advantage. A missing menu item can cause customers to switch to an item with a lower absolute profit. In considering an item or a procedure, the operation has to add or subtract some sum as the cost of having it available.

MAKING A DETERMINATION

The ten major cost factors do not all enter into every evaluation of alternative products. Only in planning an installation as either a conventional production system or a convenience system, or in contemplating a substantial conversion to convenience or from convenience does each become vitally important.

Most managers are faced with a series of continual item-by-item decisions. They have a menu or a menu cycle which is the starting point of their product evaluation. They are weighing alternative production systems for each item or item component. For instance, should the beef burgundy be made or bought? If the beef burgundy is to be made, at what degree of processing (from none to ready-to-use) should the onions, carrots, sauce, and meat be bought? The basis of the decision is the cost of the alternatives, but only one or two of the cost factors will usually make a significant difference. Unlike the planner or the person contemplating conversion, the manager's area of decision is more limited. For example, the beef burgundy may require several hours of a highly paid chef's time; the commercial product, assuming the same quality, proves to be less expensive. The manager may still elect to make the product because he needs the chef and cannot otherwise utilize his time so productively.

The manager with a large storeroom does not have to build one. On the other hand, to use large quantities of frozen convenience foods, he must have freezer space, which necessitates a capital investment to effect a long-term gain. If the capital is available, might it not be better (more profitably) invested in interior or exterior decoration or in advertising? In all probability this will not be his decision although he can certainly prepare a case for his superiors.

For a particular manager the argument may be turned the other way. The convenience item may be more expensive, but its purchase may be justified because a manager cannot hire a chef for a fraction of a day or because the ingredients for the item cannot be purchased in sufficiently small quantities to justify their being stored or inventoried.

Whatever the bases for decision, they should be readily apparent when the manager examines the alternatives with the ten cost factors in mind. Once it becomes apparent that in one instance the issue is labor and in another, storage cost, then the manager can do the calculations necessary for the determination.

INVENTORY MANAGEMENT

Inventory management principles can be very sophisticated. For the purchasing department of a large hotel or restaurant chain a sophisticated approach is necessary and profitable because of the large sums of money involved and the savings made possible by purchasing at particular times or at quantity discounts.

At this scale of operations the ideal inventory amount is determined by weighing the costs of owning the inventory against the economic advantages of purchasing the inventoried products in certain quantities at certain times.

The cost of ownership includes:

1. *Cost of the money invested in the inventory.* If the products are purchased, the money needed is either borrowed at a certain rate of interest, or the money is unavailable to earn interest or be used for investment in fields such as advertising which might have a return.
2. *Cost of carrying the inventory.* Physical possession of the inventory implies some place to store it, insurance costs for it, some labor costs in handling, guarding, and managing it. There may also be some deterioration, damage, and theft in storage. In some areas, inventories are taxed.

On the other hand, there is an economic advantage to owning the inventory, and it *may* outweigh the costs of ownership.

The economic advantage of ownership includes:

1. *Quantity discounts.* Often items can be purchased in quantity at lower unit costs.
2. *Seasonal price advantages.* At certain times of the year even non-perishable items such as canned goods and non-food items are cheaper.
3. *Decreased costs of purchasing and administration* (acquisition costs). For the large purchaser who may be employing a dozen purchasing agents fewer actual orders for the same total amount of product means lowered costs. Six or eight purchasing agents might service the operation instead of 12.
4. *Economies of scale in carrying the inventory.* It does not cost twice as much to build a warehouse twice the size, so the overhead per unit is lowered with increased inventory.

Once these factors are quantified, a number of calculations become possible to determine whether or not a certain quantity of an item should be purchased at a certain time. For example, inventory managers of large operations determine by the use of tables, or algebraically, the *economic order quantity,* the point at which carrying costs (which increase with the size of inventory) equal acquisition costs (which decrease with size of inventory). Or the advantage of taking a quantity discount can be determined by calculating the cost of the investment in the additional inventory and the additional carrying costs and comparing it with the possible savings.

None of these aspects of inventory management concern the operational manager except in their implications. In general, the inventory under the control of an operational manager is too small in dollar value and turns over too rapidly to permit a sensible application of these determinations. Certain concepts, however, are important because they concern his operational inventory management.

In make or buy analysis inventory cost has to be considered as the discussion above indicated. As well, in purchasing items which have a high dollar value, for instance, alcoholic beverages or cleaning products, the cost of carrying inventory is certainly a decision factor.

The operational manager also has to recognize that discounts can be costly unless the sum saved on buying ketchup or french fries on a special at least equals the cost of the additional investment at whatever the current rate of interest is, and whatever carrying costs are generated. Sometimes, but rarely, the operational manager may find that it pays to buy an item such as frozen french fries and to rent space in a public freezer for it.

This same reasoning should be applied to discounts offered for prompt payment of bills but with an obviously different perspective. If a bill indicates that there will be a discount for payment within 10 days, for example 2 percent, and the full payment is due in 30 days, by not paying in 10 days, the manager is paying 2 percent of the sum owed for the use of the money for 20 days.

On an annual basis, this is equivalent to paying interest of almost 37 percent.

The operational manager has certain inventory management problems that parallel but do not quite coincide with the problems of the quantity purchaser. The operational manager must juggle inventory, order quantities, and allow storage space to prevent shortages (called *stockouts*) which can slow down production, thereby increasing labor costs or inconveniencing customers.

In the hypothetical example below, for simplicity of illustration, only one commodity, frozen vegetables, is considered, but the thinking needed is dramatized adequately. The manager has a number of real concerns in juggling a possibly finite amount of frozen-storage space, his desire to eliminate stockouts, and a delivery schedule which he may not control.

1. *What amount of frozen vegetables does he actually need?* Basically, the operational manager has to analyze his production process and determine what his "working inventory" of each vegetable is, i.e., the absolute minimum of each vegetable that he needs. The manager may start with a daily sales analysis of the menu and then adjust it to take in account that many menu items are produced over several days. The result is a product list with critical levels, saying, in sum, that the operation absolutely requires this much (A) total frozen vegetables at 7:00 a.m. every morning *to function*. If the operation is seasonal or there is a seasonal demand for certain items, then he must develop several profiles of his requirements to accommodate the variations.

2. *How frequently (and when) can he expect deliveries?* If the manager is serviced by his supplier fewer than seven times a week, he must adjust his working inventory figure to take into account the need to keep at least several days' supply on hand, and the difference in usage for the days of the week. If he used the same amount of (A) every day but could only expect Monday, Wednesday, and Friday delivery, his requirements for ordering would in fact be:

Monday	2A (Enough for Monday and Tuesday)
Wednesday	2A (Enough for Wednesday and Thursday)
Friday	3A (Enough for Friday, Saturday, and Sunday)

He needs 2A storage because that is the most (Friday night) he will have to store. If the delivery days were the same, but the supplier delivered *after* the item was needed for production, then the order would be the same:

Monday	2A (Enough for Tuesday and Wednesday)
Wednesday	2A (Enough for Thursday and Friday)
Friday	3A (Enough for Saturday, Sunday, and Monday)

But there is an important difference: the operation now has to store frozen 3A instead of 2A because when Friday's order is delivered, none of it is needed for Friday's production.

In actual practice, the ordering procedure will probably have to take into account uneven distribution of usage among the days of the week. Quite possibly the pattern would be:

Monday	1A (Enough for Monday, Tuesday, and Wednesday)
Wednesday	2A (Enough for Thursday and Friday)
Friday	4A (Enough for Saturday and Sunday)

Necessarily this would mean the storage of 4A. The storage requirements for exactly the same total weekly usage, are double that of the first example.

3. *How much safety inventory does he need?* At the very least, ordering quantities which exactly respond to working inventory needs will compromise the manager's health as he worries the truck into the receiving area three times a week. Some safety inventory is obviously needed to insure against delay in shipments, missed deliveries, unanticipated business. The manager would like to have an inventory (working inventory plus safety inventory) that would allow him to miss a delivery. Using the usage pattern in the last example, to provide this margin his order would have to be:

Monday	3A (Enough for Monday–Friday)
Wednesday	4A (Enough for Saturday and Sunday)
Friday	1A (Enough for Monday, Tuesday, and Wednesday)

Storage requirements have increased. When the delivery was made on Wednesday 2A still remained in inventory and 4A arrived making it necessary to store 6A.

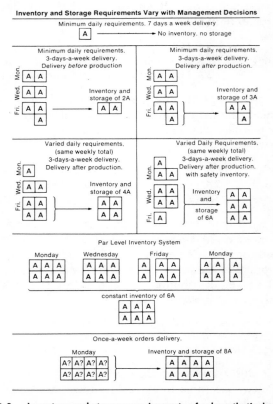

Figure 6.3. Inventory and storage requirements of a hypothetical product.

In actual practice, in an *a la carte* restaurant, the manager wanting the safety margin which obliges him to have 6A storage capabilities, would take advantage of the fact to increase his safety margin within his storage capabilities by never having *less than* 6A.

Monday	6A (1A consumed Monday, Tuesday, and Wednesday)
Wednesday	1A (Inventory built up to 6A)
Friday	2A (Inventory built up to 6A)
Monday	4A (Inventory built up to 6A)

Ordering to a par level inventory also greatly simplifies the ordering procedure. Quite obviously a form can be developed which lists the par level for each item and provides a space for the actual inventory and the order.

4. *How much can he store?* It can be seen in these examples that if the manager can in fact store 8A he can have a once a week delivery, and still have the safety margin to miss a delivery (Monday's). He simply orders to a level of 8A each Monday. Most managers would accept that this is the most desirable ordering pattern because it involves the least administration, and offers the simplest ordering procedure. The savings in administration and ordering has its costs if the freezer space is not already available. Storing 8A means that he must have twice as much storage space as he actually minimally requires (4A), and a third again as much as he requires for a "safe" inventory level (6A). Since *A,* which can be used to represent the total frozen food needs, or even all products needed, can in reality be tons of product, building and operating the additional storage space can cost additional thousands of dollars.

BUILDING CARE MANAGEMENT

Building care is expensive. Building care will become even more expensive as the minimum wage rate and the cost of materials increase. Neglect of hotels, restaurants, institutions, and commercial properties is also expensive; replacement of structural and decorative materials is costly; customer dissatisfaction with dirty, shoddy premises reduces revenues.

For management, there is only one possible resolution of this dilemma: application of the management techniques usually applied to revenue producing operations, and an intensification of management concern for the cost of cleaning and cleaning maintenance.

Building care operations are often neglected by management for three reasons: (1) they do not contribute directly to revenues; (2) building care departments are small and seem to demand only low level supervision; (3) the low wages traditionally paid building care workers seem to indicate that the labor cost is low.

While building care operations do not contribute directly to revenues, they contribute indirectly. For example, surveys of restaurant patrons continually indicate that cleanliness is their first concern. A dirty, sloppy, or shoddy establishment loses customers.

The neglect of premises also costs profits. Depreciation of furniture, floor and wall coverings, and structural elements is accelerated by neglect. Premature replacement reduces revenues.

The relative smallness of building care departments in many hotel and motel organizations seems to indicate that the cost of building care is low. The cost of cleaning and cleaning maintenance by other departments must be included in any accurate analysis. In a hotel, for example, expensive craftsmen, electricians, and painters may be cleaning. In a restaurant, cooks routinely spend part of their time cleaning. The smallness of the building care department limits the quality of supervision assigned it, while cleaning and cleaning maintenance operations in other departments have little or no supervision. If total cleaning costs are analyzed, the manager may discover that hidden cleaning costs have dramatically increased the apparent costs, and that productivity in this area is extremely low.

The low wages paid building care workers does not generally result in low building care costs. In fact, low wages ultimately result in higher than necessary costs, if the cost of inefficiency, turnover, damage to facilities and equipment, waste of materials, theft, unemployment insurance rate increases, intensive (but low quality) supervision, and diminished customer satisfaction is considered.

A distinction should be made between *cleaning* and *cleaning maintenance* as operational objectives. *Cleaning* includes such activities as waste removal from rooms and offices; straightening and arranging furniture and supplies; replenishing consumables; removal of surface dirt from furniture, walls, and floor coverings; polishing wood, plastic, metal, and glass; and sanitation in the sense of disinfection, pest control, and germproofing. On the other hand, *cleaning maintenance* is directed toward the preservation and restoration of the physical premises and includes procedures that are directed toward preventing deterioration and soiling, and toward anticipating and limiting the need for cleaning and repair.

Essentially the distinction is between a day-to-day effort to deal with the disorder and the dirt created by normal business activities and a planned program of long-term building care. Both are quite obviously necessary, but management has a tendency to ignore cleaning maintenance.

In the long term, cleaning maintenance economically justifies itself by reducing routine cleaning costs, mechanical maintenance, and major repairs and restorations. For example, if a rug is vacuumed as part of daily cleaning and piled and shampooed as part of a cleaning maintenance program, it may never be necessary to remove the rug to have it cleaned outside the operation. If exterior painted surfaces are repainted when necessary, the structural elements protected by the paint may never have to be renewed. If mineral deposits are removed from piping on a routine basis, the likelihood of the pipes becoming obstructed and rupturing is significantly reduced. If minor cracks in paved areas are repaired, major resurfacing may never be needed. If floors are periodically stripped, resealed, and rewaxed, daily buffing and polishing is easier.

The operational manager concerned with building care surely must make routine cleaning his first priority, but a program of long-term building care offers him the most opportunities for cost reduction and facility improvement.

Planning Building Care

The first step in determining the requirements of any operation is the preparation of a master list of tasks to be done. This is essentially an area-by-area survey of the premises, giving a description of every area and item of equipment and furnishing that must be serviced. An indication of what must be done is included.

If one individual is in charge of all sanitation and maintenance, the master list will include all jobs, regardless of type. If the functions are departmentalized, each manager lists the tasks he accepts for his department. These lists are compared to prevent overlapping.

The lists should be absolutely specific. A listing such as "dining room, clean floor" is inadequate for the planning procedure. Much more information is needed. What type of floor? What is the area in square feet?

Any information that might be a factor in the amount of time required for the job, the skill levels needed, or the difficulty of the job must be listed. The basic rule is: Quantify anything that is quantifiable. Include everything that can be reckoned by number: the number of square feet to be waxed, the number of cubic feet to be ventilated, the number of pumps to be serviced, the number of dishes to be washed, the number of faucets that require washer replacement, etc.

Perhaps the best way to start a master list is to examine the floor plans of a building. The requirements for floor cleaning and cleaning maintenance of stairway, corridor, and lobby can be determined. An examination of the kitchen plans will indicate what machinery was installed.

WORK DETERMINATION

Area_____Quality Standard_____

Item	Cleaning Method (Describe)	Standard Time	Amount or Number of the Item	Total Time (Minutes)	Cleaning Frequency	Yearly Time (Hours)

Figure 6.4. A work determination survey form used in plan for building care.

All windows will require washing. All lamps will require relamping. Without moving from his office, the manager can chart the broad outlines of his master list of sanitation and maintenance requirements.

A room-by-room, area-by-area, space-by-space survey should follow. The master list becomes more specific as jobs are added and defined by area requirements.

Once the master list is prepared, four other planning factors can be introduced: time standards per smallest quantifiable operation, extent of total operation, frequency, and quality standard.

1. *Time standards per smallest quantifiable operation.* How long does it take to clean one of the filters in a large air conditioner? How long

does it take to clean a square foot of asbestos tile? To clean and wax a square foot of asbestos tile? To strip, seal, wax and buff a square foot of asbestos tile? It is necessary to establish a time standard for each item on the master list. Industry standards can be used. These are generally available from the companies that offer the cleaning supplies or the original equipment.

Managers are usually confronted with ongoing operations, and the purpose of the survey is the improvement of performance, not the structuring of an entirely new program. For such surveys, actual work performance can be measured for the specific area being considered. One worker, cleaning a dining room floor of 2,000 square feet, takes a total of 40 minutes to sweep it, 80 minutes to scrub it with a 14-inch machine, 60 minutes to wax it and 30 minutes to polish it with a 19-inch machine, Using these standards, it is possible to determine a time standard for sweeping the dining room (40 minutes divided by 2,000 square feet equals 1.2 seconds per square foot), scrubbing it, waxing it, and polishing it. These time standards can be extended to other comparable areas: It should take about 1.2 seconds per square foot to sweep any area.

2. *Extent of Total Operation.* Each area or job under consideration incorporates a number of lesser tasks for which there is a time standard and a total quantity for each task to be done. For example, a guest room involves (among other tasks) floor cleaning and furniture polishing. The amount of floor cleaning in square feet, multiplied by the time standard for the job, plus the amount of furniture polishing by square foot (or piece), multiplied by the time standard for the job, plus all the other jobs, multiplied by their time standard, equals the extent of the operation to be performed in the room.

3. *Frequency.* Some jobs are done more than once a day, others are done once a day, once or twice a week, once a month, once a quarter, once a year, etc. The frequency of the work is obviously an important factor in planning the work and allocating labor for it.

4. *Quality Standard.* In establishing a time standard, the manager must decide how well the job must be done. For example, the manager determines that it takes 8 hours to clean a lawn of 90 percent of the visible paper, but it takes 16 hours—twice the amount of time—to clean the same lawn of all visible paper. To keep the lawn constantly clean (removing the paper as it is discarded) requires 32 hours—the labor of four men for an entire day. The manager must decide which standard is preferable. Is it satisfactory to have the lawn 90-percent free of visible paper? Similar decisions involve floor polishing, window washing, wall washing, rug cleaning, etc. What is the minimum acceptable standard? How does the achievement of this standard affect the time standard and the frequency factors?

TABLE 6.1. ESTIMATED PRODUCTIVITY PER MAN-DAY FOR CLEANING AND CLEANING MAINTENANCE OPERATIONS

Operation	Productivity Per Man-Day (8 hours) (In square feet or units)
Floor Care	
Sweeping unobstructed large areas (empty banquet rooms, for example)	100,000 maximum machine
Sweeping halls and corridors	50,000 manual
Sweeping dining room	15–25,000 manual
Buffing with machine	20–40,000 depending on area
Waxing	6–15,000 depending on area and equipment
Stripping	3–4,000
Wet mopping	7–12,000 depending on area
Damp mopping	15–30,000 depending on area
Machine scrubbing	10–48,000 depending on machine
Dust mopping	30–80,000 depending on area
Vacuuming	15–30,000 depending on area
Shampooing	1–2,000 depending on area
Cleaning Public Areas	
Elevators	25
Escalators	22 flights
Stairways, sweep and dust	60 flights
Stairways, mop	22 flights
Wall washing	2,000 manual 3,500 machine
Venetian blinds	16 (4′) manual, 50 machine 8 (8′) manual, 25 machine
Ceiling	1,500 manual 2,500 machine
Lobby area policing and cleaning	100,000

TABLE 6.1. ESTIMATED PRODUCTIVITY PER MAN-DAY FOR CLEANING AND
CLEANING MAINTENANCE OPERATIONS—continued

Operation	Productivity Per Man-Day (8 hours) (In square feet or units)
Office Cleaning	
Straightening, waste removal, dusting and floor care	9–15,000
Furniture dusting	30 seconds per piece
Desk dusting	1–2 minutes
Washrooms	
Cleaning	3–4,000
Water closets	4–6 minutes each
Urinals	3 minutes each
Window Washing	
Large single panes	3,000

The end product of this initial survey is a chart, or series of charts, indicating the jobs to be done, their extent, and how often they are to be done. Some indication should be given of the quality of performance required.

INTERPRETATION OF SANITATION AND MAINTENANCE REQUIREMENTS

Once the requirements for sanitation and maintenance have been established, it becomes necessary to interpret the data to produce meaningful staffing requirements. Sanitation and maintenance requirements should be divided into jobs that are performed best on an area basis and jobs that are performed best on a task basis.

For example, the cleaning of floor coverings—which includes washing, scrubbing, dust mopping, stripping, polishing, sealing, waxing, and buffing as necessary—is generally done on an area basis. Assignment of the total responsibility for the maintenance and cleaning of the floor covering is made by area. An individual (or a group) does everything pertaining to the floor covering in the area. On the other hand, refrigeration maintenance is assigned on a task basis. An individual (or a group) maintains refrigeration equipment wherever it is located in the operation: kitchen, bar, executive offices, air-cooling device areas, etc.

Some operations take what are usually area responsibilities and assign them to specialist squads. For example, the banquet rooms of an operation could be cleaned by a number of employees, each responsible for a room, or by a squad of employees who are responsible for cleaning all the rooms.

There are advantages and disadvantages to each method. Area responsibility can generate a higher interest level in the individual employee: The work is varied and a worker can take pride in "his room." The responsibility for poor performance, breakage, and theft is easily pinpointed, and labor turnover is decreased.

Squad cleaning tends to develop a higher productivity in individuals because of specialization. Close supervision is possible, the quality of the work is usually higher, equipment usage is maximized, and there is a more equitable distribution of work.

Whatever approach is chosen—area, squad, or a combination approach—the total amount of labor involved must equal the total amount of labor required. The labor requirements, as they are charted, cannot always be directly converted into actual shifts. A number of factors— worker productivity, absenteeism, disruption of routine, leave days, travel to and from the job area, time for assembling equipment, the preparation of cleaning materials, the cleaning of machines before maintenance can be done—must be considered in the conversion of labor required to labor to be hired.

For example, the master chart indicates that, on a daily basis, a floor containing 15 guest rooms requires 1 hour of bed making, 3 hours of floor cleaning, and 2 hours of washing, polishing, straightening, and similar tasks. Practical experience indicates that this is the work of one maid, working at normal productivity. This means that approximately 25 percent of her workday is not used productively. The chart is interpreted to indicate that one maid is required for rooms A1 to A15.

This same area may require a relief maid for every six days worked by the regular maid, or expressed another way, every six floors (with similar requirements to floor A) will need an additional maid. The same floor can require 3 hours of window washing a month, 2 hours of corridor cleaning a day, 1 hour of high cleaning a month, etc. All requirements are determined by a computation of the quantity of work to be done, divided by the productivity (time standard for each job), and multiplied by frequency performance. An adjustment for lost time must be included.

The individual requirements of each area indicate the total staff requirements. If floors must be scrubbed for 6 to 8 hours a day, a specialist must be hired. If this is not done, the general worker must neglect his other work in order to scrub floors.

CONSOLIDATED MAINTENANCE
REQUISITION AND WORK ORDER

TO_____ DATE REQUESTED_____

DEPT. OR SECTION_____ BY_____

EQUIPMENT NO._____

WORK TO BE DONE_____
_____

REASON_____ TYPE OF REPAIR:_____
_____   ELECTRICAL_____MACHINERY_____
_____   PLUMBING_____FIRE-FIGHTING
_____   GAS_____EQUIPMENT_____
_____   MASONRY_____TILE_____
_____   WELDING_____STRUCTURAL_____
                                  OTHER_____SHEET METAL_____

APPROVED BY   APPROVED BY
HEAD OF DEPT._____   HEAD OF MAINTENANCE_____

DATE_____   ASSIGNED TO_____
                                               DATE WORK
                                DATE_____TO BE DONE_____

ESTIMATED TIME_____   ESTIMATED COST_____

    ESTIMATED MATERIALS REQUIRED   QUANTITY   COST

_____   _____   _____

_____   _____   _____

CONSOLIDATED MAINTENANCE REQUISITION AND WORK ORDER Page 2

IF SENT OUT FOR REPAIR

TO WHOM SENT_____ DATE_____

ADDRESS_____ TELEPHONE_____

HOW SHIPPED_____

EXPECTED RETURN DATE_____ ACTUAL RETURN DATE_____

ESTIMATED CHARGE_____ ACTUAL CHARGE_____

DATE WORK
COMPLETED_____ BY_____

ACTUAL TIME_____ ACTUAL COST_____

       ACTUAL MATERIALS   QUANTITY   COST

_____   _____   _____

_____   _____   _____

JOB CHECKED BY_____ JOB INSPECTED BY_____

DATE_____ DATE_____

Figure 6.5. Consolidated maintenance requisition and work order for control of building-care activities.

In this manner the raw data of the master chart is converted into a list of jobs for individuals. This list can be summarized to indicate the size of the labor force required to meet the maintenance and sanitation needs of the operation: so many floor maids, so many electricians, so many floor buffers, etc.

PROGRAMMED SANITATION AND MAINTENANCE

The series of charts which have been developed can now be completed. In addition to the material which appeared on the master list of sanitation and maintenance requirements (task and description, time standard, extent, frequency, and quality standard) and the conversion of the list into individuals required, the charts can indicate time needs.

The manager knows what is to be done and how many people he needs to do it. Now he can impose this schema on a calendar for a definite period: 1 year, 2 years, 3 months. He can establish priorities and realistic work schedules that maximize the use of the equipment and personnel. Neither the electrician nor the buffing machine can be in two places at one time. Their use must be planned. It is purposeless to lubricate the swimming pool pumps for 2 consecutive weeks and then neglect them for a year—even though the pumps were serviced twice in the calendar year, as required.

Should all the windows be cleaned on the outside, then all the windows cleaned on the inside? Obviously not. Should guest rooms be scheduled for painting during the high occupancy seasons? Obviously not. Should the floor in the convention area be stripped before or after the farm implement show?

Proper planning includes preventive maintenance and preventive cleaning, not only cleaning that responds to dirtiness or maintenance that responds to breakdowns. The roof of the establishment should be resaturated periodically. How often depends on climatic conditions. Rugs should be removed and sent to an outside plant for cleaning on a regular schedule. Interiors should be periodically repainted for aesthetic reasons.

Each of these activities, and many others, has to be planned long in advance so that crews are available. The crews normally assigned to routine maintenance and cleaning must be reassigned. If the roof is being resaturated, it does not have to be swept; walls being repainted do not have to be washed; rugs not in the operation cannot be vacuumed.

CONTRACT MAINTENANCE AND SANITATION AS ELEMENTS IN PLANNING

After the requirements for sanitation and maintenance have been specified in terms of labor, it may be apparent to the manager that he does not have sufficient work to justify the employment of a full crew of full-time specialists. The operation may have a few demands for certain cleaning and maintenance services. Even a very healthy and profitable foodservice operation is not likely to need a full-time electrician, refrigeration specialist, floor buffer, etc. Full cleaning and maintenance can require 15 or 20 individuals, each exercising a specialty.

There are two alternatives for any operation regardless of size that does not require a full-time specialist but requires the periodic services of someone with knowledge of the specialty: the employment of a generalist or the employment of an outside firm on contract.

Small foodservice and hospitality operations employ an individual called a cleaning man (or utility man or maintenance or sanitation man) who may be called on to perform any maintenance or sanitation function. The obvious disadvantage of this system is its reliance on the knowledge, loyalty, reliability, and attendance of a single individual. The obvious advantage is the low cost of the total service.

Many operations employ contract cleaners and contract maintenance firms. A large centralized operation usually can do its own work more economically. For the small operation, or the operation with numerous small units, contract maintenance and cleaning can be economical. The disadvantages, which might be interpreted as hidden costs, are the loss of control over the quality of the cleaning, maintenance, and products used; the presence of outsiders in the facility; the loss of an immediate response to breakdowns or accidents; and the disruption of normal business caused by circumstances over which the operator has no control—the maintenance firm goes on strike, another client of the maintenance firm has a rush job, etc.

Contract services may be the only economical way to ensure full cleaning and maintenance. Many services may be purchased: window cleaning, floor and furniture refinishing, floor maintenance, toilet cleaning, carpet cleaning, machinery cleaning and repair, structural cleaning, heavy cleaning, dry cleaning, routine cleaning, snow removal, lawn and ground care, etc.

Contracts may be cost plus: The labor costs, overhead, and profit are accountable separately. This arrangement provides a measure of control for the operator. Contracts may also be fixed-sum. A fee is paid for the complete service, but the cost of each component is not itemized. The operator is guaranteed a fixed expenditure per month, plus extras which are billed separately. He loses a great deal of control over the maintenance and cleaning unless he has carefully specified the exact services he expects in the formal written agreement with the contractor. All aspects of the agreement—the functions to be performed, their frequency, the materials to be used, etc.—must be written in detail, if the relationship is to be satisfactory for the operator.

Since much of the responsibility for the facility is being placed with an outsider, the operator should investigate the contractor thoroughly. His credit rating should be determined. Other clients should be surveyed. His plant should be visited and his equipment inspected.

When contract maintenance is being considered, the original suppliers or manufacturers of the equipment might be asked for recommendations for local servicers. Utility companies may also have lists of approved technicians. A good standard for judgment is the extent of the company's testing equipment and parts inventory.

Cost Analysis and Control

Maintenance and sanitation functions do not have a direct effect on revenues. The manager in charge of these areas is therefore deprived of the best standard of his performance: how much money he is making for the operation. A dollar invested in maintenance cannot be shown to produce a dollar of revenue. The only real standard of efficiency is a comparison with past performance. If the manager constantly attacks the cost of his past performance, works to lower costs, and succeeds, he can point to the evidence of his success as a "profit." A dollar less spent on cleaning and maintenance is a dollar more for the operation.

In order to be able to improve his economic performance, the manager must be able to place dollar amounts on the activities of his department. The manager must know the amount of the total expenses used for labor, supervision, materials and supplies. He should also be able to assign dollar amounts to any specific cleaning operation in any of these areas.

Managers who are aware of costs from year to year know how much it costs them to clean a square foot of the dining room and how much it costs them to service a pump in the filtering system of the swimming pool. The figure should be less for the following year.

By using this criterion, the manager can make certain vitally important decisions. Can a machine do the job more cheaply? Should a contract service be employed? Should the equipment be replaced because its maintenance cost is too high? Should the floor covering be replaced because it is generating inordinate cleaning costs?

If a $7,000 floor-cleaning machine can be used at least 6 hours a day, the operator may find that the cost per square foot of buffing and waxing floors is reduced or he may discover that he cannot use the machine enough to justify its purchase.

The operator may find that it is cheaper to replace a carpet than to continue paying for the expensive chemicals needed to clean the present carpet.

While this procedure is fairly straightforward for the cleaning and maintenance operations in the lodging and public areas, it is more difficult in the food production areas.

It is necessary to analyze the time spent on sanitation and maintenance tasks by every individual not engaged in sanitation and maintenance. For example, if four cooks—each earning $200 dollars a week—spend one-fourth of their time cleaning, the operation is better served by scheduling three cooks and one porter.

A daily record of operations is perhaps the most effective cost analysis tool. The manager uses this record to compare scheduled man-hours, actual man-hours spent, and payroll hours for particular tasks: washroom cleaning, floor cleaning, etc. The actual dollar expenditure can also be recorded by labor category. This makes it possible to judge whether more units of lower-priced labor can economically replace more expensive labor. The efficiency of scheduling can be judged, and individual performance can be evaluated by comparison with other performances.

Although labor accounts for the most significant expenditure in sanitation and maintenance, the materials used can cost a considerable sum. The manager who is responsible for maintenance and sanitation should concern himself with the proper care of hand tools and machines and the proper use of cleaning supplies and products.

The establishment of a custodial closet for cleaning supplies and tools is highly recommended. The room should be sufficiently large with a floor-level sink fitted with a hot-and-cold-water mixing faucet and a hose for filling buckets. The room itself should be easy to clean and maintain. Sufficient shelving should be available. Enough light and ventilation are extremely important.

There should also be a set routine for the care and cleaning of equipment at the end of work. The cleaning of tools and equipment should be a part of the job. Applicators should be cleaned of wax and detergents, usable rags should be washed, mops should be cleaned, etc.

Maintenance should also include the maintenance of cleaning equipment. Casters on buckets require lubrication. Safety belts for window washing require inspection and repair. Floor machines require lubrication and servicing.

The proper storage of equipment and tools is also important. Brooms and mops should not be stored standing on their bristles or fibers. Floor brushes should be stored on their backs.

Order and routine are extremely important. The time spent in searching for equipment or gathering supplies is time lost. A place should be established for every tool and each type of supplies.

An inventory of all cleaning and maintenance materials should be made and a par level set for each product. The storage facility should be well secured.

All employees should be given instruction in the use of consumables. Many cleaning and maintenance employees believe that if a product is effective in its recommended quantity any additional amount used will increase the efficacy of the product and reduce the amount of human effort needed for cleaning. Some of the chemicals available for floor care are extremely expensive. They are worthwhile when used as directed and for the purposes for which they are formulated. When used improperly, the operation is literally pouring money down the drain.

Even items that seem inexpensive are relatively costly when used indiscriminately. Rags should be color coded by dying to indicate the purpose for which they are best suited. Worn mattress pads are good burnishing cloths and torn bath towels are good bar wipers. Color coding prevents their use for general cleaning.

As much use as possible should be made of products generated by the operation itself. In addition to rags, leftover guest soap can be grated into water and the liquid used for general cleaning. Slightly used shoe-polishing cloths can be turned into burnishing cloths for silver. Used razor blades can be fitted into special scrapers.

It is also possible to extend the life of mops and brooms by coding them for specialized uses. The newest mop can be used for the cleanest jobs (such as drying rinsed floors) while older mops can be used for scrubbing.

The packaging of items also controls cost. Many products are available both in barrels or drums and in small bottles or containers. The decision of which to buy is not based entirely on the cost per unit.

When a chemical is purchased in a drum, it is less expensive per gallon, but there is the hidden cost of storing the drum and pumping the liquid from it. Drums cannot be stored end on end because of weight, but boxes of the same product present no such problem.

Format can be another factor in considering the cost of a particular product. Detergents are always sold by weight but used by volume. When cost is considered, the price per volume unit per use might be compared. A detergent that is fluffy but more expensive per pound might be less expensive when measured by the volume unit per use.

EQUIPMENT MANAGEMENT

The operational manager has three primary responsibilities in equipment management: 1) equipment record keeping; 2) specification of new equipment for ease of maintenance and cleaning and safety of operation; 3) management of a preventive maintenance program.

MASTER EQUIPMENT RECORD   CARD NO. _____

ITEM _____ EQUIPMENT NO. _____ INV. NO. _____

MAKE _____ MODEL NO. _____ SERIAL NO. _____

LOCATION _____ DATE INSTALLED _____

DESCRIPTION _____ HORSEPOWER _____ AMPS _____ VOLTS _____

_____ PHASE _____ RPM _____ CAPACITY _____

_____ FRAME _____ CYCLES _____

PURCHASE DATE _____ PURCHASE PRICE _____ DEPRECIATION _____

GUARANTEE _____ DATE OF EXPIRATION _____

DEALER _____ TELEPHONE _____

ADDRESS _____

SERVICE CONTRACT TERMS _____ SERVICEMAN _____

ROUTINE MAINTENANCE SCHEDULE: JAN   FEB   MAR   APR   MAY   JUNE
                                  JULY   AUG   SEPT   OCT   NOV   DEC

PREVENTIVE MAINTENANCE INSTRUCTIONS _____

_____

_____

SPECIAL SAFETY INSTRUCTIONS _____

_____

_____

SPARE PARTS ON HAND _____

MAINTENANCE

DATE	REPAIR OR SERVICE	COST	DATE	REPAIR OR SERVICE	COST

Figure 6.6.   **Master equipment record form.**

Record-keeping provides the operational management and higher level management with some measure of control over the operation's considerable investment in equipment.

When the operational manager specifies new equipment for purchase or for consideration by higher level management, an attention to ease of maintenance and cleaning, and safety of operation, as well as functional characteristics, serves to promote profitability by making equipment care cheaper, and by protecting the operation against the costs of bad sanitation and poor safety practices.

Equipment Record Keeping

It is impossible to manage equipment unless accurate records are kept. A file card system on each piece of equipment, listing the data outlined below allows management to determine the actual costs of the equipment to the operation, and to monitor the various aspects of preventative maintenance.

There are a number of different systems, but all have the same basic elements: date of installation; servicing history; breakdown history; peculiarities; warranties; parts and service manuals; dealer's name, address, and phone number; serviceman's name, address, and phone number; name plate data (model number, serial number, voltage, wattage, etc.); and any business particulars.

Specification for Maintenance, Cleanliness and Safety
Maintenance, and Cleanliness

Specification for cleanliness and ease of maintenance is a fairly easy proposition for some equipment. The National Sanitation Foundation (NSF), a nonprofit organization devoted to research and education, has developed standards and criteria for equipment, products, and services that bear upon health. The NSF seal is widely recognized as a sign that the article in question complies with public health requirements.

Current standards and criteria are applied to such diverse areas as soda fountain and luncheonette equipment, spray-type dishwashing machines, commercial cooking and warming equipment, icemaking equipment, thermoplastic materials, pipe fittings, valves, traps, filters for swimming pools, commercial cooking equipment, exhaust systems, dinnerware, and cloth towel dispensers.

Standards are published in pamphlet form and can be ordered for a nominal cost. These standards can be easily converted into specifications or criteria for judging individual pieces of equipment. Even when an article of equipment is not covered by the published standards of the NSF, the manager can apply the same thinking on which the standards are based.

There are 20 basic criteria to use for judging from the general appearance of a piece of equipment the quality of sanitation and safety it offers (ease in cleaning and maintaining, safeness in use):

1. The materials used in the construction of the equipment should be durable. They should withstand normal wear and resist corrosion from food substances, cleaning products, and human contacts.
2. The materials used should be nontoxic. They should impart no appreciable color, odor, or taste.
3. The equipment should be built to resist the encroachment of vermin.
4. The equipment should not provide a harbor for vermin or micro-organic contamination.
5. The equipment should be finished in such a way as to discourage the accumulation of debris and filth that would provide food for micro-organic contaminants and vermin.
6. Any coating materials used in the construction should not be the type to crack, chip, or spall, especially when food contact is involved.
7. The equipment should permit ready cleaning; any areas which can get dirty should be accessible to the cleaner and permit sanitization with germicidal solutions.
8. Equipment should be easy to disassemble for cleaning and maintenance.
9. The equipment should be designed so that it encourages sanitary usage.
10. Sharp angles and edges should be eliminated whenever possible (to facilitate cleaning and to avoid accidents).
11. Heavy, nonportable equipment should be sufficiently high from the floor to permit cleaning under it, or it should be sealed to the floor to prevent the entrance of dirt.
12. Motors should be protected from the entrance of dirt and water.
13. If the equipment cannot be disassembled, there should be access doors to any parts that must be maintained or cleaned.
14. Permanent attachments to equipment—for example, tracks and guides—should have holes at the ends or bottoms to facilitate cleaning.
15. Removable parts and attachments should not be difficult to remove.

16. There should be an instruction plate indicating the recommended procedure for cleaning and sanitizing.
17. The equipment should be installed in such a way as to permit its sanitary use.
18. Utility connections should be easily disconnected to permit safe and efficient cleaning.
19. There should be adequate provision for the removal of waste liquids and condensation.
20. Any pipes, valves, fittings, and tubes should either disassemble for cleaning or permit the passage of sanitizing and descaling solutions.

SAFETY

The passage of the Occupational Safety and Health Act of 1970 has made the specification of safety standards for some equipment and systems extremely easy. The standards are precisely articulated in the Act, which may be obtained from the Government Printing Office or the local offices of the Occupational Safety and Health Administration.

The thrust of the thinking embodied in the Act, which is a collection of extant laws and a codification of other legislation, can be made into a series of safety considerations for the specification of equipment and equipment installation.

1. Employees should be trained, either by experienced operators or by manufacturer's representatives, in the use of machines.
2. Only authorized persons should use equipment that is potentially hazardous. Locks should be used, and warning signs should be posted.
3. Equipment should be installed with sufficient overhead and side clearance.
4. Counters, worktables, and machine surfaces should be high enough to minimize operator fatigue.
5. There should be adequate illumination, either as specified in the installation or as part of the machine.
6. Power transmission parts—such as moving belts, chains, gears, and shafts—should be completely enclosed.
7. When guards are removed (for cleaning or maintenance), the machine should be made inoperable by safety switches or interlocks.
8. Safety switches and devices should be shuntproof.
9. Starting and stopping buttons should be accessible to the worker without danger to his hands.

10. All hazardous machinery should be equipped with a deadman brake which will interrupt the power when the operator ceases to activate it.
11. Starting buttons should be recessed to prevent accidental operation.
12. The grounding of electrical devices should be adequate.
13. Heavy-duty, waterproof wiring should be specified.
14. Potentially dangerous machinery should be located outside of high-traffic areas or used when there is no possibility of interference.
15. The areas around machines should be nonskid if there is a possibility of spillage.
16. All openings to cutting or grinding devices, if they are large enough to permit the entry of a hand, should be guarded—for example, food choppers, garbage disposals, etc.
17. Pipes, tubes, valves, and fittings that carry hot grease, hot water, or steam should be insulated if they can be touched by a worker.
18. Heavy lids, covers, and parts of equipment that can be opened and closed should be counterbalanced so that they cannot fall on fingers.
19. Heavy objects should be equipped with adequate handles.
20. Heavy objects and pieces of equipment should be equipped with mechanical aids—such as built-in carts, casters, etc.—that permit transportation.

Preventive Maintenance

ECONOMIC IMPLICATIONS

There is no system, no machine, no process, no equipment, that does not require maintenance. The more sophisticated and expensive the original equipment or system, the greater the demand on the maintenance capabilities of the operation. When a realistic balance sheet is drawn, there is every economic argument (among a host of others) for good maintenance management. Bad practices and the short term economies neglect may generate are always very costly in the long run. Bad equipment maintenance practices cost an operation in at least five significant ways:

1. Accelerated deterioration of equipment
2. Increased insurance rates
3. Decreased employee productivity
4. Waste
5. Legal penalties

Accelerated deterioration of equipment. Hospitality and restaurant equipment and mechanical systems are expensive. While they will not be usable indefinitely, their utility over a period of time has been anticipated by management in creating and capitalizing the operation. For example, equipment which is neglected and has to be replaced in three years instead of five must be replaced with equipment purchased from the operation's profits. An employee (or a manager) who willfully neglects a piece of equipment is for all intents and purposes stealing from the operation. The result on the profit and loss statement, is the same as an outright theft of cash. It might be observed that an operation where there is considerable filth or neglect almost always has considerable problems in the loss of either goods or cash or both. Misuse of property is seldom specific to a single operational area.

Increased insurance rates. An operation with a history of sanitation and safety violations, because of neglected equipment, is penalized in its insurance rate.

Decreased employee productivity. Unsafe conditions and states of disrepair tend to encourage bad work habits in employees. They contribute mightily to the problem, they neglect equipment, and they work in a fashion that mirrors the general indifference of management. Unsafe conditions also contribute to high accident rates, and increased labor costs are the result.

Waste. Neglect is in itself wasteful. Unrepaired equipment soon becomes irreparable. Most important, management neglect signals its lack of concern for the economic operation. Employees soon adopt an even more casual attitude toward the preservation and conservation of food, equipment, and the physical plant.

Legal penalties. Violations of health and safety standards are becoming extremely expensive for the negligent operation because of increasingly stringent enforcement of extant sanitary, health, and safety codes and the immediate promise of extensive, rigid federal legislation. The fines themselves are costly. The average operation may have to sell $40,000 worth of food and drink to pay a $1,000 fine from profits.

If the violation is so considerable that the operation is closed until it conforms to the regulations, the cost in immediate revenues and lost clientele may never be fully recovered.

PREVENTIVE MAINTENANCE PROGRAM

Preventive maintenance in a foodservice or hospitality operation involves three interrelated activities: deep cleaning, servicing, and routine renewal.

Deep cleaning prevents the development of malfunctions in equipment and limits the damage caused by dirt and debris.

Servicing ensures the proper operation of equipment and systems by supplying continuing adjustment and inspection.

Routine renewal anticipates the possible disruption of the operation and replaces vulnerable parts before they break down and cause loss of productivity.

These three activities assure the continued functioning of equipment and systems. Only a very large operation will have a complete maintenance department staffed with plumbers, electricians, heating and ventilation specialists, repairmen, servicemen, and skilled cleaners. In smaller operations, maintenance assignments may be given to a general handyman or assigned to the housekeeping or grounds departments and performed within the operational unit. Other operations, even fairly large ones, rely on service contracts with the original suppliers of equipment. Some arrange for maintenance by outside specialists.

Each system has its advantages and disadvantages. Briefly, the manager must analyze the cost of each approach (or combined approach), considering the direct costs of labor and supplies and the indirect cost of lost revenues and productivity if the response to a malfunction is not instantaneous.

GENERAL EQUIPMENT PREVENTIVE MAINTENANCE

An electric motor is the heart of most machines: dishwashers, air conditioners, vacuum cleaners, elevators, business machines, refrigerators, meat slicers, etc. If electrical motors are kept functioning properly, and the moving parts associated with them lubricated routinely, 90 percent of equipment maintenance is accomplished. Routine adjustment pushes the percentage several points higher.

Electric motor servicing. The primary effort in maintaining motors is cleaning. Dirt and dust are a continuing danger to the correct functioning of motors. Dirt may work its way into bearings, dust may become sufficiently deep to prevent proper heat loss during operation, dirt may even impede the proper passage of current within the motor. Accumulations of dirt within the motor also tend to encourage the accumulation of grease, moisture, and decomposition products which can also cause malfunctions.

Dirt should be removed as soon as it settles on the surface of the motor or in the vicinity of the motor housing. The best method for accomplishing this goal is regular inspection and cleaning with a stream of low pressure, compressed air to blow away dust and grit. If the physical circumstances demand it, vacuum suction may be used.

Oil presents another cleaning problem. Oil where it does not belong (for example, on the motor parts which pass current) can interfere with operations because it acts as insulation. The main problem source of oil is the motor's own lubricating oil which mists onto the exterior or squirts into the interior. Care in lubricating the motor and proper maintenance of oil-holding systems are necessary.

A third concern in motor maintenance is moisture: water and atmospheric humidity. Water should be prevented from contacting the motor. In high humidity situations, motors are insulated against water. Protective housing might be used for motors that are not insulated.

When a motor has become wet it should be dried immediately. Drying in an oven is possible. Forcing air through the motor either by placing it under a hot-air fan or by using compressed air will dry it. Even covering the motor with a blanket and placing some heat source within, possibly several light bulbs, will work.

Lubrication. Most machinery and equipment comes with instructions for lubrication. The manufacturer's instructions should be followed. Machinery with moving parts generally requires a film of oil or grease between the parts to prevent wear and the development of excessive heat. An inexpensive lubricating agent can save the expense of replacing equipment.

Routine adjustment. The use of a machine or piece of equipment can change some of the blueprint specifications. Vibration or heavy usage can loosen screws and bolts. Since much modern equipment is manufactured at tolerances of a few thousandths of an inch, a slight deviation in the position of an operating part can limit function and can precipitate breakdown. A deviation in control mechanisms can increase consumption of energy, (gas, oil or electricity) or make the operation of the equipment difficult to monitor.

An inspection schedule should be established for all equipment. When the piece of equipment is inspected, it should be tested, if only by operating it and observing its functioning. The vulnerable parts should be individually considered and adjusted. For example, the gas valves in an oven should be lubricated, the burner and gas orifice should be adjusted to provide proper heat, the spring on the oven door should be examined to determine if it is keeping the door sufficiently tight, and the automatic pilot and safety cutoff valve should be regulated.

Electric motors must also be routinely adjusted. Bearings are checked for looseness; bolts holding the motor mounts are tightened; belt tension is checked; rheostat settings are adjusted, etc.

Any pieces of equipment that can wear out may need adjustment. Usually those parts which are vulnerable to wear require periodic adjustment.

During inspection and adjustment, parts which are worn are replaced before their malfunctioning damages the machinery or limits its operation. The parts to be replaced are usually inexpensive fittings, and their replacement does not require any substantial economic judgment.

PREVENTIVE MAINTENANCE OF SPECIFIC EQUIPMENT

Table 6.2 indicates the major procedures necessary for the preventive maintenance of equipment in most hospitality operation units. Precise maintenance and cleaning procedures will necessarily depend on the particular equipment. As the operational manager includes this task in his unit's work program, the manufacturer's service manual should be consulted.

ENERGY MANAGEMENT

The rising costs of electricity, oil, gas, and steam, combined with increased consumption "labor saving" but energy consuming equipment introduced into hospitality operations, make energy an important cost item. Much of the utilization of energy is directly under the control of operational managers. By effective management of energy, operating costs can be reduced.

An energy management program includes 6 basic areas:

1. Reduction of conspicuous waste
2. Energy conserving equipment utilization and operating procedures
3. Record keeping
4. Maximum utilization of energy purchased
5. Rate examination and adjustment
6. Consideration of energy requirements in equipment specification.

Reduction of Conspicuous Waste

The simplest aspect of energy management is perhaps the most difficult to implement: energy is wasted because people are simply indifferent or ignorant. Employees and often managers do not recognize that it is a costly commodity. It is used when it need not be. The most cursory survey of a hospitality operation will reveal numerous instances of waste: lights burning when rooms are unoccupied, air conditioning running in vacant rooms, deep fat fryers running full blast during periods of reduced business. There are two essential questions the operational manager should be asking himself and other employees: "Why is it on?" and "Why do we do that?" Most energy waste is due to individuals not being specifically charged with turning off equipment or lighting. Even very clever procedural instructions that tell the worker to turn on the fryer or preheat the oven don't tell him to shut it off. The second largest cause of waste is past practice ("We always . . ."). Often energy utilization patterns and procedures were established during times of cheap energy or at least when energy conservation was not being given any consideration. Nowadays it is necessary to reexamine the "always." For example, the lighting in an area may always have been

Table 6.2. ROUTINE PREVENTIVE MAINTENANCE OF MECHANICAL
SYSTEMS AND EQUIPMENT

System or Equipment	Lubricate	Clean
Air conditioner	Motor; fan bearings	Condenser, cooling coils, fans; replace filters.
Air washer	Pump	Pump, baffle, eliminator plates
Alarms	Moving parts	Moving parts
Boiler	Fan	Flue passages, interior, shell drums, gauges, siphon loops, bonnets
Burners, gas		Controls; combustion chamber, flues, chimney
Burners, oil	Fan	Electrodes; draft regulator; fan, fan housing, filets; water separators, strainers
Clocks		Cabinets
Condensate pump	Pump and motor	Receiver, vent pipe, inlet and discharge openings
Cooling tower (as needed)		Water treatment equipment, tower pans, casings, and screens; nozzles
Doors, power operated (2)	Gear box	Mechanism and unit
Dumbwaiter	Motor, controls, safety devices	Hoistway, pit, cable pulls
Elevators	Brake, gears, motor, check keys, chains, cams, door closer pivot points, sill trips, checking devices, brushes, dashpots, traveling cables, tape drive, car door, pivots, worm and gear backlash, brake cores, bearings	Brake, checks, linkages, gears, wiring, motor, check keys, contacts, chains, cams, pivot points, sill trips, checking devices, brushes, dashpots, traveling cables, chain, magnets, tape drive, broken tape switch, car door, gate tracks pivots, hangers, car grill, stile channels, leveling switches, hoistway vanes, magnets, inductors, brake drum, drive sheave, motor

Table 6.2.   **ROUTINE PREVENTIVE MAINTENANCE OF MECHANICAL SYSTEMS AND EQUIPMENT**—continued

System or Equipment	Lubricate	Clean
		worm and gear, drum buffers, rope clamps, operating box, slack cable switch, shaft, keyways, pulleys, etc.
Escalator	Handrail tension device, and drive assembly	Machine space, tracks, transfer bars, guides, switches
Emergency lights	Terminals	Terminals, vent holes, exterior
Emergency generator	Engine, generator	Fuel filter, commutator, collector rings, generator winding
Fire doors	Pulleys	Track
Fire dampers	Friction points	
Fan	Motor	Fan, housing, motor, rotor
Heaters	Motor, pump	Tanks, coil, thermometers, aquastats, valves, gauges, traps
Incinerators		Furnace, ash pit, grates, uptakes, dampers
Paper baler	Motor, drive unit	Machinery
Radiators		Trap, valve
Sprinkler heads		Heads
Sump pump	Pump, motor	Pit, strainer, controls, switch

75-watt bulbs: the lighting has to be reconsidered. The operation's garbarge trucks have always run to the dump 3 times a day; but are they always full?

Energy Conserving Equipment Utilization and Operating Procedures

Sometimes the operational manager has a choice of equipment or method which can be made with energy conservation in mind. For example, an operational manager in food service may be able to cook food items in steamers instead of open pots. He may have the opportunity to defrost food items instead of cooking them frozen. An operational manager involved with the service desk of a hotel can refine schedules for shuttle buses, or consolidate mail for fewer trips to the post office. An operational manager in housekeeping can schedule jobs to take advantage of natural light or schedule heavy electrical equipment utilization during periods when other equipment is not used so as to take advantage of off peak rates.

Record Keeping

Keeping records of the energy consumption indicated by utility bills has two purposes. The operational manager can identify unusual consumption if he can compare it to similar periods. He then can attempt to correct the situation if the unusual consumption was in fact waste and not a weather change or unusual business. The procedure is familiar certainly to hospitality operational managers: it parallels systems of labor and food cost control.

The second purpose of record keeping is to monitor the billing of the utility. There are errors in computing bills, in reading meters, in the rate applied to the particular month in the meters themselves, etc. Merely comparing two bills can show that the reading shown on the prior bill has not been made the basis of the computation for the energy used during the following period. In the conventional sense, the utility company is "honest" but a great many fallible people are involved in the preparation of a computerized billing.

Operations which are being billed for energy usage by a private concern, for instance a shopping center or a complex of buildings, have a much more difficult problem. Sometimes it is quite evident from a comparison of past figures that the operation has been overbilled for heating or airconditioning. The operation's case for a reduction may perhaps be made simply on the basis of its records. Other times it is necessary to have an engineering study to demonstrate that it was impossible to have used that much airconditioning and not to have provided the guest with arctic clothing. An error of this kind has sometimes accounted for as much as a thousand dollars a month in extra cost for restaurant facilities alone.

Maximum Utilization of Energy Purchased

Poor building care management and poor general equipment management can result in energy waste. Heat which escapes through poorly

ENERGY CONSUMPTION AND COST RECORD

Building _____

Utility Company _____

Meter Constant _____
Cubic Volume of Bldg. _____
Net Sq. Ft. Heated Space _____

Rate Schedule _____
Hours Heating (mo.) _____
Days Heating (mo.) _____

1	2	3	4	5	6	7	8	9	10
Date of Reading	Degree Days	Meter Reading	Steam Consump.	Pounds Steam	Demand	Demand Charge	Fuel & Misc. Charges	Total Bill	Remarks, Etc.
Sept.									
Oct.									
Nov.									
Dec.									
Jan.									
Feb.									
Mar.									
Apr.									
May.									

Consumption for Year _____
Consumption for Past Year _____

1. Computed from the first day of the month where possible. If steam is purchased, or if boilers are placed on line other than first day of month, indicate in remarks column.
2. Degree days for month as reported by local Weather Bureau office, if available. Otherwise from other accredited source such as ASHRAE Guide.
3. Readings of steam condensate meter, or other recording device.
4. Pounds of steam consumed. Meter reading times constant.
5. Pounds steam per degree day, column 4 divided by column 2.

Figure 6.7. Energy consumption and cost record form.

Table 6.3. REDUCING THE COST OF UTILITIES

Utility	Check-point	Action
ELECTRICAL	Capacitors	Use static capacitors to improve power factor.
	Lamps	Survey requirements to eliminate over-sized lamps and over-lighted areas.
		Develop cyclic relamping programs to avoid spot replacement of bulbs.
	Load	Schedule heavy loads for off-peak hours to reduce peak demand charges.
		Investigate feasibility of installing load control devices.
	Meters	Reduce or consolidate metering points.
	Rates	Renegotiate more favorable rate schedule.
HEATING	Condensate	Conduct surveys to determine economics of returning condensate to boiler.
	Ventilation	Conduct surveys to determine economics of using heated air vented from kitchens for space heating.
	Controls	Eliminate overheating and waste by use of automatic controls.
	Fuel	Obtain competitive bids for fuel.
		Check fuel specifications.
		Check delivery schedules and ordering quantities.
	Insulation	Check condition of existing insulation on pipes and buildings.
	Leaks	Inspect system for fuel leaks and heat losses.
	Maintenance	Improve preventive maintenance procedures.
WATER	Chemicals	Check specification on treatment chemicals; seek standard chemicals rather than high-cost brand-name products.
	Faucets	Check for leaks, especially in hot water systems.

Table 6.3. REDUCING THE COST OF UTILITIES—continued

Utility	Check-point	Action
	Fixtures	Conduct surveys to determine economics of installing toilets, showers, and faucets that use less water.
		Install automatic closing devices where possible.
	Rates	Check meters and rates applied.
AIRCONDI-TIONING	*Controls*	Install automatic controls to allow cooling with outdoor air when conditions permit.
		Conduct surveys to determine economics of automatic devices to shut-down equipment when room or area is not being used.
	Filters	Check specifications and purchasing policy.
		Check replacement program.
		Practice preventive maintenance of system.
		Investigate use of permanent filters; cleaned on premises.

maintained windows, oven doors, hot water lines has to be replaced by further energy utilization. Electric motors which have not been maintained operate inefficiently, thereby increasing electrical utilization. Poorly maintained airconditioning or heating equipment is less efficient in its use of energy.

Special attention should be paid the devices which monitor or control energy consumption: valves on gas equipment, thermostats on equipment or heating systems, etc.

Rate Examination and Adjustment

The cost of energy, especially electricity and gas, can show as much as a threefold variation throughout the United States. In most instances the public utility's *Tariff,* a schedule of rates and general terms and conditions of services, is regulated by a governmental agency. The published Tariff is often a mammoth volume which no one without specialized knowledge of this area can expect to interpret. Several different methods of rate calculation may be offered, different classes of customers may qualify for different rates, there may be rates which change when the price of coal or utility worker wages change.

Someone could examine the Tariff and discover that a different method of rate calculation for which his operation qualified would save a considerable sum. Because of the complexity of the subject, and certainly because the Tariff is subject to continuous administrative rulings by the governmental agency after it is published, this type of research by the operational manager is unlikely to be productive. Large operations employ specialized consultants. Smaller operations investigate the matter periodically with the representatives of the utility who will study the operation's energy utilization and recommend a least expensive rate basis system *if they are invited to do so.*

Often there is the possibility of switching metering systems from a single meter to several or from several to a single meter with some economies. Or the rate schedule may be adjusted so that it is computed on the basis of several different factors, for example, a flat rate on an annual basis, a rate related to the maximum demand of energy at the operations peak utilization and the total amount of energy used. The utility representative helps the manager make the calculations or makes them for him so that the decision factors are apparent.

The utility representative will also help the manager take advantage of rate differentials by working with him to reduce "demand," the maximum energy demanded, so that this factor as a rate basis is smaller. Utilization of equipment is rescheduled or scheduled at periods of the day when rates are cheaper, for instance.

Consideration of Energy Requirements in Equipment Specification

There is often a choice between equipment or equipment systems which can be made on the basis of energy conservation. Some equipment is simply more efficient than other equipment of the same type. For instance an airconditioner manufactured by one company can cool a room for far less energy cost than a similar unit manufactured by another company.

When the choice is between equipment systems the calculation can be complex. For example, the director of a restaurant may be considering the installation of a display cooking station. He has two choices of ventilation system: the conventional hood system above the station, or down draught or "proximity" ventilation next to it. On an energy conservation basis the down draught ventilation is far more efficient, not because it is very much less expensive to run, but because it does not remove the air-conditioned air from the restaurant with the cooking fumes. The cost of operating the system—the dining room and the cooking station—is reduced by the lowered air conditioning costs.

Painting wall surfaces with light colors reduces the system's demand for energy—the room is the system—by allowing the operator to use less lighting for the same amount of illumination.

A light-colored van used to shuttle guests to a golf club requires much less air-conditioner utilization than a dark-colored van.

It should be obvious from the diversity of these examples that there are innumerable possibilities for energy conservation in equipment acquisition if the manager makes energy utilization a specification factor.

7 | Management Controls

The narrowest concept of control confounds it with information gathering: the broadest concept confuses it with the entire management process. Control activities have very specific functions which are served by information gathering, and which in their turn serve the process of management in optimizing profits, maximizing the use of resources, and so on. Management control is based on information, and information is the basis of action.

CONTROL ACTIVITIES

Control activities thus encompass all the devices, procedures, and systems designed to produce such information as food and beverage cost control, departmental reports, etc. Control activities stimulate all sorts of managerial activity such as planning, budgeting, supervising, cost cutting, labor scheduling, . . .

In modern hospitality organizations the nature of control activities is the direct result of the particularities of today's industry. Control activities are not what they were 40 years ago and they are not what they will be 10 years from now. When hospitality organizations were entirely managed, and often staffed, by one individual, control activities were almost unnecessary: the needed information and the capacity to act on it were consolidated in one man's mind. When hospitality organizations reach the sophistication and the size of major industrial corporations, control activities will be designed to compensate for the inability of any one man, or even a small group of men, to assimilate enough information and to act on it effectively. Today, control activities in the hospitality industry are midway between the cigar box and the digital computer, midway between rules of thumb and dynamic programming.

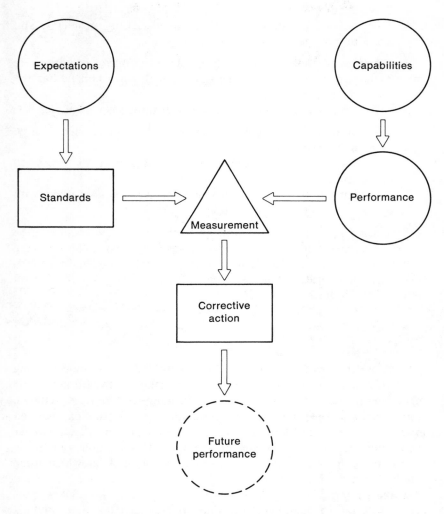

Figure 7.1. The control process step by step.

At this juncture, control activities in the hospitality industry serve five purposes.

1. They measure the quality, quantity, and performance of the operation against some standard.
2. They conform and correct the operation when it deviates from these standards.
3. They provide the decision base for managerial activity in planning, forecasting, budgeting, pricing, scheduling.

4. They communicate the operational standards.
5. They provide an internal check to limit security problems, and measure managerial effectiveness.

The operational manager is deeply involved in control activities. He gathers most of the information the operation requires and he has the opportunity to act on much of it.

In any operational unit, he is charged with three responsibilities:

1. Information gathering in specific areas such as labor, sales, quality, cash, unit performance;
2. Record keeping so that the information is sufficiently organized to be useful;
3. Reporting so that other managers not directly concerned with operations have the information they need.

Necessarily, specific control principles, the data base required, the reports generated, and the procedures implemented will differ with the operational unit, yet the functions of control activities and the responsibilities of the operational manager correspond broadly to the general needs of the industry at this time.

Functions of Control

MEASUREMENT

Control activities are diagnostic. The health of the operation is being tested in much the same way a physician tests the health of a person by measuring his heart function, blood composition, temperature, reflexes, respiration, etc. The vital signs of a hospitality organization can be seen in sales volume, cost of labor and materiel, labor productivity, customer satisfaction, return on investment, equipment utilization—all those aspects of business activity which are quantifiable and for which some standard can be established.

A measurement is taken, expressed meaningfully in dollars, percentages, a ratio to another measurement, and then compared with a standard so that the relative health of the operation on this basis can be determined.

The "standard" may be a goal. Management planned to have a labor cost percentage of 30 percent of sales. Control activities measure how nearly this standard was achieved.

The "standard" may be past performance. This month last year, 400 people were served: control activities compare this year's measurement of people served with last year's.

The "standard" may be an industry norm. Similar operations have a food cost percentage of 30 percent of sales, control activities determine how nearly normal the operation is in this respect.

The "standard" may be an organizational policy. Management has decided to serve a 12-ounce steak or a fresh appearing salad. Control activities determine if this standard is being met.

CONFORMING AND CORRECTING

In well managed operations, control activities often produce no evidence of problems. The measurement conforms to the established standard: no action is needed. Logically, control activity in this area should be reduced. Instead of daily or weekly measurements, monthly measurements should be taken. The cost of control is reduced, and management is freed to concentrate on those areas which deviate from the standard. This logic is not as pervasive as it seems, hence the confusion of control with information gathering and financial reporting. The control device or report becomes glorified as "good management," as though there were some virtue in the number of elaborate meters one could string on a pipe-line or the number of chest x-rays a doctor took during a physical examination.

When there is a deviation from the standard, managerial action is necessary. The deviation revealed by the measurement stimulates a corrective procedure planned as part of the operational system. Sales volume slips, thus marketing effort must be increased. Food costs increase, thus direct supervision must be intensified. Productivity slackens, incentives must be introduced. Ideally, the managerial reaction is part of the control activity. Just as a thermostat regulates a furnace when a certain temperature has been exceeded, managerial reaction to a deviation from a standard should be automatic.

At least it should be speedy. The worth of a control activity is directly related to how fast management can react to the information it produces, and to how fast the control reveals a deviation. Hence the attraction of pre-control procedures such as menu pre-costing which anticipate deviations.

A control activity which reveals deviations long after they occur has limited value: a great deal of damage has been done, and it might be too late to specifically isolate the problem. Financial reporting devices such as balance sheets and profit-and-loss statements provide an inadequate operational control basis precisely for this reason. The unsatisfactory results are apparent but not their cause nor the course of action necessary to affect a correction.

PROVIDING A DECISION BASE

Much control activity is directed to providing information of use to management in planning, budgeting, forecasting, and certainly in establishing standards by which future operations will be measured. The act of measuring and the articulation of the measurement serve as a reference point for operational improvement. The measurement becomes the standard to be bettered by an exploration of alternative courses of action. For example, a menu-pricing decision is based on information resulting from control activity, specifically, analysis of cost factors (through yield tests, etc.), profit margins, and sales, and directed to establishing a new standard of profitability. Likewise a make or buy decision is based on information resulting from a control activity, specifically, analysis of labor productivity, raw material costs, and equipment utilization, directed toward establishing a new standard for the product cost.

This function of control activity is especially valuable in the hospitality industry in which industry-wide standards have not yet been satisfactorily articulated. In many critical areas there is no norm by which the manager can judge his operation: no "right" labor cost percentage, no "right" food cost percentage, no "right" cost of materiel percentage for housekeeping, etc. Hospitality operations are too diverse, and the state of hospitality industry operations research too primitive to draw many conclusions which are not simply dangerous generalizations. A 30-percent food cost in one operation is acceptable, in another it is disastrous, while a third operation is highly profitable with a 50-percent food cost precisely because they are three different operations.

Lacking established standards, the operational manager must simply hammer away at his own standards in an attempt to better them. For this, he needs accurate current information.

COMMUNICATION

Control activities often communicate the operations standards so that deviations are prevented or limited, and thus do not have to be corrected. A purchase specification, a housekeeping check list, a portion control chart are control devices which communicate a standard so that people other than the manager can control quantity or quality before they become the manager's concern. Likewise a policy manual developed by higher level management controls the activities of the manager.

Pre-control communications devices of this sort prevent or limit the extent of deviations, and economize managerial control efforts. A chef who has been told to cut a 12-ounce steak does not cut an 18-ounce steak. He might if he were told nothing. Even though he may still cut 14-ounce steaks some savings is achieved. When the manager must intercede, the change to conform to the standard is not as radical.

INTERNAL CHECKING

In addition to being an analytical tool, control activities function as security and audit devices to prevent or identify fraudulent conversion of assets by employees, suppliers, outside thieves, and so on. Chapter 8 extensively treats the manager's responsibilities in implementing this control function.

When internal checks are the only function of a control device, it should be carefully evaluated to determine that the cost of control does not exceed the potential loss. It is usually possible to incorporate internal

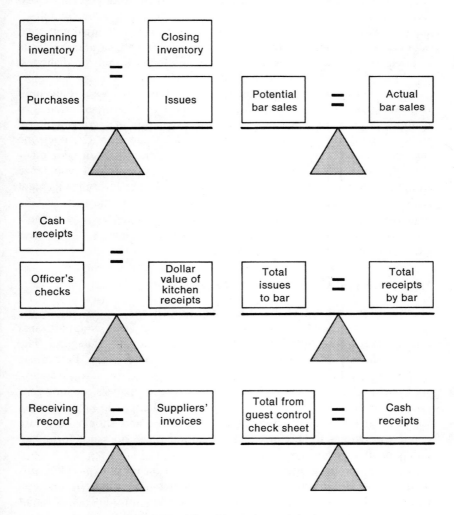

Figure 7.2.   Selected internal control checks.

check functions in a control activity which also supplies management data, or at least to derive internal check significance from accurate management data. For instance, an accurate analysis of labor costs and productivity for managerial purposes would reveal the presence of phantom workers on the payroll.

Sometimes the mere presence of a visible control system, whether or not it is particularly effective, can serve as an inexpensive internal check. A dishonest employee is not necessarily familiar with managerial control systems. A surprise change in the control procedure, perhaps in the number or routing of forms, or even in their color, keeps the dishonest individual disconcerted. Managers can ask for "meaningless" data to which the potentially dishonest employee will attribute great significance. The number of paper cups used in a cabana area has little relation to the number of guests sold chaises longues, but the dishonest employee draws his own conclusions.

Other internal checks have an entirely different purpose: they limit the damage someone's bad judgment can have on the organization. For example, a purchase order may require the signature of a craftsman and the unit manager, or the unit manager and his superior. Or, overtime may not be authorized except by written permission of a superior manager. The presence of the control procedure suggests lack of confidence in the subordinate's judgment, not his honesty. Upper level management feels that a system of control by accountability, after the fact, will be expensive to the organization. By requiring authorizations and permissions, there is an opportunity to evaluate the subordinate's effectiveness in his function without risking very much.

The Operational Manager's Control Responsibilities

Just as the elements of the managerial process are divided among the levels of management, the spectrum of control activities is apportioned among executives, administrators, and operational managers. The primary distinction is in their respective areas of concern. Percentage analysis of the financial statement, cash flow control, break-even analysis, control of collections and indebtedness, ratio analysis, do not generally concern the operational manager. Although he may supply information for control activities in these areas, and should be aware of their principles for his own self-development, he does not formulate policy or make decisions in these areas.

As the manager progresses in the organization he is exposed to different information, different control activities and different decision areas until he finds himself occupied with matters substantially different

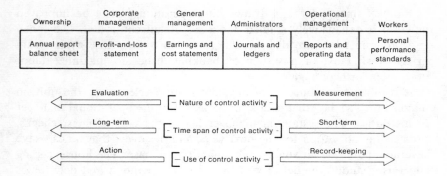

Figure 7.3. The control spectrum: control activities and information vary with the level of management.

from those which originally occupied him. Still and always he is part of the same managerial framework and control continuum.

In the day-to-day management of hospitality operations, the operational manager finds himself completing forms with information he cannot use, and implementing policy decisions based on data he does not have. The manager of one of a chain of restaurants and his colleagues may be supplying information which in aggregate will form the basis of a contract-buying decision by a central purchasing department. Or, he may be instructed to take an inventory position in a particular product as part of a commodity hedge of which he is unaware. The selective use of information is inherently part of the control process of any sophisticated organization. Otherwise, there is too much of it for any individual to handle.

INFORMATION GATHERING

The operational manager is obliged to gather the information the formal control system of his organization requires. He is given forms to complete such as a census of meals served, a recapitulation of checks, a cashier's report, charge control form, a labor analysis, and so on. Upper-level management is concerned with the business activity of his unit, his cost of sales, and his control of cash.

The operational manager also gathers information specifically useful to him as an operational manager. For example, information on labor productivity or the cost of energy, discussed in preceding chapters, properly interpreted can improve his unit's effectiveness. It is on the basis of this informal information gathering that the operational manager distinguishes himself. Creative solutions to problems and significant improvements in operations develop from a minute understanding of the way things work. A dishwashing operation cannot be improved unless it is exhaustively studied and every detail controlled. Only then is a program to reduce dish breakage, a plan to use rinse cycle steam in the wash tank, or a system of banking dishes to maximize labor utilization forthcoming.

It is difficult to conceive of any information relevant to the unit no matter how "trivial" that could not be useful to the operational manager in his duties. The restaurant manager learns the cost of guest checks, projects his utilization for the next year, and discovers that he can save several hundred dollars by a single quantity purchase. The housekeeping supervisor studies the delivery of linen to the operation and determines that he can eliminate one worker entirely if it is weighed rather than counted. The banquet sales manager analyzes the sales process and finds that he can add 20 percent to the effective selling time of his salesmen by developing a "book" of standardized paragraphs for follow-up letters.

RECORD KEEPING

Good record-keeping is the basis of planning, budgeting, decision making, forecasting, organizing, scheduling, production control, cost analysis and a score of other management activities. After information is gathered it must be organized to be meaningful. Unless the operational manager is endowed with total recall, organization means writing down information somewhere. The formal control devices of operation mandate certain record keeping but the operational manager may only be a conduit for this information. He may not be able to keep any of the forms he completes or information he supplies. A parallel system of record keeping should be established. At the very least a personal log, in diary form, lets him compare past business activity with anticipated events. More meaningfully he can construct charts and graphs which display critical control factors and relate to each other: labor cost to sales volume, food cost percentage to check average, outside temperature to iced tea sales, warewasher productivity to dish breakage, etc. Eventually, record keeping lets him establish decision rules that vastly increase his effectiveness.

REPORTING

In some hospitality organizations, reporting has been formalized. Standard forms are completed by the operational manager to communicate the statistical, accounting, or narrative data that higher level management requires. Sometimes electronic data processing equipment links the operational unit to a central computer which produces this information.

In other hospitality organizations, including many large establishments, much information, especially information other than accounting data, is communicated by means of operational reports produced by the manager.

Often the operational manager is charged with a specific operations research assignment by upper-level management. In essence, he is being asked to control an operational area which is not presently being controlled and to present the results of the control activity. The area may be very important. The upper-level management will then make a decision based on the data reported. To someone unfamiliar with hospitality organizations and perhaps familiar with industrial corporations the very process can seem bizarre: Why is this important area not always controlled? Many hospitality organizations are still growing, not only becoming larger but evolving as organizations, and control priorities change as the entire system changes.

Suddenly upper-level management decides that it must examine the menu mix to determine the profit contribution of each menu item as a percentage of total food sales. Or, the actual cost of employee meals becomes the object of consideration. Routine control data which focuses on accounting factors may not produce this information. The operational manager studies the area and produces a useful report. That is, the operational manager is asked to produce a useful report. Unfortunately, upper-level managers often discover that operational managers are incapable of presenting control information unless they are given a prepared form as simple to complete as a motor vehicle registration. As the preparation of such a form would be time consuming, superior managers vigorously protest this upward delegation of responsibility. As well, in many areas the use of a prepared form can limit the control activity, as its preparation must dictate the data basis of the control activity.

By following a few simple guidelines the operational manager can greatly increase the usefulness of the information he supplies his superiors.

1. *Include a standard of comparison in the report.* The standard can be derived from the operational manager's records: historical figures. It can be an industry standard where one exists, attributed to an authoritative source.

2. *Use current information.* Operating information stales rapidly. Sometimes special measurements, expressly for report purposes are necessary.

3. *Cover areas other than those covered by accounting systems.* Good control reports have depth beyond a presentation of income, cost, and expense. The inner workings of the operation should be plumbed in the specific report area.

```
                    RESTAURANT MANAGER'S REPORT

                              SALES

                    FOOD          BAR          SUNDRY
CASH SALES    :
CHARGES       :
CREDIT CARDS:_____
    TOTALS:
                                                           _____
                                                           Total
                                                           Sales
                          HOUSE CHARGES

                    FOOD          BAR          SUNDRY
OFFICERS'     :
EMPLOYEES'    :
COMPLIMENTARY:
WALK-OUTS     :
MISSED MEALS  :_____
        TOTALS:     _____   _____   _____
                                                           _____
                                                           Total
                                                           House
                                                           Charges

(SALES + HOUSE      _____   _____   _____
 CHARGE TOTAL)
                              GRAND TOTAL        :
                              (Sales + House Charges) _____

                    COST OF SALES: MATERIALS

                    FOOD          BAR          SUNDRY
BEGINNING INVENTORY    : $_____  $_____  $_____
ADD PURCHASES/RECEIPTS: _____    _____    _____
LESS CLOSING INVENTORY: _____    _____    _____


        COST              $____      $____      $____
```

Figure 7.4.   Restaurant manager's report: a basis for forecasting and budgeting.

4. *Limit the presentation of statistical material.* A report is not a worksheet. Conclusions not computations should be shown.
5. *Aim for communication effectiveness.* Presentation, organization, quality of preparation make the report easier to *use*.
6. *Venture conclusions.* Nobody can know the workings of the operational unit better than the operational manager. The report should indicate whether results are extraordinary or whether they indicate a trend. If a dish storage rack collapsed in the month being examined, the information on breakage for that month would have to be carefully qualified to prevent entirely wrong conclusions from being drawn.

```
                        RECONCILIATION OF FOOD COSTS

SALES:
     Total Food Sales                           $_____
     Less: Rebates                              ==========
           Net Food Sales                                    $_____

COSTS:
     Opening Storeroom Inventory    $_____
     Opening Production Inventory   ==========
        Total Opening Inventory                 $_____

     Storeroom Purchases            _____
     Direct Purchases               _____
        Total Purchases                         $_____

     Beverage to Food               _____
        Total Charges                                        $_____

LESS:
     Closing Storeroom Inventory    $_____
     Closing Production Inventory   ==========
        Total Closing Inventory                 $_____

     Credits: Food to Bars          $_____
              Gratis to Bars        _____
              Promotion Expense-
                 Manager            _____
                 Sales Staff        _____
                 Other              _____
              Misc. Sales &
                 Promotion          _____
              Misc. Credit &
                 Rebates            _____
              Grease & Fat Sales    _____
     Total Credits                  ==========  $_____
     Total All Credits                                       $_____
     Cost of Food Sold                                       $_____ ___%
     Less: Cost of Employee Meals                            ==========  ___
     Net Cost of Food Sold                                   _____  ___

     Net Food Cost at Par (From Summary of Food
                           Sales and Costs)                  $_____ ___%
     Difference Between Actual and Par Costs                 _____  ___

SUMMARY OF STOREROOM ISSUES              INVENTORY TURNOVER
     Kitchen - Main Kitchen   $_____    Dollar Inventory at Par  $_____
               Kitchen Staff  _____     Actual Inventory         ========
                                          Inventory Over/Short     _____
     Food to Bars             _____
     Steward Sales            _____     Actual Inventory
     Other                    _____        Turnover              $_____
     Total Book Issues        ========
     Total Actual Issues      _____     Total of Returns,
     Storeroom Over (or                      Corrections for the
          Under)              $_____       Month                 $_____


Signed: _____  DATE: _____
```

Figure 7.5. Reconciliation of food costs: an internal check and a data base for management decisions.

OPERATIONAL CONTROL PROCEDURES AND DEVICES

Operational control procedures and devices in areas of general concern to operational managers such as labor utilization and profit protection are extensively discussed in other chapters. (See Chapter 5, *Management of Work;* Chapter 6, *Management of Materiel;* Chapter 8, *Management of Profits.*)

Each operational area in a hospitality organization has its own specific procedures and devices which, in addition to the unit manager's general control activities, form the basis of his particular control responsibilities. Although hospitality organizations differ widely in the systems they utilize on the operational level, some consideration of the procedures and devices widely used in major operational units provides insight into the general concept of control.

Control of Restaurant Sales

In restaurant operations, control activities concern three principal areas in addition to that of cash receipts (Chapter 8): guest activity, guest checks, and menu item sales.

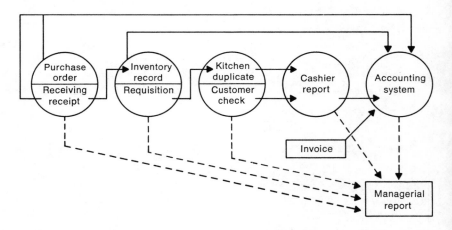

Figure 7.6. Control activities in foodservice.

GUEST ACTIVITY

Several devices control guest activity: cover forecast, reservations book, and meal census. Control is exercised before the operational activity, during it, and after it by these devices.

Cover forecast. The data base of the cover forecast provides the necessary information for scheduling personnel and food production. It is essentially an analytical management control tool which obliges the operational manager to address the various factors which will determine the volume of guest activity. It then serves as a communications device so that other individuals within the unit and elsewhere in the organization are aware of this determination.

Reservations book. The reservations book allows a measurement of guest activity during the progress of the meal and can provide the basis for on the spot managerial decisions such as a decision to accept or refuse additional business, keep the unit open past a certain hour, extend the work day into overtime for some employee, and so on.

Meal census. The meal census indicates the total number of people actually served and categorizes the guests in ways useful for planning, budgeting, improvement of forecasting, and cost analysis. Depending on the nature of the operation, categorization can include: take-out business, American Plan guests, hotel guests and outside guests, officer and employee meals, banquet and party business, and complimentary meals.

GUEST CHECKS

So that the integrity of food production control devices and cash control devices is maintained, there must be a control of guest checks. Otherwise, it is difficult to determine if food produced was actually served guests, or if the operation received payment for the food served. Check control devices include: the check itself, guest check control sheet, waiter's signature book, void record, officers and employee meal tickets, and food checker's recapitulation sheet.

Guest checks. The information on the guest check, specifically the waiter number or name, the table number, the number of persons, and the check number, permits several control procedures. The checks of an individual waiter can be compared with either duplicates of the check or "waiter's orders" in the kitchen. The number of people served allows closer control of the sales activity by allowing cover averages to be determined instead of check averages. Likewise, customer flow can be more accurately controlled for scheduling. The guest check number allows an essential control of cash receipts to be performed. If all checks can be accounted for, cash receipts (cash, charges, and credit card charges) should equal the total of all checks.

Guest check control sheet. The data base of the guest check control includes the number of each check used and its total amount. It allows the cashier to account for every serially numbered check, thereby determining if there are checks missing. The control sheet also permits a tally of the waiter's sales as a productivity index. The total dollar sales on the check control sheet can be compared with the total dollar sales computed from check duplicates in the kitchen, or with the total cash

DAILY CASH and CHECK REPORT

Restaurant_____ _____ day Date_____19___ Hour_____m.

Waiter's Number	Starting Number	Next Starting Number	Checks This Period	Checks From Previous Period	Amount	Total Checks			Nos. of Missing Checks	Paid from Register		
						Count	Void	Out				
1										FOODS	$	$
2												
3										Meat		
4												
5										Fish		
6												
7										Groceries		
8												
9										Fruit and		
10										Vegetables		
11												
12										Eggs		
13												
14										Bakery and		
15										Pastry		
High Checks										Pies		
Night Checks										Coffee		
1												
2										Butter		
3										Ice Cream		
4												
Cigars etc.										PHONE		
										SUNDRY		
										WAGES		
TOTALS										TOTALS		
												CASHIER

RECAPITULATION

				MEALS SERVED	CHECK AVERAGE (cents)	CASH RECEIPTS			CIGAR SALES	
		CASH	CHECKS			MORNING	NOON	EVENING		
This Register Reading......	$									
Last Register Reading......										
For this Period...........	$	$	$			$	$	$		
Forward last Period........										
Totals to Date.............										

Figure 7.7. Control form for checks and cash: an internal check on foodservice and cashiering personnel.

receipts to provide another control loop. Guest check control sheet is also called a check recapitulation form.

Waiter's signature book. Simply discovering that checks are missing by use of the guest check control sheet does not attribute the responsibility for them to anyone. The waiter's signature book notes to which waiter specific guest checks and kitchen duplicates were issued, and makes him acknowledge their receipt with his signature.

Void record. The void record may take the form of a sheet of paper on which void checks and their number are noted with an explanation, or it may be a printed chit that is attached to voided checks. The control premise is the same in both instances. Voided checks have to be authorized and noted so that adjustments can be made on the guest control sheet. Some operations use a walk-out sheet or chit to the same end: to separate mistakes and customer theft from employee conversion.

Officers and employee meal tickets. It is essential to the control of restaurant sales that the food delivered to the waiters by the kitchen and accounted for by "waiters orders" or duplicates (so called even when they are not duplicates of anything) be compared with guest checks either by item or total dollars. If officers or employees eat in the same dining room as guests a separate tally has to be kept of their consumption so that the kitchen accounting can be adjusted. Officers or employee meals do not appear on the guest control sheet nor are they usually rung into the cash register. (They might be on a separate "staff" key but this is rare.) This tally may take the form of signed chits or tickets which offers a further control over who is eating or, less satisfactorily, it may be kept as a running total by the cashier.

Food checker recapitulation sheet. In some kitchens it is virtually impossible to generate a duplicate check for every food item taken from the kitchen by the waiter. As a measure of control an employee is charged with examining the waiter tray and itemizing (by amount) the food on it using a printing cashier register (checking machine). The total from this machine substitutes for the duplicate or waiter's order tally. Less satisfactorily but also less expensively, the waiters operate the checking machine. Although the house is thus ensured that it receives all the money the customer pays for items on the check, there is still the possibility that waiters can *short check,* that is, not record items on a check, for "friends" or in the hope of getting a greater gratuity. Some checking machines generate printed duplicates which serve as the waiter's order. Their current use is largely confined to fast food restaurants or limited menu restaurants because of the expense of keying the machine for all the items in a full menu operation.

MENU ITEM SALES

Unlike guest-check control, which serves as an internal check, the primary purpose of menu item sales control is to provide an analytical tool for management. Knowing the number of each item sold allows the manager to compute the profit contribution of each item as a percentage of sales, allows him to control the offering of specials and the promotion of side dishes to increase check averages and profits, etc. The essence of the control procedure is simply to record the number of each item sold. Newer checking machines keep running tallies and can print out this information. Otherwise, mechanical counters can be used, or a system of hand transcription from either customer's checks or kitchen duplicates. The form on which the hand transcription is recorded is sometimes called the foodservice tally recapitulation sheet, the menu scoring worksheet or most commonly the menu scatter sheet.

Menu scatter sheet. The data base of the scatter sheet consists of a list of menu items usually categorized by percentage food cost (of selling

MENU ANALYSIS: SCATTER SHEET

DATE_____ DAY_____COVERS_____ COVER AVERAGE_____REMARKS_____

ITEM	MENU PRICE	PERCENT SOLD	TIMES SOLD	TOTAL SOLD	SALES VALUE	PERCENT TOTAL ITEMS	PERCENT FOOD COST	PERCENT GROSS PROFIT

Figure 7.8.   The menu scatter sheet: basic control device of item sales.

price) to facilitate calculation, with their sales price, food cost percentage, a recapitulation of the number of times each item was sold, and the total sales value of each item sold.

Control of Room Sales

Control devices involving room sales are divided into 2 major categories: those involved with room occupancy and those involved with charging the guest for services he purchases in addition to his room. As the control systems in these areas are extensive but largely routine, many operations are introducing integrated control systems which are based on electronic data processing. Not only is a great deal of paperwork and the personnel to do it eliminated, but the process of control is speeded considerably.

ROOM OCCUPANCY

The objective of the room occupancy control system and its dependent devices is information. The front office must know which rooms are vacant and uncommitted to guests who have not arrived so that they can be sold. The front office must also know which rooms are occupied and at what rates so that guests using them may be appropriately charged. Quite obviously the complexity and the sophistication of the control system depends on the number of rooms available and on the frequency of their being occupied by different guests. Room occupancy in a motel with just a few rooms can be controlled by the simplest record keeping

RESERVATIONS RECORD

DATE RECEIVED	NAME LAST	FIRST	HOW RECEIVED	NO. IN PARTY	ROOMS REQUESTED	DATE REQUESTED	TYPE OF ROOM	TIME ARRIVING	ROOMS ASSIGNED	RATE	DEPOSIT	BY	ARRIVED

Figure 7.9. A simple control form for recording reservations: adequate for a small property or one with little transient business.

on a sheet of paper. Likewise, a large residential hotel can be simply controlled.

Reservation booking record. When a guest contacts the hotel to purchase a room for some future date, that room must be removed from the list of available rooms for that date. The room availability on that date is communicated in a variety of ways, any of which serves as a reservation: booking record, a reservation diary, a visible display, or a computer instruction. Whatever the specific device, it provides a permanent record of the reservation so that the room will not be sold twice.

Arrival and departure record. On a given day it is necessary to determine if guests with reservations have arrived and if guests expected to depart have departed. In a small hotel a simple list with just this information suffices. In larger establishments a room rack is used so that rooms sold for that day can be blocked and rooms vacated that day can be sold. Color coding of the slips blocking the sale of a specific room allows some measure of control over how long the reservation will be honored before the room is released for sale.

Registration record. The registration record, whether it is a simple bound book or a registration packet of assorted forms indicates that a guest is in a room and the room cannot be sold. In most modern establishments the registration record is quickly duplicated or communicated so that other departments concerned with guest service are aware of the guest's occupancy: telephone switchboard, housekeeping, dining room (in American Plan hotels), etc. The registration record is also used to update the room rack and to open the guest's account with the hotel so that he can be charged on leaving for his room and the services he purchases.

GUEST CHARGES

There are two basic devices used to control guest transactions: the guest folio and departmental charge vouchers.

Guest folio. The guest folio is the continuing record of the guest's account with the hotel during his stay. Any charges to him are recorded on the folio from which his final statement is prepared. As well, if there are any credits to his account during his stay they are recorded on the folio.

Departmental charge vouchers. In most operations a guest may pay cash for products or services for which the operation asks payment or he may charge it to his room account. Departmental charge vouchers or charge control slips communicate to the front office cashier maintaining the guest folio that the guest has charged something: tennis lessons, drinks at the bar, valet services, garaging for his car, magazines and newspapers, laundry, etc. These departmental charge vouchers may be color coded or printed to indicate in which department they originated or this material may be handwritten by the departmental cashier along with the guest's name, room number, items purchased, and their amount.

Control of Beverage Sales

The general objectives of control of beverage sales parallel those of control of food sales. Fundamentally, beverage controls provide an internal check against conversion by employees, and secondarily, supply managerial data for pricing and buying decisions. Beverage control procedures and devices, however, must differ from those used in controlling food sales. Food control systems rely on independent tallies of merchandise or the cash for it at different check points: producer (kitchen), server, and cashier. The bartender may combine these 3 functions.

The basic beverage control procedure is to compare the actual revenues from a known quantity of spirits, wine, or beer with the potential revenues computed by applying a pricing factor to the cost of the product. Control by this means is most effective when the product is easily quantified such as canned beer, and least effective when the product is a variable combination of ingredients (as it most often is) such as mixed cocktails.

The devices used in beverage control support this control procedure. The beverage control system is completed by physical controls, control of checks, shopping bartenders, and other security devices discussed in Chapter 8.

It is also possible to structure the system so that an independent tally is possible. A separate cashier can be used or the liquor can be dispensed from an automatic device which meters and records the amount dispensed.

Bar sales record. The bar sales record data base provides information on the cash sales of the bar and the cost of issues to the bar. On a daily basis bar sales records can be computed to show an indicative liquor cost percentage. On a weekly or monthly basis, with adjustments for opening and closing inventory, the liquor cost percentage can be more accurately determined. In many operations control of this percentage is the primary control activity. A deviation from the established standard indicates that there is a problem. Control is not as complete as a comparison of actual and potential revenues, as extraordinary sales of items with a low cost percentage such as beer or specialty drinks during the control period can compensate for the conversion of assets by a dishonest employee. The method is widely used because its cost of control is far less than the actual-potential comparison, or the Herculean task of attempting to compare product usage derived from guest checks with actual product used.

BEVERAGE ACTUAL AND POTENTIAL WORKSHEET

HOTEL _____ LOCATION _____ PERIOD _____

	COMBINED OPERATION													
	Cost	Potential Sales	Cost	Potential Sales	Cost	Potential Sales	Cost	Potential Sales	Cost	Potential Sales	Cost	Potential Sales	Cost	Potential Sales
Opening Inventory														
Issues (Requisitions)														
Closing Inventory														
Food For Mixing														
Sub Total														
Loss and Breakage														
Price Differential Adjustment														
Cocktail Adjustment														
Cocktail Adjustment, Other														
Mineral Adjustment														
Executive Office														
Sales Promotion, Etc.														
TOTAL														
Less: Actual Bottle Cost and Sales														
= Actual Drink Cost & Potential Sales														
Less: Actual Drink Sales														
= Difference														

Figure 7.10. An actual and potential sales worksheet.

SUMMARY OF BEVERAGE ISSUES

HOTEL _____ LOCATION _____ MONTH _____

ITEM	SIZE	PRICE	POTENTIAL SALES PRICE	ISSUES Days of Month																TOTAL ISSUES	TOTAL COST	TOTAL POTENTIAL	ISSUES Days of Month																TOTAL ISSUES	TOTAL COST	TOTAL POTENTIAL
				1	2	3	4	5	6	7	8	9	10	11	12	13	14	15				16	17	18	19	20	21	22	23	24	25	26	27	28	29	30	31			

Figure 7.11. Form for comparing beverage issues and receipts.

Bar inventory and issue record: For beverage control procedures to be effective the physical inventory of the bar at the start of the control period must be known. When issues to the bar are also controlled, usage can be determined and compared with sales. (Opening inventory, plus issues, less closing inventory equals usage.) Most of the forms and devices used in beverage control address inventory or issues.

Bar requisitions. As the issue record is generated by the stores department, a control is necessary to insure that issues are actually arriving in the bar. As a procedure the bar generally prepares a written requisition for beverages (which can be compared with issue records) and acknowledges receipt of beverages on the requisition or on an issue device so that responsibility can be fixed if control activities indicate a deviation from standard.

Check control sheets, etc. Beverage sales can be compromised by the conversion of cash as well as merchandise. The devices used in food sales control are also used in monitoring bar transactions.

Control of Sales, Catering and Convention Operations

The control of sales for catering and convention operations depends purely and simply on the proper maintenance of records for past, current, and future business. These communicate essential information in condensed form to individuals and departments in the organization.

Records and files may be divided into two categories: (1) those pertaining to the sale and booking of the catering affair or convention and (2) those that are essentially operational.

SALES AND BOOKING FILES

Sales and booking files include the following: function file envelopes or folders, master cards, tickler, or follow-up cards, sales report forms, tentative booking reports, confirmed booking reports, cancellation reports, backlog summaries, reports of lost business, and contracts.

Function file envelopes or folders. Function file envelopes or folders are generally 9 by 12 inches or larger for holding all correspondence, records, forms, and reports on a particular account. They can be purchased preprinted, with blanks for essential information which might include the material on the master card, the menu, the number of guests, and the requirements for specific events.

Master cards. Master cards are the key to continuing bookings, especially of business groups. They generally contain at least the name of the organization; the name and address of the executive or elected officer in charge (or private individual); the names, addresses, and telephone numbers of local representatives of the organization; the type of affair; the usual attendance; the approximate date of meeting for a periodic affair; a history of past bookings, plus current and future bookings; and any special requirements.

A master card is necessary even to book a wedding or party for a private individual, since other customers often discuss future bookings in terms of parties they have attended.

```
                              SALES REPORT


                                    Date:_____.

ORGANIZATION _____

Name of Contact_____ Title_____

Address_____City_____

Phone No._____ In Hotel [  ]      Their Office [  ]   Phone [  ]

National File_____ I.B.M. No._____ Acct. Exec. No._____

Report in Full on Interview_____

_____

_____

_____

_____

_____

_____

_____

_____

_____

_____

_____

                                    Trace _____

Representative_____

Hotel _____

City _____

Copy _____
```

Figure 7.12. Sample sales report form: control device for monitoring marketing activity.

Tickler, or follow-up cards. Tickler cards are used by a sales staff to organize sales solicitation so that possible clients for banquets, business meetings, or social affairs are contacted at the best time. Most of the time the tickler card duplicates the essential information on the master card and is filed in a suspension file by date so that the salesman only has to pull the daily file to organize his calls.

Sales report forms. A sales report is essential in any type of sales from banquet solicitations to convention blitzes. It allows the manager to monitor the salesman's sales efforts. It should contain the following information: the date; the name of the organization; the contact's name, title, address, and telephone number; the place of the interview; and a report of the interview.

Tentative booking reports. Generally the tentative booking is the first notification to the operation as a whole that a specific party with certain requirements may be booked. It contains the same information as the confirmed booking but is marked for information, not action.

Confirmed booking reports. A confirmed booking indicates the name of the organization: the contact's name, title, address, telephone; details on the type of function; the place of the function; the number in the group; rates; and instructions. In many instances the confirmed booking is made on a contract form.

Cancellation reports. A cancellation report may be issued after a tentative booking, after a confirmed booking, and even after a contract has been signed. It simply notifies the individuals or departments concerned that the affair has been cancelled, using the same headings as the confirmed or tentative booking. At this point, depending on the terms of the contract and the operation's particular business policy, the manager can decide to return deposits in full or in part.

Backlog summaries. The backlog summary, which recapitulates the catering business of an operation by the week or by the month, is essentially a management tool. It presents sufficient information on the money value of business in a given period to allow the manager to make decisions on the immediate profitability of accepting additional business at specific rates.

Reports of lost business. The report of lost business, which indicates in detail the reasons why a potential customer elected not to use the organization's services helps the management to evaluate its market position and its competition. It is filed by sales personnel who have followed up a "good lead."

Contracts. Most operations use a contract form that provides space for filling in information about the specific menu and arrangements, and contains the legal stipulations on the back. It is in effect an order blank *and* a contract.

BACKLOG SUMMARY

Year _____ Month _____

Enter every booking (except repetitive functions, such as Civic Clubs, etc.) in Total only.

NAME OF GROUP	BOOKING OR REVALUATION DATE	NUMBER OF GUESTS	VALUATION OF BOOKING							
			ROOMS	FOOD		BEVERAGE		RENTALS	TOTAL	
				FUNCTIONS	REGULAR	FUNCTIONS	REGULAR			
Total Monthly Value of repetitive functions										

Numbers in Valuation columns refer to Totals recorded in "Booking Value Recap" on Booking Report.

To record revaluation: Cross out original entry and enter new data in next available space.

Figure 7.13. Backlog summary: provides data for control of sales.

OPERATIONAL RECORDS AND FILES

Standard forms and records, or at least standard formats for forms and records, are generally used to reduce verbal communication in the operational units. Such standard-format communication travels throughout a hospitality organization as work orders, departmental work orders, purchase orders, schedules, event resumes, and weekly function sheets.

The forms and records are as detailed as necessary, but probably, after a time, certain details can be considered routine. For example, the components of a place setting for a specific banquet menu need not be specified each time, since the individuals concerned learn them or consult past records.

```
                                             Date_____


                        REPORT OF LOST BUSINESS


Name of Group_____

Contact:_____Title_____

Address_____

Date of Functions or Convention_____

Type of Business_____

Size of Group (No. Persons; No. Rooms, etc.)_____

_____

_____Hotel Selected_____

Source of Lead and Date Received_____

_____

_____

Reason for Losing Business_____

_____

_____

Report of Solicitation_____

_____

_____


cc: General Manager          Name_____
    Director of Sales
    File                     Title_____
```

Figure 7.14   Report of lost business: a method of evaluating sales productivity.

Copies of all forms are kept in the function envelope or file. As they are needed, they are sent to the bookkeeping department or the individual who bills the function.

Function work order. The various individuals or sections concerned with the function are given specific instructions as to their responsibilities and roles. In a very well organized operation, a duplicate of the function work order may suffice if the individuals concerned are sufficiently expert to abstract what they need. Otherwise, a separate sheet is prepared for the kitchen, for the individual who will run the dining room crew on- or off-premises, for the steward in charge of equipment, and for anyone else involved. Very often these sheets are mimeographed or photocopied for the information of all parties.

```
                          SPECIAL FUNCTION FORM



    FUNCTION:                                    NO.

    DATE  (DAY, MONTH, YEAR)

    TIME:                       ROOM:       NUMBER OF GUESTS _____

    SPECIAL ARRANGEMENTS:

                            FLOWERS
                        ENTERTAINMENT
    BEVERAGES:              OTHER




          FOOD MENU:




          TOTAL

    PAYMENT:

        It is agreed that the undersigned will provide a minimum guarantee on the
    number of guests to be served 24 hours in advance of party.  A variation of 5%
    is permitted, and the undersigned agrees to pay for all guests who attend but not
    less than 95% of the guaranteed number.  Cash payment of charge will be made only
    to an open mess cashier.


                              _____
                                    Customer's Signature

    _____
          Booking Party
                              APPROVED BY _____
```

Figure 7.15. Form for recording data for social functions.

Purchase orders. Purchase orders, requisitions, and similar forms may be issued by the individuals concerned in each department, or they may be entirely prepared by the managerial personnel coordinating the function. Very often there are purchase orders for special equipment, rentals, flowers, and entertainment to be issued by someone other than the production department or the equipment, serviceware, and napery steward. Such purchase orders would be handled by managerial personnel.

Schedules. As the actual date of the event approaches, accurate and detailed schedules have to be prepared. These are necessary so that the individuals concerned will know when they must schedule personnel, complete production, have equipment available, call for transportation, and complete the rest of the arrangements.

Event resumes. Event resumes are issued in large operations to update function work orders that may have been prepared months or years before the actual event. Various individuals can then plan their work for the month on the basis of the event resume.

Weekly function sheets. A weekly function sheet relates all the operation's activities to each other in summary form. Its purpose is to avoid duplicate commitment of rooms, personnel, equipment, production facilities, et cetera; to remind all concerned of upcoming events; and to offer a master checklist.

Control of Food Production

Although the control devices used in food production operational units provide internal checks and operational data for managerial decisions, their primary emphasis is the pre-control of quantity and quality. Deviations from the control standard are prevented by measurement before food products are actually committed to the customer.

Yield tests. The food production operational manager measures the quantity of usable or salable products in a purchased or prepared item so that he can compare that measure with an establishment standard, and can provide himself with a data base for menu pricing, production scheduling, and internal checks on food production and foodservice personnel. For example, in measuring the yield of 8-ounce portions of a cooked prime rib, he measures the quality of the meat the purveyor supplied, determines information for pricing and menu pre-costing, and provides himself with a check point for comparing kitchen duplicates and guest checks. Yield tests directed to different products are called, also butcher's tests, carving tests, canned food tests, and cooking loss tests.

Standard portion sizes. Charts, displays, and handbooks communicate

FORMAT	SIZE PORTION	UNIT COST	PORTION COST	ADJUSTED COST TO DATE		ADJUSTED COST TO DATE	
				DATE	COST	DATE	COST
1							
2							
3							
4							
5							
6							
7							
8							
9							
10							
COST ADJUSTMENTS FINISHED COST							
SELLING PRICE DEDUCT FINISHED COST GROSS PROFIT GROSS PROFIT %							

COST TEST FORM

ITEM_____   VENDOR_____

DATE_____   BY_____

Figure 7.16. Cost test form: purchasing decisions must be frequently reevaluated.

the established portion size of food items so that employees other than the manager can pre-control the product.

Standard recipe. The use of standardized recipes in cards, books, and charts protects the integrity of the control system by pre-controlling the preparation of items which cannot be easily controlled after they are prepared.

Menu precost. The menu precost is a planning device which obliges the manager to forecast the number of portions to be sold of each item on the menu that day. He extends forecasts to the total sales for that day by multiplying the sales price by the number of each item sold. As he can also incorporate the cost per portion and food cost percentage for each item (based on the sales price) into the forecast, he can control his managerial judgment in placing certain items on the menu. He may find

BUTCHER TEST CARD

ITEM_____ GRADE_____ DATE_____

PIECES_____ WEIGHING_____ LBS._____ OZ._____ AVERAGE WEIGHT_____

TOTAL COST $_____ AT $_____ PER_____ SUPPLIER_____ HOTEL_____

BREAKDOWN	No.	WEIGHT		RATIO TO TOTAL WEIGHT	VALUE PER LB.	TOTAL VALUE	COST OF EACH		PORTION		COST FACTOR PER	
		LB.	OZ.				LB.	OZ.	SIZE	COST	LB.	PORTION
TOTAL												

ITEM_____ PORTION SIZE_____ PORTION COST FACTOR_____

Figure 7.17. Butcher test card: for control of portion yields and analysis of actual yields of as-purchased products.

DAILY LUNCH COUNT SHEET

CENTRAL KITCHEN _____

UNIT _____

DAY _____

LUNCH COUNT TIME _____
TIME CALLED _____

DATE _____

COUNT GIVEN BY _____

Menu Item	Portion Sent	Quan. Sent	Size of Portion	Serving Utensil	Size and Type Pan	Carrier	Temp. at Central Kitchen	Temp. at Unit	Excess Portion

Pick Up Time: _____
Time Picked Up: _____
Transported By: _____

Delivery Time: _____
Time Delivered: _____
Received By: _____

COMMENTS: _____

WHITE - S.L. OFFICE COPY
YELLOW - RECEIVING SCHOOL COPY
PINK - CENTRAL KITCHEN COPY

* Temp of food when placed in carrier
** Of last pan of food

Figure 7.18. Daily lunch count sheet: device incorporating data on both quantity and quality.

	A	B	C	D	E	F	G	H
						PERCENT OF SALES		PERCENT GROSS PROFIT
			TOTAL		TOTAL	OF SALES	GROSS	PROFIT
	COST	NUMBER	COST	SALES	SALES	(% OF	PROFIT	(% OF
ITEM	PORTION	SOLD	(A TIMES B)	PRICE	(B TIMES D)	TOTAL E)	(E MINUS C)	TOTAL G)
TOTALS XXX						100.00		100.00

ENTREE MIX COST PERCENTAGE (FORECAST OR REPORT)

$$\text{GROSS PROFIT PERCENTAGE} = \frac{\text{TOTAL G}}{\text{TOTAL E}} \times 100$$

$$\text{GROSS PROFIT AVERAGE PER ENTREE} = \frac{\text{TOTAL E}}{\text{TOTAL B}} \times \text{GROSS PROFIT PERCENTAGE}$$

Figure 7.19. Chart for comparison of forecast figures with actual performance.

that if his forecast is correct, he cannot achieve the food cost percentage to which he is committed. He can then adjust the menu (by changing it entirely in American Plan hotels, cafeterias, or institutions, or by adding or removing specials in à la carte restaurants) so that the forecast and the food cost percentage is acceptable.

Menu abstract. The menu abstract exactly parallels the menu precost (and may appear on the same form) except that it is performed after the meal as a control of the accuracy of the forecasting.

Production order. Production orders, production schedules, cook's work sheets, and food preparation orders, communicate the manager's forecast of business—his expectation of the number of each item that will be sold—so that production is pre-controlled to meet this standard.

Food portion control report. When food items are prepared in a single kitchen but used in several service units it becomes necessary to introduce an internal check that compares the total number of portions prepared with the total number sold in the units. Each unit is made accountable by means of reports, which are summarized as the food portion control report. In addition to fixing responsibility for lost portions, the report also provides a management tool for production plan-

MENU PRECOST AND ABSTRACT

DEPARTMENT_____ MEAL_____

DAY_____ DATE_____ WEATHER_____

| ENTREE | SELLING PRICE | COST | FORECAST | | | | | ACTUAL | | | | | |
			NUMBER	REVENUE	COST	COST %	Ratio to TOTAL	NUMBER SOLD	SALES	COST	COST %	Ratio to TOTAL

Figure 7.20. Menu precost and abstract: control which allows a manager to improve on an operational activity before it occurs.

PRODUCTION ORDER AND RECORD

DATE TODAY_____ BY_____ FOR DATE_____

DINING ROOM MENU	ITEM	PORTION SIZE	PORTIONS PER	PAR LEVEL	ON HAND	MAKE	MADE	RETURNS	USED	EXTENSIONS	DISPOSITION OF RETURNS

Figure 7.21. Production order and record form: such control devices allow pre-control by the manager.

DAILY AND WEEKLY FOOD COST REPORT

Week Beginning

| Date | Purveyor | Items: Dollar Costs | | | | | | | | Total Purchases | | Total Sales | | % Cumulat. Purchases to Sales |
		Meats	Poult.	Sea Food	Veg.	Dairy Prod.	Ice Cream	Groceries	Bakry Goods	Misc.	Daily	Cumulat.	Daily	Cumulat.	
Mon.															
Tues.															
Wed.															
Thu.															
Fri.															
Sat.															
Sun.															

Figure 7.22.   Daily and weekly food cost report: a valuable tool in institutional foodservice.

ning. Identical menus need not sell identically in different rooms or units. The food portion control report isolates the differences in menu acceptability.

Daily food cost sheet. The data base of the daily food cost sheet is the total cost of food during the day assessed by food group. The managers who use this control device interpret deviations in the cost of particular items as indicative of a general deviation from the operational standard. For example, if the butter cost increases in absolute amount or as a percentage of the total dollar cost for food, they react. As a control procedure, costing food on a daily basis has its limitations. It is somewhat effective in operations with an unvarying volume of business and a cyclical menu carefully adjusted to produce standard meal costs. Prisons or schools might use it. In commercial restaurants, other control devices, based on food cost percentage standards or menu analysis, are more effective because of the variable factors involved.

Control of Inventory

Inventory control procedures primarily serve as internal checks. The control devices used signal management if an item purchased and received has been fraudulently converted or wasted by inappropriate handling in storage. The secondary use of inventory control devices is to provide management information so that purchasing can be economical and efficient, and so that other control procedures for other areas such as food production can be initiated.

The basic control procedure consists of a reconciliation of items received with items issued, with adjustments for those items in stock at the beginning of the control period and at its end. The beginning inventory plus the items received less the issues should equal the closing inventory. The inventory and issues figures can be expressed in actual units of items or in total dollar figures depending on the purpose of the procedure. Most operations express inventory and issues in both units and dollars on different control devices. Control of units allows isolation of conversion and waste. Control of dollar costs allows a determination of the dollar cost during a period for use in control of cost of sales in food and beverage operations, and of costs in housekeeping, maintenance, etc.

Receiving records. If the inventory control procedure is to be meaningful the key elements of its data base must be accurate. Receiving records, receiving clerks' reports, or receiving entries on control devices are necessary. Receiving records are also an element in purchasing control (see below).

Issuing records. Issuing records may take the form of entries on con-

RECEIVING RECORD AND REPORT

LOCATION____

DATE____

SHEET NUMBER____ OF____

ITEM	PURVEYOR SHIPPER	P.O. #	I.N. #	QUANTITY ORDER	RECEIVED	UNIT	UNIT PRICE	TOTAL AMOUNT	# OF PKGS.	DISTRIBUTION DEPT.	DEPT.	DEPT.	DEPT.	COMMENTS	REC. BY

Figure 7.23. Receiving record and report: an internal check of suppliers' invoices.

STOCK NUMBER__________
CARD NUMBER__________

INVENTORY AND PURCHASE RECORD

ARTICLE:__________ SECTION:__________
UNIT:__________ AISLE:__________
PACKAGE:__________ BIN:__________

DESCRIPTION/SPECIFICATIONS:__________

INVENTORY DATA	YEAR	CONSUMPTION DATA: MONTHLY											
	19	1	2	3	4	5	6	7	8	9	10	11	12
MINIMUM:	19												
MAXIMUM:	19												
PAR LEVEL:	19												
ORDER QUANTITY:	19												

VENDORS

	FIRM	CAT. #	DELIVERY TIME	HOW SHIPPED	BRAND	REMARKS
0						
1						
2						
3						
4						
5						

PURCHASE RECORD

ORDERED				RECEIVED						
DATE	FIRM	P.O.	QUANT.	DATE	I#	QUANT.	INVOICE AMOUNT	UNIT PRICE	BRAND	REMARKS

PERPETUAL INVENTORY

DATE	P.O./ REQ.#	IN	OUT	BAL.	DATE	P.O./ REQ.#	IN	OUT	BAL.	DATE	P.O./ REQ.#	IN	OUT	BAL.

Figure 7.24. Inventory and purchase record: data base for purchasing decisions.

trol devices such as perpetual inventories, or copies of the requisitions used by production units. In common with receiving records, the issuing records form an essential element of the data base of the control procedure.

Perpetual inventories. Perpetual inventories, either in unit quantities of particular items or in dollars or both, provide bases for control of inventory at any time. There is a continuous up-date of the beginning in-

REQUISITION   NUMBER_____

TO:
FROM:
BY: DATE WANTED:
DATE: IMMEDIATE: ( )
CHARGED TO: REGULAR DEL.: AM ( ) PM ( )

CODE	ITEM/DESCRIPTION	UNIT	ON HAND	QUANT. ORD.	QUANT. DEL.	BACK ORD. DELIVERY	QUANT. REC.	COST PER UNIT	TOTAL COST

APPROVED BY: FILLED BY: RECEIVED BY: TOTAL COST
                                                                 OF REQ.
DATE: DATE: DATE:

COPY CODE:
    WHITE: ORDERING DEPT. RETAINS
    BLUE: TO SUPPLY DEPT., RETAINS
    PINK: TO SUPPLY DEPT., USED AS RECEIPT: TO CONTROL
    GREEN: SHIPPING DEPT.

Figure 7.25. Requisition sheet: essential to the control of inventory and ultimately of costs.

ventory by the addition of the items received and the subtraction of the items issued. A perpetual inventory is not necessary to the control procedure. Rather it allows the flexible application of the procedure, as no definite control period has to be used. At any time, a reconciliation of items issued and items received can be made. The control procedure is however, limited, as the inventory on paper may not correspond to the actual number of items or the dollar value of items in stock.

Physical inventories. An actual count of items in stock at the beginning and the end of the control period allows the surest adjustment of the reconciliation of items received and items issued. After items are counted they can be priced and the inventory of specific items and the total inventory expressed in dollar terms. In addition to providing the other elements in the data base necessary for the control procedure as an internal check, costing the physical inventory also allows control of

DAILY REQUISITION SHEET

ITEM	UNIT	A OPEN INVENTORY	B REC.	C TOTAL (A+B)	D CLOSE INVENTORY	E USAGE (C-D)	F PAR LEVEL	G REQ./ ORD.

Figure 7.26. Daily requisition sheet: a departmental system of controlling inventory, ordering, and usage.

inventory judgments. The value of an inventory in dollars at the end of one control period can be compared with a standard to determine if inventory carrying costs have become excessive. (See Chapter 6.)

Control of purchasing. Purchasing control devices have two purposes: pre-control to communicate the standards of the operation to suppliers and to limit the extent of purchases by persons with only limited pur-

PHYSICAL INVENTORY

LOCATION:_____ BY:_____ DATE:_____ SHEET NUMBER____OF____

CLASSIFICATION	SHELF IN	ITEM DESCRIPTION	UNIT	QUANTITY	UNIT PRICE	EXTENSIONS TOTAL COST	TOTAL VALUE

Figure 7.27. Physical inventory: insures that control data is accurate.

PURCHASE ORDER

Item No.	Name	Specifications	Quantity Needed	Unit Cost	Total Cost	Justification

Signature _____

Date   Department _____

Figure 7.28. Sample basic purchase order.

chasing authority; and internal checking on receiving by employees and billing by suppliers so that fraudulent conversion and fraud are prevented. The same control devices serve both these purposes.

Purchase order. The data base of the purchase order provides the basis of the control procedure: item being purchased, quantity wanted, unit cost, vendor identification, and purchasing authorization by signature. From this information the receiving clerk can control the arrival of merchandise. With this information and the receiving record, purveyor bills can be examined. As well, by the routing of the purchase order within the operation before it is sent to the purveyor, management precontrol of the purchase itself is possible.

Purchase specification. The purchase specifications, a detailed description of the operation's standards for a particular item, allow the purveyor to pre-control the merchandise he sends the operation. The specification also communicates this standard to receiving personnel so that the quality of merchandise arriving can be controlled.

Quotations. Economy in the acquisition of products and services requires the comparison of prices charged by several suppliers. A record of prices of different purveyors for identical or comparable items provides an internal check on the individual purchasing. In addition, the quotation sheet displays the data necessary to make the buying decision.

FIXTURE ORDER FORM

Vendor's Copy
FIXTURE ORDER

Send 2 Copies (White and Pink)
To Equip. Div., N.Y.O.)

| Order Not
Valid Without
Equipment Div.
Approval
Stamp | ⌐   ⌐
                      F8326
  ⌐   ⌐ |

ORDER DATE _____

Vendor _____

Street _____

City _____

TERMS: NOT FOR RESALE
Ship AT ONCE unless later
Date is specified here _____

SHIP VIA - Ship in accordance with our
TRAFFIC DIVISION'S shipping
directions unless a route is
specified below:

_____

Item Number	Item Description	Qty. Wanted Show Unit	Unit Cost	Total Cost	Is This A Replacement Yes or No	IF A REPLACEMENT		
						Item Replaced	Yr. Orig. Purchased	Cost (Leave Blank)

TOTAL
COST

STORE NOTE: All orders over $50 must be approved by Regional Office.
            All orders under $50 send direct to Equipment.

IMPORTANT
VENDOR NOTE
1. SEND INVOICE DIRECT TO ABOVE
2. No order is valid without rubber stamp approval of the Equipment Division of the New York Office.
3. Original bill of lading or express receipt must be attached to all invoices.
4. It is understood that unless we are notified shipment cannot be made within thirty days, you will assume responsibility for all special damages incidental to your failing to adhere to the shipping date shown, or transportation expenses arising therefrom. Such special or other expenses may be deducted from the invoice.
5. The vendor, by accepting this order shall be deemed to warrant that the goods furnished under this order shall not infringe on any patent rights of third parties.

Figure 7.29. More complex purchase order: restricts purchasing authority of the operational management involved.

Control of Business Activity

The data from the control devices used on the operational level is summarized in departmental reports to provide the basis for more generalized control procedures by higher levels of management. From accounting journals and ledgers and the control devices used in these more generalized control procedures, reports such as profit and loss statements and balance sheets are prepared. The owners or their representative board of directors can apply the ultimate control standards to the entire operation.

The operational manager may prepare departmental reports or they may be prepared from the information his unit supplies by a separate controller's or accounting office. The reports required by general management differ substantially from operation to operation, but certain major reports are widely used. Table 7.1 lists these reports, and indi-

Table 7.1. REPORTS TO THE GENERAL MANAGER

Report	Data Base	Prepared by
Payroll report	Daily labor cost of operation	Controller
Departmental payroll report	Daily labor cost by job category and/or rates	Department operational manager
Daily sales report	Complete summary of operations, sales by all departments, room statistics, accounts receivable, bank balance, etc.	Controller, accounting department, night auditor, depending on operation
Operating report	Financial transactions: income and expenses, checks drawn and bank balance; cumulative figures, month and year; and comparative figures for same day and month in prior years	Controller, accounting department, night auditor, depending on operation
Departmental sales report (Daily statement of business in restaurant)	Summary of daily business by predetermined categories such as beverages, food, cigarettes, etc. Generally prepared by machine or supplemented with machine totals	Department operational manager or designated employee such as night auditor (Hence *Night Auditor's Report* is front office departmental sales report.)
Steward's report	Summary of receipts and issues by stores department	Departmental manager
Turnover report	Employee terminations and hirings	Departmental manager or personnel department

Table 7.1.   REPORTS TO THE GENERAL MANAGER—continued

Report	Data Base	Prepared by
Projections and forecasts	Anticipated sales volume, business activity, manpower needs, price changes, etc. for definite control periods to provide higher level management review and information	Departmental operational managers, controller, accounting department, depending on nature of forecast
Budget reports	Comparison of actual expenses and purchases with budgeted expenses and purchases. Both operating and capital expenses are covered.	Departmental operational manager, controller

cates their general data base and suggests by whom they are usually prepared.

The general management of the operation can apply its own control procedures to the data presented in these reports to determine if the operation is meeting the control standard. For example, food inventory turnover may be expressed as the ratio of the total cost of food sold to the average food inventory. If this ratio changes, that is, if inventory increases in proportion to total cost of food sold, general management may attempt to correct the deviation. Likewise the occupancy percentage, the total rooms sold compared with the available rooms, may be compared with an acceptable standard, for example 70 percent, and the operation found wanting.

Average room rate, average restaurant check, beverage inventory turnover, food and beverage cost, percentage of accounts receivable turnover, and the other operational indicators revealed by the reports may be controlled.

Ultimately, the same data appropriately restructured as ledgers and journals is developed into financial statements such as a complete monthly report or a monthly balance sheet and in the longer term as a profit and loss statement or annual report. To this data other control standards are applied from the perspective of the owners of the property. They measure the operation's return on owners equity, return on assets, profit margins, solvency, against either industry standards or their expectations.

```
                    SELECTED OPERATING RATIOS


ROOM                        ROOMS OCCUPIED
OCCUPANCY                   ROOMS AVAILABLE


AVERAGE RATE               TOTAL ROOM REVENUE
PER OCCUPIED               ROOMS OCCUPIED
ROOM


AVERAGE RATE               TOTAL ROOM REVENUE
PER GUEST                  TOTAL GUESTS


RESTAURANT                 MEALS SERVED
OCCUPANCY                  NUMBER OF COVERS


AVERAGE MEAL               RESTAURANT REVENUE
CHECK                      MEALS SERVED


AVERAGE BANQUET            BANQUET REVENUE
CHECK                      MEALS SERVED
```

Figure 7.30. **Selected operating ratios: control device used by upper-level management.**

```
                    SELECTED FINANCIAL RATIOS

Current Ratio              Cash,Accounts Receivable,Inventory
(Times)                    Accounts Payable and Taxes Payable

Quick Ratio                Cash & Accounts Receivable
(Times)                    Accounts Payable & Taxes Payable

Accounts Receivable        Sales
Turnover (Times)           Accounts Receivable

Average Day's Accounts     Days in Year
Receivable and Outstanding Accounts Receivable Turnover

Inventory Turnover         Cost of Goods
(Times)                    Inventory

Operating Profit           Operating Profit
(Percentage)               Sales

Net Profit (Percentage)    Net Profit
                           Sales

Return on Investment       Net Profit
(Percentage)               Net Worth

Debt to Net Worth          Accounts Payable, Taxes Payable
(Percentage)               Net Worth
```

Figure 7.31. **Selected financial ratios: used by general management to control business activity.**

CLUB FINANCIAL REPORT

DAILY FINANCIAL SUMMARY			AS OF	

	TODAY	%	MONTH TO DATE	%	LAST MONTH MONTH TO DATE	%
SALES						
1. Bar						
2. Food B$ L$ D$						
3. Other Activities (Includes package sales, bulk sales, bingo, parties, etc.)						
4. TOTAL						
GROSS PROFIT						
5. Bar						
6. Food						
7. Other Activities (Includes package sales, bulk sales, bingo, parties, etc.)						
8. Dues (Dues income computed on an estimated basis.)						
9. Other Activities Revenue (Income derived from concessionaires, barber shops, amusement machines, etc.)						
10. TOTAL						
EXPENSES						
11. Bar Salaries (Dollar amount and as a percentage of sales.)						
12. Food Salaries (Dollar amount and as a percentage of sales.)						
13. All Other Salaries						
14. Total Salaries (Dollar amount and as a percentage of total sales.)						
15. Entertainment (Dollar amount and as a percentage of sales.)						
16. All Other Operating Expenses (This figure can be estimated by taking the past several months' operation and after establishing an average monthly expense, divide by 30 for a daily expense (overhead).)						
17. TOTAL						
18. NET PROFIT FROM OPERATION						
19. OTHER INCOME						
20. OTHER EXPENSE						
21. NET PROFIT TO SURPLUS						

RESTAURANT ANALYSIS										
	B	L	D	Total Today	B	L	D	Total to date	Total to date last month
CUSTOMERS									
AVERAGE CHECK									

REMARKS: (Reason for unusual high or low sales, costs of goods, costs of labor, and other operating expenses.)

Prepared by:	Secretary:

Figure 7.32. Sample financial report: provides ownership with control data for decision-making.

```
                    RESTAURANT OPERATING STATISTICS


                         Item


Annual sales ------------------------------------- dollars        _____
Daily sales:
    Food ----------------------------------------- dollars        _____
        Proportion of total sales ----------------- percent       _____
    Liquor---------------------------------------- dollars        _____
        Proportion of total sales ----------------- percent       _____

        Total daily sales ------------------------ dollars        ===========

Days per week open for business -------------------- number       _____
Hours per day open for business -------------------- number       _____
Menu size:
    Luncheon entrees ----------------------------- number         _____
    Nonrepetitive luncheon entrees --------------- number         _____
    Dinner entrees ------------------------------- number         _____
    Nonrepetitive dinner entrees ----------------- number         _____
Dining room seating ------------------------------- number        _____
Daily customer count ------------------------------ number        _____
Seat turnover per day ----------------------------- number        _____
Daily check average per customer ------------------ dollars       _____
Daily income per seat ----------------------------- dollars       _____
Daily income per square foot of dining area ------- dollars       _____
Daily income per square foot of kitchen area ------ dollars       _____

        Total ------------------------------------ dollars        ===========

Ratio of food cost to sales ----------------------- percent       _____
Ratio of payroll cost to sales -------------------- percent       _____
        Total ------------------------------------ percent        _____

Average hourly rate ------------------------------- dollars       _____
Employee turnover per month ----------------------- percent       _____
```

Figure 7.33. Operational statistics: for comparison with pre-determined standards to evaluate performance.

8 | Management of Profits

Every competent restaurant and lodging manager relentlessly strives to build net profits by increasing sales and reducing costs. Unfortunately, his best efforts may often be negated by great losses through poor security.

The new cashier who accepts a bad credit card because she was not taught the method of verifying cards; the bartender who deposits payment in his pocket instead of in the cash register; the guest who is robbed in the operation's parking lot and sues the operation for insufficient lighting in its lot; the new night porter whose references were never checked and who is later discovered to be a thief—all are costly.

Theft, fraud, and pilferage losses are paid for with net profits. A $1,000 theft or a thousand $1 merchandise losses directly attack the bottom line: With that loss, in an operation with a net profit of 2 percent on gross sales, the profits from $50,000 in sales would be eliminated. Conversely, preventing $1,000 in losses is equivalent to increasing sales by $50,000—an accomplishment that should be as praiseworthy as selling a convention for that sum or reducing the meat bill by the same amount.

In their enthusiasm for the management of getting and spending, qualified professionals often neglect keeping. Most hospitality operations, like most businesses, are vulnerable to loss, as employees, guests, and professional thieves have laid siege to the bottom line. A few managers are doing something about the problem, a great many know about it but don't know what to do, and the majority are not even aware of what's happening.

A manager will not be able to protect his operation entirely by instituting a security program or upgrading an existing program. Hospitality operations cannot become fortresses. Maximum security and "hospital-

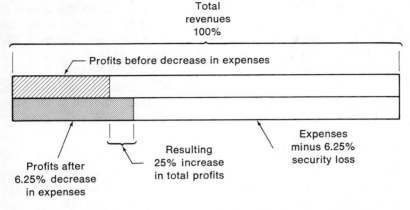

Figure 8.1. Chart showing increase in profits brought about by eliminating security losses.

ity" probably can't exist side by side, but security problems can become manageable with proper handling.

Management of profits by the operational manager should encompass a six-point program:

1. Establishing a preventive security program that includes education of employees, maintenance of security alertness, apprehension and prosecution of malefactors.
2. Setting up internal security systems that protect the operation from hiring potentially dishonest persons and that limit opportunities for "honest" employees' transgressions.
3. Monitoring business activities by proper control and audit procedures to discover abnormalties of any type.
4. Protecting against fraud, including theft of services, bogus negotiable instruments, counterfeit money, and so on.
5. Protecting against theft of stock, merchandise, or guests' valuables by shoplifters, dishonest employees, burglars, robbers, and other such types.
6. Protecting against cash losses from cash revenues, sales, holding areas, and so on.

PREVENTIVE SECURITY

From the general manager to the head porter, every hospitality manager has a definite role in the protection of the operation's revenues and premises and of the customers' property and well-being. Every aspect of the operation is entirely vulnerable to poor security. Responsibility and area of concern increase with managerial authority. The general manager, for example, must consider whether he has protected the operation against conversion of funds by the members of the executive committee through manipulation of the computer accounting system. He must also worry about the housekeepers' not turning in items guests have left in rooms.

On any managerial level, the manager has three major responsibilities: (1) education of all employees under him (2) maintenance of a security alertness, and (3) apprehension and prosecution of any malefactors.

What Employees Should Be Taught

Security education of employees is a primary management responsibility that must take two directions: (1) Employees have to be taught not to steal, and (2) employees have to be able to recognize theft in order to prevent it. Any training means is acceptable: classroom lectures, brochures, audiovisual demonstrations, in-house newsletters, posters, personal interviews, and so on.

Numerous arguments will convince the "honest" employee that crime does not pay: He will not get away with it; he will be caught and sent to jail; he will lose a rewarding career; he risks public disgrace; thefts can bankrupt a business with small profit margins; the thefts could cause everybody to lose his job.

Specific education is necessary for persons with particularly vulnerable jobs: The cashier should be able to spot counterfeit bills; the receiving clerk should be aware of the common ploys used by dishonest truckers; the doorman should have a profile of the likely room thief; the housekeeping department should be searching for guests with "light luggage" who are likely to leave without paying the bill.

What to Keep an Eye on and the Questions to Ask

Management must always think about security. A questioning attitude on the part of all management is an operation's best protection. The general manager might ask if it is really necessary for the book-keeper to take records home to copy them over "so that they are neat." The restaurant manager might ask why produce deliveries come from only 2 vendors, when neither the produce nor the price is very attractive. The head bellman might question the frequent "disappearance" of his bellhops for 30 or 40 minutes. The food and beverage manager might wonder why a bartender employed for five years has never asked for a raise. The chef might consider how a porter can afford a $4,000 car and why he refuses a promotion to pantry man.

The desk clerk can certainly wonder about the guest who misspells the name of his hometown or the athletic individual who prefers the stairs to the elevator. Any golfer on the staff might have doubts about the guest who has well used, expensive clubs but appears to be a complete duffer. The switchboard operator might certainly refuse to connect a hotel guest with room 224 if the guest does not know who is occupying 224.

Apprehension and Prosecution of Malefactors

The prospect of punishment is the ultimate deterrent. If a minimum-wage porter is caught looting rooms and he is not prosecuted but only fired, every other minimum-wage employee in the operation might as well steal, because he has nothing to lose. If trespassing teenagers are merely chased from the motel pool and neither the authorities nor their parents are informed of continuing offenses, the pool might as well be made public. Every teenager who can dog-paddle will consider it his private domain. If an operation overlooks the transgressions of a person because he is a fantastic baker as well as a thief, then all his not-so-fantastic co-workers will take advantage of the same fringe benefits.

Hospitality operations quickly gain reputations as being easy "marks." An operation that does not prosecute is a marvelous training ground for the aspiring crook. If a transgressor does happen to be sent to jail by an operation that does prosecute, the word will surely spread.

When there is theft of any kind, the police should be called in, the suspected thief should be arrested, and the operation should prosecute and take advantage of the normal and customary publicity that may accompany the procedure.

LEGAL PROBLEMS

In their zeal to catch a thief, managers and other employees sometimes overlook the legal protections the law affords even guilty persons, and they infringe on the person's rights. Apparent criminality—for example, that of a strange person caught looting the office safe—does not present problems, except perhaps that of restraining the person without using undue force until the police come. Neither do continuing employee thefts, which should be documented with the cooperation of the police, private security officers, or auditors before official action is taken.

On the other hand, hospitality management should look for guidance from the police authorities or private counsel in such matters as citizen arrests, arrests by peace officer guards, false arrest, slander, false imprisonment, and the local state's definitions of what particular acts constitute a prosecutable crime. For example: When can a manager detain an employee for questioning? Is a postdated bad check a fraudulent instrument? What is criminal trespass? What is the difference between trapping and entrapment?

It is possible for a manager's or supervisory employee's injudicious action to cost an operation more than the action saves it, sometimes by many thousands of dollars. For example, a manager who brings about the arrest of an innocent person without reasonable cause may subject the operation to a possible successful lawsuit. Even verbally abusing anyone in public should be avoided.

It would be a grave mistake to conclude from these observations that prosecutions should not be undertaken because of the legal difficulties that may follow. Although the Constitution and the laws of the states protect the individual, they also protect property and other people. Only in a few gray areas, which can be discussed with an attorney, and only in a few instances is there a possibility of conflict between individual rights and doing right.

SELF SURVEY: 100 SECURITY SOFT SPOTS

A program of preventive security limits the manager's need to play detective. Wrongdoing that is kept from occurring does not have to be discovered. But the magnitude of hospitality security problems might be dramatized significantly if the problems are considered from the investigative perspective. The 100 questions below, which could as well be 1,000, point to situations that may be security problems. A manager's answers to these questions can indicate circumstances worthy of consideration as security vulnerabilities in his operation.

1. Are all register drawers, everywhere, always closed except during an actual transaction?
2. Do bartenders make change from their pockets?
3. Are employee's lockers covered with see-through but secure steel mesh?
4. Do kitchen employees wear their street clothes into the kitchen and then change?
5. Do room-keepers inspect rooms immediately after the guest has left?
6. Can every key to the manager's office be accounted for?
7. When were the room door locks last changed?
8. Are records kept of missing room keys?
9. Who audits the bell captain's log of his time spent on guest floors?
10. Can the subheads of a newspaper be read on the loading dock at night under present lighting?
11. Is the trash or garbage inspected by a trustworthy employee?
12. Does the receiving clerk weigh sealed cases of whiskey?
13. Who checks the number of cases of soda for the bar?
14. Will business records be lost in a fire?
15. Will a riot in the lobby engulf the switchboard and isolate the hotel or is there another line or citizens' band radio?

16. Is there a security check at the employees' entrance?
17. Is there a back door to the operation? Who uses it?
18. Why is that large table necessary in the boiler room?
19. Who audits petty cash vouchers?
20. Does the night clerk have a friend of the opposite sex?
21. Is there a time lock on the storeroom?
22. Does the valet collect and deliver clothing?
23. Does night management know the hours of police patrols?
24. Are empty safes left open?
25. Where are the operation's unused checkbooks?
26. Are the checkbooks intact and in a secure place?
27. What happens to lost and found articles that nobody claims?
28. Are identification cards of terminated employees turned in to the timekeeper?
29. Are basement storerooms adequately ventilated, or are the doors left open?
30. How many people know that the security officers go to the bank every day at two o'clock?
31. Who audits the no-sales on the cash register?
32. Are telephone bills and telephone charges cross-checked?
33. What happens to the fat from the kitchen?
34. Do bookkeepers, purchasing agents, or clerks have systems that are too difficult to explain to others?
35. Does anyone not take a vacation?
36. Do employees' payroll checks come back endorsed to other employees?
37. Are breakfast charges immediately telephoned to the cashier?
38. Are employees ever seen socializing with purveyors?
39. Is management aware of all employees who are related?
40. Do fire stairs exit only to the street?
41. Does management ever actually count the people on the grounds crew?
42. Are last year's vouchers, receipt duplicates, and checks securely stored?
43. Does the morning cook leave the door open for the bakery delivery?
44. Are inventories checked without notice?
45. Can all allowances, refunds, and discounts be accounted for?
46. Are guests being charged properly for their laundry?
47. Can room doors be opened with a credit card?
48. Where are the airline ticket blanks locked?
49. Does every cashier know how to verify a credit card?
50. Are all guest folios updated every night?

51. How does the waitress indicate to the cashier that a party of ten has two separate checks?
52. When were employees last asked to produce the keys they are supposed to have in their possession?
53. Why is he content to be a porter? desk clerk? parking lot attendant?
54. For what does the cashier need a notebook?
55. Who actually saw the exterminator?
56. For how much, and how, are the contract cleaners bonded?
57. When was the receiving dock scale last checked?
58. Do bartenders return to the bar on their day off?
59. What doesn't the room-keeper see?
60. For what services is the John Doe Company billing without an itemized bill?
61. Does the entertainment director really pick up that many checks? Does he audit them?
62. Why did the little girl guest need a dollar from her mother to go swimming?
63. Why does the kitchen order butter in quarter pound packages?
64. Why is that blue car parked outside the employees' entrance every payday?
65. Do all the bottles in the bar belong to the operation?
66. Does the bakery weigh the ice cream it receives?
67. Who checked the night auditor's five-year-old reference?
68. Who argued for abandoning the independent audit because it cost too much?
69. How secure is the lock on the key room?
70. When the receiving clerk opens the padlock on the liquor stores, where does he put it? Who has access to the lock?
71. How is whiskey tested for added water?
72. Is room service always to occupied rooms?
73. Who is authorized to order and receive restaurant checks?
74. Do guest doors automatically lock when the guest leaves the room?
75. Do cashiers ask guests to return keys?
76. Are telephone vouchers for guest charges serially numbered?
77. Does the operation cash third-party checks?
78. Do security officers have irregular patrols through halls?
79. Do some waitresses consistently have more voided checks than others?
80. If there is a fire elsewhere in the building, who will remove the accounts payable and receivable from the bookkeeping department?

81. Does the local police department know anything about bombs?
82. Can the police see into the bar when it is closed?
83. Where does the receiving clerk park?
84. Is the operation sharing computer facilities with a competitor?
85. Are employees' packages inspected?
86. Who audits uncollectable accounts?
87. Where does the grounds crew get gas for their machines?
88. Are critical security employees cross-trained and rotated?
89. In the event of a bomb threat, who has what security responsibilities for cash?
90. When legally possible, is the credit rating of cash-handling personnel checked with the local credit bureau?
91. Are maids routinely notified that a double room is to be occupied by a single individual?
92. Is safety glass used for all windows in vulnerable areas?
93. Are customer and employee parking lots well lighted?
94. Does cash go to the bank regularly and promptly or is it allowed to accumulate?
95. Are cars parked in the garage or parking lot by employees automatically counted?
96. Are skylights and roofs secure?
97. Do trash, garbage sheds, or dumpsters hide rear entrances?
98. After banking hours, can surplus cash be put in a section of the safe that cannot be opened by anyone until morning?
99. When was the last time the security guard was tested on the shooting range?
100. Is the combination to the safe in the tray drawer of that desk over there?

ACTIVE INTERNAL SECURITY

A hospitality operation's employees present the greatest risk to its security. They have every advantage over the outside thief: opportunity, knowledge of the operation, varied possibilities of theft, ability to control the amount of thefts, assistance of other employees with specialized skills, and so on.

In many respects, the operation's defenses are passive. The operation limits the employee's opportunity to steal by effective physical security, control and audit systems, and monitoring of employee movements. Increasing the risk of apprehension by using detection devices is another passive yet admittedly effective measure, especially if the employees are aware of the devices and are unable to compromise them readily. A program of prosecution when employees are apprehended offers a further passive defense.

Perhaps the purchase of honesty insurance is the ultimate passive protection. Insuring, or "bonding" employees does not prevent wrongdoing, but it does prevent or limit loss.

It is also possible for the operation to implement a program of active internal security. High-risk candidates for employment can be identified and rejected, and high-risk current employees can be identified and eliminated or controlled as part of a preventive security program.

How to Spot High Risk Candidates for Employment

There is definitely an element of unfairness to applying universal standards to individuals. Undoubtedly honest candidates are rejected because their backgrounds include elements that have been frequently identified with backgrounds of dishonest persons. Similarly, there are ex-convicts who have been rehabilitated, mental patients who have been cured, and alcoholic bartenders who will never touch another drop.

The problem for the manager is in weighing the possibility of unfairly and unnecessarily rejecting an individual against the possible risk to the operation. When the manager considers his responsibility to employers, shareholders, partners, guests, and honest employees, the operation's interest and their interests must take precedence over the interests of a single individual, who may, then, have been unfairly evaluated.

Legislation that protects the individual by limiting what can be investigated during his application for employment may hinder the candidate with only an apparent problem. For example, if the interviewer suspects that the person has been arrested but cannot ask directly for the details of the arrest, then caution may cause him to reject an individual who can reasonably and satisfactorily explain a police mistake.

Erring on the side of caution and prudence is by necessity a vice that becomes a virtue in a manager hiring people for a hospitality organization.

For security reasons, the manager or the personnel officer attempts to identify and reject persons who are unstable, intemperate, previously dishonest, subject to unusual financial pressures, chronically ill, given to gambling, addicted to drugs, involved in litigations, or subject to influence or coercion by lawless persons.

In addition, the manager or personnel officer is on the lookout for persons who apparently do not have any of these problems but who are "too good to be true." For example, highly skilled persons who are seeking semi-skilled or menial employment may genuinely need the work, but they may have some nefarious purpose in mind—theft of the operation's assets or victimization of its customers. Over-qualified individuals may simply be restless, or they may be clever enough to limit their thievery and be harder to detect.

Management has three basic tools for identifying high-risk candidates: (1) the employment application and questionnaire; (2) the interview, and (3) the background investigation.

THE EMPLOYMENT APPLICATION AND QUESTIONNAIRE

The employment application that the operation uses must conform with current state and federal regulations, principally legislation prohibiting discrimination on the basis of race, color, religion, sex, national origin, or age and the judicial decisions that interpret it. If necessary, the manager should seek legal counsel in deciding what questions can be asked of every employee and what additional detailed questions can be asked for the purpose of arriving at an evaluation of a person's bona fide occupational qualifications.

Within the limitations that the law imposes, the application should provide management with information in several critical security areas: residence, education, past employment, military service, references, and illnesses. The facts themselves, for example a dishonorable discharge from military service, or five addresses in two years, or the absence of fact—significant gaps such as no indication of military service or status or a chronological gap in residency listings—can be important. The problems that caused separation from the military or initial rejection— physical, mental, or moral disqualifications—can also make the person a high-security risk. No address listed for a significant period may mean that the person was incarcerated or confined and is reluctant to admit it. The application may be revealing, or it may provide information for discussion during the interview, or it may be the basis for a background check.

In addition to factual or supposedly factual information, the application also provides an opportunity for the management to oblige the candidate to give his permission for a personal background check, to agree to conform with the security regulations of the operation if he is employed, and to acknowledge that he understands that offering any false information in connection with his application for employment is cause for dismissal.

The net effect of these avowals, which should be specifically couched by an attorney, is to allow the operation to confirm the information of the application readily, to act on the information even if the person has been employed, and to react if there is a breach of security.

THE INTERVIEW

The interview allows the management to discuss important application points and perhaps expose some falsehood. The interviewer might know the general manager of a hotel listed among the applicant's employers. The applicant may not.

The main purpose of the interview is to evaluate the candidate's personality and background. The discussion should be general and free-wheeling enough so that suspect activities and proclivities are possibly revealed. For example, a discussion of prior employment can lead to a discussion of prior employers. An applicant's overreaction to a question about his past bosses can indicate that he is a person likely to avenge himself on his superiors by thefts to "pay them back." Frustration at his inability to advance can be dangerous if the interviewer does not feel the person will advance beyond his entry job. Some thieves steal to prove how smart they are.

Personal problems that make the man a risk should be revealed during the interview. A limited individual in a limited job may not be able to legitimately support a rich man's daughter. An applicant's sexual problems may be a direct threat to the operation's reputation, or they may cause the individual to be blackmailed beyond his means. An excessive need to be liked may lead him to condone illegal acts. Chronically sick children or parents may be more than he or the operation can afford.

The area of conflict of interest should not be ignored. The man in charge of the linen room should not have a summer bungalow colony. The receiving clerk's brother-in-law should not be a major purveyor.

The manager should be alert to psychological clues that will indicate that the applicant's stability is only apparent or temporary. Reluctance to talk about certain vulnerable background items might be covered by coughing or sneezing. The candidate may suddenly become argumentative or defensive about a seemingly minor matter. Mention of dishonesty in general or security problems may prompt him to twitch, scratch, wink, turn away, lick his lips, rub his toe on the carpet, tremble, or sprinkle himself with cigarette ashes. The psychological trigger may not be that apparent, but any manifestation of nervousness beyond the normal emotions anyone feels in applying for a job is suspect. If the operation is still interested in the applicant, the matter should certainly be pursued in a background check.

BACKGROUND CHECK

Hospitality operations with seasonable labor demands find it almost impossible to check an employee's background exhaustively. Unfortunately, these operations are the most vulnerable. Often they must rely on passive devices and undercover agents for protection. At the least, something should be checked. A telephone call to the last employer can confirm some facts on the application blank and may give the manager some indication of the person's character and personality. Maybe the last employer was able to be more thorough.

Employees in job situations with a high probability of grave consequences of loss by employee theft should be investigated. All the points on the application blank should be checked. The employee has given permission for interviews, consumer credit checks, police checks, neighborhood investigations, and examination of school transcripts. If necessary, reproduce that portion of the application which grants permission and send it with written requests.

How to Pick Out the High-Risk Employee

Management will discover that some persons with undesirable personality traits, activities, or backgrounds have not been eliminated during the application and hiring process. If there was misrepresentation, either by omission or commission, the employee should be discharged.

If management simply did not discover that the employee was deeply in debt to professional gamblers, was a chronic alcoholic, or was associating with undesirable persons, his employment should be evaluated. A great deal may depend on the prevailing union contract and whether the employee actually violates any laws or rules on the premises. Although he is definitely a high-risk employee, management may be limited to transferring him to noncritical activities or controlling his movements in the operation. Most likely, the person who would have been rejected during screening, but was not, will eventually be terminated for cause.

Dishonest employees who were basically honest and who had acceptable backgrounds when hired present more of a problem. These persons have changed since employment. They can be identified as high-risk employees (although not all high-risk employees are dishonest) either by their current behavior or by evaluation of the changed circumstances of their lives.

CURRENT BEHAVIOR

An employee's excesses in any area usually cause problems that can only be solved by money, often somebody else's: gambling, automobiles, clothing, drinking, hobbies, attractive companions.

The first symptom of financial problems is evidence of the person's financial disorder. Although he may not have stolen anything and may not even be contemplating stealing at this point, he may start to borrow small sums of money, default on loans to junior employees, speculate on stocks, buy lottery tickets, run out of money early in the week, or postdate checks.

At the next step, his behavior is still not illegal. The employee may violate minor rules and discover ways to augment his income somewhat or offset his expenses. For example, a barman may entertain his personal friends or a clerk may begin to make personal telephone calls or accept unauthorized gratuities.

Defensive behavior is the next symptom. If the employee is stealing, he is now concerned with covering himself. He may suddenly change his behavior pattern: His financial problems are now momentarily resolved; he does not have to borrow small sums; he is wary of calling attention to himself by minor rule violations. Within a short time, the free-spending, blatantly amoral employee may become the soul of rectitude. In fact he may start to criticize the honesty of others.

The employee acts like a man with something to hide. He resents normal questions of superiors and juniors. He makes errors that confuse records. He covers his errors. He takes books and ledgers home. He refuses vacations and promotions. He discovers and implements work-saving systems that do not seem very efficient and that only he understands. He is very jealous of procedures and routines that involve merchandise or cash movements. He is suspicious of repairmen, government auditors, new clerks, and the manager's college-student nephew.

CHANGED CIRCUMSTANCES CHANGE PEOPLE

The high-risk employee may not identify himself readily. If his stealing is only symptomatic and he is clever, he will not carry a wallet bulging with fifties, nor will creditors suddenly appear.

For example, the long-term employee with a real or fancied grievance against management is definitely a high risk. Management can identify him by recognizing the circumstances that have made him a high risk. There seems to be much naivete in this area: Some managers feel that a pat on the shoulder and a short chat on the good of the team will placate a worker who has been passed over for promotion. He has become a high-risk employee.

Management may hire a plain girl with an acceptable background. When she finds herself a plain middle-aged spinster fifteen years later, she becomes a high-risk employee.

Employees' personal lives deeply affect their attitudes toward their company. Death of a relative, divorce, sickness, disillusionment—in sum, any human event that can cause depression, maladjustment, or a disorganization of the person's values—can result in stealing. Those who have suffered personal catastrophes in addition to their other problems have also become high-risk employees.

In addition to learning of changed circumstances, management can also benefit by noting changes in attitude and behavior that may not be associated with honesty or dishonesty. In a small operation, there is usually enough contact with employees for the alert manager to notice that a person has become sarcastic, down-on-life, significantly overweight or underweight, sloppy, cranky, or abrasive. A larger operation can either experiment with psychological evaluations through testing designed to identify high-risk employees or employ undercover investigators who can profile the high-risk employee as well as detect actual theft.

PROTECTION AGAINST FRAUD

Elaborate frauds and confidence schemes perpetrated by outside thieves are not a major hospitality problem. Frankly, there is little protection against the professional confidence man, because he never proceeds unless he can actively involve the victim through his own avarice and cupidity.

Rather, hospitality operations are repeatedly cheated by the "workers" of the confidence game, not the princes, and by the amateurs who do it now and then but do something else for a living.

The four major problems of the hospitality operation are bad money, bad checks, bad credit cards, and bad business.

Bad Money: How to Spot Counterfeits

When 2,000 people are checking out of a resort hotel on a summer Sunday afternoon, the cashier, the coffee shop, and the bellman may be able to assemble several kinds of counterfeit money: a few pesetas; a twenty-dollar bill fabricated from a five-dollar bill and a corner from each of four twenties; a genuine counterfeit twenty; a number of miserable photocopy bills; and a clutch of coins that jangle when they should tinkle.

In essence, three types of bad money are represented: (1) quality professional counterfeits (2) amateur practical jokes that still work, and (3) real money from another country. Given a moment, and exerting something less than monumental indifference, the employee should be able to spot the amateur efforts and the foreign money.

Professional-quality counterfeit money is not easy to identify. The sophistication of photo-offset printing processes has made it possible to make good-looking counterfeits if the counterfeiter takes his time and invests substantial sums of money. Many counterfeiters are caught because of the difficulty they have in passing large quantities of bills, not because of the quality of their work. Wholesaling the money and then retailing it involves them with unreliable characters.

All but the very best work can be identified as counterfeit if a bill is carefully examined. The quality of the paper and the printing processes give the counterfeit away. Genuine treasury money is printed on paper shot through with actual fibers of red and blue thread—not lines—fibers. Counterfeit money is not printed on this kind of paper, even though there may be some effort to print red and blue lines. Genuine money is printed from engraved steel plates. All fine lines are distinct, clear, and unbroken. Pointed objects have points; portraits are life-like. Counterfeit money does not have the sharpness, contrast, or detail of genuine money. Backgrounds are dark and merged with the portrait. Crisscross lines are not clear or distinct.

Some devices are available that identify counterfeit bills by their glow under an ultraviolet light, on the premise that counterfeit bills must be printed on paper that will glow; government paper does not have to be.

Counterfeit coins are best compared with genuine coins. Genuine coins (10¢, 25¢, 50¢ $1) will have even and distinct reeding, or corrugations on the outer edge. The reeding on counterfeits is uneven and broken if it is present at all. The coins struck after 1965, made of copper clad in nonsilver alloys, will have a clearly visible copper band in the middle. Genuine coins will not cut easily; many counterfeit coins will.

When a counterfeit is discovered, it should not be returned to the passer. Only the United States Secret Service or police should be given the bill. It is unlikely that the passer will be the counterfeiter or a criminal. The criminal will have left in a hurry. Only the counterfeiter's last victim will remain, patiently waiting for the change that will never come. If possible, he should be detained because he may help the Secret Service identify the source of the bill.

Bad Checks: What To Watch For

It is more likely that restaurants, bars, and shops in hotels will be victimized by bogus checks than hotels themselves. The need to make credit arrangements in advance, or at least a sign posted to that effect, discourages the professional bad-check artist. It is simply easier to pass a bad check in a store or restaurant.

Three types of bad checks are generally encountered by hospitality operations: the entirely spurious check, the forged check, and the uncashable legitimate check.

The entirely spurious check has been totally manufactured by the forger or by the forger and an accommodating printer. The company does not exist, nor does the account; the name is fictitious; the bank and even the town may be contrived.

The forged check is legitimate except for the signature. Blank checks may have been printed or stolen, and the check is genuine in all respects except that the holder of the account did not make the check. If the forger is really good and the bookkeeping of the account holder very casual, the check may pass as genuine.

The uncashable legitimate check is written on an account that was properly opened (except that the bad-check artist may have lied about his name, business, and so on) but does not contain enough money to cover the check. Although the check is bad, if it was innocently written by a customer who thought there was enough money in his account to cover it, in most cases no crime has been committed. Unfortunately, many of the bad checks passed are deliberately written on accounts without sufficient funds.

Unlike European banks, which are far less casual in allowing individuals to have checking accounts, American banks offer special checking accounts that do not have to be secured by even a minimum deposit to almost anyone who can show any identification. A person depositing a small amount will often immediately receive a folder of checks while checks with his name are being imprinted. Obviously, there is little need to steal checks or have them printed except when the criminal wants to presume on the credit rating of a well-known person or large firm.

ESTABLISHING A CHECK POLICY

Hospitality operations can limit their risks by simply limiting the checks they will accept, while still cashing checks normally presented by legitimate customers (see following section). The policy might incorporate the following guidelines:
1. No out-of-state bank checks unless verified by telephone at the customer's expense.
2. No foreign bank checks.
3. No postdated checks.
4. No third-party checks (checks not made out by the person presenting them), except perhaps payroll checks.
5. No checks from intoxicated persons.
6. No checks beyond a certain amount.
7. No checks cashed for minors.

HOW TO APPROVE CHECKS

Checks should be approved by some managerial employee if possible. In addition to enforcing the check policy, he can inspect the check itself and see that it is properly made. All the necessary elements to make it legal and collectable should be present: valid date; correspondence of the amount in numbers and the written amount; acceptable appearance, including letters and numbers and color and feel of the paper.

It is also a good idea to stamp the check at the time of the transaction with either the words "For Deposit Only" when the check is accepted in payment, or "For Deposit Only" and the word "Cashed" when the check is being cashed for a customer who will later be presented with a bill.

Stamping a check "For Deposit" makes it impossible to cash if it is lost or stolen. Banks will accept it only for deposit.

When possible, the maker of the check should be asked to prepare the check in front of the managerial employee. Several problems are avoided: In this way the operation will not be cashing a valid check with an altered amount; the managerial employee can compare the signature of the maker with the signature on whatever identification is presented; he is sure he is not being presented with a stolen check and stolen identification. He can also judge the person who is making the check. People should not have difficulty in writing their own signature. There should be no hesitation apparent in the signing or in the signature.

When the check has been completed, it should be compared with proper identification. Driver's licenses are widely accepted because they include a brief description of the person and his signature. Passports and employee identification badges with photographs also establish that the maker of the check has represented himself properly. If the person is suspect, the manager might ask for "weird" identification. Few professionals have library cards in their assumed names.

Many persons who are experienced in check cashing and can detect check frauds make it a point to delay when there is anything suspect about the check or the person presenting it—sometimes by leaving the room or the cashier's counter. As the thief has a pocket full of blank checks he will not wait to see if the manager has gone to call the police.

Any effort to distract the manager by compliments, threats, protestations, indignation at being asked for identification, jokes, singing, and conversation with other people should make his check suspect.

The operation can also subscribe to a verification service, which may have the "bad-check artist" listed. Or, everyone can be asked for a thumbprint; there is even a commercially available inkless system. The thief will have second thoughts about cashing the check.

HOW TO LIMIT LOSSES THROUGH BAD CHECKS

The simple verities of recognizing bad checks and bad-check passers must be implemented if the operation is to limit its losses. A check-cashing policy should be established with definite penalties for employees who depart from it. Perhaps any losses incurred through their violations of policy can be charged against their salaries.

Employees should be trained to examine critically all checks and identification. The well-prepared professional will not be stopped, but the amateur and the petty crook who has stolen someone's wallet will be. Businesses, including banks, are reluctant to admit how much the cashing of bad checks has cost them or what percentage of the checks they cash are bad. But of the two billion dollars per year estimated as lost through the cashing of bad checks, a significant sum could be saved if employees who cash the checks could be made more conscious of the problem. Bad checks without any signature, with the signature of a dead president of the United States, or with a signature forged on a photocopied blank have all been passed.

Bad Credit Cards: How to Avoid Trouble

Operations that do not have their own house credit cards but accept national credit cards or oil company cards cannot suffer losses from the theft or misuse of the cards unless the operation violates the essential rules of their agreement with the credit card companies: The card must not have been cancelled, and the signature of the customer must match the signature on the card.

Under these conditions any losses will be borne by either the credit-card company or the person who lost the card, depending on their agreement.

Hospitality operations encounter problems with national cards when their personnel do not properly verify the card either with the circulated list of cancelled and stolen cards or by the telephone procedure indicated in the specific agreement. If the card has been reported stolen or has expired or been cancelled and this information is available to the operation in the agreed-upon manner, then the operation suffers the loss.

Understandably, but regrettably, in the press of business, many cashiers do not take the time to look through the credit card company bulletins or verify the card.

The operation's only real defense against the negligence of its employees is to make a point of dismissing anyone who does not follow the proper procedure and, periodically, to "shop" the cashiers to make sure that the procedure is being followed. On occasion, either a professional service or "friends" of the establishment should be asked to make credit-card purchases with legitimate cards, and then to report whether the cards were properly checked.

Operations that issue their own cards have all these problems, the problem of bad business (see below), and the problems of the credit card companies. A number of factors must be rigidly controlled if the operation is to protect itself against losses.

1. Cards must be issued only to a person with an acceptable credit rating and, at the least, a verified name and address.
2. A dollar limit should be set on the use of the card without identification.
3. The operation or the credit-card holder or both should be insured against misuse of the card.

4. Cards should be made so as not to be easily counterfeited.
5. Billing of credit-card accounts should be regular and frequent so that misuse is quickly spotted.
6. Customers should be taught by the operation—especially if charges on the card will be their own responsibility, no matter who makes them—to protect their cards on their person and in their homes as though they were cash.
7. Lists of stolen cards and cancelled cards should be made available to all cashiers.
8. Cards should be reissued at frequent periods.
9. Control employees should be aware of the spending profile of card holders. An account that averages $200 a month should not suddenly become active enough to generate $500 in charges in a week.
10. The operation should employ or engage a trained investigator to interview card holders whose cards have been misused, so that everyone concerned—employee or customer—is aware of the seriousness with which the operation considers its offering of credit-card privileges.

Bad Business: How to Minimize the Losses

In their efforts to attract business and please customers, hospitality establishments may neglect some of the common sense aspects of business operations. They allow themselves to be victimized by legitimate customers who are overextended, and by confidence men posing as customers.

"LEGITIMATE" BAD BUSINESS

Legitimate customers who have accumulated charges they cannot pay are not genuine security problems. In a large operation the credit manager, accounting department, or the comptroller have probably not done their work well. Initial investigations of credit references, personal bank accounts, and business references should have established a credit limit that would protect the operation. Since debt is not a crime, collection of monies owed may involve civil suits, the use of a collection agency, or more often, the operation's acceptance of the customer's note for the uncollected balance and the institution of a long-term payment plan.

Some individual owners of restaurants and small hotels are much too generous with the privilege of signing. In their efforts to attract and keep business, especially when the operation has just opened, they accept almost anyone as a house account.

Many of their credit clients are simply bad credit risks and should be refused credit. Others have the means to pay but purposely delay in paying their bills and, in effect, work their own subtle legal confidence game.

The owner of a new establishment is often short of credit himself and requires cash to meet current expenses. Yet he is reluctant to pressure "good customers" because he also needs the business and he feels that by importuning them he will lose their patronage. In every urban area there is a group of people aware of his dilemma who exploit it. They do not pay in the expectation that the business will fail simply by losing favor with the public after the initial flush of business that advertising and publicity have generated. In fact, they may precipitate its failure by not paying their bills. Very frequently, a restaurant will close holding forty or fifty thousand dollars in good but overdue paper.

Many of the sophisticates, jet setters, and beautiful people who sign in the best places (and pay later) have been attracted by good publicity, perhaps a good operation, and the generosity of the host. When he begins to feel the credit squeeze, in part generated by their delayed payment, the quality of the operation is compromised. The gourmet butcher will not deliver; the better help leave because they are not paid promptly. Then, both cash and credit customers depart, and the fragile credit structure collapses completely.

Unless the operation is sufficiently capitalized to extend long-term credit, it should not. Rather, only national credit cards should be accepted. Periodically, all house accounts should be reviewed, and even at the risk of alienating some customers, credit on overdue accounts should be curtailed. In actuality, the situation can be successfully explained to genuine card customers, many of whom are businessmen who have had similar problems at some time in their careers. Bonhomie should work both ways.

"ILLEGITIMATE" BAD BUSINESS

Minor Fraud. Hospitality operations can be victimized by fraud without the use of checks or credit cards. Losses can range from a room bill to the price of a banquet.

All the old ploys still work because there are always new thieves and new employees. The man without any luggage is probably legitimate; it's the man who has purchased a ten-dollar suitcase in the hotel sundry shop and loaded it with hotel telephone books before going in the front door who will leave without paying his room and restaurant charges.

Every morning countless operations lose out on breakfast costs because customers pay room charges before the meal charge arrives at the cashier's counter.

Hurried night auditors do not compare signatures on signed checks with those on the registration cards. If the cheating guest is caught (his charges would have been billed to another guest's room), he simply admits his stupidity at "forgetting" his room number.

Bartenders accept signed checks from the big tippers who are not even registered in the hotel.

Spurious billing addresses, often backed by equally false personal and business identification, cost countless thousands.

Unfortunately, although the "Innkeeper's Laws" in various states protect the operation against fraud, it is very often difficult to prove a suspect's "intent."

The professional is well aware of the law and avoids manifestly fraudulent documentation of his identity. If he is caught, he probably will pay and will offer haste or even "the crowd at the cash register" as an excuse. If he does not pay, his name and address are probably legitimate. Unless the operation can prove fraudulent intent, he will simply become a debtor against whom there is little recourse. Only a few states have laws that list refusal to pay or neglect to pay or even surreptitious removal of luggage as evidence of fraudulent intent.

The vigilance of all employees is the operation's strongest defense. If a guest, his luggage, or his actions do not seem normal, management should be alerted.

The room clerks should be wary of those individuals who hesitate in writing registration cards or attempt to hurry the clerk through the formalities of registration. Asking for credit identification, such as a credit card, may limit fraud to some small extent, but it is unlikely that anyone intending to defraud the hotel has not prepared himself adequately. Asking for an inkless thumbprint is effective, however.

Room housekeepers can report light luggage or shabby luggage, as it is likely that the thief will abandon cheap valises rather than attempt to sneak them from the hotel. Guests with luggage who are not accompanied by a bellman should be reported to the service desk.

All personnel in lobby areas should survey elevators constantly for hurried departures of guests with luggage. Legal exits should be limited to the front door. Any emergency exits from the operation can be equipped with alarms that sound when the door is opened.

Major Fraud. Frauds for small sums can add up to a considerable amount, but a major fraud for a significant sum is always more disheartening.

For example, many hospitality operations have good active accounts with business firms for lodgings, convention business, or restaurant charges. On occasion they are victims of subtle legal frauds. Control of a company may have passed from its original owners to illegal operators who are busily converting the assets into cash or resalable merchandise, to the eventual detriment of shareholders and creditors. The illegal operators may even hold the annual stockholders' meeting in the hospitality operation besides, continuing to charge to the company account. When the company is finally bankrupt, the hospitality operation receives a few pennies on the dollar if anything at all.

Some completely illegal operators may establish a favorable credit rating either by paying promptly or by having accomplices manipulate company records for credit verification. For example, a confidence man in the vicinity for another business swindle may be a good cash or credit customer, averaging a few hundred dollars a month. On the basis of this credit, he escalates his purchases by ordering outside catering, suites of rooms for members of his company, or a banquet for sales presentations.

The operation can protect itself by continuing independent verification of credit accounts; by requiring significant cash deposits, even from long-term customers; or by being wary of escalating charges; by being suspicious of any accounts that seem too good to be true, of ostentatious company names, or prestigious companies or individuals who happen to discover little restaurants or hotels.

SECURITY THROUGH AUDIT AND CONTROL

Audit and control are essential in limiting theft of cash and merchandise, but while cash and merchandise can be protected by physical barriers and surveillance, only audit and control can protect the operation against embezzlement, conversion of assets, misappropriation, and misuse of funds. Audit and control protect operations from so called "white collar" crime.

The sophistication of the modern hospitality industry has made it possible for someone to manipulate the instruments of record, communication, transfer of funds, and cash and merchandise control to his own advantage. To steal, it is not necessary to reach into the cash drawer or smuggle valuables past security guards. For example, any employee who has exclusive and unquestioned purchase approval can have the operation billed for services never rendered by a company with which he has colluded, by a company he owns, or by a company which does not exist except as an accommodation address and a billhead. Or, any person who makes payments or takes receipts that are not somehow verified can make those payments or divert those receipts to himself. The ability to make discounts or grant refunds offers the same opportunity.

Control and audit procedures that are independent of the procedures used for business forecasting or cost analysis can severely limit any misappropriation by removing responsibility from those who might misuse it.

General Security Audits and Controls

Although each department of a hospitality operation has its own vulnerabilities that should be countered by specific audit and control procedures, some general rules might be applied throughout the operation.

1. Treat all paper and forms that record the movements of cash or merchandise as though they were cash or merchandise. Requisitions, purchase orders, receiving records, rack slips, bank checks, and all other forms pertaining to transactions should be physically secured and accountable at all times. In an operation, many of the employees never see a guest room, a bottle of whiskey, a dollar bill, or a roast beef. All they see is the paper that represents movement of these things. If they are given the right paper with distorted information they can be prompted to act in ways that benefit the wrongdoer.

2. Separate all bookkeeping functions. The employee who issues a check should not reconcile the bank statement. The one who formulates a purchase order should not receive the merchandise. The person who prepares the time cards should not make out the payroll checks.

3. Schedule irregular, independent audits of books, cash, and merchandise. Whenever possible, outside people or management personnel from outside a particular department should verify current figures, including computer records.

4. Number everything. All instruments, forms, papers, and record pages used in the control of cash or merchandise should be independently controlled by being sequentially numbered and logged: for example, registration cards, refund receipts, allowance book pages, and rolls of cash-register tape.

5. Log checks and invoices. All checks and invoices should be date-stamped and numbered as they are mailed or received in the mail, and their description noted with the number. This procedure should be separate from the processing of checks and invoices.

6. Make all payments by check. There should be no cash fund of any type. If necessary, a special petty-cash checking account can

be opened for disbursements when persons authorized to sign checks on the major company account are not available.

7. Have all checks examined when returned to compare invoice name and endorser. This should be done by someone other than the person who prepared or otherwise handled the checks.

8. Cross-train and transfer all control and accounting employees. The night auditors should be trained in food and beverage control, payroll employees should be trained in hotel accounting, and so on.

9. Require at least two authorizations for allowances, reductions, discounts, credits, etc. Any activity that establishes the opportunity to neutralize full dollar-control procedures should be double checked.

10. Have management do it. All control procedures, handling of cash and checks, mailing of statements, employee payments, and posting of charges should be done periodically by management to identify irregularities and to isolate vulnerabilities.

11. Duplicate, separate, and cross-check forms. Movements of merchandise from the operation to the outside, from the outside to the operation, and within the operation should be controlled by the transmission of duplicate forms to all parties to the movement. For example, a shipment of food from the main kitchen to the bar restaurant should be controlled by sending records of requisition and receipt to the departments concerned, who will compare them as a control.

12. Cancel paperwork on completed transactions. When invoices have been paid or checks received, all the records and forms that pertain to the transaction should be cancelled either by a perforating machine or by indelible stamping to avoid the possibility of reuse of the same instruments.

13. Separate control, accounting, and operational functions. Responsibilities of managers and employees in each of these areas should be independent so that cross-checking is possible and manipulation of records is not.

14. Stress the system. Remove a blank check from the book; file a receiving slip for merchandise for which there has been no purchase order; add ten dollars to the bank balance by making a cash deposit. See what happens and how long it takes to happen.

15. Write it down. All control, audit, accounting, and bookkeeping systems should be clearly recorded so that they do not become the province of a single person who is too busy (doing what?) to explain them.

Measuring the Efficacy of General Security Audits and Controls

The manager should test the effectiveness of audit and control procedures by hypothesizing any larcenous ploy that might occur to him and determining if his control could be neutralized. The following table suggests how ten common hospitality problems might be exposed only by the general security audits and controls just listed, which are not all-inclusive. Some problems require specific countermeasures.

Table 8.1. TESTING GENERAL SECURITY AUDITS AND CONTROLS

Method of Theft	Control or Audit Countermeasure
Reusing previously used invoices	Perforation of invoices after completed transactions
Payment to own company or in collusive arrangement	No record of receipt of merchandise or inventory record
Falsification of inventories	Spot inventories by management
Failure to make cash deposits	Reconciliation by independent person
Diversion of legitimate checks to suppliers	Comparison of check log with accounts
False payment of claims by guest	Payment only by check; comparison of endorsee's signature with records
Carrying payroll ghosts	Management distribution of pay on occasion
Removing or inserting ledger sheets	Numbering ledger sheets
Collecting debts, then writing them off as bad	Need for two signatures
Diverting payment by using fictitious account	Independent auditing

Specific Audit and Control Procedures

The security audit and control procedures which might be instituted by a major hotel for its various departments can be adapted to restaurants without lodging facilities and to small hotels and motels without restaurant facilities. The large hotel has all the problems; other hospitality operations have only some of them.

The large hotel, however, usually has the specialized audit and accounting personnel to implement the solutions. There are enough people involved to separate functions and this offers the most potent measure of control: independent processing of the records, requisitions, purchase orders, sales receipts, and so on. The smaller operations usually have to consolidate functions and create a minimum number of "bookkeeping" positions. Their vulnerability increases as the number of persons involved decreases. For example, if one person does the purchasing and receiving, limiting the possibility of collusion with suppliers is difficult. If one person reconciles the bank statements and prepares checks for suppliers, there is virtually no control over the payment procedure. Unfortunately, trusted, hardworking, valued employees who find themselves in these special situations sometimes steal. Temptation from opportunity, and not greed or need, prompts most dishonesty.

The manager has an obligation to himself and to the business to limit the possibility of theft, thereby he must limit the temptation to steal. He also has an obligation to the employee. Perhaps the logic is sophistic, but given the moral context of the time, the victim as well as the perpetrator is responsible for the crime. Many employees are "honest," at least by the accepted definition of the term, when they are hired. If the manager can avoid creating situations that strain their moral fiber, he can keep satisfactory employees, save the operation a cash or merchandise loss, and, ironically, protect the employees from themselves.

In a small operation, the manager's only recourse is to perform key tasks himself, at least on a frequent, irregular basis. The temptation of collusion will be neutralized if the purchasing agent and receiving clerk, in the person of the chef, realizes that any day the manager may receive the merchandise. If every check is examined for completeness before it is signed and the manager reconciles the bank statement, the bookkeeper will not be tempted by the easy opportunity to write himself money.

SECURITY IN PURCHASING AND RECEIVING

Separation of the three essential functions in the purchase of merchandise—ordering, receiving, and paying—is the key to security. When these functions are combined or when any person has access to all the "paper" that surrounds the process, problems occur.

At least five major theft opportunities can be identified:

1. Short merchandise or merchandise in variance with specifications is received and accepted.
2. False invoices are submitted and paid.
3. Merchandise is diverted.

4. Inventoried merchandise is stolen.
5. Bills are padded and there are kickbacks.

The ideal purchasing, receiving, and paying system provides several independent opportunities to check whether the operation has received the merchandise it ordered and is paying for the merchandise it received. For example, when a department head or the purchasing agent initiates an order, copies should go to the control department, to the accounting department for the vendor's file, to the vendor, and to the receiving department. The copy to the receiving department might only indicate the items, not their quantity. When the merchandise is received, the receiving clerk would count and weigh the items and prepare his own receiving slip, essentially ignoring the packing list and the duplicate purchase order. Duplicate receiving slips would be sent to all departments (or individuals) who would compare the goods received with the goods ordered. Accounting would hold payment until the vendor's invoice could be compared with the goods received. Finally, when payment is authorized, all the existing paper on the transaction would be cancelled by indelible stamp or perforation so that none of it could be reused to support a spurious transaction at any level.

Although the system is not 100 percent perfect—it does not provide for the control of intangible purchases like exterminating, for example —it is practical even in small operations, because they can generate sequentially numbered carbon sets.

Putting the system under stress periodically keeps it alive. The manager might add a case of beer to a shipment or have a lettuce case filled with onions shipped to determine if items are being counted and inspected as well as weighed.

SECURITY IN RESTAURANT TRANSACTIONS

Strict accountability for checks on the one hand and food on the other limits the possibility of theft by waiters, cashiers, or food production personnel. Security procedures are directed to at least five major theft opportunities.

1. Service employees pocket revenues and destroy or alter checks.
2. Service employees short-check—collude with customers to present checks for less than the amount for items ordered.
3. Cashiers under-ring, pocket even money payments, or falsify checks.
4. Food production personnel steal merchandise.
5. Food production personnel and service personnel offer food without payment to the operation.

Protection of the operation has five distinct elements:

1. All checks must be accounted for at all times. The cashier should sign for checkbooks; the waiter should sign for his individual books; and checks used and checks received by the cashier should be reconciled. Several opportunities for theft are forestalled: The cashier must ring checks and cannot run her own book; the waiter must present checks and cannot void them or destroy them without accounting for them.
2. Checks must be compared with register tapes. Machines that number the check and the tape sequentially make the process easier. The checks should match the tapes, and they should show no signs of alteration or erasure.
3. Food produced by the kitchen must be compared with food delivered to the dining room and food paid for by customers. There are a number of methods for independent totaling of food sales: After orders are taken by dining room personnel and before they are presented to the kitchen, the check is priced by the cashier; duplicate checks are used so that the waiter's sales and the kitchen's delivery to him are reconcilable; a food checker is interposed between the waiter and the kitchen, and he prices the items delivered to the waiter either by retaining a duplicate check or by using a check register machine.
4. Checks are audited periodically for incorrect pricing by an independent control.
5. A portion-control system is instituted in the food production department so that a sales analysis of waiter checks can be compared with food requisitions.

SECURITY IN ROOM TRANSACTIONS

As the sale of a room is a transaction that involves an intangible, it is difficult to control or audit by comparing revenues with consumption of merchandise—the action hinges on the manager's ability to interrupt the theft while it is in progress. The thief becomes vulnerable because the "stolen" item must be used on the premises for a period of time.

There are three basic situations which allow theft of room revenue:

1. Clerks destroy registration cards and bills for guests who check in and check out during a shift when they are both desk clerk and cashier.
2. Without using registration cards, clerks sell rooms for use for short periods to guests who collude with the clerk to lower room rates or violate the law or policy.

3. Clerks hold rooms, turning away legitimate customers who do not offer them gratuities.

The operation can be protected effectively by a program that includes five elements:

1. Accurate and complete housekeepers' reports of rooms used.
2. Distinctive, numbered room-registration slips and cards and strict accountability.
3. Frequent, independent inspection of the room rack, or a computerized system from which information can be recalled at various terminals.
4. Security personnel to spot-check officially unoccupied rooms.
5. Shopping desk clerks with paid or volunteer operatives.

In addition, if union contracts and local laws permit, electronic surveillance of desk operation can be instituted.

PROTECTION AGAINST THEFT OF STOCK, PROPERTY, AND GUESTS' VALUABLES

A hospitality operation, unlike a fertilizer plant or a cable factory, is full of articles that anyone can use. The temptation to steal and hence the possibility of theft is vastly increased by the ease with which bath towels from linen stocks, cashmere sweaters from guest's rooms, sunglasses from the sundry shop, and cases of ketchup from the kitchen can be absorbed.

Hospitality operations also suffer from a history of condonation. For example, when food was inexpensive, wages low, and profits high, managers tended to consider minor thefts of food with the attitude of a father discovering his nine-year-old in the cookie jar. With today's economic conditions, however, managers are often faced with situations in which theft has become an employee's "right."

There are three distinct problems: (1) theft of stock, linens, liquor, or food by either employees or outside thieves; (2) theft of property from retail stores and items from guest rooms and restaurants, generally by guests or outsiders and occasionally by employees; and (3) theft of guests' possessions from their persons or their rooms by other guests or outsiders, and sometimes by employees.

How to Discourage Theft of Stock

Wherever inventory is stored, issued, or received, it is vulnerable to theft, but analysis of the movement of items shows that most theft can be countered by three measures: (1) control and audit (2) physical barriers, and (3) employee control.

CONTROL AND AUDIT

Control and audit procedures do not prevent employee theft, but they make it possible to discover it quickly and to assign responsibility before too many persons have become involved. If the potential thief is aware of the control and audit procedures, he will realize that any theft will soon be noticed and quickly attributed to the wrongdoer. Even if the evidence against him is not conclusive, his dismissal will be likely. More important, the thought of theft will not occur to the "honest" employee: He will not be stimulated by a tempting situation.

Effective control procedures make somebody responsible for stock at all times. Stored articles are in the charge of the staff in the storeroom. Articles are issued to the one person who will transport them. That person then assigns responsibility for the items to the persons who will use them. In practice, then, there must be a system of overlapping receipts backed by perpetual inventory systems wherever items are held. For example, linen is received from the outside laundry by the linen room. Receipt is acknowledged by duplicate slips to the vendor's delivery man, the housekeeper, the accounting department, and an internal control unit. Perpetual inventory records note the receipt of the linen and its issuance to floor supervisors who sign for it and maintain inventories of linen closets. They in turn issue the linen to room housekeepers who acknowledge its receipt. Returns of soiled and unused linen are also noted. Every sheet and towel is always someone's responsibility. More important, the process can easily be audited by a comparison of the actual linen count anywhere in the chain with what the records show the count should be.

Internal movement of food, beverages, supplies, and furniture can be similarly monitored if management is willing to enforce control procedures and stage periodic irregular physical audits to demonstrate its earnestness. Physical audits must not be desultory, however, or the system is virtually neutralized. As an example, the food and beverage manager of a large operation with several bars would stop his inventory for a dinner break. Employees would then move already counted bottles to another location, where they would be recounted. A second manager eventually discovered that the first one was not only counting the same bottles twice, he was counting empty cases as full ones because he never actually examined pallet-loaded merchandise.

PHYSICAL BARRIERS

Audit and control procedures can be effective only if responsibility for goods can fairly be assigned to the persons in charge of the goods. If anyone is able to march into a storeroom at any time and take what he wants, shortages cannot be blamed on the storeroom attendants. The seven rules for physical security of storerooms are common sense.

1. There must always be someone on duty in the storeroom when it is open. This person may not leave the storeroom and should not be assigned other responsibilities at those times.
2. Only authorized personnel—designated runners—may be sent to the storeroom.
3. Only storeroom personnel should handle merchandise, and all carts, boxes, etc., should be checked against the issue slip each time stock leaves the storeroom.
4. Whenever the storeroom is closed, it should be physically secured.
5. Keys should be strictly controlled. Ideally, the storeroom door should have a time lock that will record the time the storeroom was opened (after hours) and by which key.
6. No supplies should move without written indication of issue and receipt.
7. All records should be maintained on at least a daily basis.

EMPLOYEE CONTROL

Certain situations in hospitality operations make security through control and audit and physical barriers difficult. When items are consumed by guests and there is no way of determining exactly the extent of consumption, it is possible for dishonest employees to divert goods. At a banquet, for example, customers are often billed for the number of bottles of liquor consumed. Even if empty and full unused bottles are counted, a dishonest employee can pour liquor into his own bottle. Employee theft may also be impossible to detect when there is a normal amount of loss expected. For example, some flatware is always lost and some serviceware is always broken by negligence in washing. If the volume of pieces handled is large, thefts of $100 a day may be hidden by normal loss and breakage.

In these and in the other situations that cannot be fully controlled, the operation can introduce a measure of security by limiting the employees' ability to remove articles from the premises. An employee control program should include nine elements:

1. There should be a single employee entrance and exit manned by an intelligent, trained, able guard.
2. Complete package control should be strict. No items may be brought into the establishment; they must be checked with the guard. No items may be removed from the establishment without being opened and completely inspected by the guard.
3. No articles which are sold or used in the operation may be passed

by the guard, even if they are the employee's own property, without a specific property pass.

4. If local laws and union contracts permit, detection devices should be used. Two examples are metal detectors and scales over which the employees must pass so that any unusual weight change is noted.
5. As local laws and union contracts permit, random body searches should be instituted if the operation has discovered security problems.
6. Employees' cars should be parked away from the employee's entrance and certainly away from kitchen doors, loading docks, and other such areas.
7. Undercover agents should be used to identify employees who are working in collusion with "guests," consuming foodstuffs and liquor on the premises or selling them to other employees, or stealing or receiving merchandise.
8. Lockers should be made of wire mesh so that their interiors are visible, and employees should be required to sign a blanket permission for the inspection of lockers by management personnel.
9. In order to enter the premises, employees should be required to show passes that should be identified adequately—ideally with a photograph—and marked with shift hours and days off. If no permanent passes are used, the guard should have up-to-date lists of employees authorized to be in the building.

Property Thefts

Thefts of property from hospitality operations are a continuing problem. Restaurants lose silverware, peppermills, ashtrays, bud vases, and expensive menus. Hotels and motels must absorb the losses of room items ranging from bath mats to television sets. Two types of thieves are responsible: the systematic professional and the souvenir-hunting amateur.

In addition, operations with retail stores or even a single counter with retail merchandise are victimized by professional and amateur shoplifters.

HOW TO LIMIT THEFT OF PROPERTY

The key to minimizing theft of property by both amateurs and professionals is a vigilant staff. When a guest leaves a restaurant table, the table should quickly be checked by the waiter for the theft of valuable articles. Similarly, when a guest leaves his room, the room housekeeper should inspect it right away. If an article is missing, management should be informed before the guest has left the premises. The manager can then make the rather critical judgment whether to risk offending an innocent guest by suggesting that the guest has "accidentally or mistakenly removed some of the operation's property." When an item of significant cost such as a television set has been stolen, he must pursue the matter. When an item whose cost is equal to the profit from the guest's meal or his stay is missing—a wine carafe or a bath mat, for example—the manager might consider whether the guest is a regular customer or a transient with no prospect of returning. In most cases, the operation can absorb the loss and assign it to "public relations" if the guest is a frequent customer and if the theft is his first. On the other hand, a transient might be politely queried, and the habitual collector strongly discouraged.

It is possible to embarrass a customer into paying for the items without immediately losing him as a customer. For example, one manager discovered that the wife of a frequent customer was collecting a demitasse set. He sent a very polite but slightly wry letter to the customer suggesting that he might like to surprise his wife with the rest of the set to "complete her service" at the operation's cost.

In many instances, the theft of small items can be reduced if the items are offered for sale by the operation. Many souvenir hunters do not realize the value of what they take. A list with accurate prices for commercial china and room accessories places the theft in a new perspective. "Honest" guests who steal bedspreads would never dream of stealing forty dollars.

Management may show some prudence by removing temptation. The best lamps should not fit into suitcases; smaller lamps might be bolted to tables. The wide-bottom captain's decanter and the three-foot peppermill are preferable to the convenient-to-carry conventional items.

Major hotel room items such as television sets can be protected by quality locks and alarms. Even an impressive sticker indicating that there is an alarm when there is none is effective: "Please call the service desk if you want to move this television."

SHOPLIFTING

Hospitality operation retail stores—sundry and tobacco shops, or liquor, jewelry, and clothing stores, for example—have several advantages over outside establishments. In many instances, the thief cannot exit to the street but must walk through the operation past employees and guards. The professional who would prefer to disappear quickly into a crowd is thus discouraged. Most hospitality retail stores attract only transient customers. The local amateur shoplifter likely to make an impulse theft when legitimately purchasing merchandise is probably shopping elsewhere; local teen-agers are out of place in a hotel shop and are more likely to forage in a department store.

These differences from outside shops can be used to advantage by the hospitality operation. For example, signs, real and mock television cameras, mirrors, observation windows, and other similar devices that are useful in hospitality operations do not work in most retail establishments because the shoplifter has time to analyze them and discover their weaknesses. He may even be given some incentive to shoplift to "beat" the protection devices. A guest is not likely to slip a pair of sunglasses into his pocket if he thinks he can be seen in a convex mirror. Even a sign indicating that "Shoplifters will be prosecuted" is menacing to him: He usually has no local connections, and his normal fear of the law is compounded by his fear of a strange court system.

Employee vigilance can further limit shoplifting losses. Attentive sales personnel who immediately greet customers and browsers deprive the shoplifter of his feeling of anonymity. Even asking the question "Is there anything else?" of every customer can panic the amateur shoplifter into bringing forth an article he has pocketed.

When a theft has occurred and an employee has observed it, the hospitality operation has an advantage over many retail establishments: The item can be charged to the guest's bill. The clerk phones the thief's description to a security officer who spots and identifies the guest by name and room. The guilty amateur usually welcomes the opportunity to pay.

Theft of Guests' Valuables

Although in some states the innkeeper's traditional absolute liability has been limited by statute, loss due to theft of a guest's property is usually the responsibility of the operation, unless the loss was caused by the guest's negligence or some uncontrollable circumstance. Common sense public relations and good business practice also argue for the protection of guests' cash and property under any circumstances.

Some of the elements of guest protection have already been discussed: employee screening and general managerial vigilance especially.

Other specific measures complete the security program:

1. The guests' cars should be protected against theft by proper physical security in hotel garages and lots and by an adequate control system over delivery of the car. At the very least, the front door should be adequately manned to prevent thieves posing as hotel employees from stealing cars. Guests should identify themselves with more than the claim check when the cars are delivered.

2. All personnel movement of any type on guest floors should be

logged. If a maintenance man is sent to replace a light bulb, there should be a full record of his visit to the guest floor. Likewise bellhops, room-service waiters, and housemen should all account for their time.

3. Identification should be presented by persons asking for room keys.
4. Front desk personnel should urge guests to place valuables and cash (up to the statutory limit) in hotel vaults or safes.
5. If there have been frequent problems on guest floors, floor security personnel or even floor clerks should be assigned.
6. Room housekeeper hours should be staggered so that someone is present on guest floors for as much of the day as possible.
7. Telephone operators should not connect a caller with any room unless he knows the name of its occupant, and operators should not give the room number of a hotel guest to a caller when completing a connection.
8. Security forces should take special precautions when guests make a public display of cash or jewelry.
9. Night personnel, especially elevator operators and desk clerks, should be alert to strangers in the lobby or corridors.
10. Security forces or outside consultants might stage a mock "attack" on guest rooms to expose the operation's correctable weaknesses, such as rear doors left open, guest floors that can be reached from public concourses, or easy access from adjoining buildings to guest room balconies.

HOW TO PROTECT AGAINST CASH LOSSES

The possibility of theft of cash is an ever-present problem in the hospitality industry, because much of its business is in cash. Unfortunately, the high labor turnover of the industry increases its vulnerability: Casual employees may be robbers or burglars; cashiers and bartenders may be hired without proper screening because of immediate need; former employees may discuss protective systems with those currently employed.

There are three major threats to cash: (1) theft by cashiers and other cash-handling employees; (2) robbery or theft by violence or with the threat of violence in the presence of witnesses, and (3) burglary, the surreptitious entry and removal of cash.

Employee Theft

Embezzlement of cash by the manipulation of records must be countered by control and audit procedures. Although the sums stolen by embezzlers are often dramatically large, this type of crime is hardly as menacing as continual small thefts by cash-handling employees. If most cashiers and bartenders were not honest, few hospitality operations could survive. The goals of management efforts to control theft are to isolate the few dishonest employees and to keep the majority honest.

SECURITY IN CASH TRANSACTIONS

Theft from a cash register is very simple. The employee figures out a way to avoid ringing total revenues from all sales and thus can pocket the difference between true sales and sales recorded on the register.

The operation has three defenses: (1) the establishment of a strict system to which cashiers must adhere, plus observation and enforcement; (2) auditing the register, and (3) the use of undercover agents.

Rules for cashiers. Although the operational details of each type of register will vary, basic rules should be established for all cashiers. Even the most casual overt management observation will identify cashiers who consistently violate the rules. Very infrequent violations can be interpreted as human error, but frequent disregard of the rules makes the cashier suspect; repeated instances should be cause for termination.

1. The cash drawer should remain completely closed except when a transaction is actually in progress. If a drawer remains open between easily observable transactions, the cashier may be able to slip revenue from a quick even-money sale into the drawer unobserved without ringing it. Leaving the drawer open also allows the cashier to count the money in such a way that underrings can be adjusted to make the amount stolen leave the register balanced at the end of the shift.
2. All transactions must be rung immediately as they are received. Collecting transactions allows the cashier to steal easily and yet keep the register in balance.
3. A receipt should be thrown with every transaction or the machine should at least display the amount rung, and the cashier should announce the total being rung. The customer then becomes an auditor.
4. All overrings and voids should be initialed on the tape by the manager and noted on a control form. Cashiers should never be allowed to adjust for errors, as these adjustments are indistinguishable from adjustments for theft.
5. Employees' packages, pocketbooks, coats, and the like should not be kept on or near the cash stand. Ideally, cashiers should wear uniforms without pockets. Sometime during the day, the dishonest

cashier must remove the stolen money to some hiding place so that the register balances.

In addition to observing the cashier's compliance with these rules, the manager should also assure himself that there is always tape in the register, that the register tape area and back are locked, that the cashier is using the proper key if several people use the register, and that the cashier does not seem to be engaged in continuing computations, which would indicate that he is balancing the cash drawer against the register tape.

Auditing the register. Only the manager or control personnel should be able to either "zero" the machine or read the totals. Otherwise a dishonest employee can easily balance the cash and the register tape while still stealing large sums. Some machines, for example, can be zeroed in the middle of a long tape, and only the most careful auditing would discover that money representing only the last half of the transactions was turned in.

The tape compartment itself must be protected against insertion of a fresh tape, ringing a spurious tape, or blocking the registering of certain transactions by preventing the printing dies from striking the tape. The compartment should be locked at all times, and only management should have a key. If there is any doubt about key control, the lock should be changed.

When the register tape is audited, comparison with sales checks that should be sequentially numbered and sequentially stamped by the machine is the primary control. If a numbered check is not used, or if the cashier is also a salesperson, the tape can still be revealing. Managers should be suspicious of cashiers whose tapes show any of the following five irregularities:

1. Consistent sums over or under. Often the dishonest cashier will be over because he is afraid of being under. He will have stolen money but will have left too much in the register.
2. Any break in the sequence of transaction numbers. Some transactions have been recorded elsewhere, obviously to the employee's advantage.
3. Frequent no-sale transactions. The cash drawer is being opened without any legitimate reason (except if it is obvious that the cashier must give change frequently). Perhaps sales are not being recorded; perhaps a very nervous thief is constantly counting the money to make sure that his adjustments are in order.
4. Unusual voids or overrings for the operation. Individual cashiers should be checked. Tapes of a cashier and his relief should be compared. Too many overrings and voids, even when they are

authorized, indicates either poor training or complicity with the person authorizing the overrings.

In addition to auditing the tape at the end of the shift, management should conduct surprise audits of the cash and tape during the shift. Few employees are stupid enough to pocket money as they steal it. Rather, they collect their takings once or twice a day; at all other times the register is unbalanced.

Use of Undercover Agents. In a variety of ways the undercover agent sets up a situation in which the dishonest cashier has the opportunity to pocket money from a transaction without registering it. Whether the transaction was registered can be determined by an examination of the tape, because the agent is able to bracket it. The undercover agents, generally called "honesty shoppers," can be given a standard fee per shopping or can be retained at a fixed salary. Most often they are used to document cases against cashiers already suspected of dishonesty so that their time is maximized.

SECURITY IN BAR TRANSACTIONS

Traditionally, bar transactions have presented an area of high vulnerability for hospitality operations. If the bartender is the cashier, all observations made on security in other cash transactions must be applied. Whenever possible, hospitality operators separate the two functions of cashier and bartender as a defense against theft.

The operation's second defense is strict control of bar stocks. There are several accounting methods, but basically actual sales must equal the revenues that are projected on the number of bottles supplied to the bar. Projections, which take into account spillage and evaporation, must equal revenues, or some of the bar stock has been sold for the profit of the bartender and not the operation. Also, bottles may be identified with marks that will be visible only in ultraviolet light so that bartenders cannot bring in their own bottles. In addition, management should be prepared to test the bottles for alcoholic content. By watering stock, the bartender can keep the revenues from the extra drinks he gains per bottle. Theft by selling liquor without recording the transaction is made much more difficult, of course, by automatic dispensing machines.

Check control is the operation's third defense. In many well-run bars a double ring system is used. The bartender writes the order on the check, leaves the check in front of the customer, mixes the drink, serves it, registers the price on the check and then presents the check to the customer. When the customer pays, after one drink or after several, the check is rung again. Then the check is deposited in a locked box, so that it cannot be presented again. Obviously no checks must be missing, all first-ring totals must equal all second-ring totals, and the cash received must equal the total revenues rung (less charges).

Finally, observation of bartenders by undercover agents assures the operation that they are not violating any of the procedures indicated and that they have not begun to steal from the customers in order to steal from the operation. For example, a bartender who shorts customers on drinks has that amount of liquor in the bottle to divert to his own unrecorded transactions.

Robbery

A hospitality operation is particularly vulnerable to robbery: It accumulates large amounts of cash when banks are closed; "loitering" for the purposes of consuming food and beverages is encouraged; and experienced robbers have ample opportunity and complete freedom to "case" the job.

There is very little protection possible against the robber who walks into a restaurant late Saturday night, approaches the cashier's station, which is often out of view, threatens the cashier with a gun, and tosses over a paper bag to be filled with large bills.

Perhaps the management has been wise enough to remove sums from the register during the evening and secure them in a safe, but in most operations the money will be right there in the register. Perhaps the cashier has a silent alarm but it is unlikely that the police will reach the operation in the few minutes that it takes to complete a theft.

At best, the cashier will be able to describe the robber accurately and aid the police in his identification and apprehension. At worst, the cashier will be fool-hardy and attempt to brain the robber with the Diner's Club machine and get shot.

Large hospitality operations share this problem—their bars, coffee shops, and night clubs are equally vulnerable—but they also have the additional problems of the security of their cashier areas, which sometimes contain as much money as a branch bank, and of moving significant sums to and from banks. Fortunately, they usually have the space, money, and personnel to defend themselves rather effectively against robbery on the premises and robbery in transit.

ROBBERY ON THE PREMISES

An individual hotel cashier might be robbed by an amateur, a dope addict, or a petty thief, but the robbery of the cashier's department in a large hotel would probably be undertaken only by a professional team capable of some planning. The team might have an inside accomplice who will open a fire door, or at least an informant. As they want to minimize their risk and maximize their gain, they will undoubtedly observe the operation to assess the possible amount of their take, the difficulty of the robbery, and the possibility of interference with their getaway.

The operation can create conditions that will discourage robbery attempts by professionals by following these procedures:

1. Limit the amount of cash that will be available to the robbers by depositing it in the bank or the bank's night depository. Other sums can be secured in safes or safe compartments to which persons present do not have the keys or combinations. Robbers are not safe crackers; they are frustrated by measures that will delay them even for a few minutes.

2. Establish the policy of having a limited amount of cash on hand and available, enforce it, and advertise it. Make sure that potential professional robbers know that robbing the operation would not be worth their while. The same sources who will inform them of large sums of money lying around for the taking—porters, part-time secretaries, and clerks—will tell them about the low ceiling on cash.

3. Harden the cashier's area. It should at least give the appearance of a secure area, as true invulnerability is probably too expensive for most operations. It is possible to install attractive burglar-resistant or bulletproof glass around the whole area. Access to it should be limited to a single metal door with a view window that opens outward.

4. Install obvious detection devices that cannot be controlled by either the employees in the cashiers' areas or the robbers. For example, a closed-circuit television camera overlooking the area with a monitor in a basement switchboard room would make a robber quite reluctant to tackle the operation. Even if he initiates the robbery, he knows that the police will be called and that there will be a video tape record of the crime.

If the operation should be robbed, even with these precautions, proper employee indoctrination can save lives and aid in both apprehension of the robber and recovery of the stolen money. Employees should be instructed to cooperate with the robber and not to attempt to defend the operation. By maintaining their calm they can accurately note the robber's description and help the police.

Passive alarms rather than alarms that require activation by an individual protect employees and still signal the police. For example, cash drawers may be equipped with an alarm trigger that must be switched off before opening the drawer. Or, a procedure may be established for signaling the switchboard operator at intervals if there is no problem. Safes that employees can open can require an initial dialing sequence that will deactivate the alarm.

ROBBERY IN TRANSIT

When cash is moved from the operation to the bank, conditions that may have limited possibility of robbery on the premises are absent. Robbers know that a sum worth transporting is probably worth stealing; there are no alarms; there are only a few witnesses; they themselves can be prepared for flight; and the person carrying the money is not prepared to follow them.

An operation can hire an armored car service to make the robbers' task more difficult, but the expense cannot be justified except by a very large operation, and even then substantial cash must be accumulated to warrant the expense.

Sometimes, routine but effective security is ignored. An effective program can include varying the departure time for cash; using several different bonded messengers from among trusted employees; scheduling frequent trips so that no sum carried is significant; and asking the local police to protect the money in transit. This method effectively forestalls robbery, because the potential robbers cannot plan adequately; they do not know when the money will move or who will carry it. They risk apprehension, and—most important—the potential gain is unattractive when it must be divided among the three or four men necessary to stage a robbery in transit and a successful getaway.

Burglary

It may be necessary for a hospitality operation to keep significant sums of money or protect guests' valuables in a vault or a safe. Thieves may contemplate robbery when there are few of the personnel near the vault, or they may attempt a surreptitious entry when the vault is not under observation.

Maximum security is assured if four conditions are met:

1. It should be impossible to open the safe or the vault until a time when there is protection for the contents and when witnesses are present. In other words, even if the thieves have been sold the combination or keys by a dishonest employee or are prepared to menace the life of an employee who knows the combination, they will not be able to enter the safe or vault legitimately because of a time lock.
2. The construction of the unit itself should meet defined standards of burglar resistance as specified by the Underwriters Laboratories

or insurance associations so that it will frustrate the burglars long enough either to discourage them or facilitate their detection and apprehension.

3. Physical barriers to penetration should be supplemented by several silent alarm systems that cannot easily be neutralized, so that security forces or police can respond while the burglary is in progress.

4. Control procedures are developed and enforced so that employees cannot inadvertently or deliberately leave the safe or vault open or neutralize the alarm systems. Essentially, independent double and triple checks are necessary.

9 | Management of Business Activity

Marketing, sales promotion, advertising, and other activities directed toward increasing total revenues are not primary concerns of operational management. Most often they are the responsibility of executive or corporate management, staff specialists, or outside advertising or marketing firms. Operational managers concern themselves largely with "bottom line" activities such as improving profitability through better labor utilization, more effective controls, and cost effectiveness.

His emphasis on bottom line activities, however, does not absolve the operational manager from responsibility in this area. The operational manager, especially the individual involved in foodservice, beverage service, and front office management can contribute mightily in the total organizational effort to increase revenues.

INTERNAL SALES MANAGEMENT

The operational manager is principally concerned with business activity within the operation. Rather than working toward attracting new customers, he concentrates on internal sales, i.e., sales to customers already in the operation.

The operational manager has to make his unit an active rather than a passive sales organization. He has to invite and encourage business activity within the operation rather than simply waiting to service whatever customer external marketing efforts produce.

A comparison of state liquor stores and private liquor stores offers extreme examples of the difference between passive and active sales organizations. Both offer the same products for sale. The private enterprise obviously has an effective sales organization because it has remained in business in a market where it competes with many other outlets that offer the same products at more or less the same prices. The state store was deliberately designed and structured to discourage the sale of its only commodity: If it were any less effective as a sales unit, it would have to close the doors.

The differences in approach between these two enterprises provide an essential lesson for hospitality operational managers. The private store displays its wares; the state store does not. The private store employs sales personnel; the state store seemingly recruits retired toll takers. The private store merchandises in the store; the state store does not. The private store suits the convenience of the market in arranging its hours, products, and aisles; the state store makes it difficult to buy and difficult to see. The private store creates the impulse to buy with promotional techniques and devices; the state store smothers that impulse by obliging the customer to know what he wants. Most important, the private store makes liquor buying fun and friendly; the state store makes the customer feel slightly guilty and offers him as much fun as he might get from purchasing a license for a hay baler.

In more specific terms, in the hospitality industry sales oriented operational managers have made the slogan of the National Restaurant Association, "We're glad you're here," a working formula that is immediately communicated to the customer in a hundred ways. Operational managers unconcerned with sales seem to be saying "Be glad we're here."

The current customer is an excellent prospect for additional sales. The person who walks in the door of a restaurant or hotel has prequalified himself. He is there to buy. The television campaign, radio spots, billboard ads, direct mailings, and telephone solicitations have worked.

The operational manager has the internal sales market before him in the flesh. Unlike the individual concerned with overall marketing he is not faced with the prospect of deciding whether some of the pellets from his shotgun blast of external media advertising will strike potential customers. He has the customers; he has to decide whether he can fire a bullet that will hit them in their desire to buy.

The operational manager looks over the dining room or the lobby and asks himself: "What do those people want that I am offering but that they are unaware I am offering? What do they want that I can offer? Do they want intangibles, such as excitement, adventure, value, comfort, convenience, service information, and prestige? Or do they want tangibles, such as menu specialties, theme nights, buffets, sauna baths, all-night coffee and in-house secretarial services?"

The customers of an operation are definitely a market for something more, but not for everything. In addition to analyzing their needs and isolating the benefits the operation can offer them, the operational manager might consider a very realistic approach to determining areas for internal sales: What are his customers buying elsewhere? If a restaurant customer spends any money on food or drink within an hour of arriving at the restaurant or leaving it, that money "rightly" belongs to the restaurant manager. He only has to be clever enough to get it away from the outside bar where his customers go for cocktails and the ice cream parlor where they go for dessert.

For lodging operations, this kind of thinking can produce dramatic revelations about the deficiencies of the operation from its customers' point of view. Once corrected, a deficiency becomes a market benefit and conceivably a plus on the bottom line. For example, how many thousands of guests in downtown luxury hotels do not eat breakfast in the hotel but go to the cafeteria and coffee shops next door? How many travelers do not eat at least once in the hotel dining room? How many people buy liquor on the street? How many business-men take their associates to lunch in other restaurants and to drinks in other bars? Where are they having their haircuts, buying their newspapers, arranging for their theater tickets and hired cars, having their shoes shined, giving their dictation, and getting their sore feet massaged? It is bad enough if the operation loses these revenues because it cannot supply the guests' wants, but it is an immediate internal sales problem if the operation does have the facilities and the guests are not using them.

Every Hospitality Employee Is a Salesperson

Hospitality vs. huckstering? Hospitality and hustling? Con and comfort? Slick salesman and service employee?

Some hospitality employees, and some operational managers, conveniently excuse their unwillingness to sell by saying that sales efforts are inconsistent with their roles in a *service* industry. They miss a very important point: Nobody is sold anything that he does not want to buy. Sales is a communications process. The good salesman tells the potential customer about something he would like to buy. The salesman renders a service. He offers actual samples or a verbal or graphic description that lets the customer sample the pleasures or the usefulness of the product.

When a waitress suggests a bottle of wine to a customer, the customer accepts the suggestion because he feels that the bottle of wine will enrich his meal. Had the waitress not suggested it, his meal would have been less enjoyable. She made the suggestion for the house's benefit, perhaps for her benefit, but certainly for the customer's benefit. When the elevator operator announces that breakfast is being served in the dining room until 11 a.m. he is selling breakfast. But he is also assisting the fellow who must decide when to eat his breakfast. When management has installed a vending machine containing toilet articles in some convenient and tasteful space, who benefits most—the operation, which makes a few hundred dollars a year, or the scores of guests who, when they wake up with a bad taste in their mouths, can do something about it?

Any employee of a hospitality operation can proudly bar the "s" in service, making it $ervice, because he can rightly presume that his sales efforts result in a positive good for guests. They can afford anything they are sold. And they want it, or they would not buy it.

Establish Program Objectives

Some internal sales objectives are crisis objectives; others have high priorities; and still others imply a long-term developmental program.

An operation that does not have an active, positive, sales organization on the operational level is in the throes of crisis. That room clerk must sell. That waitress must sell. That telephone operator, bartender, bell captain, lobby, window area, menu, guest room, brochure, and elevator must sell. At least they have to sell the operation if repeat customers are to be made. At best they are building restaurant checks and room revenues and selling the operation. This is the first priority.

Items with high priorities include facilities that are not earning their potential: bars that are half empty, four-chair barber shops with one barber, and newsstands with yesterday's newspapers. There are also potential profit areas: retail sales where there are now none, added services, sales of future bookings, and so on.

Some organization of priorities is necessary, because internal sales efforts require time, energy, and expenditures. Even if the cost is minimal, focused objectives mean the best use of managerial time and the success that comes with a definite campaign rather than an unstructured, limited assault.

Operational managers generally have priority concerns in seven major areas:

Developing a regular clientele
Bigger profits from food sales
Boosting beverage sales
Building up restaurant checks
Selling guest rooms

Increasing profits from retail sales

Making in-house sales efforts effective

DEVELOPING A REGULAR CLIENTELE

Hospitality operations cannot afford the cost of attracting customers for one time only. Even if a profit can be made on the one-time guest, despite the high cost of attracting him, the operation eventually exhausts the market's potential for producing new customers.

A hospitality operation has to keep its customers so that the initial cost of attracting them is spread over numerous visits. And these regular customers become an operation's best advertising medium. They communicate the merits of the operation to its precise market, the people like themselves: their friends, neighbors, business colleagues, and social peers.

When a clientele has been developed, external advertising and sales efforts may no longer be necessary; at least they can be reduced. Generally, the hospitality operation has three phases of development. In the first, there is a broad expensive advertising effort that attracts many customers, all new, only some of whom are offered any real benefit by the operation. Second, there is the period of consolidation, with advertising and sales selectively directed to the group that has emerged as the prime market. In the third, the operation concentrates on advertising to reinforce its market image; it can no longer be "news" to the market. It directs its effort toward maintaining the clientele and market position.

There is ample counsel available from public relations, promotion, and advertising agencies for the first two phases. In the third phase, the most important one, the operation is virtually on its own. There is a presumption that, if a customer who likes hot dogs gets a good hot dog, he will remain a hot-dog customer until he dies, moves, or becomes a vegetarian. Unfortunately, he can get a hot dog just as good down the street. He can get bored with hot dogs. And he can get insulted and decide to make his hot dogs at home. Keeping him is a matter of keeping him happy.

A customer is happy when the operation has established itself as uniquely "his place." The customer identifies with the establishment. He feels that between his visits all activities cease; when he returns, he animates the operation again. He has the impression that he is the focus around which the operation revolves. His patronage gives it purpose. When he buys a drink or a meal or rents a room, his actual purchase is almost incidental. He is having his psychic batteries recharged, his wobbly sense of self-importance propped, and his passport validated for another ego trip.

Restaurants

The restaurant is increasingly limited in the ways that it can keep customers happy. Product distinction becomes harder and harder as rising labor costs and the lack of skilled personnel oblige the operation to purchase prepared foods. High food costs prevent loading plates to give customers the feeling they are in their own dining rooms. Service personnel often place their own ego needs ahead of the customer's. In sum, it becomes a management problem to keep the customer happy. Management creates, plans, and implements the internal sales program that keeps customers coming back.

A combination of three approaches, adapted to the specific restaurant's operational needs, can have significant results:

Customer accommodation

Promotion

Hostmanship

CUSTOMER ACCOMMODATION

In addition to a value-for-the-money meal, every operation can offer its particular special market benefits and services that the customer will not get at the competing establishments. The benefits and services that will develop a regular clientele are those that help meet definite customer needs.

For example, there are a dozen lunch facilities on a small city's main street. Most of the lunch patronage of a particular operation comes from professional men and businessmen. They do business by telephone, yet at lunch they are out of touch with their offices. To keep them as regular customers, the operation can establish a message center with pigeon-hole boxes at the cashier desk. It can provide them with printed stickers for their office telephones—"At lunchtime transfer my calls to . . ."—and it can have the telephone company install telephone jacks near all tables. If one or two particular companies account for most of the operation's business, or could, an arrangement can be made to link their switchboards with the restaurant line. In an industrial park area, for example, one restaurant, by offering special accommodations to businessmen, can virtually capture the business market.

Accommodations for other markets may be less involved. The executive would prefer to sign rather than pay cash or use a national credit card. Selected patrons can be given house accounts. If shoppers are a major market segment, the operation can provide facilities for holding packages. The key lockers seen in bus and train stations can be altered to operate without charge. The customer then can make the operation his base and finish his tour with a meal there.

In many operations, children are merely tolerated. Yet families can be extremely loyal patrons if the children like an operation. Accommodate the family patron by offering a children's menu of items that children like to eat. Have booster chairs and high chairs available. Supply bibs and bottles of warm milk. Give the kids toys to play with so they leave the salt and sugar alone. Let them burrow in a box of inexpensive toys when they leave, or give them candy, small toys, balloons, coloring books, or comics.

PROMOTION

Promotional efforts are really the operation's way of rewarding its customers who have remained loyal, in the hope of inducing them to continue their patronage. These efforts are intended to say: "It pays to be our customer."

Meal tickets, for example, are the most direct form of reward for continuing patronage. Either the customer purchases at a discount a book of meal tickets or coupons worth a certain amount, or he is given some as a bonus when he has spent a certain sum or has visited the operation a certain number of times. In any kind of value-for-the money operation this approach works extremely well. The young secretary and the junior executive appreciate saving that 5 or 6 percent—which, in dollars, is most often less than the cost of attracting new customers.

The same approach may work in a high-check-average restaurant, but it requires a little more sophistication. The management invites selected patrons to special gourmet dinners on an evening when the restaurant is normally closed. Or it presents them with food or beverage gifts, such as crocks of homemade pâté, or an interesting wine. Perhaps the sophisticated customer would appreciate receiving a series of recipe cards with a photograph of the specialty on one side and the recipe on the other.

HOSTMANSHIP

While it is impractical to consider developing every waiter into the type of worker who builds his own faithful clientele, most operations can develop a host. By force of personality and a few simple devices, that host can make the customer identify with the restaurant. The host can be a manager or a service worker. He can also be an individual hired specifically to host the operation. There are several successful restaurants that pay their hosts $30,000 and $40,000 a year to give distinction to four ordinary walls and run-of-the-mill food. Even for some lesser amount excellent results are possible. The key to hostmanship is remembering the customer's name. It impresses him, and it impresses his party. Some expert hosts spend several hours a day reviewing business cards and visualizing customers' faces. Standard memory devices such as relating a physical characteristic with the name may work for some hosts: Mr. Appel's hair is apple red; Mr. Smith has a grip like a blacksmith's pincers; and so on.

Accurate records can be kept on a guest's likes and dislikes. When the guest makes a reservation, he can be assigned the table he prefers and a reserved sign with his name can be placed on it. It might be possible to see a pattern in his ordering: If he always has a bottle of champagne, it can be iced and waiting for him. If he needs salt-free vegetables, they can be prepared ahead of time. Tables can be reserved for regular guests without their making prior reservations, at least until a certain hour. Eating in a particular restaurant becomes a habit. Some operations have napkin rings made with regular guests' names. Certainly the host can make sure that the regular guest experiences active hospitality. For example, when circulating among the diners, the host may find that a particular customer likes a certain brand of steak sauce, diet crackers, or mineral water. And the next time he comes in, his restaurant has the product for him.

A guest book can often become a vehicle of hostmanship. The host has the guests sign, so that they may be "invited to our spring wine tasting." Throughout the year they are sent invitations, recipe cards, and holiday cards. Personal cards are sent on birthdays and anniversaries —and if possible are sent far enough in advance so that the guests may celebrate the occasions at the restaurant and enjoy the "little treat" indicated on the cards.

Even if the operation is not forewarned of a birthday, anniversary or other celebration, a competent host or professional service worker should be able to spot a celebrating group. The host can always have on hand a few splits or half-bottles of champagne to toast the customer, or a few small decorated cakes in the freezer.

Bars and Cocktail Lounges

Bars and cocktail lounges must develop a regular clientele in order to survive, yet product distinction is virtually impossible for them. As a rule people do not think of a bar or cocktail lounge as a place where they make great drinks—unless the drinks are an especially good value or when brand names are used as bar stock.

In most instances, bars and cocktail lounges develop clientele because of the personalities of their bartenders or their success in identifying with the customers.

DRINKS WITH PERSONALITY

The manager of a bar or cocktail lounge without a really sensational decor concept that is, in effect, an entertainment, relies on his bartenders and service personnel to establish the atmosphere, the ambience, of the operation. The neighborhood tavern is a typical example. Often it has no decor and no distinction: It has the usual tables, stools, backbar, television set, and hardboiled eggs. Yet the customers keep coming for 40 years because the bartenders are there for 40 years.

They remember each customer's name, what he drinks, how he drinks, whether he likes to chat, where he works, and the ages of his children. They also keep track of such vital information as ball game results, the name of the current Irish prime minister, the high cost of living, the good old days, and the general decline of everything.

The management of other bar and cocktail operations often ignore the lesson of the neighborhood tavern. They hire bartenders with good references and the ability to make drinks but without any capacity to relate to the customer. The management should decide on the type of man it wants, what he should look like, and what personality he should have. The bartenders should be as alike as Tweedledee and Tweedledum. It may take a regular customer months to be able to tell them apart.

However, the personality of the customer is the primary criterion. With whom will he feel at home? This is the most important consideration, for the objective is to make him feel comfortable and relaxed. In the neighborhood tavern, which often has a middle-class, blue-collar clientele, the bartenders share upbringing attitudes and interests with the customers. On their days off they drink in the same type of bar.

As millionaires and their butlers often resemble each other, the businessman or the clubman appreciates a barman who seems as though he could be sitting on their side of the bar. And a man who looks like a retired prize fighter and has a hearty personality is certainly a better choice for a men's bar than a modish youngster would be.

In sum, management must decide on a clientele (late night, free-spenders, after-theater patrons, commuting businessmen, singles, older married couples, cocktail drinkers, or swingers) and give them a partner in dialogue who has the lines they want to hear.

IDENTITY CONCEPTS

Between the featureless neighborhood tavern and the million-dollar re-creation of a Polynesian Village, there is the possibility of creating a decor with which the market can identify. Whether the regular customer articulates it or not, he sees the operation as his kind of place. When he walks in the door, he finds the kind of stage set on which he can role-play a little. A bar in a financial area, for example, can make all its customers, including the junior clerks, feel like investment bankers about to buy a small country. Dark wood, leather, brass, and copies of financial newspapers can do the trick.

Autographed pictures, movie stills, and cartoon caricatures of stars bring the tinsel world of Hollywood stardom to an operation near the theaters and movies. Black glass and red velvet are sufficiently sinful-looking to make married couples feel as if they are cheating. Safari paraphernalia, sporting pictures, or American West accent notes allow the customer to "daydream" while he drinks.

Lodging Operations

To keep customers coming back, lodging operations must battle against their built-in impersonality. However dramatic and unique modern hotels and motels are on the outside, inside they are almost indistinguishable. Many veteran business travelers (the market segment with the most repeat potential) wake up in the morning without immediately realizing where they are or in what hotel.

MAKING A GUEST WANT TO RETURN

Certainly the guest appreciates the efficiency and organization that are parts of standardization and modernity, but he knows that he can expect the same quality of lodging in any major operation. On this basis, he has no reason to name a particular operation. "Get me a room in Detroit" is about as specific as many businessmen are in their instructions to their secretaries. Even the occasional traveler, vacationer, and convention guest can try the competition next time, because lacking substantial identification with any operation, he might as well enjoy whatever superficial variety changing hotels offers. To sell the customer on coming back, the operation has to give him something unique to come back to. It has to make him feel like a V.I.P.; it has to make him feel that the operation is a home away from home.

The V.I.P. treatment. A great many Americans travel, but many, many more never leave their home states. Few people travel so extensively that they no longer consider a trip something special. If a lodging operation can make the traveler feel as though he is a special person doing something special, it can win him as a regular. Most operations reserve their V.I.P. treatment for a few individuals. Other operations feel so secure in their prestige that they think they don't need a V.I.P. treatment at all.

The V.I.P. treatment has to be democratized. How far it can be spread from the presidential suite toward the minimum singles depends entirely on how much repeat business is worth to the operation. In other words, it depends on how much the operation is willing to spend to attract a new customer to replace the guest who just drifts away. There are degrees to the V.I.P. treatment, and each degree carries its own price tag.

Management presence. Someone in management should meet the guest just after he arrives and ask him if there is anything he requires. In most instances, the guest will be perfectly satisfied. In the rare instance that he has a complaint, management's attentions will win him for the hotel. It is possible to divide the task among several managers, each of whom calls guest rooms and meets guests for an hour a day.

Anticipation of guest needs. If the guest has already been in the operation and has returned for a second time, the hotel has an excellent chance of making him a regular. The guest is already in the process of doing that for himself. Guest records can provide the key. Most business travelers would welcome a pre-registration procedure. Instead of waiting in the lobby and filling out the forms, guests could go straight to the bell captain and be taken to their rooms. If a guest has special requirements—for example, if he needs extra towels or nonallergenic soaps—guest records would help the operation to prepare the room to his satisfaction before he arrives. The guest will be spared a half-hour on the telephone to housekeeping.

Regular-guest privileges. The operation can make regular-guest status desirable. An attractive booklet outlining a regular-guest club can be placed in each guest room. Members (second time guests) can be given signing privileges, the right to a free drink in the main bar, message service, free local telephone calls, and other advantages as well.

Courtesy cars. The operation might investigate the cost and local regulations of picking up and delivering guests at major transportation terminals, either on call or on a regular schedule. The operation that can save the guest the problems of retrieving his luggage and finding a porter and a cab has a distinct competitive advantage.

Party concepts. In most operations the management can invite the guests to something: coffee, a drink, a cocktail party, a midnight swim, a movie (perhaps in an empty banquet room), a lecture on local history, an encounter session or a yoga lesson.

Home away from home. "Homelike" comfort and convenience need not be homelike at all. A hospitality operation is in a position to offer the guest a style of living he wishes he enjoyed at home. Almost every embellishment of the quality of the lodging—almost everything beyond a decent bed and a clean room—is a selling point. For example, a guest will return to an operation that offers him an in-the-room sauna bath, just because of the bath. Lodging managers might consider any number of enhancements, each of which, necessarily, has its price tag. Such conveniences might include:

1. A small refrigerator in every room, with or without food items
2. Efficiency units: sinks, stoves, and refrigerators
3. Coffee service in rooms
4. Free continental breakfasts
5. Closed-circuit movies
6. A health club
7. Saunas in the rooms
8. Valet units in the rooms
9. Shoe shining during the night
10. Extended check-outs and early check-ins
11. Guest privileges for guests in hotel pools and facilities
12. WATS lines to major cities
13. Arrangements for guests to use golf courses, tennis courts, and other facilities
14. Secretarial service (which might not be self-sustaining)
15. Living rooms on every floor
16. Baby sitting
17. True concierge services from the bell captain: theater tickets and running errands, for example
18. Hometown newspapers on breakfast trays
19. Loans of typewriters, hair dryers, office calculators, and clock radios
20. Car service to sporting and other events

BIGGER PROFITS FROM FOOD SALES

The customer in a food operation, whether it is a hot dog stand or a white-tablecloth restaurant, is there because he wants to buy. He does not have to be sold the operation, because he has already been sold by external advertising, word of mouth, or his past experience. Nor is it possible to sell him more than his stomach can hold. Three sales objectives thus remain for internal sales efforts:

1. Selling the customer more than he intended to buy: pie as well as coffee, a dinner instead of an entree
2. Selling him on coming back
3. Selling him the items on which the restaurant makes the most profit

Selling the customer more than he intended to buy is the primary objective of internal selling. The operation makes the customer aware that he would like food-and-drink items that he had not thought of when he entered the operation. The most passive, catalog-like menu can prompt some customers to buy by making them aware of an item, but other selling efforts are obviously more effective.

Selling the customer on coming back is a twofold approach. First, the customer must find what he expected to find, including satisfaction with the quality of the food, service, and cleanliness. Second, the operation must combat that inevitable boredom that even satisfied customers experience, by selling the customer on the idea that the operation is vital, changing, always interesting, old (which he likes), and new (which he wants at the same time).

Selling the customer items on which the restaurant makes the most profit is the most sophisticated use of internal selling. In essence, the object is to increase the profits from a restaurant full of well-fed customers. More customers cannot be packed in, and the customers cannot be sold two dinners, yet they can be induced to switch to the high-profit items. For example, an operation offers a steak dinner for $7.50 and a chicken dinner for $5.50. The food cost on the steak dinner is $4.50 and only $1.50 on the chicken. On the steak the operation realizes $3 gross profit, while on the lower-priced chicken it realizes $4 gross profit. The objectives of an internal sales effort would be to sell more chicken or all chicken and no steaks by placing the chicken high on the menu (because people often read only the first few items), by using stunning graphics for the chicken item and a neutral presentation for the steak, by promoting the chicken with table tents, and so on.

Internal sales techniques can help realize this objective for any type of operation. The fast-food hamburger drive-in; or the coffee shop that would benefit from selling more eggs than corned beef sandwiches. The same techniques can even benefit operations which do not have menus or prices. An American-Plan hotel, for example, profits more by lower food costs if low-cost items can be sold against high-cost items: a Mexican specialty against a roast beef plate, for example.

Menus that Sell

Most operations have the type of menu that suits their style of business. Few drive-in operations present their customers with folded, thick-paper menus, and few white-tablecloth restaurants use signboards with changeable type. Sometimes a quality operation will make the error of buying an expensive but poorly printed or poorly designed menu, but most of the time the package is right.

Usually the contents, not the package, is the problem when the menu is not being sold. It may be so badly wrought on the inside that it neutralizes the positive impression of the restaurant that the decor and accessories have helped create in the new customer.

When menus do not sell, it is because they have not been written from a sales perspective, using selling techniques. Instead, the chef makes the menu in the interests of culinary art or his convenience; or the manager copies the competition; or the printer takes the responsibility, because he wants to get the job done. Nobody thinks about how menus can make the restaurant a dollar or two more.

SELLING DESIGN

It is very possible to confuse a pretty menu with a selling menu; they are not necessarily the same. Operations are sold beautiful printing jobs or expensive signs that are frankly admired by the customers but don't do the job. The well-designed menu will incorporate three vital features:

1. It will establish the mood of the operation. It will encourage the customer to make the buying decision the operator wants. For example, an extremely elegant menu with velvet-textured paper and gold stamping says to the customer that he has arrived and should be eating the very best (most expensive) items. A menu with homey graphics, featuring a family around a loaded table, says "value for the money." A fantasy menu promotes fantasy items.
2. The graphic presentation will feature items the manager wants most to sell. At the very least, the highly profitable items will be listed first, so that the customer is captured before he has a chance to read on. Items that offer additional revenues (check builders) will be presented: Appetizers, desserts, wine in carafes, and side dishes will not be hidden.
3. The graphics will communicate the operation, so that the menu becomes a not-so-subtle sales pitch for the restaurant. The manager wants the customer to remember the place as friendly, convenient, economical: The design gives that impression, or the menu announces these attributes in so many words. Graphics designers are immensely capable in this area. Consider how precisely magazine advertising design and graphics communicate that Caribbean Island countries are fun for everyone and that big steel has only the public interest at heart.

SELLING LANGUAGE

The selling language. It is a piece of advertising material for the items the operation wants to sell.

There is only one rule for menu writing: Say something. Nobody is sold by a list. A "phone book" menu or signboard passes the sales initiative back to the customer, who then makes his buying decision on bases that may not serve the operation's interest.

Obviously, the menu should communicate information about the items the operation wants to sell, so that those items are absolutely enticing. The language should be to the point, but clever, memorable, almost poetic. If it is not, then the cliches that are universally used, abused, and overused will have to serve. On the one hand, such common descriptions as "chilled sweet melon" and "young, tender veal" and "fresh fish" can be mocked. What restaurant would serve warm melon or admit to stale fish, or be able to obtain veal—young beef—that is not young? On the other hand, the customer is not a sophisticated literary critic. He thinks in exactly these terms. He speaks in cliches. Cliches have become cliches because of their effectiveness. If he were asked about the melon, the customer would be more likely to say that it was cold and sweet than to quote elegant prose in praise of the melon.

In addition to some expression that whets the customer's appetite, menu descriptions of items can include other selling points:

1. A listing of the ingredients so that the customer knows what he is getting and will not feel obliged to play it safe. For example, the customer should be told that paella includes lobster, mussels, shrimp, spicy sausages, chunks of chicken, saffron rice, green bell peppers, and plum tomatoes.
2. An indication that the item is special, customized, cooked à la carte, or at least painstakingly prepared. For example: "Paella: lobster, mussels, shrimp, spicy sausages, and chunks of chicken, baked together with saffron rice, green bell peppers, and plum tomatoes in our brick oven in an individual cast iron pan."
3. When possible, an indication that the item is value for the money: "Paella: a heaping platter of lobster, mussels . . ."
4. Some excitement: "Exotic Spanish Paella: a heaping platter of lobster, mussels . . ."
5. Cleverness, if possible, to catch the customer's attention. For example, Beef and Reef instead of Surf and Turf.
6. Cooking-time information. Long cooking times stimulate cocktail and appetizer sales and sell the customer who wants to make an evening of dinner or feels that anticipation is greater than realization. The customer who wants to eat quickly is not frustrated. At the end of the paella description, the operator might add: "Every dish is cooked to order. Allow at least 20 minutes for your paella to be prepared."
7. Special market information. For example, a dish can be described as high protein, low calorie, diet, or weight watchers.

MENU SELLING DEVICES

Menus can be designed with enough flexibility to permit intensive selling. For example, it is not necessary to list desserts on the main menu.

A separate dessert menu presented at the time the customer is ready to order dessert, lets the operation highlight its offerings.

When the operation has certain items it wants to sell because they are especially good or especially profitable (particularly leftovers), the menu can be supplemented by an attached or inserted piece of paper featuring this item. Some menus have clips glued to them, others have panels with slots that accept cards. In any case, the operation can offer a special sale in much the same way that any retail merchant offers certain items at a discount or promotes certain articles. When the sale is over, the card is removed.

A further benefit of the insert, tip-in, or clip-on addition is the variety it offers. Regular customers do not have the feeling that they know the menu as well as the cook knows it. They are pleased to see something new, even though they may continue to order their old favorite. Customers enjoy reading a good description of a game pie before ordering their sirloin steak. It's part of the adventure of eating, just as trying on a tattersall vest before buying a blue suit is part of the adventure of shopping.

Point-of-Sale Merchandising

Even a strong selling menu can be supplemented effectively by other materials or sales devices. When there is no menu or when the menu cannot sell intensively, other point-of-sale materials take on additional importance. For example, an expensive gourmet restaurant must rely on its menu and its personnel to sell because a promotion tent on the table or a lapel badge on the maitre d'hotel's dinner jacket would be unseemly. The counter operation, on the other hand, limited to a menu signboard which must be simple because it must be large and legible, can effectively use everything from a lapel badge to a specially painted barrage balloon.

There are three types of point-of-sale merchandising: (1) printed materials (2) displays (3) gimmicks.

PRINTED MATERIALS

Printed materials can be extensively used as long as they do not offend the customer, neutralize the decor, clutter the operation, or destroy the mood. In actuality, this means that the ceremonious hotel dining room may have to limit itself to discreet advertising matchbooks, while the fun-fast-food operation can go all out.

Table tents. The table tent is a traditional point-of-sale printed piece that, when folded, stands on a level surface like a tent. At its simplest it is a folded single sheet of paper with graphics, illustrations, photographs or a sales message on it. Table tents have been sophisticated considerably. Those available from liquor companies and product promoters include three-dimensional cardboard antique cars, miniature liquor bottles, pop-up cartoon figures and so on.

Topper cards. Many operations use a wire holder with a cliplike handle for sugar, salt and pepper. A topper card can be fitted into the clip. Like the table tent, it may be plain or dramatically designed and cut.

Super graphics. Type can be beautiful. Giant-sized letters on walls, ceilings, and floors, spelling out, for example, house specials, are as much decor as they are advertising.

Place mats. Paper place mats can advertise menu items, promote other facilities, and entertain customers.

Lobster bibs. When worn by customers eating lobster, lobster bibs remind other customers that seafood is available.

Lapel badges. Lapel badges on service personnel in informal dining rooms and on counterservers can be straightforward or clever. For example, a strawberry-shaped badge that says, "Strawberry Shortcake, Parfait, Sundae, Soda," sells these items. A badge that says "Kill the Pudgies!" invites the customer to ask how and allows the waiter to answer, "By ordering our diet platter."

Banners, poster signs, mobiles. Some operations have the opportunity to use the same point-of-sale techniques as retail establishments: display advertising of all forms. It is also a good idea to post the same signs in the kitchen and the pantry, so that personnel gets in the selling mood.

DISPLAYS

Good-looking food sells itself.* If the operator can somehow contrive to display his menu items, or at least the items he wants to sell, customers will be tempted to order them.

Displays are used in both white-tablecloth and fast food operations. Many classical French restaurants greet their customers with an hors d'oeuvre display of smoked salmon sides on a marble slab, colorful hors d'oeuvre salads, platters of preserved fish, caviar set in ice, and the like. Or a dessert cart can be positioned near the door, so that the customer can anticipate a helping of fresh raspberries or a chocolate mousse while he is finishing his meal.

Counter installations often include refrigerated glass cabinets which could be used quite effectively for display. Unfortunately, individual boxes of wrapped cereal and wrapped convenience cakes too often seem to be "featured."

---

* See *Showmanship in the Dining Room* and *Adding Eye Appeal to Foods,* both part of the Focus Series by Bruce H. Axler (Indianapolis: ITT Educational Publishing, 1974).

The restaurateur might consider a number of different displays as part of an internal sales effort: a dining room cooking station, a main entrée wagon, open hearth cooking, a salad bar, a self-service hors d'oeuvre buffet or lazy susan, racked wines, a giant soup kettle, a dessert bar, and an internal espresso cafe.

GIMMICKS

Since food is fun, most successful selling gimmicks are also fun. They can range from an Italian theme with straw hats, checkered handkerchiefs, mustaches, wine bottle candles, a push cart, and an organ grinder to sell a pizza burger, meatballs on a stick (skewer), or a takeout paper cone of round spaghetti and mini meatballs, to a visit from a celebrity doing missionary work for a brand of whiskey. Gimmicks, when they are well done, which means well planned and adequately funded, really sell, and perhaps more importantly, they get the customers involved.
Some gimmicks are:

1. Two-for-the-price-of-one specials
2. Give-away serviceware (suitably identified) with certain items
3. Hidden prizes in several items of a batch
4. Free portions of any main dish their parents order to kids under 12
5. Trading cards with purchases
6. Purchasing a certain item means a contribution to a local charity by the operation
7. Balloons
8. Balloons with different prices inside: Customer picks and pops for his price
9. Breakfast with Santa
10. All the whatever the customer can eat
11. Strawberry festival
12. Christmas in July, complete with fixings
13. Free dessert if the waitress does not ask
14. Free dessert if service takes longer than five minutes
15. A raffle (where legal)
16. Fashion shows
17. Midnight breakfast in bars (dinefest?)
18. A soft-drink happy hour for kids
19. Parking lot banners, barrage balloons
20. Themes: ethnic themes, holiday celebrations, birthdays of fantasy characters
21. Five- or ten-cent coffee with the purchase of some other item
22. Eating contests: beat the record, eat for free

23. Prizes for kids who finish their dinner: a free dessert
24. A free cocktail for anybody named Pat
25. Dessert after the theater with dinner before

Quite obviously, good internal sales gimmicks are the basis for successful media advertising campaigns. They keep the place alive for regular customers, make transients into regulars, and help attract new business if by nothing more than word of mouth.

BOOSTING BEVERAGE SALES

Every hospitality manager would like to sell more alcoholic beverages. The money from the sale of spirits, wines, and beer is only slightly dented by labor and product costs. The percentages are so attractive that some restaurants price their menus at a loss in order to appeal to serious drinkers.

Internal sales efforts are especially suited to selling more alcoholic beverages, as well as other products the operation wants to sell. External selling founders because it is extremely difficult to establish the difference in quality among widely distributed brands of liquor. Internal selling, however, reaches the customer when he is ready to buy and lets him sample an operation's unique but difficult-to-advertise extras, such as service, decor, and atmosphere.

Selling Beverages in Foodservice and Lodging Operations

An operation that legally qualifies can make money selling spirits, wines, and beers. Having the product available is the primary sales device; though this is obvious, it is often neglected. Some food operations that are able to obtain licenses do not sell beverages because of the "investment" or "space" problem. For example, many restaurants with cocktail lounges and barrooms do not sell wine in the dining room because the manager overestimates the cost of offering it. He does not realize that he does not need a wine list, a cellar, or even a waiter who can pull a cork. All he needs is a handful of all-purpose glasses and a case of red wines and white wines in gallon jugs: a total investment of $50. If he can sell a gallon a day at 50¢ a glass, he makes about $2,500 a year profit—clear profit, without increasing his labor costs or overhead.

The restaurant without a cocktail lounge can, of course, offer wine and beer with great success, but it can also find some place to stick enough bottles to have a service bar. It may be the world's most poorly managed bar—it may have anyone and everyone making drinks—but it will make money.

Self-contained bar units allow restaurants without cocktail lounges, as well as lodging operations, to economically offer beverage service. There are very few operations that do not have a porch, entranceway, or lobby that will accommodate an 8-by-3-foot bar. The couch in the motel lobby is not making any money; a bar manned by even the most inept part-time desk clerk will.

A hotel can change that lobby full of chairs into a bar full of chairs and tables. The space then becomes a profitable court or cafe, because in these days of air conditioning and room televisions, it is not needed for after-dinner Bible reading and cribbage.

Simply stated: The best way to build beverage sales is to sell beverages, anywhere, any time, and any way.

WINE

In some restaurants wine sales need little stimulation. The customers habitually take wine with their lunch and dinner. In those establishments that cater to customers who have the money and the interest but who have only lately graduated from the wine-for-weddings-only school, wines need selling.

If they are to sell, wines must be priced fairly. Unfortunately, many operations attempt to realize enormous profits in wine. (Some mark them up 300 to 400 percent.) These managers fail to consider the ideal price-volume relationship. The mark-up goal should be the largest final profit on wine, not the highest profit per unit. Considering that there is little, if any, added labor cost in putting two glasses and a bottle on a table and that investments can be minimized, especially in areas where distributors deliver overnight, 100 percent mark-up is more profitable for most operations.

Anybody who wants a glass of wine with his meal or food snack should be able to have one for a price that appears reasonable when compared with the cost of the food item. A glass of white wine or a wine cooler with a fried fish sandwich is a great idea if the wine can be sold for 30¢. Instead of worrying about offering a great many different wines with names that neither employees nor customers can pronounce, the manager who wants to sell wine (and not especially to impress the gourmet club) should stock a variety of formats: wine by the glass, wine in pitchers, wine in carafes, half-bottles, splits, and so on.

There is at least as much money in selling bulk wines in attractive glasses or carafes as there is in selling bottles. The manager can use gallon jugs to fill his glasses or pitchers, or he can invest in a barrel-like chilled or unchilled dispenser unit.

Even fast food operations catering to the younger market can begin to experiment with wine: Their customers do. The wine dispenser filled with a wine-and-fruit-juice combination or a flavored wine will eventually become as common as a carbonated drink machine. The manager who installs one now in his chicken take-out, hot dog stand, pizza parlor, or diner will start making profits from wine now.

The manager offering wines can supplement the sales efforts of his service personnel with a variety of sales aids, including wine lists, displays, and merchandising materials. Considerable assistance is generally available from wine distributors and domestic wine companies.

Wine Lists. The formal, leather-bound wine list is an excellent selling tool if the customer can relate to it. Merely reading the names is a sufficient sales pitch for the customer who knows the wines. On the other hand, most customers who have to be sold wine don't know wines very well. The wine list should include descriptions of the wines, perhaps labels from the bottles themselves, and menu matches.

The printing of wine lists on the actual dinner menu is often a better selling tool. The restaurant suggests that the lobster dinner would be complemented by a bottle of Pouilly-Fuissé, or a glass or carafe of the operation's own dry white wine. The customer who is really unsure of himself orders with the confidence that the wine will suit the dish, and without the fear that his lack of knowledge will be exposed to his companions or the waiter.

Displays. Wine displays help sell wines. They can range from a simple table of bottles, decanting baskets, and fresh or artificial grapes to cellar-like combination displays and storage areas at one end of the dining room. Many operations use wine racks as room dividers. Others have rolling carts fitted to accept bottles and glasses, and perhaps they also have a small wine barrel for carafe wines or by-the-glass sales. The waiter rolls the cart to the table and can actually show the customer the bottles. One operation has a number of wines in glass barrels on the cart. The waiter actually offers the house wines to the customer to sample. Even on the rare occasion that a glass or carafe is not sold, the operation has been well served by the goodwill that was earned.

Direct Merchandising. Not every merchandising device works well for every operation. In essence, the operator must understand his market. For example, promoting a Wine of the Month, unless it is a very exciting wine, has little effect on the sales of wine in a gourmet restaurant. Customers have their own preferences. On the other hand, in operations where the customer and the operator may be learning about wine together, a Wine-of-the-Month promotion works wonderfully.

Some direct merchandising techniques are:

Table tents: Table tents and other similar materials are available from wine importers and producers.

The Wine-of-the-Month promotion: A particular wine is offered at an attractive price throughout the month. Often theme decorations are used, perhaps featuring posters from the wine-producing country.

Wine drinks: Wine drinks such as Sangria (red wine, fruit juices, and sliced fruit) are immensely popular.

Wine on the table: Some operations find that by placing a bottle of wine or even a bottle each of both red and white wines on the table helps sales. If the customer does not order the wine, it is removed, still unopened, before the main course.

Wine-and-food combination: Wine can be sold as part of a package with a food item. Examples are wine with cheese and fruit for dessert, a glass of dry white wine with a seafood appetizer, and a bottle of sauterne with a multiportion order of Baked Alaska.

Wine cocktails: People who do not drink spirits can be offered, as cocktails, glasses of table wines, aperitif wines (such as sherry and white port), or name-brand blended wines.

COCKTAILS

Habitual cocktail drinkers do not have to be sold the first two cocktails. They can be sold a third cocktail if the operation offers attractive nibbles with it. Other customers, those who do not usually have a drink before their meal, offer the most sales potential. Since they do not require a drink to stimulate their appetites, or to relax, as do the habitual cocktail drinkers, they have to be sold on another basis.

The waiter, table tents, or a special cocktail menu can tell them about sherry and port, which are genteel drinks; about tall wine drinks and coolers, which are refreshing; or about the blended-wine drinks, tropical cocktails, and house specialties, which are fun, exotic, and perhaps exciting.

It is possible to sell a rum drink in a pineapple to the customer who thinks martinis taste like turpentine. The middle-aged lady whose husband is belting manhattans might take a little cream sherry just to keep him company. Five young secretaries celebrating somebody's marriage would love champagne cocktails.

AFTER-DINNER DRINKS

After-dinner drinks have an increasing sales potential, as more and more guests consider restaurant dining an evening experience instead of merely dinner. They willingly prolong the meal with coffee and dessert. They can easily be sold high-profit liqueurs, dessert wines, and spirits.

The restaurateur might reconsider his bar stock and purchase some of the more interesting after-dinner drinks. Although a great many customers will order crème de menthe or Drambuie, many can be introduced to such items as chocolate orange liqueur, clear pear alcohol, port and sauterne wines, or apple and cherry brandy.

Selling after-dinner drinks is a matter of communicating the fact that they are available and that they are exactly right for the moment. To the man who has been drinking a name-brand scotch as a cocktail, the waiter can say that the operation has just received some unblended scotch. The dessert menu can list liqueurs, brandies, and after-dinner cocktails such as Benedictine and brandy (B and B) and stingers. Some operations find that they can increase sales considerably by placing a rolling cart full of liqueurs and glasses near the customer's table just as he is ordering coffee.

BEER

Ironically, the popularity of beer has led to its neglect by restaurant operators. Most male and many female customers like beer and drink it at home, at meals, and when they are thirsty. Yet it is seldom merchandised in food facilities. A coffee shop in an office building could sell hundreds of bottles or glasses during a noon lunch hour. If premium beers were tastefully displayed in a refrigerated case, a great number of iced-tea drinkers could be converted. The manager might well consider listing premium and imported beers on a page of the menu or on a separate beer list. The major brewers and importers have a wide variety of materials available for promotion. These include beer recipes, glasses, displays, draft beer dispensers. Many brewers offer attractive arrangements for the acquisition of these dispensers.

Selling Beverages in Bars and Cocktail Lounges

Internal selling in bars and cocktail lounges has three objectives: (1) selling the customers more (2) selling them the drinks on which the operation realizes the most profit (3) selling them on coming back.

Variety and novelty are the keys to internal sales in beverage operations. Almost any merchandising device that is consistent with the mood of the operation works for a while; then it is time to try something new. Bars and cocktail lounges that do not merchandise can still be very profitable operations. However, every time anyone in the neighborhood moves or dies, they lose a customer that they cannot replace from among the transient customers who order a drink only once.

Hotel and restaurant bars effectively use merchandising as a means of entertainment and attraction, so that they can earn the beverage dollars of their food-and-lodging customers.

Five major internal sales approaches suggest themselves:

Themes and entertainment

Service concepts
Food promotions
Advertising and advertising novelties
Specialty drinks

THEMES AND ENTERTAINMENT

Some operations have decor concepts that are so stunning that customers stay and drink just to participate in them. For example, there are several million-dollar Hawaiian-theme bars complete with grass-skirted waitresses, ukulele bands, and tropical indoor waterfalls. These operations continuously sell themselves: "The price of a drink is a ticket to paradise." Even more modest theme decors have the same selling effect. Customers enjoy English pubs, Old West saloons, German beer houses, circuses, flea markets of mismatched chairs and tables, Swiss chalets, and so on.

Entertainment, with or without a theme, allows the customer to justify the evening's costs. The piano bar, which has never really been popularized on the East Coast, is the simplest entertainment concept. The guests eat around a large grand piano, which serves them as a table, and are entertained with music, songs and light chatter. The lounge is the most complex concept. Major nationally known singers and comedians entertain the drinkers. Between these two extremes are endless variations: singing waiters; a singing barman; a guitar, accordion, or mandolin player; a jazz group; a rock and roll group; a mood singer; a succession of cafe acts; and so on. It is sometimes possible to have the entertainers join the customers to stimulate drink sales.

SERVICE CONCEPTS

The beverage operator cannot improve on the customers' drinks, but he can improve or at least vary their service for product distinction and interest. For example, offering beer and ale by the yard, perhaps in the special glass in a wooden stand that was used to hand drinks to English coachmen in their high seats, distinguishes an operation from others offering the same beer. The yard may or may not actually be a "bargain." It always seems to be a buy, however, because of the presentation. Some other service concepts are:

1. Two-for-one cocktails: every drink a double.
2. Drinks by the ounce or pound, weighed on a scale.
3. Beer and other drinks by the pitcher, rather than by the glass.
4. Cocktail specials at lower prices.
5. "Happy Hours."
6. Specialty glassware: frosted mugs, German beer steins, wine glasses with stems for all drinks, or fish bowls.

7. Pour your own from a bottle: Either the operation trusts the customer or the bottle is marked.
8. Individual permanent beer mugs or cocktail mugs for regular guests.
9. Explore the grounds with a giant-sized insulated glass.
10. Drinks for two for lovers.

FOOD PROMOTIONS

People leave bars because they are hungry. They go home or to a restaurant instead of to a bar because they want to eat and drink. The bar that offers some food broadens its market appeal.

While the famous free lunch of the past is impossible today, the cheap lunch is not. A bar will be packed if it offers a different popular sandwich with a drink or beer every day for about what it costs to make the sandwich. Some customers will have the sandwich and one drink but most will have at least two drinks or two beers.

Cocktail hour giveaways can be lent some distinction if the manager offers more than the customary pretzels, peanuts, popcorn, and potato chips. Hotel and restaurant bars have unlimited opportunities to enhance their offerings, but even the bar without a restaurant can manage such items as fried chicken drumettes, chunks of hot sausage, barbecued riblets, tiny fish cakes, bits of meat and vegetables on toothpick skewers, stuffed mushrooms, cheese snacks, bits of herring, dips, liver paste spreads, and crackers.

The prospect of something to eat for free or for a reasonable price after the bar closes or just before it closes for liquor service will keep customers drinking through the night. A single item suffices: spaghetti, knockwurst and kraut, pizza, fried chicken, a 6-foot-long hero sandwich, and so on. If necessary, the bartender can arrange with a local fast food outlet to deliver food items to him early in the evening.

ADVERTISING AND ADVERTISING NOVELTIES

Beverage sales can be promoted by advertising materials, to the extent that the decor, atmosphere and lighting of the bar permit their use. Table tents, back-of-the-bar signs, calendars, lights, illuminated signs, ashtrays, coasters, napkins, stirrers, speed pourers, aprons, water pitchers, and other items can be collected from liquor companies and beer distributors. They are only useful to the operation, however, if they can somehow be demonstrated to contribute to the bar's revenues and not merely to the revenue of the supplier of a particular product. Material advertising a premium whiskey or beer, for example, benefits both the operator and the supplier. Specialty-drink advertising materials (like glassware and accessories) supplied by the manufacturer of one of the ingredients, can be profitably used if the drink costs less than brand-name whiskeys or if it increases sales.

SPECIALTY DRINKS

Specialty drinks add some excitement to a bar's offerings, especially if the bartenders can make them seem exciting and dramatic. Attractive glassware adds immeasurably to the presentation. Customers seeing the specialty drink served may ask for "one of those." Some operations develop a cycle of specialty drinks and offer them at regular intervals throughout the year. A long-term program justifies an investment in glassware, accessories, attractive table tents, and advertisements. Other operations post a sign indicating the Special-of-the-Month or -Week. With the right market of tourists, young people, secretaries, or vacationers, a menu of specialty drinks is a viable possibility. Tropical drinks, hot toddies, coffee specialties made with espresso coffee from a machine, fruit concoctions, an ice cream soda "spiked" with liqueurs are all workable menu possibilities.

THE ART OF BUILDING CHECKS

The good foodservice worker is automatically a good salesperson. Sales and service are indivisible, because successful selling is based on the helpfulness of the waiter, waitress, or counterman to the customer. The least aggressive sales pitch and perhaps the shortest is also the most helpful and successful: "Will there be anything else, sir?" This question can be asked of the same person five times in succession with an additional sale each time. If it were asked of every person in drive-ins, coffee shops, gourmet restaurants, and bars, the impact on revenues would be tremendous. There would also be a great many more customers satisfied with the service they received.

The salesperson assists the customer by selling. He also benefits the operation and himself—first, by increased gratuities based on a percentage of the check and in monies from incentive programs and, second, by helping ensure the survival of the operation and his job.

The professional dignity of the service worker should be founded on his success as salesman. Rather than just delivering food and drink, the service worker functions as a representative of the operation and as a limited business associate of the proprietors. He can take pride in food-and-beverage sales. He can see in them his own contribution to the operation's success. They can be an accurate measure of his abilities as a waiter. Customers cannot be sold check-building items by a waiter who forgets their water.

Direct Food-and-Beverage Sales

Training foodservice workers to sell involves five major areas of understanding:

1. Acting the part of a salesperson
2. Understanding the psychology of food-and-beverage sales
3. Knowing the customer
4. Knowing what to sell
5. Acquiring specific sales techniques

ACTING THE PART OF A SALESPERSON

A salesperson's personality and appearance must be consistent with his product. The food salesperson representing the operation and its wares to customers must reinforce the customer's best expectations. Specifically, restaurant guests expect cleanliness and professionalism.

A waiter may or may not provide his own uniform. When management provides the uniform, it has a responsibility to supply him with a clean, good-looking, well-fitting uniform and sufficient changes so that he can always be impeccably dressed. When the waiter provides his own uniform or parts of his own uniform, he should be no less exacting. A salesman should look presentable. Shoes should be shined, shirts starched, collars unfrayed, socks clean and matching and so on.

Individuals in food-and-beverage sales cannot appear any more extreme in their personal grooming than the most conservative of their customers. The middle-aged gentleman from Wall Street, not the young advertising executive, should be the model for hair length and facial hair. A waiter who acts contrarily is, in effect, making a management decision on what clientele the operation should attract.

Food-and-beverage personnel should look clean and be clean. Hands and nails that are close to the guest's food have to be absolutely spotless. Because of the close contact with the guests and the somewhat vigorous physical activity of the service, daily bathing with a medicated soap and the use of a neutral-scented deodorant are necessary. Perfumes, strong after-shave lotions, and strong smelling hair oils should not be used. Teeth should be presentable and clean, and the breath sweet smelling. Only regular professional care and several daily brushings will guarantee that the waiter will not lose the sale by offending the customer.

In the presence of customers, personnel should also be careful to avoid sneezing or excessive nose blowing and should, in general, avoid touching their faces, facial blemishes, hair, and underclothing.

General politeness and amiability are obviously expected of food-and-beverage personnel. All remarks such as "thank you" and "good morning" should include the guest's name, title, or the word "sir" or "madam."

UNDERSTANDING THE PHYCHOLOGY OF FOOD-AND-BEVERAGE SALES

The food-and-beverage salesperson has a tremendous advantage over sales personnel in other fields. The customer has come to the operation to buy; nobody browses in a restaurant. The customer is probably motivated by an elemental urge: He is hungry. Nobody is compelled to buy socks three times a day. The customer wants to be sold; few people who are eating out are practicing stringent economies. They are treating themselves, even if they are simply buying a hot dog, because "they deserve it" after a tough morning or after shopping.

In sum, the food-and-beverage salesperson has the ideal customer: positively motivated, pre-sold, and ready to buy. All he has to do is help the customer make the choices he wants him to make.

Ideally, the salesperson establishes a relationship with the customer, even in a fast food operation. There can be enough in a smile and a "good morning" for the customer to feel that the person behind the counter has his interests at heart.

In a tableservice restaurant, the salesperson has more opportunity to establish the context for the sale. He does his job well. When the waiter helps the customer with his chair, he gets partial credit for the pleasure the customer has in finally sitting down. When the waiter brings the menu and fills the water glass, the customer recognizes him as someone concerned with the customer's basic needs. What used-car salesperson would not like to pick up a good prospect at home and drive him to the lot? What encyclopedia salesperson would not welcome the opportunity to mail a letter for a potential customer?

Prompt service, common courtesy, and the appearance of concern establish the context for the sale. The customer puts himself, at least for the duration of the transaction, in the salesperson's hands.

KNOWING THE CUSTOMER

When the salesperson approaches the guest and has the first exchange of conversation with him, he should be able to make some sort of evaluation of the guest as a potential customer. Every salesperson types the prospect. The used-car salesman asks himself if the prospect is a Cadillac, Ford, sports car, or station-wagon type. The food-and-beverage salesperson looks for the customers who are out on the town, celebrating an anniversary, anxious to impress their tablemates, obviously fond of food, venturesome in their drinking, bored with their tablemates, new in town, and eating and drinking on an expense account. And he looks for these customers because they can all be sold food and drink beyond their basic meal requirements.

The food-and-beverage salesperson attempts to type the customer, because he can only make subtle pitches. He can ritualistically attempt to interest the customer in appetizers, wines, desserts, and tableside cooking, but he cannot intensively sell them. For example, the customers on the town, or celebrating, are good champagne prospects. The person attempting to impress his tablemate, perhaps a female companion or a business client, would like the waiter to help him order the best without the waiter's seeming to participate. Someone who is bored with his tablemate might like to spend a half-hour watching the waiter prepare dinner or dessert in the dining room. The newcomers in town are receptive to a try-this-everybody-hereabouts-likes-it approach. The man on the expense account definitely would like a pitcher (not a glass) of iced martinis, a platter of hors d'oeuvres, a cooked-to-order specialty, a bottle of vintage wine, and some of the manager's special reserve cognac.

KNOWING WHAT TO SELL

Knowing what to sell has two aspects: (1) The salesperson must know his products, all of them, and (2) the salesperson must know what is best to sell from the perspective of the operation's profit.

Knowing the menu is an absolute obligation for the food-and-beverage salesperson. He must be able to identify the ingredients and explain the preparation of each item including the time involved. His primary opportunities to sell come when he is discussing the menu with the customer. When a customer who is allergic to onions asks whether the chopped steak has onions on it, the waiter may have to answer "yes." But then he can recommend the mixed grill as being excellent, cooked to order, and onion-free. When the customer who must catch a four o'clock train asks how long the chicken sauté will take, the waiter might have to answer "45 minutes." But then he can suggest the lamb curry, which is ready. In each instance the waiter was able to "trade up," because he knew the menu. Much more basically, if the waiter does not know about a menu item, what credence can his recommendation of praise be given when he is trying to build the check?

Knowing what items are best to sell means being able to identify those items, such as daily specials and roasts, which could become leftovers. A good waiter is in constant communication with the kitchen either directly or through the captain. An hour before closing, selling the last table the remaining orders of roast lamb means the difference in profits between the roast lamb, selling at $7.50 today, and the lamb being used in Scotch barley soup, selling at 50¢ a bowl tomorrow.

Salespersons should also know which items represent the most absolute profit: the steak that sells for $7.50 but only returns a $3 profit vs. the chicken that sells for $5.50 but returns $4.

ACQUIRING SPECIFIC SALES TECHNIQUES

Selling food and beverages is "soft" selling; calm, polite, informal, and nonaggressive. It is a natural extension of helpfulness by the salesperson to the customer. The fundamental technique can be reduced to four short rules: (1) start selling early (2) listen carefully (3) think quickly (4) be prepared.

The skilled food-and-beverage salesperson finds numerous opportunities to sell by starting early. If he is unable to sell a cocktail, then wine, appetizers, special courses, desserts, and after-dinner drinks still remain as sales possibilities.

Whenever he can, the waiter takes his lead from the customer. The least indecision or query is an invitation to sell: "How is the veal?" What soup do you suggest?" "Are the green beans fresh?" Whatever the waiter's direct response, he has been invited to give a pitch. He can switch the customer to another item, sell an accompaniment, or do the customer a tremendous "favor" by suggesting that a certain item might not be to his taste.

When a lead is presented by the customer, the salesperson has to think quickly, so that his response makes the sale the salesperson wants. Given the lead, he is prepared to sell. For example, when a customer orders a hamburger, the waiter automatically suggests French fries. When the customer orders a piece of pie, the waiter automatically suggests ice cream (pie à la mode). He has prepared himself by reading the menu carefully and developing tandem items. If the customer does not want French fries, he can try for onion rings. If the customer does not want ice cream with pie, he can try for cheese.

Preparation and quick thinking also help the waiter develop automatic selling responses to customer conversation and byplay with the salesperson. For example, when the customer does not want a cocktail, the waiter automatically suggests wine with dinner. When the customer comments that he is on a diet, the waiter automatically suggests a special salad with low-calorie dressing, instead of the main-dish starch garnish. A "no-dessert" order prompts the waiter to suggest a liqueur.

Whenever the waiter addresses the customer, he should make a positive suggestion, not a negative or neutral suggestion. When a customer does not order dessert, it is not because the thought has not occurred to him. Asking "Would you like dessert?" invites a negative response. Instead, the waiter should suggest a specific dessert, which prompts the customer to order the alternative if it is not acceptable: "May I suggest our deep-dish apple pie, sir?" Even at a fast food counter, the positive question "Is there anything else?" sells better than the negative question "Will that be all?"

Whenever the customer has a problem, the solution provided by the waiter can mean an additional or better sale. For example, if the customer is rushed, the waiter suggests an item that can be quickly prepared and is among those he wants to sell. If the customer cannot drink because he must drive, the waiter solves the problem with a coffee specialty.

The progress of the meal can be seen as a succession of sales opportunities: cocktail, appetizer, wine, side-dish, dessert, and after-dinner drink sales opportunities.

Cocktail sales. Established cocktail drinkers are not a problem. They will habitually order one or two cocktails before dinner. Some operations even offer complimentary canapes at the table to encourage such diners to linger and order a third. Selling the individual who does not habitually order a drink is the challenge. Simply walking to his table and asking "Cocktail, sir?" is seldom the answer. Guests who do not take the initiative in ordering drinks do not usually respond positively to an outright question. More sales are made by saying to such a customer: "May I suggest some of our very fine (name) sherry?" The waiter has taken the initiative. Yet, he has also complimented the guest, because drinking sherry is associated with refinement. In addition, he has left the guest an opportunity to order something else. In the same way, the waiter can offer an aperitif wine or even a bottle of champagne for a large party.

Appetizer sales. Every order of a long-cooking item should prompt the waiter to mention the cooking time without exaggerating and suggest that if the guest is especially hungry, the waiter would recommend a specific appetizer that would be just right. One of the ways to communicate this is to discreetly offer to bring the salad as a first course with the offer of a specific appetizer as an alternative.

Side dishes. Items like onion rings, garlic bread, specific salad dressings, chives, and sour cream dressing for potatoes are great moneymakers for the operation. Most waiters are successful in selling these items by announcing their existence as though the guests want them but have somehow missed them on the menu: "We have both Roquefort and Caesar salad dressings, sir."

Desserts. Desserts are always profitable and excellent check-builders. Unfortunately, they are sometimes hard to sell to calorie-conscious, fairly full guests. The waiter has to make dessert exciting, not just another course. He gives the customer the impression that dessert will be the perfect ending, the crowning glory of the meal. Many waiters find that focusing on a particular dessert, as though the guest's meal were a composition that required that certain finishing touch, is the finest way.

To be successful in convincing guests to order a specific suggestion, the waiter has to have analyzed his guest carefully; it is better to sell a dish of sherbet than nothing at all.

An effective technique is to go through the motions of preparing the table for coffee and dessert. The table should be cleared and the water glass refilled and the ashtray emptied as though the meal were beginning, not ending. Stains should be covered with a clean napkin, as though the guest were going to be there for a long time. Ordering dessert is the next logical step.

Wines. In some operations, wine sales are a matter of course at both lunch and dinner. In others, only a concentrated, full-scale promotion will begin to sell bottles of wine regularly. The waiter's opportunities for salesmanship come in the operation that has some wine sales but not too many.

In these circumstances, the waiter can sell wine instead of a cocktail with the main course, as a dessert beverage, or at all three times. None of the hard-sell approaches—such as asking the guest whether he wants red or white wine with his dinner, thereby assuming that he wants wine—really works. The question is in itself absurd. No sensible person orders wine by that qualification alone, and moreover the guest is likely to be offended. A tentative suggestion is much more effective after taking the food order: "Our guests have really enjoyed a glass of muscadel with the Fra Diavolo, sir." If the customer makes no response, the waiter can politely make another try at dessert: "Our California sauterne is the perfect accompaniment to the baked Alaska, sir."

Management's Responsibilities in Check Building

Management of restaurant operations contributes to service personnel sales efforts in three ways: (1) training (2) recognition (3) incentives.

TRAINING

Although management must place a priority on the serving techniques and productivity of employees, sales training should be an important part of orientation and continuing instruction. The best sales training combines pep talks by management with practice sessions that duplicate actual work situations. The employees playact at being customers and salespersons; the group criticizes the performance.

RECOGNITION

Management can increase the effectiveness of service personnel sales efforts by recognizing professional performance on this basis. When the manager recapitulates the waiter's checks, he should be looking for the number of customers served and the check averages. Promotions, better stations, and similar rewards should be given for sales volume—at least on an equal basis with customer turnover, which presently receives more emphasis.

INCENTIVES

The management should be willing to pass some of the additional profits to the employees who generate extra sales, especially those in nongratuity service stations, such as counters and cafeterias.

Even when the waiter will earn additional gratuities by building the check, a dollar incentive or a prize is a productive stimulus.

There are numerous devices and formulas to relate sales volume to rewards. Some are:

1. A cash commission for sales beyond a certain level
2. Check-average contests with cash or gift prizes
3. Progressive sales incentives on specific items, such as wine or dessert
4. Point systems for the sale of side dishes, with prizes or cash for achieving point totals
5. Quota systems for specific items, with incentives for exceeding the quota

SELLING GUEST ROOMS

Guest rooms are a hospitality lodging operation's most important commodity: The front office personnel must be trained to sell them, prepared to sell them, and willing to sell them. Sometimes it seems that room salesmen (front desk clerks) have misunderstood which of their job tasks has priority. Unless there is a deposit on a specific room, they should be salesmen intent on making a sale. Only after the room is rented can bureaucratic inclinations, natural hauteur, or other interests be allowed to reassert themselves.

Even a minimal sales effort can have astounding results. An extra $10-a-day room sold each day is $3,650 more in revenue each year, with only a minimal increase in costs: Selling "up" on the room, even if there is only the difference of a dollar, means the same amount in net profit.

This kind of potential profit might prompt management to reconsider the organization of the front office and its personnel. An enthusiastic salesman—paid substantially more than a room clerk, but with a commission on certain sales—could easily return his salary several fold. He would also be much more successful in promoting good guest relations, because salesmanship is virtually indivisible from customer pleasing.

The Room Salesman

The successful room salesman has a selling attitude. He knows the operation, because he is selling an experience, not just a room, and he knows his product.

Successful selling is often a matter of courtesy and consideration. Simply by treating potential customers decently, a room salesman disposes them to buy. Unfortunately, on the basis of their experience with many front desks, most customers don't expect such treatment. These low expectations help the wily salesman to stun potential customers with hospitality and graciousness and then to sell them the presidential suite.

GUIDELINES FOR THE FRONT DESK SALESMAN

1. Greet all who approach the desk. Address them as "sir" or "madam" until their names are known.
2. Attend to the guest in front of the desk before attending to paperwork or telephone conversations.
3. Honor reservations promptly.
4. Assign unreserved rooms on a first-come-first-served basis. Do not engage in private "enterprises."
5. Be extremely tactful, helpful, and polite when the operation is overbooked or full.
6. Listen to the person in front of the desk for sales leads.
7. Do not argue with potential customers; sell them, oblige them, or apologize for not being able to serve them.
8. Speak politely and pleasantly, without being affected, patronizing, or officious.
9. Maintain a scrupulously high level of personal hygiene and grooming.
10. Do not lean on the counter, slouch, eat, smoke, chew gum, or talk loudly on duty.

KNOW THE OPERATION

The room salesman is not just selling rooms, he is selling the operation as a place to spend a period of time, to eat, to play, and to work. He is selling all the hotel services—those which are included in the room rate and those which are available but extra. He may have only a broom closet with an army cot and a bucket left, but he still has the world's largest indoor swimming pool, a 24-hour health club; a celebrity nightclub show, five great dining rooms, 36 holes of golf, free ice, color television, coffee service, courtesy cars . . .

If necessary he can "give away" the room and let the customer buy the operation's incredible leisure-and-fun package—for the price of the room, of course.

KNOW THE PRODUCT

The room salesman should have visited every room in the operation and spent several nights in typical facilities in different price ranges. He should be able to say with complete honesty that a minimum single is small but that he knows from his own experience that it is charmingly decorated, compact, efficient, and very comfortable. He should know the luxurious feeling of padding around the better suites in his bare feet and of breakfasting on the balcony overlooking the interior court.

In a well-designed operation, each room will have some virtues. Certainly each will have quality beds, a functioning television, and ample hot water. It will have enough simple comfort to commend it to the tired traveler who wants a place to spend the night.

The salesman must also know what he has immediately available. He cannot pitch a room only to find that it is occupied. If he is a good salesman, the client will not be switched easily, and if he is switched, he will regret having "lost" the first room. Ideally, the operation will have a modern system that shows which rooms are available. The salesman can glance over that system while talking to the prospect. Otherwise, whenever he has a moment, the room salesman should prepare his own handwritten room-status reports.

Selling Across the Front Desk

The room salesman encounters basic sales situations: (1) a potential customer is making an inquiry—he is shopping; (2) an individual has made a reservation and has arrived but has not specified a room or a rate.

ROOM SHOPPER

The room shopper is prepared to get back into his car or cab and try another operation. The room salesperson has to sell him the operation and the best room he can. In the first few moments of the conversation, the salesman should learn as much as possible about the customer and his reason for being in the area. A polite question or two usually elicits the needed information: "Are we expecting you?" "Have you been with us before?" "Is this your first time in Detroit?" Ideally, the room salesman will have at least some idea of the type of accommodation that will suit the customer. When he suggests a room, he should make every effort to sell the room and the operation, not the rate.

The first principle of room salesmanship is to start high and watch for reactions. Several rooms can be described attractively, so that the customer can choose between alternatives, perhaps between a medium-priced and a high-priced room. The sales emphasis should be on the higher-priced room. If there is a negative reaction, the room salesman can sell down. Whenever possible, the customer should be shown the rooms or color photographs of them. The room salesman can accompany him. A bellman, who should have been instructed by management to simply guide the customer, can also perform this task. Only as a last resort or when the customer asks outright should the minimum room be offered. It should be sold by an attractive description and recapitulation of the comforts of the room as well as of the facilities of the operation.

The best closing for the sale is most often a question proposing that the customer choose between the rooms discussed: "Do you think 209 or 311 would suit you best?" "After seeing the rooms, Mr. Black, do you prefer the room overlooking the pool or the room on the 12th floor?" Or a positive suggestion can be made: "I think you'll be very happy with the Georgian suite. If not, we can move you tomorrow."

SELLING UP

The guest who has made a reservation is very unlikely to pick up his bags and try to find another hotel. In essence the room salesman is selling against his own minimum room. However, he should not assume that the guest wants a better room.

The salesman should first try to confirm the guest's good judgment in choosing the operation: "I am sure you will enjoy your stay with us, Mr. Black. The gardens have never been more beautiful." Or: "There is a fine comedian in the lounge." Or: "We have just started a breakfast buffet." He then tries to understand the guest's needs and to anticipate them. Conversation should bring out such information as the guest's wanting a quiet room to work in, or fearing heights, or liking interior rooms. The key to selling the room the salesman wants to sell is then a glowing description of the room, emphasizing the guest's desires. In very many instances, the customer will not dispute the room salesman's choice or query the price. He probably formed a good idea of the rates and accommodations at the time he made his reservations.

Some room salesmen unsell customers who are quite willing to stay in deluxe accommodations. They do this by interposing their own values. The young couple on vacation and the fatherly-looking businessman are not necessarily looking for bargains.

INCREASING PROFITS FROM RETAIL SALES

Aggressive, continuing promotion of retail sales outlets to the operation's customers is the key to developing profitable new outlets and to profitably sustaining stores which are necessary for the convenience of hospitality guests. Unfortunately, hospitality management is often reluctant to venture out of food service or lodging (its areas of expertise) and into retailing. But rising costs of food, beverages, labor, and construction make it important for managers to make just such a venture. Restaurants have to maximize their square-footage revenues. Lodging operations must at least break even on convenience sales: They need the money.

A retail sales outlet allows the hospitality operation to realize profits from unused space. For example, a hotel can use part of its rather considerable basement area for an arcade of retail stores, while a restaurant can open a compact convenience food store with access from its parking lot. Such a store has good profit possibilities, provided it is not treated as a stepchild. A lodging operation obliged to provide retail sales outlets can also make them profitable if management brings to them the same energy, talent, and business acumen it devotes to room, food, and beverage sales.

Restaurants

Restaurants are essentially retail stores selling a very limited product line. To offer their items for sale, restaurants remain open long hours, sometimes seven days a week, and maintain a facility and a staff. There is a considerable amount of money to be made by expanding the product line so that the primary sale of food and drink consumed on the premises is followed by the sale of a product for use elsewhere. Since the sale of secondary items does not normally increase overhead or operating costs, revenues from these items are especially attractive. If a restaurant realizes an annual net profit of $2,500—that is, $7 or $8 a day—from secondary sales, on a sales volume of $5,000 or $10,000, it could mean the equivalent on the bottom line of increasing food and beverage revenues as much as $60,000 or $100,000.

In fact, in some cases, managers have found that secondary sales were so profitable that it made economic sense to remove several tables to increase their volume. For example, one operation established a 6-by-8-foot takeout counter that makes as much as any ten tables in the place.

There are five major secondary sales approaches the manager might consider:

Takeout offerings
Menu items for home consumption
Vending
Cashier "stores"
Total merchandising

TAKEOUT OFFERINGS

Drive-in and fast-food restaurants are already well committed to take-outs, but gourmet restaurants are not likely to be able to sell their customers expensive *à la carte* portions of sauce dishes, because the customer has little reason for buying them.

It is the restaurants in the middle, the majority of American restaurants, that miss the takeout profits. For example, the operation offering a quality breakfast has the opportunity to sell its customers their coffee break and their lunch. Modern disposable containers of foam plastic will keep hot foods hot and cold foods chilled and appetizing for several hours.

On a spring day, half the secretaries in a coffee shop having breakfast or coffee could be sold a packaged picnic for the park: a cold chicken leg, an individual French loaf, a piece of cake, cheese and fruit, and a chilled punch-type beverage (perhaps a split-of-wine option), with a plastic combination tablecloth and blanket and a checkered paper napkin.

Almost every early-morning customer is potentially a coffee-break customer. If he cannot be sold the coffee itself, he can be sold food items the coffee cart or the office refrigerator is not likely to have: gelatin salads, cheese, puddings, fresh fruit, quality freshly baked cakes, and so on.

The restaurant that attracts travelers can easily sell customers car food. Car food can be anything: a full meal in an insulated hamper; a breakfast kit for campers consisting of blanched bacon, raw eggs, rolls, and portion packs of accessories; fresh fruit; disposable thermoses of coffee for night drivers; or a succession of little trip treats for kids, so that they can be amused with something more nourishing and healthful than a candy bar.

Whatever the takeout offering, the menu provides an ideal means of communicating it to the customer. While the customer is eating, service personnel can put together this takeout order. Table tents work well, especially if they can be marked by the customer to indicate what he wants and then converted into a check.

MENU ITEMS FOR HOME CONSUMPTION

The greatest salad dressing, cheddar cheese soup, delectable hors d'oeuvre items, and any other dish that customers prize, can be packaged for purchase. The customer sells himself superbly: He samples the product. When he sees it on the way out of the restaurant, or sees on the menu that it is offered for takeout, he readily buys.

Cakes and other baked products can be offered from display cases. The operation might even undertake producing some entrée items in either boil-in-the-bag formats or in aluminum pans. They can be displayed in a small upright or chest freezer or brought from the kitchen. Items that sell because of their appearance, like preserves, dessert sauces, and relishes, can be prepared in the operation and packaged by a local canner in glass jars. Or the formula can be produced by arrangement with a packer. Often a few bottles sold in the operation are the start of a successful food-manufacturing endeavor. The local supermarket or bakery can be induced to accept frozen products such as hors d'oeuvre platter arrangements on disposable serving trays with clear plastic covers.

VENDING

A restaurant already has two vending machines as an accommodation to the customer: a cigarette machine and a telephone. Vended offerings can be expanded without making the hallway look like a bus station. The fronts of many modern vending units can be customized to seem consistent with the restaurant decor, or the units themselves can be built in.

The vending possibilities for each operation differ. The office area restaurant can position vending machines in the lavatory facilities and sell such items as plastic rain hats, nylons, sanitary napkins, sewing kits, and eyeglass-repair kits.

Late-night restaurants have a ready market for vended, early-morning newspapers, toilet articles, breath sweeteners, caffeine tablets, ice, milk, and other small items. Restaurants frequented by tourists and travelers have a market for games, toys, novelties, paperback books, souvenirs, and so on.

If an operation has the space for a vending machine, there is little argument for not installing one. The machine can be purchased at a low cost, or sometimes borrowed from a company anxious to sell its products, or leased from a vending company which will participate in the revenues. Whatever the machine sells, there is a profit the operation would not otherwise earn.

CASHIER "STORES"

The cashier's area of a restaurant can be made to produce substantial revenues instead of remaining wasted space. The situation is ideal for retail sales. The customer has money in his hand, and there is a responsible, presumably intelligent, personable employee on hand to assist him.

The "store" can be as simple as a rack of chewing gum or as complex as a novelty store. Several companies offer a complete range of retail deals designed especially for secondary sales in restaurants. They offer free-standing tree-like stands hung with bags of candy, countertop display cartons, and even large, attractive cupboards with candies, relishes, salad dressing, and novelty items.

Any high-profit item can be worth merchandising: perfumes, cigarette lighters, writing accessories, jewelry from a local craftsman, leather goods, or even hunks of polished rock.

Certainly, tobacco products and smokers' articles, in addition to cigarettes, have a ready market in almost every operation. The manager whose establishment is the best in town might consider that he is offering his sophisticated customers a genuine accommodation by stocking quality cigars, especially if their only alternative is a drugstore stogie.

Lodging Operations

A lodging operation has more than an opportunity to sell; it has an obligation. Unlike hotels in Europe, which maintain 24-hour personnel who can be sent for items not sold on the premises, American hotels and motels frequently abandon their guests after selling them a room. For example, an operation in a small city which frequently receives guests from the last flight of an airline at 11 o'clock at night should have some way of feeding them. The business traveler who started his journey in another state cannot be expected to have a cheese sandwich in his pocket. Nor would he have any way of knowing that the dining room closes at 10 o'clock. While he may be prepared to drink his dinner that evening, he will blame the operation when he is not able to eat his breakfast the next morning.

There has to be something for him; and some way of getting him the toothbrush he forgot, the newspaper he wants, the baseball tickets he would like. Even if the operation does not make a dime, this is hospitality.

FOOD AND DRINK

While recognizing that food-and-drink sales are an important part of total revenues, sometimes even exceeding room sales, many operations restrict their food-and-beverage service to limited-hour, conventional, four-wall restaurants and bars.

It is possible to sell food and beverages anywhere and any time at a profit and with a minimal space and labor commitment. That lobby becomes a cafe once a portable bar and a refrigerator are installed. That college student is a mobile barman as soon as he is given a golf cart fitted with bar accessories, a fancy uniform, and a coin changer. Thus equipped, let him patrol the tennis courts and swimming pool of the resort hotel or the parking lot of the ranch-style motel.

That linen room on the ninth floor can become a floor store. Install vending machines with ice, soda, sandwiches, coffee, cakes, and miniature bottles of whiskey. Perhaps volume will justify making it into a mini, in-house takeout. Perhaps it can be manned by the bell captain's wife, who is willing to work for a percentage of the profits just so she can maintain the same hours as her husband.

For guest rooms, several companies make vending units that offer both food and drink. They can be geared to simply keep count or to make change from deposited money.

Every time there is a convention, sporting event, or meeting, the operation should be prepared with mobile equipment to offer coffee, snacks, and drinks for cash.

Hospitality suites are another great opportunity for big-profit sales, but most sell only a few liquor setups or a platter of canapes. When the booking is made or when the guests have just arrived and not yet had a chance to go down the street to the liquor store and the supermarket, sell them self-service bar cases of soda and liquor, and provide them with a refrigerator stocked with cold cuts. Buy a couple of second-hand residential style refrigerators, paint them or cover them with wallpaper, and wheel them right into the room. The customer is not too proud to walk through the lobby to his suite with a brown paper bag; the operation should not maintain any false sense of dignity, and high room-service price, if it is not going to get his business.

VENDING

The cost of labor involvement is the biggest operational argument against late-night food service and retail sales counters. The traffic does not warrant or justify the 4.2 to 4.8 people it may take to cover a sales center 24 hours a day, seven days a week. A vending machine is constantly open for business: It can be serviced by anybody as part of his normal job.

Machines can be placed anywhere: in niches in hallways, in parking lots, in special self-service stores. The modern vending machine is attractive, efficient, maintenance free, and reliable. Machines that will vend virtually any product can be purchased, leased, or borrowed on arrangement with vending companies or product suppliers. The lodging manager might make a list of the articles his customers are buying elsewhere and make some arrangements to accommodate them. The average list includes toilet articles, paperback books, tobacco products, novelties, and such small articles of clothing as handkerchiefs, socks, stockings, plastic rain hats and coats, as well as writing materials, snack items, soft drinks, spirits, beer, milk, hot beverages, sandwiches, flowers, and souvenirs.

Even employees are a potential market. Instead of stimulating or condoning arrangements among the foodservice and food production employees and the other personnel, arrangements that may not always be in the operation's best interest, the operation can install vending machines for soda and snacks in the employee locker, meal, and rest areas.

Coin-operated games open another revenue-producing area. If there is a space for a game room, it can be equipped with half-a-dozen money machines. Both children and adults enjoy the very sophisticated games available today, games such as club pool, tabletop European football, computer games of skill, and space-age electronic pin-ball and shooting galleries. There is no product, often no investment; only profit.

If operations catering to family groups and business travelers do not have valet services, they should certainly consider laundry rooms with washers, driers, pressing machines, and dry-cleaning machines. Even the most affluent traveler's pants get creased in his suitcase. Unless the operation accommodates him somehow, perhaps with a coin-operated unit in his room, he may waste a couple of hundred gallons of hot water trying to steam his suit in the shower.

RETAIL SALES OPERATIONS

Substantially diminished overhead is an advantage the hospitality retail operation enjoys over many other retailers. As the operation does not normally occupy space that could be used for restaurant tables or guest rooms, it is virtually rent free. As a result, it becomes profitable at a much lower sales volume. As the hospitality retail manager does not anticipate or require large volume, he can be much more modest in his commitment to facilities and fixtures. Hospitality retail outlets can vary from counters manned by restaurant cashiers to a series of small boutiques.

Four operational formats are most common:

Incidental stores
Impulse-sales centers
Boutiques
Special sales activities

Incidental stores. In addition to maximizing from square footage, incidental stores maximize the productivity of some labor by giving a hospitality worker a second job as a retail sales person. The cashier in a restaurant is the most common example. While management may succeed in ensuring that foodservice and production workers have a full 8 hours work, it is extremely difficult in many instances to keep a cashier fully occupied. While the cashier may be given telephone answering chores or some light bookkeeping, these are not revenue-producing activities. Putting the cashier "in business" makes the dollars paid him in wages work for the establishment.

With the cashier store concept in mind, the manager might consider other personnel who are only partially occupied and could be providing both a service to the guest and a source of revenue to the operation. The night bellman, for example, is a necessity for most operations, but he may make very few trips. He could man a convenience counter that could be easily secured when he did have to leave it. In motels and small hotels, the obligatory night auditor/room clerk/switchboard operator might as well wear still another hat.

Impulse-sales centers. The guest on vacation or on an expense account buys readily. Impulse-sales centers give him the opportunity. He comes upon an indoor or outdoor specialty kiosk, attractively decorated, filled with desirable merchandise, and attended by a pretty girl. And he buys funny hats, sports equipment, leather goods, wrist watches, costume jewelry, writing materials, gag gifts, candles, or toys.

Almost any high-traffic area can make an impulse-sales center pay for itself. The margins on the items are sufficiently high and the labor cost often is a minimum salary to a part-time worker or student. Active lobbies, convention halls, exhibition areas, bar areaways, and sports facilities can all provide space for impulse-sales centers. In addition to potential profits, these centers can help bring an area to life. They also provide guests with an employee who can answer queries and refer them to other personnel for assistance.

Boutiques. A series of boutiques is simply the traditional newsstand or sundry shop exploded. While the newsstand or sundry shop might sell nylon stockings and handkerchiefs, a small clothing store sells both necessities and a limited line of quality clothing.

Successful hospitality retail outlets owe some of their success to their unique relationship with the operation's market. Although they are open to the public, they are not general retail stores, serving the public at large. They can carry items which appeal directly to the operation's primary market. They can create an atmosphere that is consistent with the operation's image and they can employ sales personnel who seem to be service employees.

The luxury-hotel shop specializing in crystal figurines does not have to excuse its prices or the limited appeal of its products. The operation's guests have the money for such fragile luxuries, and they are precisely the people to whom those luxuries appeal. On the other hand, it would be an error to open a luxury-hotel shop offering novelties, card tricks, funny hats, and lapel flowers that squirt water. This type of shop would better suit a convention hotel.

The selling atmosphere can also fit the circumstances. The luxury hotel could maintain a cigar and pipe store that resembles the smoking room in an exclusive club: The shop could be complete with leather furnishings, brass cuspidors, and cedar humidors. A self-service store with free-standing rack fixtures would be more suited to a high-traffic commercial hotel.

In many instances, the personnel in the luxury-hotel store can assume the role of counselor rather than salesperson. When the guest walks into the jewelry store, there is an assumption that he or she will buy. The employee simply tries to help the customers make their selections after a consideration of their requirements. Certainly, the employees in a bridal shop can make sales incidental to assistance.

The number of boutiques an operation can open depends primarily on the volume and profit potential and on the operating arrangement. Many operations have found that they can establish parallel interests with local merchants who will establish outlets in the operation. The operation has the advantage of the expertise of the merchant, his reputation, and his purchasing power. The merchant has a prequalified market, overhead that can be related to volume, the opportunity to spread his management costs over additional unit sales, and the added prestige of association with a high quality hospitality operation.

Boutiques can handle jewelry, clothing, quality ceramics and glass, tobacco products, cutlery, tableware, leather goods, luggage, silver, paints, sculpture, oriental rugs, and similar luxury items.

Special sales activities. Retailing can be combined with entertainment. The hospitality operation has ideal facilities for auctions. Even a restaurant or bar can hold a colorful, exciting, and profitable auction (where legal), perhaps with some of the proceeds going to a charitable organization. A closing-hour gag-item auction, for example, has the possibility of stimulating publicity. Nothing prevents a restaurant or a hotel from using part of its grounds for a flea market or bazaar of colorful tents and booths.

Traditionally, hotels have used demonstration sales as a combined entertainment and retailing device. A cosmetician gives a beauty demonstration and sells makeup and other products; a tobacconist discusses pipes and cigars; a jeweler cleans rings for free while displaying other merchandise.

MAKING IN-HOUSE SALES EFFORTS EFFECTIVE

When a guest is enjoying one of the operation's products or services, the operation has the best opportunity for selling another: crisscross selling. A full-scale program of crisscross selling, a combination of advertising, promotion, and communication, lets the operation make the most of its opportunities. The restaurant sells the nightclub, which sells the coffee shop, which sells weekend package-plan rooms, and so on.

Most often the sales message is low-key; there is no need to hard-sell a satisfied customer. Crisscross selling emphasizes information and services: "We are sure you would like to hear about our . . . . It will help make your stay more pleasant." "Having enjoyed our . . . , we are sure you will want to try our . . . ."

It almost seems unnecessary, yet crisscross selling is the single most effective way of increasing revenues. The guests of a lodging operation do not know about the swimming pool, coffee shop, nightclub, health club, airline agencies, and room-service express breakfast unless someone tells them. Practical experience demonstrates that something is more reliable and consistent that someone.

Although restaurants have fewer facilities to sell, crisscross selling is equally necessary for them. Half a restaurant's dinner customers may be totally unaware that it is open for breakfast. Guests will not know about banquet facilities or outside catering services or midweek theme nights unless they are told. If they are already relatively happy customers, they definitely want to know. Why should they have an office party or a business meeting elsewhere?

All hospitality operations, restaurants, and lodging facilities use two selling techniques with success: display advertising and printed advertising. Lodging operations have further opportunities: They can sell in guest rooms, and they can promote by personal communications.

Display Advertising

A hospitality operation has a definite need for signs and poster advertisements as guest aids. Even if there were no selling intent, they would be necessary to keep guests informed. The best display advertising answers some guest questions that can normally be anticipated and combines the information with a selling message. For example, the guest asks himself, "Is there a nightclub?" And then, "Who is appearing in it?" Signs in the lobby and elevators tell him that there is a nightclub that opens at 11 p.m. and does not have a minimum or cover charge. The signs also make the point that it is worth trying because of its cabaret revue, exotic oriental decor, fabulous supper snacks, celebrity clientele, and so on. A life-size cutout or a poster-sized photograph of the entertainer shows the guest who he is, and a selection of quotes from complimentary reviews tells him that the show is worth seeing.

Display advertising in public areas successfully answers major questions and promotes major facilities. The guest needs a bottle of liquor? The operation has a fully stocked liquor store. The guest wishes to eat?

The operation has five restaurants, each with individual attractions. The guest wants to be entertained? The operation has a nightclub and a lounge with first-rate acts. The guest wants to play tennis or golf? He wants to swim or roller skate? Display advertising tells him where and how good it is.

As display advertising must be limited, first because space is limited and second because the operation must not appear to be a bus station arcade, priorities must be assigned to different facilities. Only major facilities such as restaurants, nightclubs, golf courses and swimming pools can be advertised with free standing lobby signs or large wall posters. Other facilities and services are usually advertised together in wall-panel advertising displays, elevator display cases, or a single free standing "fun" display such as a mock Parisian kiosk, an oversized beach umbrella, a mobile, or a standing tent.

Often there is an effort to give the operation a feeling of thematic unity, so that an attractive combined display will be carefully examined by the passing guest. For example, an operation with eight restaurants might want to suggest that the guest could have a gourmet tour of the world without ever leaving the hotel. This idea might be expressed by constructing a stylized globe or world map, highlighting the restaurants. Sports facilities can be advertised by a display of actual sports equipment and perhaps a series of pictures of a "Joe Typical Guest" in varied professional-style sports clothes.

Moving and electronic displays are quite effective when they can be used with good taste. A part of the lobby wall area could be devoted to back projections of colored slides of sports facilities. An electronic directional map is an effective display and a real aid in a large, sprawling resort hotel.

Corridors, reception areas, entranceways, and outside walls flanking doorways are prime display areas in restaurants and hotel dining facilities. They can be devoted to other facilities, such as the bar, banquet rooms, or unrelated services and products. Or they can be devoted to features of the dining room within, such as a buffet, a special package dinner, free wine, unlimited salad, a house specialty, specialty cuisine, room decor, and service concepts (waitresses in sarongs, for example).

Printed Advertisements

Anything the guest has to read, wants to read, or is likely to read can inadvertently contain a crisscross advertisement. Since an operation may expend two or three pounds of paper a day on a guest, in such forms as menus, table checks, or paperware, there is ample opportunity to exploit the written word.

MENUS

The backs of menus, side panels, and tip-in cards can all be used for other advertising with good effect, because the guest may have it in his hands and before his eyes for several minutes. Typical menu advertising subjects include: brunch promotion, banquet and office party facilities, bar services, and other facilities, and takeout service.

TABLE TENTS

The table tent should combine a striking illustration or headline with strong text. Because it remains on the table in the dining room, bar, or lobby, or on the cashier stand, front desk, or service desk, the customer has ample time to read it, if he notices it. Unlike a display advertisement, it does not have to make its point to a passing viewer. But its appeal must make up for its lack of size.

CHECKS

Guests examine checks and bills closely. The manager can give such items an added message as well as a thank you.

PAPERWARE

Every piece of paper that the operation uses can be imprinted with an advertising message. Most of the time, however, incidental paperware is used for an awareness message. An attractive, brightly patterned wrapping for men's shirts, overprinted in large type with the words "Hotel Luxury Valet," makes everyone aware that the Hotel Luxury has a valet service. Instead of a dull brown bag or even an attractive but common paper bag, a custom bag for takeout makes the customer an unpaid sandwich-board man for the operation until he finally discards the bag in his office. The wrapping should be used for maximum advertising effectiveness: "Fine Food Restaurant" on the bag sells nothing. Inch-high letters all over the bag, repeating POW-WOW BURGER: FINE FOOD, are much more effective. There is no reason why wrapping material and disposables with which the customer will have a lot of contact should not tell a lengthy story. Most restaurant customers dining alone read the ketchup bottle's label ten times. Let them read the place mats, cocktail coasters, napkins, and doilies.

Other vehicles for printed advertising might include: baby bibs, bureau scarfs, matchbooks, key tags, meal tickets, doggy bags, and paper tablecloths.

REPRINTS

The monetary return from the rather considerable sums spent on display advertising in newspapers and magazines can be somewhat increased by using these publications in the operation. An arrangement can easily be made with the publisher or the operation's advertising agency to print this kind of material on signboards or single pieces of paper.

The signs can be made free-standing. The papers can be left on countertops, cashier stands, and lobby tables. If anybody reads them, and somebody waiting for somebody else undoubtedly will, the minimum expense is justified.

Single leaves of paper can routinely be stuffed in all other printed materials, such as daily menus, brochures, TV magazines, room-service menus and so on. They can also be left in an attractive, small but conspicuous rack on the service desk or the front desk. The lonely traveler, bored with television and unable to get a newspaper, will read anything.

Selling in Guest Rooms

The hotel guest room is the primary marketplace of all the hotel facilities and services and whatever products the operation sells. The customer has voluntarily committed himself to contact with the sales materials in his room. Like any other animal bedding down for the night, he is likely to carefully examine his surroundings. The most ill-wrought room-service menu may be read line by line while the guest waits for his socks to dry.

The basic precept of crisscross selling in guest rooms is to pack the room. Assume that the guest will go on a veritable Easter-egg hunt for materials. Use any advertising vehicle possible: Sell everything.

PROMOTIONAL ROOM GIFTS

Most operations supply the guest with a collection of useful and pseudo-useful items which can be printed with advertising messages. Messages can range from one line promotions, "Hotel Luxury, Home of the Boom Boom Room," to clever or amusing one-line headlines relating the item to the product offered, with a message that pitches the product. For example, the operation can give the guest a sponge wrapped around a bar of soap and imprinted with: "Are dining expenses getting out of hand? Visit our buffet breakfast." or, "Don't let the good things in life slip by. Visit the Boom Boom Room." Or the operation might supply a key for squeezing toothpaste: "The Boom Boom Bar is good till the last drop, at 4 a.m.

MENUS

Attractive dining room, coffee shop, and bar menus can be left in guest rooms. If they are well done and are full of merchandising copy and attractive art work, the guest will be tasting the food hours before he reaches the dining room. Even if they are simply informational, the guest will become aware of the services available to him. A room-service menu left on the pillow, even if it is simply a modest card, tells the guest that he can have breakfast in his room when he wants it by calling the operator before he goes to bed.

DIRECTORIES

Most guests look for directories of hotel services. Most operations could improve their selling messages considerably if they made use of color photographs, advertising graphics, and external advertisements in their directories. Even a very fancy directory with a lot of color could be printed at a relatively small per-unit cost and in large quantities if it were designed so that those pages with changing information were printed separately, and just bound with the color pages.

TABLE TENTS AND PRINTED MATERIALS

A number of table tents advertising various facilities and services could be placed on the bureaus, nightstands, desks and bathroom-counter areas of rooms. Nonwoven-cloth bureau scarfs could be printed. Paper doilies can be used under ashtrays. Wrappers, shopping bags, and paper laundry bags can also be printed with advertising messages.

TELEVISION AND RADIO

Guest televisions and radios can be designed to offer closed-circuit advertisements and information. A notice can suggest that the guest turn to Channel 10 for weather information, a recapitulation of the flights to and from the area, a guide to local events, and so on. Advertisements for the operation can be interspersed with the guest service announcements. It is also possible to offer closed-circuit broadcasts to a block of rooms. Convention proceedings or nightclub acts (with promotional messages, of course) can be transmitted to these smaller groups.

The operation can also program its advertisements in the advertising spots in commercial programming. Instead of the guest seeing the nationally broadcast commercial, he sees the operation's specialty prepared closed-circuit commercial.

Personal Promotion

Even those employees who do not have jobs in revenue-producing departments can make a contribution to profits by crisscross selling. In almost all instances, they render a service to the guests by promoting a facility. For example, the room salesperson who advises a guest that the dining room or bar will close in 30 minutes has advertised the facility, hopefully with a small selling message, and has perhaps ensured that a hungry guest will have some dinner there.

By merely mentioning the 16th-floor cocktail lounge every time the elevator passes it, the elevator operator sells it. The switchboard operator making wake-up calls might ask, "May I connect you with room service?" Or, even more positively, he might say, "Good morning. It's 10 o'clock, time for our minute express continental breakfast." At night the operator can suggest that the customer order breakfast when he receives his wake-up call.

Every employee who is even likely to come into contact with an inquiring guest should be prepared to tell him what he wants to know. If employee turnover prevents training some workers as salesmen, at least they can all be given small directories of the operation to hand the guest. It is worthwhile to offer a small incentive to employees and to establish a mysterious-guest program using an individual who will test the salesmanship and, incidentally, the courtesy of employees in non-revenue-producing departments.

Merchandising, using products that are for sale in the operation itself can stimulate sales. Restaurants and bars can make use of decorative items, tableware, accessories, and the like. Items used in guest rooms, including such consumables as individual soaps, can be sold in the retail outlets. A small sign in the bathroom or a table tent in the dining room would stimulate a visit. Personnel can wear particularly distinctive jewelry or clothing that encourages guest inquiries.

Fashion shows and demonstrations of products in public areas also advertise a retail outlet's products. In some instances, the guest can involve himself in a demonstration. For example, if the operation is selling massage chairs, several models can be used in the lobby. Sample packs of special-blend cigarettes can be offered without charge in the dining room. The guest can be encouraged to use dart boards, ping-pong tables, and desk calculators while he remains in the operation, in the hope that he may order them for his home.

10 | Management of Guest Relations

Hotels and restaurants should not become homes away from home. The modern customer looks to hospitality operations for a quality of life that he cannot obtain himself. Even the wealthy do not routinely enjoy the benefits of so many people's involvement in their welfare, comfort, and pleasure.

They can buy the same brands of whiskey, often the same convenience entrées, the same electronic gimmickry, and the same designer furniture as the modern hospitality operation, but they cannot begin to employ so many service professionals. Only the domestic staffs of the royal households of prosperous monarchies can genuinely offer this much personal service.

The marketability of this life style and the profitability of this service depend entirely on how it is delivered. One operation makes the customer "feel like a king," and another "does him a favor" by renting him a room; but chances are that both make his bed in the morning, and both offer him a television, air conditioner, and free shoe-polishing cloth. The difference between them for the customer is as dramatic as the difference in packaging a brand of $100-an-ounce perfume in a plastic bag or in a crystal flacon: It is not important to the quality of the product, yet the difference is vital to its enjoyment.

Restaurants and hotels are the principal purveyors of the luxury of human involvement, aesthetic behavior, and plain, ordinary courtesy, but it is apparent that hospitality managers often find that their inventories of these low-cost, high-profit commodities are nearly exhausted. Hospitality workers and managers may do their jobs without being the least bit gracious. They may be so lacking in the social graces that they offend customers. Not only are they losing the potential profits of courteous and mannerly behavior, they are losing the functional advantages of common courtesy and ordinary good manners.

MAINTAINING THE RULES OF SOCIAL CONDUCT

The hospitality industry is essentially a people business. Action and reaction between people is the basic element of the industry and determines its success. Profits depend on the quality of interpersonal relationships.

It is as possible to "specify" this quality as it is to specify the thickness of the stainless steel, the weave of carpeting, or the grade of canned peaches. The manager needs to understand its characteristic: etiquette— the quality standards of the people business; hospitality, courtesy, attractime behavior, and good manners.

Hospitality

The word hospitality is not just a semantic convenience that allows discussion of restaurants, hotels, motels, fast-food operations, etc., as similar business enterprises. All hospitality establishments should be committed to being hosts and considering their customers as guests. Obviously, there are important pecuniary aspects to the relationship for both parties, but the hospitality relationship departs significantly from that of a hardware merchant and his customer, for example.

A guest room, or for that matter, a hot dog, becomes superior when the people offering it make the pleasure of individual purchasing seemingly more important than the purchase price. A resort or vacation hotel, for example, could be virtually indistinguishable from a fabulous private residence if the personnel considered themselves extensions of the "host," intent on pleasing his guests, in other words, as employees of a private individual entertaining on a lavish scale, rather than as corporate workers.

Obviously, the fast-food operation will have more difficulty in dividing hospitality and business, but it can be done. When a second cup of coffee is offered and the price of the first cup at 20 cents has allowed for a certain percentage of refills, the customer has more of the feeling that he is a "guest."

Even when there is no bonus of food or drink, the employee's attitude can mean the difference. The good fast-food employee gives the customer the impression that he has happened upon a family picnic or a church supper and has been invited to join the group: the hot dog that he pays for is handled as though it were somebody's food, and not a pound of roofing nails.

Courtesy

Courtesy is essentially the collection of little mannerisms, small actions, and meaningless remarks by which one person communicates to another that he understands their momentary relationship, and will be helpful if he can, and at least not menacing.

This is the difference between "Good morning" and "What?" or a gentleman's entering an elevator before or after a lady.

Courtesy in a hospitality operation is of pivotal importance because it signals the customer that he is being received as a "guest" and not as a business adversary.

Attractive Behavior

Certain behavior is aesthetically pleasing, other behavior is distasteful. While, often, behavioral standards to which a hospitality worker must conform are logically inexplicable to him or her, they must simply be accepted. A hospitality operation's behavioral standard must be slightly more conservative than that of the most conservative guests. For example, reasonably long hair does not interfere with a bellman's performance as it might a machinist's or pose a health hazard as it would for a cook. However, it may displease certain guests, and this gives the operation the right to limit its length. The same hair-length might be acceptable for a bellman in an adult camp or a sailor on an informal fishing boat.

When employees are working they should assume roles appropriate to their situations. Often, it is difficult to convince workers that their democratic inclinations have to be suspended when they wear a service uniform, or assume a service title. Young single men cannot court young single girls during working hours though it is their constitutional right. Uniformed employees who can sit anywhere anybody else can outside of work, cannot sit in the presence of a guest.

Some employee behavior can be offensive because the employee has not realized that he is in contact with individuals of a different background. Even executives of stature sometimes find themselves in difficulties with foreign visitors because they unknowingly deviate from that individual's national customs. For example, a Japanese without much western experience does not really like to shake hands extensively.

Even among fellow Americans, gum chewing, whistling in public, certain vocabulary usage, or physical contact can be offensive.

Finally, there is behavior that is almost universally objectionable, even to the individuals guilty of it. Often they do not realize what they are doing. For example, a waiter may tuck the service cloth with which he handles plates under his arm or in the top of his trousers, or he may blow his nose in the dining room in a loud, conspicuous, and obviously unhygienic manner.

Manners

Formal rules of conduct are much more extensive for individuals than for business enterprises in their contact with other individuals; as individuals, of course, hospitality personnel must abide by general social rules. In most business activity, company policy, politely explained when necessary, includes most of the concerns of formal etiquette. For example, to whom shall greeting cards be sent, or from whom shall gifts be accepted?

The need for a knowledge of formal manners is of more concern for hospitality operations than for commerce in general. Often, individuals purchasing catering services for weddings, banquets, and conventions look to the hospitality operation for guidance in etiquette. The worker in a hospitality operation is much more likely to encounter someone who should be formally addressed by a title other than "Mister" than is a clerk in a hardware store.

Most important, guests in a hospitality operation are often on their best, formal behavior, which means that they expect service personnel to to supply the right cues and make the appropriate moves. For instance, a woman who usually falls into her chair and pulls herself to the table will, in a restaurant, stand poised before the chair until someone helps her. The formalities of a restaurant meal between a courtly customer and a mannerly waiter can proceed with the ritual cooperation of an elegant dance.

It is vitally important that the pretensions of the operation *equal but not exceed* the pretensions of its customers. Basically, informal individuals are as offended by excessive politeness or diffidence as they are by violent breaches of ordinary conduct. They feel patronized. On the other hand, conservative, well-mannered people are rightly intolerant of casual manners. The room clerk is obliged to approach different guests on different levels of formality: one level for an informal married couple his own age and another for the conservative type guest; another for a small child; another for an oriental visitor; and so on.

Management's Role

Presumably the manager and the career hospitality employee can conform readily to the dictates of etiquette. But as many as 80 or 90 percent of the employees do not share their motivation, and most (in all probability) have not had life experiences that emphasized hospitality, courtesy, and attractive behavior or manners.

Management is faced with two considerable problems: educating a large group of basically indifferent people, the typical hospitality training situation; and the wholesale resistance to etiquette of many workers who confuse service with servility and politeness with pandering.

Often the wrong people take hospitality jobs; the free spirits, the drifters, and the mavericks. Unfortunately, these jobs are often open because the public wrongly considers them "demeaning," and potentially acceptable candidates take less-well-paying white-collar jobs.

The hospitality manager can seldom right either of these two wrongs. Although the attitude of some employees is understandable, perhaps even justified, from the operation's perspective it is entirely dysfunctional. The customer cannot be educated except as part of a general program of a professional hospitality association.

The only course is to "correct" or "terminate" the employee. A bellman in a luxury hotel would not be permitted to wear blue jeans and a sweatshirt: The manager cannot permit his attitude to be clothed in comparable casual raiments.

The most effective approach seems to be clear, specific, and definite policy statements by management. For example, the management may issue a directive indicating that all guests are to be addressed as "Sir" or "Madam" and that the employees must therefore say "Good morning, Sir" or "Thank you, Sir." Management might support this position by calling everyone "sir," from the dishwasher to the chairman of the board to indicate that the title has no social weight but is simply more polite and pleasant sounding than a single word or short sentence response, or query.

ESSENTIALS OF GUEST RELATIONS

The guest in a hospitality operation has a special relationship with the people who work there. He trusts them with his health, comfort, and property. He passes moments of his private life in their presence, relying on their discretion, presuming their integrity. He reveals himself in ways that compromise his public image. The room housekeeper knows he wears elevator shoes; the desk clerk knows he asked for a minimum single; the waiter knows he has ulcers.

Hospitality employees maintain the special relationship by developing a sense of exquisite propriety. It allows them successfully to tread a razor-thin line between mechanical efficiency on the one side and disastrous intimacy on the other. It also permits them as individuals with no extraordinary expectations of beatification to tolerate some guests' bizarre behavior, idiocyncracies, and breaches of etiquette.

Successful hospitality workers who please guests and earn generous gratuities have mastered the art of not going too far, just far enough. In guest relations they have learned the difference between a massage and a beating, suntan and sunburn:

Friendliness, not familiarity
Service, not servility
Courtesy, not courtliness
Helpfulness, not hustling
Personal attention, not prying

Friendliness, not Familiarity

The employee-guest relationship can have many of the aspects of friendship but should not have any of the intimacy, at least to the extent that the employee can control it. A guest and an employee can be glad to see each other and pleasant on meeting for the first time each day. They can chat about sports, movies, books, or weather. The guest can find the employee's company pleasing and may talk to him on his station. The employee must not confuse the manifestations of friendliness with true friendship and become familiar with the guest, for example, by calling him or her by his or her first name even when he or she uses first names; by meeting the guest socially, by revealing personal problems, and controversial opinions, or by dropping the polite formality which is his best protection.

Once he ventures beyond the polite formality of his role he may make a friend or he may make an enemy. No man objects to being called "Sir," some 30-year-old business executives will welcome being called "Jack," "man," or "guy," as an indication that the "with it" bellman thinks they are "swingers," but others will be offended. It's not necessary.

Service, not Servility

Service is lighting a guest's cigar, servility is blowing on the end to get it started for him.

Most guests appreciate professionalism and competence and do not understand or welcome fawning attentions. Airline stewardesses and stewards, who are actually airborne front desk and service persons, manage to serve admirably under difficult conditions, without compromising their roles as members of the team that flies the plane.

Americans are too democratic to really want slavish servants, perpetually bowing and scraping like windshield wipers. They want the service but not the toe shuffling and the forelock tugging. Many American millionaires ride in the front seat of their chauffeur driven cars. Essentially believers in the equality of men and the American dream of rags to riches, American hospitality guests prefer that every employee act in a way that maintains his or her eligibility to marry their sons or daughters.

Courtesy, not Courtliness

A great deal of American business has become self-service, automated, and computerized. The hospitality industry alone requires really intense human involvement. Hospitality workers therefore may never have experienced the commercial courtesy that was part of the stock and trade of the small retailer, bank, and craftsman of a generation ago. Nobody says "good morning" when the customer enters the supermarket, and the refrigerator does not tip its derby like the man who delivered the ice.

Deprived of a practical education in courtesy, hospitality workers sometimes learn mannerisms instead of manners. The late night television movie has had its influence: Pretensions are purveyed as polite behavior. The service worker learns from the drawing room farce butler, the B movie nanny, and the "faithful family retainer" to the ill-fated heroine.

On the job, the worker is awkward, in action and speech. At first he is also astounded that the "rich" do not act as he expects them to. Language usage offers a very good example. In addition to addressing guests in the third person ("Would madam like some ketchup with her cheese burgers"), he uses pseudo polite words that polite people avoid. He says "side dish" they say "separate plate," he says "wraps" they say "coats," he says "lavatory," they say "ladies' room," he says "allow me," instead of "let me," etc.

Helpfulness, not Hustling

Although gratuities are an important part of many hospitality workers' incomes, often the major part, they cannot charge guests for their services, refuse any legitimate service for which a tip is not promised, or solicit gratuities before or after helping guests. Even subtle solicitations such as a cup with "Tips" or "Thank you" written on it, or a plate full of coins is offensive. It says, in effect, that the guest is a boor who does not know enough to follow the polite custom of rewarding good service with a small sum.

If the guest *is* a cheapskate, or a "stiff," the hospitality worker has an obligation to his organization to treat him exactly like the best tipper in the establishment. The worker's self-respect depends on his professionalism. If he works only for the tips he can hustle he loses his right to identify himself with the success and reputation of the enterprise as a whole. He no longer works for a major hospitality operation, he works for a two-bit operator: himself.

Personal Attention, not Prying

A person cannot maintain his dignity before a room housekeeper, the housekeeper who sees his dirty socks and soaking dentures must maintain it for him. In varying degrees, the hospitality worker shares parts of the guest's private life. The more personal attention they offer, the more likely they are to penetrate the guest's public image. Obviously, they must make every effort not to pry.

Suggesting a wonderful new brand of denture cleaner is prying. Discussing the attractiveness of the lady with the guest last night and this morning but not tonight is prying.

Even sympathetic responses to ailments, or consoling anecdotes when the waiter discovers that guests cannot tolerate fatty foods are objectionable. Ideally, the waiter will remember the salt substitute and remember not to tout the homemade ice cream the next time the guest eats.

HANDLING SPECIAL SITUATIONS

A hospitality operation is a public facility, open to virtually anyone who gives the appearance of being able to conduct himself reasonably and pay the bill. Most guests are nice and normal. A few of the nice and normal people have problems which professional hospitality managers and workers handle wtihout losing their cool or compromising the operation. Continuing courtesy to the nice and normal people trains them to deal effectively and politely with delicate situations, including those that might cause them personal offense.

Celebrities

Celebrity guests help an operation get its name in the newspapers; therefore, they are worth the trouble. The ordinary V.I.P.—business man, academician, clergyman, author—may not expect anything more than a basket of fruit from the manager and a little special attention when checking in and out. The true celebrity from the arts or politics may require a great deal more even though he is fundamentally nice and normal.

Howling bands of teenagers necessitate extra security as a courtesy to the rock star, and for the protection of the property and other guests' persons and sensitivities. Since, often, the popular celebrity cannot venture into public places, management and employees may have to offer him additional services: extra telephone lines, 24-hour room service, visits from the barber, emergency valet, etc.

Foreign dignitaries and very important politicians may be protected by a branch of the United States Secret Service, and the operation's co-operation must be extended to them, including ham and cheese sandwiches and coffee in the hall at 5 a.m.

Resisting the temptation to join the admiring throng is the individual hospitality employee's greatest courtesy. Requesting an autograph for a niece, of course, is an imposition. Obviously, employees must refrain from assuming that the celebrity will be overjoyed to find a fan carrying his luggage, or bussing his table. The celebrities who want attention deliberately invite it. The others value their privacy.

Full House

Sometimes a guest arrives without a reservation to find the hotel full. Other times, the hotel has overbooked (computer error, naturally) and cannot honor a reservation. The situations are not identical: The hotel may have legal obligations to the guest whose reservations were confirmed. In both cases, however, the front desk clerk can save the situation with courtesy, tact, and helpfulness. He should not say: "What can I do, lady, I am only a desk clerk." He has to try to find a room for the guests with valid reservations. He should try to find a room for the guest without any, because this individual has clearly demonstrated that he wants to be a customer. The clerk checks nearby units of the same chain, or fellow participants in a reservation system, and then other hotels. While he is telephoning, the non-guests should be made comfortable, not left standing with their bundles, like deportees.

If the situation warrants it, an invitation to coffee, a drink, or dinner may be in order. When a room is found, the operation is almost obliged to transfer the guest who was overbooked in a house car or a prepaid taxi. A note of apology from the manager can follow the next day.

Children

In restaurants and hotels, employees should neither fuss over children nor ignore them because they seldom give gratuities. In effect, they are extensions of their parents and have the right to courtesies appropriate to their age. By the same token, the parents have a responsibility to the operation and the other guests. Problems should be referred to the parents, when they are not present to witness an incident, by a management employee, preferably one who can take a "one parent to another" approach. Junior personnel should not remonstrate with guests' children or attempt to discipline them in any way, or directly approach the parents.

Operations which cater to family groups are generally equipped to assist them with baby sitters' phone numbers, or baby sitters, high chairs, booster chairs, cribs, cots, bottle service, and sometimes even counselors and kindergartens. Every hospitality operation that does not post a sign saying "No dogs or children" can expect that some day they will be called on to supply the needs of a child. Management should have at least booster chairs, a crib, and an idea of how they would warm a bottle.

Complaining Guests

If a guest complains, rightly or wrongly, he has to be calmed, and the thrust of his complaint neutralized. Junior employees cannot even properly discuss the matter with the guest. The junior employee says only: "I am sorry you were inconvenienced, let me. . . ." If the complaint is complex, and reasonable, or totally unreasonable, the junior employee refers the guest to a manager. The most polite way is to make the guest comfortable and bring the manager to him; then, if necessary, they can both go to a private office. The guest should not be given the impression that the buck is being passed or that he is being brushed off.

The manager listens to the guest's complaint. His best course is to listen without responding until the guest begins to see some humor in the situation or at least runs out of steam and disarms himself. If the manager can solve the problem he does it immediately: "I am sorry the construction inconvenienced you. I'll have your room changed" (picking up the telephone). Or, "I am sorry that the lobster was stringy, would you care to try the devilled crab which I am sure is excellent tonight. Waiter!"

When the complaint cannot be addressed, the manager can still solve the problem: "I'll attend to Miss Black in the morning (by keeping her out of sight until the guest leaves) but would you care to join me for a moment or two in the lounge?" (polite, effective non sequitur).

Intoxicated Guests

An intoxicated guest is not necessarily a problem. In a resort or vacation hotel, many guests take the opportunity to get thoroughly and pleasantly smashed because they know they do not have to drive home or get up until sleep has dissipated their hangovers. In some states, they technically must not be served when they are intoxicated, but most bartenders, unable to take blood tests, allow an individual to drink as long as he holds up well.

The disruptive intoxicated guest, who is a menace to himself or vulnerable to others, is a problem. Junior employees cannot deal properly with problem-some individuals; a manager must be consulted. Often he will be able to enlist the aid of others in the person's party by talking with them out of the presence of the intoxicated individual. If the man is alone, the manager usually has a private office to which he can invite him. Surprisingly, an invitation to "talk business" or "help me with a problem" works very well, as the disruptive drunk undoubtedly thinks he is the Delphic oracle and Bernard Baruch combined. A business office, with bright lights, and the manager's sober mien, plus some straight talk (but polite) and black coffee helps the individual regain his emotional control.

Requests for Illegal Commodities

A request for illegal liquor, a sex partner, or drugs has to be denied. An employee who supplies illicit commodities is dismissed if he is discovered. He may also risk arrest. The operation's reputation can be severely compromised.

There is no reason, however, that the request, in the context of these times, when the same commodities may be had legally or with official condonation elsewhere, should invite a lecture on the law or on morality. The commodity is "unavailable" says the employee. He cannot help the guest, and no one else can, he is sorry. The discussion is polite. The employee responds as though the guest had asked for a back issue of the "Literary Digest" or a jar of moustache wax.

Pets

The presence of animals in dining or lodging facilities may be regulated by state or local law. The hospitality employee politely explains to the guest that the LAW forbids pets. The truly polite employee will be able to suggest an alternative. Major hotels can have kennels or at least an association with a boarding facility. A restaurant can suggest that an animal be left with the parking lot attendants, or may provide a small enclosure for pets.

When pets are allowed in a facility, their owners should be politely asked to keep them on a lead in public areas as a courtesy to other guests. Employees should never handle the animal as this usually excites it. As well, other guests rightly object to having their possessions handled by a room housekeeper who has just left the embrace of a St. Bernard. If an operation accepts pets and expects them, it must provide for them: Food and water should be available in the appropriate vessels; employees should accustom themselves to walking pets for guests; the housekeeping department should learn how to deal with pet stains and hairs.

Souvenir Hunters and Guests Who Damage Property

A guest in a private home would never think of packing a couple of ashtrays as a remembrance. Unfortunately, the guest in a hospitality operation thinks it is a splendid idea to take pepper mills, ashtrays, glassware, even bedspreads, if his initials match the monogram.

When a guest damages something in a private home, he offers immediately to pay for it or replace it. His host politely refuses and expects to receive a note and a check or replacement in the mail, and does. In a hospitality operation, guests inadvertently or purposely damage property worth several times the price of the room and think nothing of it.

The manager is faced with a dilemma. The maid reports that the bedspread is missing, the waiter whispers that the peppermill has disappeared. The cashier or preferably the manager has to make the attempt to recover the item without offending the guest.

Some managers are very successful in suggesting that the guest has "inadvertently or mistakenly" placed the article among his possessions when leaving. They pose this improbable premise as though similar occurrences were every-day events because of some design fault in the item. Others cannot escape letting a "caught in the cookie jar" note creep into their voices. Instead of directly confronting the guest, they write. In some cases they write to the spouse, suggesting that the individual might like a complete set as a surprise gift, mentioning the price of the single article.

It is more difficult to politely suggest that a guest pay for damage. When the damage is truly horrendous and seems to have been intentional, management can simply add a fair sum to the bill. The truly guilty guest does not protest.

Payment for small, inadvertent damage can be asked by indirection: "Excuse me but the room housekeeper noticed that the rug in your room was rather badly burnt, can you recall noticing it when you arrived?" Hopefully, the answer is: "I have been meaning to speak to you about . . ." If the guest *did* notice it, the manager has lost.

Saying No

Hospitality managers and employees have to say *no* fairly often. "No, the bar is closed, Sir." "No, I am sorry we cannot cash a personal check that large." "No, we will not be able to extend your stay."

There are a number of ways to say no. A few are more polite than others. The person saying no is always personally regretful. He would keep the bar open all night; he loves to cash checks. Unfortunately, he seems to say, a mysterious "they" who have the power of life and death over him, have decreed that the answer is *no*. The person saying *no* may mention the "management" or "company policy" or the "law" as making the guest's request impossible to grant.

The glee that some people notice when a fairly junior employee can refuse a rich guest something he wants, should be avoided. Everybody is very unhappy about the whole situation but nothing can be done. Too much explanation is a mistake, it makes the person refusing seem sympathetic to policy and makes it seem as though he had the authority to grant the request if he were convinced by logical argument. An argument, logical or otherwise, follows.

Rude Guests

In general, rudeness and stupidity should be ignored: A polite response to rude remarks is much more cutting than a spur of the moment insult, and far less disturbing to other guests than a slanging match. People from groups that are frequently the targets of the bigoted, prejudiced, and impolite have usually decided that they have better things to do with their time than correcting narrow-minded people who make broad statements.

Few hospitality operations are in such dire financial condition that management in a private office cannot politely ask a particularly objectionable guest to "make other arrangements next time."

Breaches of etiquette, bad table maners, lack of courtesy is another matter. Unless the guest's behavior is so gross that it significantly offends other guests, it is not a management concern.

Addressing V.I.P.s

Hospitality workers frequently encounter dignitaries, celebrities, the titled, and important personages from the church and from educational institutions. It is important that every employee from the bellman to the general manager address these individuals in a way that does not offend them. Fortunately, the hospitality employee, unlike the social host, is seldom, if ever, called upon to correspond with V.I.P.s (commercial correspondence is usually handled by their assistants or secretaries) or introduce them to other people or large groups. Calling every man *Sir,* and every woman *Madam,* even ordinary American citizens, substantially limits the possibility of error in addressing anyone. Only a very few people cannot properly be addressed as *sir* or *madam* and the impregnability of their exalted positions makes it unlikely that they will take offense.

The polite practice for most Americans, when the individual's title cannot be easily substituted for mister, as in *doctor, dean, governor, senator,* etc., or used *with* mister, as in *ambassador, president, attorney general,* etc., is to honor the individual with his title and then carry on using sir. For example, by first saying, "I hope Your Royal Highness will enjoy his stay" to a monarch, the speaker offers evidence that he does not harbor any anarchism or some mushy democratic notions. He then can address the gentleman as *Sir* with perfect propriety. It must be remembered that Mister and Sir are absolutely legitimate expressions of respect that every free man equally merits. In France, for example, there is no one who cannot be called "Monsieur" and no one who should not be.

Many people err when they attempt over-elaborate diffidence. For example, a Marquis in the English peerage is addressed as Lord Norfolk (*not* My Lord), as is any peer below the rank of Duke. Calling someone Earl Norfolk, Count Norfolk, Baron Norfolk is an error. By the same token, referring to any British peer as "Your Grace" is an error unless the individual is a non-royal duke and the relationship has become that of a master and servant.

While it is certainly permissible to address natives of other countries by the equivalent of *Mister* or *Sir* in their own languages, the speaker should be able to pronounce the title correctly. Otherwise, the individual should be addressed by his official title or "Mister," followed by his name. This problem frequently occurs with the wives of individuals with official titles. He is addressed as Ambassador or General, she is addressed as Madam in her language (Mrs., obviously, in English), if the speaker can handle it or by the French title *Madame*.

Academic titles are not generally used off-campus, but if the hospitality manager is aware of them, it generally indicates that the holder of the title wants it used, otherwise he would have reserved his room or table as Mr. Black, not Professor or Dean or Dr. Black.

The lower military ranks can properly be called "Mister" and addressed as "Sir" at all times. Upper echelon officers in civilian circumstances in uniform and in mufti can also be called "Mister" but individuals in service industries please the customer by acknowledging these titles even in the higher non-commissioned ranks. It is much more appropriate to use the title and the man's last name. Too many "Yes, Captain,"s "No, Captain,"s make for musical comedy, not politeness.

Any member of the catholic or protestant clergy who is less than a Cardinal can be addressed by his title in place of Mister: Bishop Black, Monsignor Black, Father Black, etc. Cardinals can be called Sir, or Your Eminence but the former is more likely in a non-religious circumstance. "Reverend" should not be used alone as the term is an adjective.

Assisting the Handicapped

Any handicapped person who appears in a public restaurant or hotel is usually quite capable, or he would not be there. He requires some additional attention but there is no need to smother him or mother him with over-attention.

A blind person, obviously, may have some difficulty in locating the front desk of a hotel, especially if he or she has never been to that hotel before (in a crowded lobby people who *can* see may have the same problem). The doorman may accompany him. More often, the doorman calls ahead to the service desk or the front desk for someone to greet the blind person as he enters the lobby. Other handicapped persons, people on crutches or in wheel chairs, for example, may be similarly treated if difficulties are anticipated, such as a flight of stairs. In each instance, the employee greets the individual and offers his assistance: "Good morning. May I help you?" or, "Can I be of assistance?" If the individual is blind or if the employee is not uniformed, the employee should identify himself so that the handicapped person knows he is being assisted by an employee.

If the guest says he requires assistance, the employee should present his arm to the person, rather than touch him, and then walk at an appropriate pace, preferably in step, to the handicapped individual's destination.

In a restaurant, after the waiter, maitre d' hotel, or hostess has conducted the blind guest to his table, the table waiter pulls out a chair and helps the guest seat himself, as he would when helping anyone else. The guest will cooperate more readily than most other customers. Generally, a sightless person using a cane will lay it across his lap, or fold it. The waiter has only to remove any clutter from the table, for example, a tall flower vase, otherwise the table is left intact. In such cases the waiter asks if the guest wishes a menu. Many legally sightless individuals can see well enough to read at close distances. If he does not, the waiter quietly reads the items and the prices without making suggestions. The guest will order and ask any necessary questions or make any necessary comments. He may ask that certain dishes be boned, or that his bread be buttered. The waiter announces quietly what he is putting on the table: "Your coffee, sir." Otherwise, the waiter performs normally.

In a bar, the barman either places the drink on the bar or announces it and waits until the blind guest has extended his hand before placing the drink in it.

Accidents and Illness

When a guest (anyone on the premises who is not an employee) has an accident or falls ill, junior personnel encountering the individual stay with him, while sending another guest or employee for a supervisor or manager. The employee should speak calmly and reassuringly to the victim, and attempt to make him comfortable if he is ill. If he has had an accident, he should be covered but not moved.

The manager or supervisor, when advised of the problem should notify the police, who will dispatch an ambulance or a physician depending on the nature of the illness. It is extremely important that the manager err on the side of prudence, caution, and conservatism, rather than economy, even if it means occasionally that the operation will be obliged to pay the bill of a doctor, who the guest, now well, decides was not necessary. If a serious event should become a tragedy of some sort, the operation must be in the position to demonstrate that its employee took all actions available to judicious individuals.

Foreign Visitors

The mounting prosperity of nations all over the world has made it possible for their citizens to travel to the United States as tourists. As well, foreign businessmen, the foreign employee of United States companies, and members of international bodies with headquarters in the United States patronize hospitality operations.

While most foreign visitors limit themselves to large urban centers, their genuine interest in the United States, and the government's active promotion, prompts a significant number to venture everywhere. It is possible for two Russian journalists to step off a bus in Kansas, or a French tourist to check into a Fort Lauderdale hotel because he finds the Mediterranean too polluted for swimming.

A hospitality operation and its employees are expected to be somewhat less insular and provincial in regard to foreign visitors than a pocket of moonshiners. While no one expects a hotel to stage a bonfire to help a Finnish guest celebrate Juhannusaatto or Midsummer's Eve, or a restaurant to produce a dish of Kim-Chi (pickled vegetables) to delight a wandering Korean, there should be an effort to understand the foreign visitor, accommodate him, and please him. In addition, hospitality employees should be at least aware of the things easily offending foreign visitors.

LANGUAGE

Many foreign visitors will speak understandable and sufficient English. Those who do not may choose to frequent hospitality establishments listed in *their* guide books as speaking their language.

Most of the individuals who speak English with difficulty understand that they are creating problems, and often treat the situation with mild humor. Patience, courtesy, and helpfulness on the part of the operation's employees are all that is required.

A very few foreign visitors expect to find that everyone will speak their language. They offer the hospitality industry in every country but their own the same problem. It is difficult to please them. Management might try obtaining newspapers in their language, either editions printed here or airmail editions of foreign papers, as a mollifying gesture, albeit a weak one.

Most problems with language occur *in English*. For example, individuals from South and Central America may strongly object to anything being described as "American," including, of course, the flag and the citizens of the United States of America. They feel they have an equal claim on the adjective. As there is no comfortable way of making "United States" into an adjective, the locution is best avoided in their presence.

Foreign visitors are also offended or startled by greetings and responses which are addressed to no one in particular. In many areas it is in bad taste to say "Good morning," "Thank you," "You're welcome" without adding the name of the addressee.

As well, foreign visitors do not usually expect to be addressed first by employees except when they have a business mission, or are making a courtesy remark ("Good morning, Sir"). They may not welcome the friendly banter, the jokes and the put-ons that American travelers expect from pleasant hospitality employees.

Certainly, employees and management in a lodging operation must learn the proper pronunciation of a guest's name, and its proper form. It may mean a call to a local consul, but is obligatory to avoid nonsense names, and social affronts. For example, a man's Spanish name may be written "Juan Lopez y Garcia" and his wife's, "Maria Santiago de Lopez". He is "Mr. Lopez" and his wife is "Mrs. de Lopez." Garcia is his father's name, and Santiago is hers. People with less common constructions are accustomed to having them mangled. If the operation does make the effort to correctly couch the man's name he is especially pleased. For example, a Chinese man's last name is first. He should be addressed by that name plus Mister. An individual may have "Mister" built into his name in English. U Thant, for example, is already Mr. (U) Thant.

Table manners differ substantially country to country. Less than one third of the world's population uses a knife and fork. Most visitors are at least familiar with the difference in customs, and may, in fact, be anxious to explore our mores. When they purposely or inadvertently commit a breach of ordinary table manners, obviously no service employee should interfere, demonstrate, or comment. For example, most Europeans eat with the knife always in the right hand and their napkins in their collars instead of laps. Both are more practical than the American procedures and hardly need defense.

When possible, the establishment should aid the guest in maintaining those table practices which he finds convenient. Large napkins should be provided, and chopsticks might be available for small children who have not learned to eat with a knife and fork as their parents probably have. If the guest has asked for toothpicks at the table, for discreet hygiene behind his napkin, they should be present at the next meal. Some guests may want to save their wine from meal to meal.

SERVICE EXPECTATIONS

The foreign visitor expects considerably more service than most American establishments routinely provide. In hotels abroad, there is usually a department charged solely with maintaining the guest's comfort and assisting him. The service desk or the bell captain has some of the same functions but not all of them. The conciege of a Paris hotel can be asked to do almost anything from arranging for a guest pass to a tennis club to changing money.

The foreign visitor really expects that someone will buy him theater tickets, fetch a package from across town, and have his shoes repaired. Once the bell captain gets over his initial shock, he may find that it is possible for him to oblige, especially if he realizes that the guest expects to pay well for really extraordinary services. If the operation cannot oblige the guest, his telephone call should be transferred to a managerial employee who can suggest possible arrangements. The hard-pressed business traveler might welcome the idea of using a temporary office employee from one of the agencies which specialize in this type of personnel. A college student (or several) might be hired as a runner. Or, the manager can help the guest develop a list of telephone numbers, including a messenger service, so that goods and services can be sent in, instead of sent for.

The English visitor will miss the "Boots," the individual who cleans shoes during the night in English hotels. It may be hoped he will have read a guide book warning him not to leave them in the hall. Arrangements can certainly be made for him, and a note left in his room indicating that a call to the bell captain will start the process.

Many visitors will prefer a continental breakfast, of beverage and bread and accompaniments, to hearty American food. Although they probably realize that no maid or waiter will arrive with it in their rooms as a "wake-up call" they may not be aware that they can order it the night before from room service to be delivered when they want it. Some operations have small "menus" which the guest completes and hangs on his door. Others leave a menu card on the guest's pillow when his bed is turned down at night suggesting that he call room service before going to bed.

Sometimes foreign visitors will surprise front desk personnel by asking to see the room before they sign the register, a very common practice in

Europe. Obviously, they must be shown the room or a series of rooms if they wish a choice, while their luggage is carefully kept in the lobby. If they ask for a room with a "bidet," a plumbing fixture used for minor bathing, the desk clerk or bellman accompanying should not be dumbstruck. He explains that bathrooms are not equipped with them but that he can have a portable *bidet* placed in the room. The operation catering to foreign guests would do well to buy several.

ETIQUETTE

American hospitality personnel commonly make what are considered errors by other people's standards. The American whose family came from the guest's native country may feel a kinship that the guest does not. It is an error for the employee to begin to discuss the foreign country, his parents, his relatives, or in any way presume on the coincidence. The guest should not even be aware of it. If the guest initiates the conversation, on hearing the employee's name, that is another matter.

Guests should not be subjected to language experiments by high-school and college scholars. It is a courtesy to attempt to help a guest who cannot speak English, it is an insult or imposition to bother one who can manage with an instant mini-lesson.

Managerial employees may be somewhat bewildered by some guest's handshaking or reluctance to shake hands. Europeans may as a matter of course shake hands as a way of greeting someone or saying good-bye. Orientals may shake hands with reluctance. The manager should neither leave the guest with his hand outstretched, nor grab the hand of a guest who does not offer it. Women's hands are not shaken unless they offer them, and then very lightly.

Managerial employees should not attempt to kiss a lady's hand. Even if this were still the general practice in Europe, it would be very unusual in a commercial situation.

TIPPING

No individual employee can himself assist a guest in conforming with American tipping practices. Restaurant and hotel workers silently suffer and occasionally benefit from the difference. For example, a waiter may find that he has been left no tip by a party who thought that service was included in the price of the meal. On the other hand, a bell captain may be surprised by a very generous tip when the guest is leaving, for his cumulative services.

Management can protect its employees and assist guests who would prefer to follow the American practice but do not understand it, by leaving a card in guest rooms *suggesting* a tipping schedule. Perhaps it can be left, along with some other information on using the telephone and the difference in electric current, so that the schedule does not leap out at the guest.

RELATIONSHIP TO WOMEN

Women's liberation has not reached many parts of the world. Guests, especially business travelers and members of international organizations who are not pre-qualified by their willingness to experience new customs, and tourists from middle-eastern and eastern countries may prefer to deal with male managerial personnel. As well, they probably would prefer male waiters, room-service waiters, bellmen, and carhops.

Religious Requirements

A guest whose religion limits his diet or activities cannot expect that a hospitality establishment for the general public will be able to fully serve him. He is in much the same position as the guest whose doctor has prescribed a salt-free diet: He can expect the operation to attempt to assist him by not adding salt to his food, but cannot expect it to meet hospital standards.

Unfortunately, the religious guest, like a guest requiring a special diet, often encounters a colossal rudeness compounded of ignorance and indifference.

A *hospitality* operation employing *service* workers should be able to produce reasonable food items which are not on the menu without the guest having publicly to defend his beliefs. It does not really matter if a guest wants a vegetable plate because he is a practicing Hindu or because he likes vegetables, or because he is dieting for medical or aesthetic reasons. He should get the vegetables without a fuss.

Likewise, individuals who request disposable serviceware because their religion forbids the combination of certain foodstuffs or the ingestion of others and these taboos are extended to serviceware which might have contained these items, should be served on disposables.

Service personnel should know enough about the ingredients of the dishes they serve to be able to assure a guest that it does not contain a food his religion proscribes, or his doctor forbids, for that matter.

An operation which is likely to have extremely religious guests or guests with severe medical diets, might consider stocking complete convenience dinners, made to various religious and dietary specifications by several companies with national distribution. While this is unnecessary if the guest has numerous alternatives, it is a genuine service that will not be forgotten if the guest's only other alternative is an orange for dinner.